DISCRETE EVENT SIMULATION IN C

THE McGRAW-HILL
INTERNATIONAL SERIES IN SOFTWARE ENGINEERING

Consulting Editor

Professor D. Ince
The Open University

Titles in this Series

Portable Modula-2 Programming – Woodman, Griffiths, Souter and Davies
SSADM: A Practical Approach – Ashworth and Goodland
Software Engineering: Analysis and Design – Easteal and Davies
Introduction to Compiling Techniques: A First Course Using ANSI C, LEX and YACC – Bennett
An Introduction to Program Design – Sargent
Object-Oriented Databases: Applications in Software Engineering – Brown
Object-Oriented Software Engineering with C^{++} – Ince
Expert Database Systems: A Gentle Introduction – Beynon-Davies
Practical Formal Methods with VDM – Andrews and Ince
SSADM Version 4: A User's Guide – Eva
A Structured Approach to Systems Development – Heap, Stanway and Windsor
Rapid Information Systems Development – Bell and Wood-Harper
Software Engineering Environments: Automated Support for Software Engineering – Brown, Earl and McDermid
Systems Construction and Analysis: A Mathematical and Logical Framework – Fenton and Hill
SSADM V4 Project Manager's Handbook – Hammer
Knowledge Engineering for Information Systems – Beynon-Davies
Introduction to Software Project Management and Quality Assurance – Ince, Sharp and Woodman
Software System Development: A Gentle Introduction – Britton and Doake
Introduction to VDM – Woodman and Heal
An Introduction to SSADM Version 4 – Ashworth and Slater
Discrete Event Simulation in C – Watkins
Objects and Databases – Kroha
Object-Oriented Specification and Design with C++ – Henderson

DISCRETE EVENT SIMULATION IN C

Kevin Watkins

McGRAW-HILL BOOK COMPANY

London · New York · St Louis · San Francisco · Auckland
Bogotá · Caracas · Lisbon · Madrid · Mexico · Milan
Montreal · New Delhi · Panama · Paris · San Juan
São Paulo · Singapore · Sydney · Tokyo · Toronto

Published by
McGRAW-HILL Book Company Europe
SHOPPENHANGERS ROAD · MAIDENHEAD · BERKSHIRE SL6 2QL · ENGLAND
TELEPHONE: 0628 23432
FAX: 0628 770224

British Library Cataloguing in Publication Data
Watkins, Kevin
  Discrete Event Simulation in C. – (McGraw-Hill
  International Series in Software Engineering)
  I. Title   II. Series
003.35133
ISBN 0-07-707733-4

Library of Congress Cataloging-in-Publication Data
Watkins, Kevin
  Discrete event simulation in C/Kevin Watkins.
  p. cm. – (The McGraw-Hill international series in software
  engineering)
  Includes bibliographical references (p.   ) and index.
  ISBN 0-07-707733-4
  1. C (Computer program language)   2. Discrete-time
  systems – Computer simulation.
  I. Title.   II. Series.
QA76.73.C15W39   1993
003′.83′01135113–dc20   93-17755 CIP

1234 CUP 9543

Typeset by The Alden Press, Oxford

Printed and bound in Great Britain at the University Press, Cambridge.

To my parents, Albert and Lyn

CONTENTS

Preface   **xi**

Acknowledgements   **xv**

1 Introduction   **1**
   1.1 Modelling   1
   1.2 Simulation   5
   1.3 Summary   8
   1.4 Exercises   9

2 Methodology   **10**
   2.1 The simulation study   10
   2.2 Workloads and performance metrics   18
   2.3 Choice of modelling units and time scales   19
   2.4 Documentation   20
   2.5 Summary   22
   2.6 Exercises   23

3 Implementation   **24**
   3.1 Simulation software   24
   3.2 Requirements of a general-purpose language   26
   3.3 Modelling approaches   28
   3.4 Summary   40
   3.5 Exercises   40

4 Simulation in C   **42**
   4.1 The C programming language   42
   4.2 Simulation model structure   43
   4.3 An example—the alternating bit protocol   47
   4.4 Summary   57
   4.5 Exercises   58

5 Random numbers   **59**
  5.1   Randomness   59
  5.2   Probability   61
  5.3   Generating random numbers from the uniform distribution   66
  5.4   Generating random numbers from other probability distributions   78
  5.5   Goodness of fit   108
  5.6   Selecting a distribution   111
  5.7   Summary   114
  5.8   Exercises   115

6 Entities and resources   **117**
  6.1   Entities   117
  6.2   Resources   127
  6.3   An example—the dining philosophers   128
  6.4   Summary   135
  6.5   Exercises   135

7 The scheduler   **137**
  7.1   The job of the scheduler   137
  7.2   Types of algorithm   138
  7.3   Dynamic algorithms   138
  7.4   Performance comparison   141
  7.5   Implementation   142
  7.6   Simultaneous events   144
  7.7   Summary   146
  7.8   Exercises   146

8 Queues   **148**
  8.1   The structure of a queuing system   148
  8.2   Basic queuing theory   149
  8.3   The implementation of queues   157
  8.4   Queue behaviour   159
  8.5   An example—a batch computer system   169
  8.6   Summary   174
  8.7   Exercises   175

9 Gathering results   **177**
  9.1   Histograms   177
  9.2   Recording results   182
  9.3   Measurements   184
  9.4   Outputting results   186
  9.5   Summary   193
  9.6   Exercises   193

10 Results analysis   **196**
   10.1 The dynamic behaviour of simulation models   196
   10.2 Transient effects   202
   10.3 Detection of the steady state   202
   10.4 Estimating accuracy   214
   10.5 Realizing accuracy goals   226
   10.6 Analysis of transient behaviour   239
   10.7 Summary   240
   10.8 Exercises   241

11 Experimental design and regression analysis   **244**
   11.1 Introduction   244
   11.2 Terminology   245
   11.3 The analysis of variance   246
   11.4 Some types of experiment   246
   11.5 Regression analysis   261
   11.6 Summary   269
   11.7 Exercises   270

12 Case study   **272**
   12.1 CSMA/CD protocols   272
   12.2 Ethernet   273
   12.3 The simulation   274
   12.4 Summary   313
   12.4 Exercises   313

Appendix A: Simulation library   **317**

Appendix B: Simulation library reference   **325**

Appendix C: Statistical tables   **355**

Answers to selected exercises   **368**

References   **374**

Index   **379**

PREFACE

The aim of this book is to provide a complete stand-alone coverage of discrete event simulation modelling which is both comprehensive and practical. The focus is on the use of ANSI C for model development. The choice of a general-purpose language such as ANSI C rather than a special purpose language is made for pedagogic as well as pragmatic reasons. Computer languages like C are far more widely known than their special-purpose counterparts such as GPSS and SIMSCRIPT. So, for the majority of readers, models implemented in C will be understood with less effort than models in these more esoteric languages. Moreover, there is likely to be a C compiler available on a convenient machine to test out directly the ideas presented. This book is not, however, intended to be an introduction to programming in C. For this, the reader is strongly recommended to obtain a copy of Kernigan and Richie (1988).

Example models and a C simulation library are included on the accompanying DOS formatted disk on the premiss that the best way to understand the principles involved is actually to develop and experiment with some models directly. No listing of the complete simulation library is provided in the book, but since all the source is provided on the accompanying disk, a hard copy listing can be readily obtained if required.

The simulation library is complete and powerful enough to be used for real simulations and has no inherent restrictions as regards its modelling ability. The appendix describes what needs to be done to compile the software on particular systems but there should not be too many problems since most compiler-dependent code has been avoided. The software has successfully compiled and run unmodified with the ANSI C compiler under HP-UX and SunOS and the Mix Power C, Borland C++ and Microsoft C compilers under MS-DOS.

The intended readership includes those wanting to learn about simulation modelling and have a complete but detailed and thorough introduction. It is also intended to be used by experienced professionals needing to build a model but being unwilling or unable to acquire a dedicated simulation modelling environment for the job.

The choice of what to include by way of mathematical statistics is difficult. Failure to include most of the statistics forces the reader constantly to refer to other texts. I personally find such a chore annoying. On the other hand, including too much mathematics can be off-putting and is certainly out of place in a book of this nature. I have tried to steer a middle course and include the basic mathematical material, but without any formal proofs or derivations. For the most part, the required level of technical ability requires only a nodding acquaintance with basic mathematics and statistics theory. The statistics material in Chapters 10 and 11 and some of the material in Chapter 5 is a bit more involved and some of it requires undergraduate level ability. It is hoped that this should not be too serious a deterrent to those more concerned with the pragmatics of model building since I have tried to make the book essentially practical.

I hope that the net result of this approach is of benefit both to those wishing to learn about simulation and those wishing actually to apply it to real-world problems of considerable size.

STRUCTURE

This book consists of twelve chapters. The first nine concentrate on various elements that are necessary for the development of C programs to perform discrete event simulation. The next two chapters are more technical and the last chapter contains a case study.

Chapters 1 to 4 provide a general introduction to simulation modelling and to the use of C. Chapter 1 sets the background. Chapter 2 describes the methodology of simulation. Chapter 3 overviews the implementation of simulation models and outlines the simulation library. Chapter 4 introduces C as the implementation language and presents a template for C simulation models.

Chapter 5 concentrates on random numbers, covering the nature of randomness and the generation of random numbers from various probability distributions.

Chapters 6 to 8 explain the implementation of modelling primitives and give some examples to illustrate their use.

Chapter 9 covers the generation and presentation of results. The facilities provided by the simulation library are described and the underlying statistical theory explained.

Chapters 10 and 11 describe the theory and application of statistics in simulation. This covers the design of experiments and the analysis of simulation results. These chapters are more mathematical in nature than the previous chapters.

Chapter 12 features a case study concerning the performance of the Ethernet protocol. The development of a model is described along with the experimentation and analysis involved.

There are also three appendices. Appendices A and B contain a synopsis of the contents of the library. Appendix C contains the tables of statistical functions which are referred to in the text.

Each chapter concludes with a summary and exercises intended to reinforce the principal topics covered in the chapter.

Some suggested reading patterns are as follows:

- For those wanting a complete general coverage: Chapters 1 to 12 in that order with reference to the source code
- For a basic introduction: Chapters 1 to 9
- For those interested in a specific topic: the relevant chapter among Chapters 2 to 11.

ACKNOWLEDGEMENTS

First of all, I would like to thank my wife Lesa for her patience and support through numerous lonely weekends and evenings during the preparation of this book.

For reading early drafts of this book and making many incisive suggestions and comments I would like to thank Don Hughes, Phil Day and John Smith.

I would also like to thank all at McGraw-Hill, in particular Jacqueline Harbor.

In addition, I am grateful to the publishers and authors of the following texts for allowing me to use extracts from their work:

- MIT Press for permission to use algorithms for binary trees in *Introduction to Algorithms* by T. H. Cormen, C. E. Leirson and R. L. Rivest (Chapter 7 and disk)
- Prentice-Hall for permission to base exercises on protocols described in *Computer Networks* by A. S. Tanenbaum (exercises Chapter 10 and disk)
- Addison-Wesley for permission to publish extracts from *The Art of Computer Programming, Vol. II, Semi-Numerical Algorithms* by D. E. Knuth (Chapter 5)
- W. H. Freeman and Co. for permission to publish extracts from *Modern Statistical, Systems and GPSS Simulation* by Z. A. Karian and E. J. Dudewicz (Chapter 5 and disk)
- Numerical Recipes Software for permission to publish extracts from *Numerical Recipes in C* by W. H. Press, B. P. Flannery, S. A. Teukolsky and W. T. Vetterling (Chapter 5 and disk)
- Dover Publications for permission to publish extracts from Table 26.1, pages 966–972 in *Handbook of Mathematical Functions*, edited by M. Abramowitz and I. A. Stegun (Table C.1)
- Biometrika Trustees for permission to publish extracts from Tables 8, 12 and 18 in Biometrika Tables for Statisticians, Vol. 1, Third edition (1966) (Tables C.2, C.3.1, C.3.2, C.4.1, C.4.2).

The following trademarks have been used in this book. UNIX is a registered trademark of UNIX System Laboratories. MS-DOS is a trademark of Microsoft Corp. HP-UX is a trademark of Hewlett-Packard Corp. SunOS is a trademark of Sun Microsystems. Power C is a trademark of MIX Software. Borland C++ is a trademark of Borland International. Ada is a registered trademark of the US Department of Defense Joint Ada Program.

1

INTRODUCTION

In this chapter we overview modelling and simulation in general. We start by looking at the widespread use of modelling as a method of systems analysis and then discuss the types of model that exist.

1.1 MODELLING

The use of the word *model* has been used to describe almost any attempt to specify a system under study. In its everyday connotation it is usually understood to mean some physical replica of a system, typically a construction such as an architectural scale model, but when used in a scientific or engineering context it has a more specific meaning. In this setting, a model is the name given to a portrayal of the interrelationships of parts of a system in precise terms. The portrayal can be interpreted in terms of some system attributes and is sufficiently detailed to permit study under a variety of circumstances and to enable the system's future behaviour to be predicted.

The use of models in this way has long been a popular technique in many technical disciplines, from management science to theoretical physics. It is possible to appreciate just how broad this range of applications is by scanning technical journals in the science and engineering disciplines. A more or less random sample of such literature reveals the following applications:

- the performance evaluation of a transaction processing system (Salsburg, 1988)
- a study of the generation and control of forest fires in California (Parks, 1964)
- the determination of the optimum division of labour along a continuous assembly line in a factory (Killbridge and Webster, 1966)

- the analysis of long polymer molecules (Wall *et al.*, 1954)
- a study of cloud formations (Fox, 1965)
- the analysis of a distributed network (Sauer and Woo, 1977)
- a study of the progression of employees through various grades of promotion in a hierarchy (Dill *et al.*, 1965)
- the evaluation of the performance of a multiprocessor operating system (Teheri and Askins, 1991)
- the analysis of the UK economy (Klein *et al.*, 1961)
- a study of water pollution control (James, 1978)
- planning the renal health care services in Europe (Davies and Davies, 1987)
- a study of stock market behaviour (Cootner, 1964)
- the analysis of a steam generator (Kwatney and Konopacki, 1977)
- the planning of a refinery (Newby, 1964)
- a study of the formation of social groups (Horvath, 1966)
- an analysis of ship boilers (Tysso, 1979).

This list could be extended almost indefinitely. There is probably no branch of science or engineering that has not benefited from the application of modelling techniques.

1.1.1 A taxonomy of models

The previous section touched upon the broad application base applicable to modelling. Not surprisingly, it is a vast subject and consists of numerous techniques and methods that are optimized for use in different domains. However, this book is only concerned with a specific subset of these domains. To help clarify the bounds of interest it is useful to consider a classification of models based on their principal characteristics. A set of convenient, but by no means unique, characteristics consists of the following:

1. *Predictability*. This refers to the degree to which fixed values assigned to inputs produce the same set of output values. Here it is possible to identify two complementary model types: *deterministic* and *stochastic*. In a deterministic model, all data and relationships are given with certainty. An example of this type of model is the determination of the efficiency of an engine based on temperature, speed, load and fuel consumption. Each of these factors can be measured to some specified accuracy and substituted into an appropriate equation in order to calculate the predicted efficiency.

    In a stochastic model at least some of the quantities involved have a value which is made to vary in an unpredictable or *random* fashion. For example, a company may use a stochastic model for financial planning where the aim is to study the financial behaviour of the company in relation to its shareholders, customers and suppliers. The uncertainty in the purchasing decisions of customers and the investment made by shareholders can be represented by selected random numbers. The 'spread' in the value of these random numbers indicates the degree of risk attached.

Purely stochastic models are rare; nearly all models contain some degree of determinism. Sometimes we find stochastic behaviour in a deterministic system, like the random patterns of traffic on a fixed communications network; sometimes the system itself is partly stochastic as in an economic model.

2. *Solvability*. For simple systems it is possible to perform a completely analytic solution of the model, although the level of skill required is often quite daunting. These models can be said to be *solvable*; but for a much wider class of systems such a treatment is impossible. Either a set of equations can be developed which is too difficult to solve, or the problem is so complicated that an appropriate set of equations simply cannot be found. In such circumstances we can *simulate* the behaviour of the system under a set of different assumptions and, as it were, form a picture of its behaviour by sampling from all the ways it might respond.

3. *Variability*. Another useful yardstick is whether time is incorporated into the model, and this fact can be used to distinguish between *static* and *dynamic* models. In a static model the results can be considered to apply at a particular moment but this point is not made explicit. For instance, consider a spreadsheet in which sales and costs are input and a value for company profit is generated. This can be viewed as a model of economic performance because it relates, in a mathematically precise way, the various economic factors relevant to company profit and loss. However, the instant at which the profit was supposed to have been made is unspecified. It is obviously the time at which the input data was valid but we can only infer this, the model itself gives us no clue.

In many cases, the analyst is more interested in seeing the result after a specific event has taken place or certain conditions are true. For instance, a biologist may want to model an ecosystem in which the principal factors of interest are animal population and a finite food resource. As the animal population increases, the food supply diminishes which tends to reduce the population. But, as the animal population decreases, the strain on the food supply is less severe and so it can increase again. Now the increase in food supply permits the population to grow and so the system tends to oscillate as a function of time. Thus we are dealing with system dynamics, and a dynamic model in which any time value is possible is required for analysis.

4. *Granularity*. Dynamic models can also be differentiated on the basis of the granularity of their treatment of time. Two contrasting notions exist: *discrete* models and *continuous models*. Discrete models concern systems involving clearly distinguishable events such as the arrival of a customer, the delivery of

some goods or the transmission of a data packet in a communications network. Here the concept of the event is fundamental. An event represents a significant moment in the course of the simulation. When an event occurs, some actions are performed and the system state, as determined by the current value assigned to variables in the model, changes. The time between events is generally non-uniform and unpredictable and during this period the system state is fixed. Discrete models are nearly always stochastic. Continuous models, on the other hand, may be deterministic or stochastic. In continuous models it is impossible to distinguish between specific events taking place. Time is considered to be an unbroken flow and 'events' are allowed to happen at very short intervals. Moreover, the occurrence of each event causes only a marginal change in the system attributes. The trajectory of a missile (i.e. the path it travels) can be viewed in this way. There will be the ever-present forces of propulsion, gravity, air friction and so on to contend with, as well as the changing mass of the rocket as fuel is expended. The trajectory can be thought of as a continuous process described by a set of differential equations. It is hoped that the set of differential equations can then be solved to give the path travelled and the point of impact, etc.

Numerous other categories are possible. One example is the time span involved, referring to the period that is modelled (e.g. microseconds versus years). Another example is level of detail, referring to whether the model is on a macro or micro level (e.g. gas pressure and temperature versus the Brownian motion of molecules). However, the classifications identified above are adequate for defining the class of models that are of interest to us. First and foremost, we are interested in discrete models. Interesting models in this class are invariably stochastic in nature and we shall be concerned with the largest set of such models: simulation models.

1.1.2 The structure of simulation models

Discrete event models are composed of essentially two different parts, one of which is *logical* and the other of which is *mathematical*. The logical part is concerned with the rules governing the behaviour of the various components of the system. Thus, we may have a rule, in the form of a conditional statement, to test whether a queue is empty or not and to perform some appropriate action if it is. Obviously, the set of rules incorporated into the model must accurately capture the logical interactions existing in the system to an adequate degree of detail for our modelling purposes. This means ignoring rules which are not relevant and incorporating those that are. Although this is an easily stated maxim, in practice it is a difficult distinction to make. Sometimes it is not possible to ascertain exactly which rules and behaviour are relevant when model construction starts. It is not until the model is relatively sophisticated that we have enough information to judge whether additional detail is necessary or whether some simplifications can be made, typically as a result of comparing model outputs with measurements from the real system (if it exists) and input from a technical authority who has detailed knowledge and experience of the subject system.

The mathematical part refers to those aspects of the system that can be expressed analytically or numerically. An important part of the mathematical structure is statistical. This should be no surprise since randomness is purposely introduced to capture the uncertainties in the behaviour of the system being modelled. Unfortunately the addition of randomness makes it more difficult to determine the relationship between input and output because the variability of our outputs now contains an unpredictable error component. However, relatively straightforward tools for this purpose have been developed and we will be looking at some of them later.

1.2 SIMULATION

As with 'model', the word 'simulation' can also lead to many different interpretations. What we refer to as simulation in this book is the execution of a discrete model, in the guise of a program residing on a digital computer, which provides us with information about a system that we are investigating. In fact this definition does not distinguish one, but two important methods of analysis: discrete event simulation and trace-driven simulation.

The idea behind *discrete event simulation* is illustrated in Fig. 1.1 in which a model is represented as a box that has an internal source of random numbers. The random numbers drive the components of the simulation model; they are used to determine the occurrence time between system events, branching probabilities and so on. The essential feature is that the model is self-contained, it requires no external inputs to operate.

On the other hand a *trace-driven simulation*, as illustrated in Fig. 1.2, is controlled by input sequences stemming from trace data generated from a real system. The trace data is a profile of the dynamics actually observed. Such an approach is very common when dealing with computer systems since they generally have built-in *tracing programs* which monitor the activities of the system and the sequence of processes pertinent to the planned simulation. For more details of the trace-driven simulation method see Sherman (1976).

The big advantage of trace-driven simulation is that it avoids much of the statistical work. This removes a potentially difficult and cumbersome activity. For example, in a discrete event simulation model inter-arrival times are normally generated from independent, identically distributed, random variables.

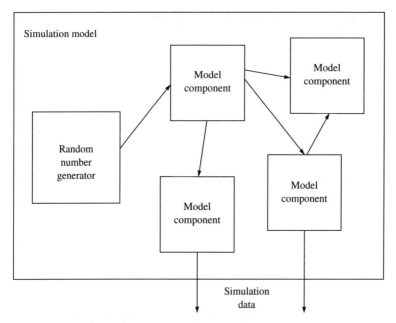

Figure 1.1 A discrete event simulation model.

However, if significant interactive effects between the underlying processes are present, then detailed statistical analysis must be performed in order to discover their characteristics. This information must then be used in the model to adjust the random variables. In trace data all such effects will be preserved, even if we do not realize that they exist. Thus trace-driven simulations are ordinarily more realistic than discrete event simulations.

A second advantage of the trace-driven approach is that it is relatively easy to verify the model. At the same time that the trace data is generated, performance measures can be obtained without too much additional effort. The availability of trace data and performance data for the same time period enables us to do a simple comparison when we run the model to establish its credibility. In comparison, model validation of discrete event simulation models can be very difficult. Problems such as selecting an appropriate level of detail, determining the modelling assumptions and fixing model parameters will all complicate the task. There are also problems of a statistical nature due to the fact that a discrete event simulation tends to have more 'variability' than a similar trace-driven one.

The main problem with trace-driven simulations is that the scope of application is small. They are really only applicable to the performance modelling of computer systems and even then they can only be used when the aim is to make moderate changes to a currently running system. In contrast, discrete

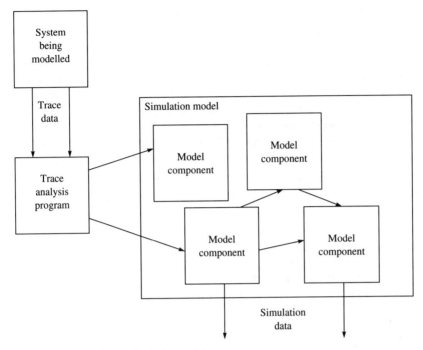

Figure 1.2 A trace-driven simulation model.

event simulation can be applied to many types of system, both existing and conceptual, and the approach is constrained only by the availability of resources (i.e. a fast enough computer, enough memory and so on). We will be wholly concerned with this latter type of model.

1.2.1 The benefits

Despite the problems of performing an accurate simulation exercise that were outlined in the previous section, the discrete event simulation method of systems analysis is still very attractive for the following reasons:

1. *Cost effectiveness.* It is feasible to perform on small computers with general-purpose languages such as Pascal, C and BASIC. With the explosive increase in the computing power of modern systems this makes even the home computer capable of handling small- to medium-size models.
2. *Accessibility.* No deep mathematical aptitude is necessary on the part of the modeller. Certainly it is necessary to understand basic mathematical statistics but the degree of understanding only needs to be at the level of the practitioner

sufficiently adept to apply the many standard mathematical tools that 'true' mathematicians have provided.

3. *Power.* The domain of application extends to systems which, in the past and even today, cause significant analytical problems for researchers and designers. These 'hard' systems share some or all of the common traits of complexity, poor definition and mathematical intractability. Discrete event simulation is a tool that can address all of these problem areas.

4. *Scope.* Discrete event simulation is very general in the sense that there are few restrictions on the type of systems and range of disciplines to which it can be applied.

The benefits of discrete event simulation normally outweigh any disadvantages and sometimes, for complex systems, we may even find that it provides the only feasible means of analysis.

The following chapters will describe how models can be developed and analysed to examine large and intricate systems. As a notational convenience from now on we will drop the long-winded 'discrete event' suffix so that all use of the terms 'model' and 'simulation' should be understood to refer to discrete event models and to discrete event simulation.

1.3 SUMMARY

Modelling concerns the portrayal of the interrelationships between the parts of a system in a precise way, which can be interpreted in terms of selected system attributes.

In order to classify the types of simulation models available we can use the following set of characteristics:

- *predictability*: whether stochastic or deterministic
- *solvability*: whether amenable to analytic treatment or whether simulation must be used
- *variability*: whether dynamic or static, and
- *granularity*: whether the treatment of time is as a discrete or continuous quantity.

This book is concerned with discrete event simulation models which involve stochastic and dynamic processes and which treat time in a discrete (i.e. a granular) way.

Simulation models are composed of a logical structure which describes the rules governing the behaviour of the system and a mathematical structure which describes the analytic components of the system. The operation of the model under specific conditions is the simulation of the system.

Simulation has significant benefits in terms of the following:

- *cost-effectiveness*: the ability to perform cheaply
- *accessibility*: the ability to be performed by non-mathematicians
- *power*: the ability to apply to difficult problems, and
- *scope*: the ability to apply to diverse problems.

1.4 EXERCISES

1.1 Classify the following models according to the categories described in Sec. 1.1.1:

(a) A model of a rabbit population based on an equation which relate population size and food supply as a function of time.

(b) A model, in the form of a set of equations, which gives the efficiency of a gas turbine generator as a function of input parameters such as engine temperature and speed.

(c) A spreadsheet model which gives the net worth of a company as a function of its current assets and liabilities.

(d) A model of a packet switch network which treats the transmission and reception of individual packets.

(e) A model which describes the variation due to osmosis of the concentration of salt suspended in a liquid as a function of time.

(f) A model of a supermarket checkout which simulates the arrival and departure of customers.

(g) A spreadsheet model which gives the projected return on investment of a company based on an estimated rate of growth of sales and costs.

(h) A model of the stock market which treats the fluctuation in share price as a random walk.

(i) A model which gives the stress in various members of a rigid wire frame for a given load distribution.

1.2 What changes do you think would have to be made to the model described in Exercise 1.1(c) in order to obtain a model like that in Exercise 1.1(g)?

2

METHODOLOGY

In this chapter we look at the steps to be taken in performing a simulation study. We also discuss how models at different levels can be combined and the sort of documentation required for a simulation exercise.

2.1 THE SIMULATION STUDY

A simulation study consists of a sequence of steps during which time a model is developed and used to analyse a system. The starting point for the study is invariably a person who has identified a problem somewhere that needs a solution. There are basically four general categories that the identified problem can fall into:

1. *Optimization*. In this type of problem there is some criterion for judging the quality of a system based on a number of observable parameters and we desire the particular combination of parameter values that maximizes quality.
2. *Forecasting*. In this type of problem the behaviour of a system is to be extrapolated into the future based on its current and previous pattern of behaviour.
3. *Analysis*. In this type of problem we want to understand the cause-and-effect relationships that a system exhibits.
4. *Comparison*. In this type of problem we want to see how a number of systems compare in terms of a defined set of metrics.

   Having decided what the problem is, the next decision concerns the best method of solution. The adoption of discrete event simulation is by no means automatic, it may be that analytic methods such as queuing theory or mathematical optimization techniques such as linear programming are possible. Alternatively, direct measurement may be made. However, for the reasons outlined in Sec. 1.2.1, we may decide that a simulation study is the most appropriate approach. It should be stressed, however, that this decision is not to be taken lightly. Successful simulations, especially of large systems, can be difficult and expensive activities to undertake.

As can be seen in Fig. 2.1, the simulation study can be split into five phases which are common to nearly all such exercises. The first is the *study definition phase*. This is where the goals of the study are identified and the input and output requirements stated. The second phase is dedicated to *systems analysis*, in which we ensure that we understand the subject system. Systems analysis may lead to a data-gathering exercise for *parameter estimation* if system parameters have been identified that need quantifying. The next phase is concerned with the *development* of the model as a computer program. The final phase consists of *experimentation and analysis*, in which the model is exercised and output data collected for investigation. From the analysis of the output data conclusions can be drawn which, it is hoped, satisfy the study goals.

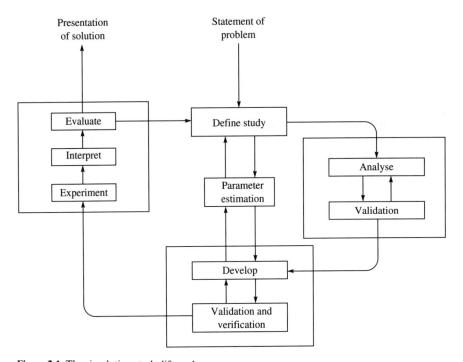

Figure 2.1 The simulation study life cycle.

Although the steps are described as a linear sequence, in practice they may involve considerable iteration and backtracking. For example, several iterations may be necessary before the goals of the simulation study are agreed between the client and the analyst, or the preliminary results of experimentation may suggest an important avenue of exploration that was not considered originally. Let us consider each of these steps in a little more detail.

2.1.1 Study definition

The scope of the simulation is expressed by the *study definition*. This describes the goals of the study and its bounds. It also identifies the assumptions made, the input variables, the output variables, the requirements for data collection activities, the accuracy and resolution required of results and the experiments to be performed (that is how the model is to be used).

The *goals* of the simulation define the basic objectives and it is important that they are formulated with the implications for the eventual experimentation in mind. The reason for this is that, if the goals are too broad, the experimentation may take far too long to perform or may not even be feasible. Hence, goals must not only cover what is to be modelled, but they must also clearly state the subject population to which the results are to apply. For example, we may have decided to evaluate the performance of a multi-user computer system under different page replacement algorithms. This is not difficult, but it is then necessary to decide to what population the results are to apply. The total possible population may consist of all applications that a group of users can run, and the whole range of conditions under which they could run them, i.e. every possible mix of user types (development, secretarial, managerial) and associated work loads, system software, communications, resource contentions and so on. Increasing the size of the population to which the results are to apply by increasing the number and combinations of input variables will require longer and more complex experimentation. It is important, therefore, to consider carefully the limitations to be placed on the goals in order that attainable targets are set.

It is useful if the internal detail of the simulation model is ignored when the input and output variables are identified. Thus, the model can be thought of as a black box giving a mapping f between a set $\{x_1, x_2, ..., x_n\}$ of *input* or *controlled variables* to a set $\{y_1, y_2, ..., y_m\}$ of *output* or *response variables*. This is depicted in Fig. 2.2. If the model is designed to support management decision making, then there will be a subset of input variables that represent parameters in the system over which management have direct control. The aim of the simulation in this case will normally be to maximize or minimize the output variables with respect to the controllable input variables or *decision variables*. The other input variables will be present in order to establish the changing conditions over which the

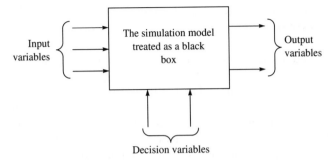

Figure 2.2 The variables relevant to a simulation.

optimum values are to be obtained. For example, if a simulation study is conducted to analyse the operation of a warehouse with the objective of determining the minimum cost, then the system input variables may be the number of vehicles to be unloaded per day and the amount of labour available for unloading. The decision variable, however, is the amount of labour available for unloading, since this is controlled by management by their deployment of staff.

2.1.2 Systems analysis

The *analysis* phase can be thought of as establishing the groundwork for model development. It should establish the principal components and dynamics of the system. The components can be categorized as entities, queues, events or resources, and each of them described and labelled for ease of identification. The dynamics define how the components behave and interact with each other. They can often be described in a graphical notation which makes it easier for non-technical personnel to understand.

In simple models *entities* are elementary homogeneous objects. In more complex models, entities have a particular set of values that characterize their individual structure or identity. For instance, in an X.25 packet switch, data packets have a logical channel number and a sequence number. The set of values is probably different for each class of entity. The requirements for this information must be recorded so that appropriate data structures can be designed when the model is developed.

Queues should have their organization specified. The most common and easiest to deal with is first in first out (FIFO) but other disciplines may be necessary and this may even require extensions to the simulation library. For example, Chapter 8 describes service pre-emption and queue swapping which may be present in the system and, if so, should normally be included in the model.

All the significant *events* in the system must be described. For example, the presence of queues implies the presence of events to insert and service members of the queue. This normally involves the entry and exit of entities from queues, the acquisition of resources and the delays incurred, all of which must be included in the event description.

The size of *resources* must also be defined. Resources represent passive objects that are used by entities and so we must determine which entities use each resource. The acquisition and release of resources will take place during significant events and so this too should form part of the event description.

The task of model construction and verification is simplified if the different components of the system under study can be assumed to have little effect on each other. This is an assumption of *independence*. However, the temptation is to assume that there is more independence than there actually is. Therefore, assumptions of independence should be tested in those situations where it seems suspect using techniques that will be covered in Chapter 10. It is not necessary to perform this exercise for all possible dependencies as this would take too much time. A sensible judgement must be made as to which dependencies are likely to be most significant and these checked analytically. The result of checking will either be the validation of the assumption of independence, or the characterization of the dependency in terms of correlation functions which must be taken into account in the model.

The result of system analysis should be checked by consulting the client. Checking seeks to ensure that all the major components of the system are covered, that the behaviour described by them is accurate and that the relationships between them are correct. The best client representatives to consult in this regard are management, designers or technical experts.

2.1.3 Parameter estimation

To obtain a convincing model, the values of parameters that quantify the effect of the different elements of the model must be similar in magnitude to the corresponding elements of the real system. For example, parameters of service times are of course vital because they determine the performance of the model and so affect the outcome of the study. Parameter estimation, therefore, should fix these values accurately enough for the purposes of the simulation. The problem is compounded when the system being modelled is still under development since, at the study stage, there is often no direct experience of the system to draw on and it is difficult to obtain these values from theoretical considerations alone. The following alternative schemes are available for estimating parameter values:

1. *Use existing client information.* Very often usable information already exists in the client organization, such as billing records, time and motion studies and

internal monitoring reports. Ideally, this will be computer based and so can be efficiently processed to determine the salient statistical features. However, if the information is out of date then it may be misleading and should therefore be carefully checked.

2. *Use manufacturers' specifications.* Sometimes it is sufficient to use manufacturers' figures. For instance, disk access times are fairly well established for certain types of commercial disk drives. It may be quite safe to use these values in the model directly. On the other hand, manufacturers' figures have a tendency to be over-optimistic or obtained from a very restricted system configuration or workload which is not relevant and so their use can be dangerous. In any case, the reason for the study is often to provide an independent opinion of performance!

3. *Make path-length estimations.* This method can be useful in some circumstances—for example, in a real-time system where there are some paths that are critical to the success of the system, perhaps because they are dealing with critical sensor data. The approach involves making an estimate of the workload by estimating the activities involved. In a computer system, for example, a rough design and code of the logical path taken through the software can be established which takes into account the number of times the path will be traversed when the software is run. This value can then be divided by the speed of the processor to give the execution time of the software (see Smith, 1990).

Care has to be exercised when using this method because it is easy to build in a degree of undue optimism. For example, it is easy to forget aspects which, in the real system, will have to be included. A large number of assumptions must also be made along the way. For instance, the assumption that the figure taken for processor speed is valid for the mix of instructions that will be used and so on.

4. *Run benchmarks.* This is really the only satisfactory method of parameter estimation in many cases. A carefully designed benchmark can take into account most of the factors involved and give a good indication of the sort of figures that will be experienced when the system is put into operation. It is far less likely to be optimistic than a figure obtained from theoretical considerations alone. It may be possible to use an early prototype or even a similar design from another system that already exists. This then enables accurate direct measurements to be taken.

Benchmarks need to be reliably designed if they are to yield the data needed. Typically, an unloaded system would be used so that no queuing effects are included. Specific transactions can be applied to the system and the transit times noted. The latency, that is the processing delay, can then be measured. From this the parameters of interest such as mean service time may be determined.

Once parameter estimates have been obtained they must be verified. Management and technical experts in the client organization can be consulted to help confirm and refine the findings.

2.1.4 Model development

Model development is concerned with the production of software and is best done progressively. Stepwise refinement of the design should start by implementing the active components as simply as possible. All detail should be eliminated and a framework established which can be embellished later. In particular, complex distributions can be replaced by constant or exponential distributions to start with and all random number streams can be replaced by a single stream.

At each step the model should be *verified*. Verification is concerned with the correctness of the *code*. There are many good textbooks dealing with this subject in varying degrees of formality such as Jackson (1983), Jones (1980) and Wirth (1986). What they essentially boil down to is that implementation starts with a specification of *what* the software is to do which is gradually refined into *how* it is to do it (in other words the actual code).

Testing is an important part of model verification. *Test data* should exercise the model in normal system states and also in extremes. In all cases the model should behave reasonably and should not crash or lock up.

Once a working framework has been obtained, the statistical aspects of the model can be introduced. Normally steady-state conditions (see Chapter 10) will be of interest, therefore steady-state analysis should be performed and results collected in histograms to confirm that they look sensible. This normally involves special-purpose code which can be removed for the experimentation phase once estimates of transient duration have been determined. Having determined in the analysis phase which measurements are required, data-collection routines should be added and the model probably generalized somewhat so that the necessary experimentation can be accommodated. This may involve allowing various model parameters to be input without having to recode. Several alternatives exist for this. One method is to enter values interactively or, alternatively, via command-line parameters. A better approach, though, is to use a model *configuration file* that contains the names of variables and the values they are to be assigned on start-up. Such a file can be read during an initialization phase when the model is executed.

The model must also be *validated*. Validation is concerned with logical correctness where we make sure that all necessary rules are embodied in the model, that unnecessary ones are excluded, that the assumptions are valid and that sound statistical methods have been used. The aim is to show, often to the client, that the model behaves like the real system. Communication is vital here. A client is normally unable and unwilling to get involved at the code level. It is necessary, therefore, to abstract the essentials and present them in a comprehensible form. Graphics such as timing diagrams, flow charts and state-transition diagrams very often provide a good means of presentation.

Once the model is running and debugged, it is possible to take measurements and compare them to those taken from the real system if it is available, leading to additional data-gathering requirements. It may also be possible to compare model predictions using *historic data* if this data is consistent with the current system, but this must be carefully checked because it is possible that conditions have changed so much over the intervening period that the data is no longer applicable.

Sensitivity analysis may also be used to verify whether an input variable is critical or unimportant. We assess how much the output variables change in value when some of the input variables are varied. If there is negligible effect on the magnitude of the output then model reduction may be possible. This should attempt to simplify the model without compromising the accuracy of the results. The principal benefits will be lower development costs, easier maintenance and a reduction in running time.

It is important to know when to exit the development loop. Adding detail which is inappropriate or unnecessary is at best time consuming and extends the model development time. It can also make the model difficult to modify should it be necessary for some related but different problem in the future. More importantly, the additional complexity makes errors more likely and the deficiency of computer resources such as processor speed and memory more problematic.

2.1.5 Experimentation and results gathering

Once the model has been developed and confidence has been established that it is a reasonable representation of the modelled system, then a period of experimentation can take place. This consists of a series of parametric simulation runs which are performed to satisfy the aims of the simulation study. Each simulation run is termed a *replication* or simply a *run*. A run generates a set of *samples* or *observations*. Each sample generated is the value of a model variable at some point in simulated time. Several runs are normally performed in order to test alternative hypotheses and to cover various combinations and levels of input variables. A run can also be repeated to increase confidence in the results of the simulation, a point which we will come back to in Chapter 10.

The experimentation performed and the analysis of the results should be guided by sound statistical theory. The important point to note in this regard is that simulation modelling will never allow anything to be proved. What we can do, however, is to ascertain the likelihood of error in a statement or the degree of confidence that can be placed in an experimental value. There is always some degree of 'doubt' surrounding the value itself. The use of statistical theory will not remove this doubt, but it will enable the experimenter to quantify the reliability of his results.

When the results have been generated then they can be used to draw conclusions. The conclusions should reflect the objectives established at the beginning of the study and they should offer quantitative support in the form of confidence intervals for all important output values as discussed in Chapter 10. In addition, when dealing with a system under development, model predictions can be compared against measured behaviour as the system evolves and the available data becomes better defined and more accurate. Current results can also be compared with results from earlier, less detailed models, to see if the additional accuracy still leads to the same decisions. This allows the model to be enhanced as the system becomes better defined.

After modelling and experimentation has been completed, output data generated, and conclusions drawn, we are in a position to evaluate the success of the simulation. In short, we can decide if the simulation study has satisfied the goals established at the outset. If the answer to this question is no then we may be able to look again at some of the previous steps to try and discover what, if anything, can be changed to rectify the deficiencies. It is possible, for example, that the results obtained lead the modeller to redefine the objectives of the simulation study because they have shown an unexpected aspect of system behaviour which needs to be investigated.

2.2 WORKLOADS AND PERFORMANCE METRICS

The *workload* of a system refers to the degree to which the system is active. This is a particularly important factor in performance evaluation since there is clearly a strong relationship between performance indicators and the simulated system activity. The quantitative description of the workload is termed a *workload characterization*. The characterization is usually specified in terms of *workload parameters* that can affect system behaviour and that are defined in a form suitable for a desired use. Thus, for example, instruction frequency may be seen as a workload parameter for a cpu, and vehicles repaired per day as a workload parameter of a service depot.

Normally, workload parameters will be related to input variables in the model so it is common to see parameters specified in terms of average resource usage and arrival rates. The selection of appropriate workload parameters can best be accomplished by considering the system as a provider of a service (or services) to external clients. A client of a communications network, for example, may be a user at a remote terminal, and the clients of an operating system may be applications programs. The first step then is to identify the services provided and the clients involved. The second step in is to choose parameters which indicate service behaviour. In the case of the cpu above, the instruction mix was chosen because the service involved is the execution of machine instructions on behalf of various system and application programs. In the case of the service depot, the vehicle repair rate was chosen because the service involved is the repair of vehicles on behalf of customers.

Similar remarks also apply to the selection of *performance metrics* (see Chapter 8). However, performance metrics will normally be related to the output variables of a model. They must therefore reflect the performance of services provided by the system. It is of little use, for instance, to specify the effect of a database server in a transaction processing system by considering its speed of response to particular database queries and updates alone. Rather, it is necessary to consider the overall effect on system performance. This is because a typical workload will involve various sorts of reads and writes, in different combinations, at unpredictable times. It is only by trying to incorporate realistic usage scenarios that the average overall effect of these different activities can be determined in the context of the particular system.

In comparative analysis it is important to remember that the workload parameters and comparative performance metrics should also be determined by how external users interface to the system under study. It is all too easy to forget this rule and allow the different alternatives to have an undue influence on the selection. For instance, in selecting parameters for a simulation model which is to be used to evaluate the effect of different disk drives it would be a mistake to focus primarily on relative disk performance. Instead, the comparison should be made by considering the effect of each disk drive to the overall system performance for as complete a set of system services as possible.

2.3 CHOICE OF MODELLING UNITS AND TIME SCALES

In simulation studies there is normally a range of time scales involved, varying from the coarse, such as users logging on for terminal sessions, to the fine, such as instructions being executed in the cpu or data being fetched from cache. It is not a good idea to mix these time scales. Obviously, events at the coarse level look like extremely rare events at the fine level. How many instructions or data fetches would have to be simulated before a log on occurred? In one study, the analyst had to wait for an hour of simulation before any coarse event took place at all. At first it was thought that something was wrong with the model, until it was realized that this was quite a reasonable result given the type of model that had been constructed.

One of the first tasks to perform when starting a modelling assignment is to choose the time scale and type of events that will be modelled. Often it is

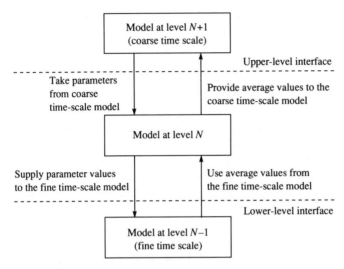

Figure 2.3 Models with different time scales.

necessary to formulate several models to handle the problem at different granularity. But if so, these models should be kept strictly separate. However, the *results* may be freely passed between models but an attempt to connect them up within a macro model will hit the problem outlined above.

If there are several time scales then it is possible to proceed as follows. At each level a model is constructed which contains some parameters which relate to higher-level models such as the number of users logged on during the simulation. These parameters are held constant during any particular run, but varied between runs. This is illustrated in Fig. 2.3 as the upper model interface.

For the lower model interface it is necessary to take average values because it is not practical to deal with the effects in detail. In other words, we take a macro view of the lower-level world. For instance, in the 'user level' model we would not represent individual computer transactions, but treat them as the average effect of loading the cpu and communications links by a certain percentage. So we might say that when a user logged on he consumed, perhaps, 5 per cent of the available cpu time and 1 per cent of the network bandwidth.

2.4 DOCUMENTATION

Any significant modelling exercise has to be documented. The results of simulation may be required by management to provide quantitative support for decision making. For example, management may need to decide between various options for upgrading a company's communications and data-processing infrastructure and have elected to evaluate the cost–benefit trade-off of the alternatives via a simulation study. In this case it will be necessary to form the results in management's terminology so that the most suitable option can be selected. This is important because often the final decision on a proposal will be made by someone who has only the report upon which to base the decision.

Producing good documentation can be difficult and time consuming and should certainly not be underestimated when planning a simulation study. The problem is that the model itself can be quite complex and will need to be described to people without a modelling background. If too much detail is included, readers may be put off and conclude that they cannot understand the model and therefore must take it on trust.

What is needed for documenting the simulation is a top-down approach, in which the general conclusions are stated up front and the material from which they have been derived given a bit at a time, in progressively more detail, so that the reader never gets lost. The detailed material should cover the structure of the model, the assumptions made, the input and output variables and the experimentation and analysis performed. Diagrams are a help in explaining the design and dynamics of the model. If the transaction or data flows can be sketched out they can usually be understood by the system designers at least. Other techniques such as state-transition diagrams and timing diagrams can also be useful, especially for describing complex logic such as a communications protocol as is illustrated in Chapter 12.

The following layout forms the basis of such a report:

1. *Introduction.* A statement of the problem stating the goals addressed, the existing conditions and the alternatives evaluated.
2. *Management summary.* A brief description of the procedures followed and the conclusion reached, written after the rest of the report has been written. Sometimes a hard-pressed manager may read no further than this section so it should be succinct and to the point.
3. *Methodology.* Describing the simulation software and the methods used for data gathering.
4. *Model structure.* A description of the composition of the model. When the implementation system involves actual coding, the details should be covered by separate technical documentation as for conventional software development. Such additional documentation is not required when the implementation system uses a generic model, such as a network analysis package that only requires data to be input.
5. *Parameters and inputs.* A description of the assumptions, important simulation parameters and inputs to the model.
6. *Model execution.* A short account of how the simulation model behaved, the runs performed and the values assigned to input parameters for these runs.

7. *Simulation results.* A discussion of the important output statistics and their analysis.
8. *Conclusions and recommendations.* The conclusions and recommendations of the analysis team, each point being written in a separate, numbered, paragraph.

The above document structure should allow a client to obtain the essential information he requires quickly and easily. If the client does not want to pursue the modelling minutiae only the first few sections need to be read. On the other hand, if the assumptions made are of vital interest, the details are available.

2.5 SUMMARY

The decision to use simulation begins with the identification of a problem which falls into one or more of the following classes:

- optimization: to maximize the quality of a system
- forecasting: to predict future behaviour
- analysis: to understand cause-and-effect relationships, and
- comparison: to compare systems in terms of a set of metrics.

Simulation modelling has five main phases. The process starts with the study definition which leads to the formulation of goals and objectives. The system is then analysed so that the requirements for the model are understood. Then follows data gathering and parameter estimation in which quantitative information is obtained which will be used to dimension the model. Model development follows and involves the translation of the specification of the subject system ultimately into executable code. The translation is done iteratively, starting with a very simplified, working framework which can be embellished. The experimentation phase is where the model is exercised and the results generated. These must be statistically analysed and conclusions drawn which satisfy the objectives set at the beginning of the study.

Workloads and performance metrics should be selected from a consideration of the services provided by a system to clients. Workload parameters should specify the service behaviour and performance metrics must reflect the performance of the services.

Various time scales are normally involved in a simulation study, ranging from the very coarse to the very fine. It is in general not possible to mix these time scales in a macro model but instead we can pass the results between the submodels executing at different granularity.

Documentation is an important part of a simulation study that must not be overlooked. Good documentation should present the conclusions of the study first and then the material from which the conclusions are based later, including details of the model and the experimentation and analysis performed with it.

2.6 EXERCISES

2.1 In what way does the development of a simulation model differ from the development of conventional software? Are there any problems that might be encountered in one but not the other?

2.2 What differences might exist between a simulation study whose objective is to evaluate the performance of a system and a simulation study whose objective is to explore the probable future behaviour of a system.

2.3 In a simulation of a distributed data-processing system two models are developed. The first is a simulation model of the protocol which allows the remote user terminals to communicate with a central database server over *radio channels*. This model predicts bit-error rate and end-to-end through-put/delay performance for various network topologies and terrain profiles. The second model predicts the performance of the server for various types and frequency of queries. How could these two models be used successfully together if the objective of a simulation study was to investigate the performance as perceived by the end-user in different network configurations and propagation conditions?

3

IMPLEMENTATION

In this chapter we overview the software used to implement simulation models. We begin by reviewing the various forms of simulation software available: dedicated simulation packages, special-purpose languages and general-purpose languages. We focus on the use of general-purpose languages and the provision of a simulation library that can be reused in different models. We then discuss the overall structure of a model.

3.1 SIMULATION SOFTWARE

Software for implementing simulation models has undergone gradual evolution from the programming languages derived in the early 1960s. The result is that the modeller these days can choose his means of implementation from three types of software: dedicated simulation packages, special-purpose languages (SPLs) and general-purpose languages (GPLs), each of which has particular strengths and weaknesses.

Dedicated simulation packages attempt to de-emphasize the programming aspect, allowing a model to be produced very quickly. These systems are usually generic models which are data-driven rather than programming languages *per se*. The model is normally represented graphically as a series of connected blocks whose parameters are specified via a forms type menu. A user defines key parameters related to entities in the model such as the queue discipline and inter-arrival times and by specifying the reports and outputs required.

The major drawback of these systems is the imposition of a rather rigid modelling framework. Given an instance of a problem, it is generally necessary to choose a system specifically geared to that particular problem domain. Hence, for example, there are systems such as XCELL (Conway *et al.*, 1986) for modelling factory systems and COMNET (CACI, 1991) for modelling communication networks. For obvious reasons these tools are often referred to as *domain specific*. Also, the cost of such systems can be quite high, which may be difficult to justify for the occasional simulation project. However, they do permit the rapid construction of simulation models and completely avoid the problems of actual code production.

SPLs are designed specifically for discrete event simulation. Their principal benefit is that they provide transparent facilities for queue management, simulated time management, resource handling, scheduling and statistical functions. They also tend to be problem oriented, providing a high level of abstraction from the mechanics of queue management and scheduling. This can make them effective tools once the initial learning curve has been overcome.

One of the early SPLs is SIMULA (Birtwistle *et al.*, 1973) which is a very elegant language based on ALGOL-60 and applicable to a wide variety of applications rather than simulation specifically. However, probably the best known SPL is GPSS (Stahl, 1990). GPSS requires the user to specify his problem in terms of a sequence of blocks for which there is a standard diagrammatic notation. The original version was developed by IBM in the sixties, but has since undergone numerous revisions and is now available as GPSS/PC (Karian and Dudewicz, 1991) for the IBM PC and compatibles, GPSS/H (Schriber, 1990) for mainframes and workstations and GPSS V (Gordon, 1975) for IBM mainframes.

With care, a simulation written in a GPL can provide a level of abstraction approaching that of an SPL. Traditionally, the GPL which has been used most for this purpose is FORTRAN, but more recent languages have also been used such as Pascal (Jennergen, 1984), Ada (Bruno, 1984), PL/1 (Hac, 1984) and C (Pidd, 1989), to name but a few.

There have also been several attempts to provide standard extensions to GPLs to provide simulation facilities. Some of these have been quite successful. GASP (Pritsker, 1975) for example is a library of FORTRAN subroutines which provide discrete and continuous simulation facilities. Another language extension, this time to an ALGOL base, is SIMON (Hills, 1966) which provides event-oriented simulation facilities and includes some results analysis tools.

A GPL has several advantages over an SPL. In the first place, SPLs tend not to be as well known as GPLs and in a new simulation project there will not be the time to learn an unknown language. GPLs are also more widely available and often provide more flexibility in terms of both the expressiveness of the language itself and its ability to link into external systems such as a relational database. A GPL implementation is also normally more efficient because the simulation components are less general, and should it be necessary to move to a different hardware platform the portability problems will be far less severe. Another significant advantage is that it will be easier to add to, or modify, the modelling primitives should it be necessary to model an unusual facet of a system. This ability allows the environment to grow and adapt as the needs of the user evolves. Such an adaption would be difficult or downright impossible with an SPL.

3.2 REQUIREMENTS OF A GENERAL-PURPOSE LANGUAGE

In this book we focus on C as an implementation language for models. However, this choice is not essential to the application of the techniques discussed. More or less any modern computer language can be used for simulation, but a potential implementation language should have the following features if it is to be used with a simulation library similar to the one described in this text:

- the ability to create dynamic data objects at run time
- the ability to pass procedures or functions as arguments
- support for separate compilation and the use of libraries of precompiled modules.

The first two features are necessary because of the way the simulation library schedules the activation of different parts of the model as the simulation proceeds. The last feature gives an effective mechanism for reusing core components from one model to another. We will explore this in a little more detail next.

3.2.1 The use of simulation libraries

The emphasis when writing simulations in a GPL should be the provision of software components that can be reused. This generally means that there should be some form of *simulation library* that can be linked into the rest of the model.

The library concept has been adopted by most current computer languages as an excellent means of allowing modules of code to be designed, implemented and tested once but used many times. As a result less code is developed from scratch and the code we reuse is known to be reliable. The net result is improvements in yield and precision. Therefore, we should provide a library of components for discrete event simulation which enables the modeller to concentrate on the logic of the model without worrying about the details of the implementation. To achieve this aim, the components must be flexible enough to permit a wide variety of systems to be modelled. In addition they must be efficient, allowing each new model to be written without being too concerned about maximizing the run-time performance. A library should also be open-ended and allow new modules to be incorporated if required. Such modules can be added to the base functionality, or provide additional services on top of those already present. The base functionality should encompass the following:

1. *Random number generation.* For the most part our models will involve stochastic processes and so it is essential that a mechanism for generating random numbers is provided. Such a set of functions should provide random numbers drawn from various probability distributions and allow many uncorrelated number streams to be active in a simulation.
2. *Entity modelling.* Entities and resources essentially model objects in the system being scrutinized. Entities normally only have a temporary existence. In a typical model many entities will be created, they will interact with each other in some way and eventually be discarded. In the simulation environment, therefore, we must have some mechanism for creating and destroying entities. We should also be capable of modelling the characteristics of such an object in the real system in terms of its attributes. Ideally, there should be no imposed restriction on the structure of this information.
3. *Resource modelling.* Resources normally have a more permanent existence in the model. They represent aggregates obtained and released by entities. Resources are essentially passive structures, used to represent real-world quantities such as an amount of storage available on a computer or the availability of a server in a queuing system.
4. *Scheduling.* The scheduler is responsible for controlling which components of the model are to be run next. It is the occurrence of an event which drives the model so the scheduler maintains a calendar of scheduled events which are to occur at some future time. When the occurrence time arrives an appropriate routine is called. Associated with this is the need to provide a simulated clock that measures the progress of time in the model, so that the instant can be determined at which future events become current events and must be actioned.
5. *Queue modelling.* Queues are an implicit part of (nearly) all discrete event simulations. They allow entities to be grouped into ordered sets whenever the limited availability of a resource causes contention. When customers arrive at a checkout for example, and the checkout is busy, they must wait in line. It is necessary then to ensure that an effective means is provided to manage queues. In particular, we require routines to insert entities into the front and back of a queue and to make insertions that are based on priority.
6. *Results collection.* The results generated from a simulation are statistical in nature and function to characterize the output variables of a model in terms of probability distributions. Ordinarily, the samples from which the characterization is constructed must be recorded as well in the form of a graph or table. It is, however, up to the analyst to add the statistics gathering functions at selected points in the model. The simulation system cannot automatically

record samples of all variables because of the performance penalty and it has no knowledge on which to sensibly base the selection of a subset.

7. *Results analysis.* When a set of results have been obtained they must be analysed in order to draw conclusions and make hypotheses concerning the behaviour of the real system. Detailed results analysis is best handled by a dedicated analysis package. However, the simulation library should be able to provide for the basic analysis of results.

Other more general, but no less important, requirements of a simulation library are that it places as few restrictions on the modelling process as possible and that it requires little, if any, customization from model to model. It is preferable that any limitations are a function of the hardware or operating system rather than an intrinsic limitation imposed by the library itself. Such a library, implemented in C, is included in source-code form on the disk enclosed with this book.

3.3 MODELLING APPROACHES

In accordance with the software engineering view that modularity is an important goal in the development of software, simulation models are generally implemented in terms of the events or processes that occur in the real system. This approach to modularity not only makes sense from a software development point of view, but it also makes it easier to see how the model relates to the system. This is of great help when we have to perform validation.

There are several structures in common use today that are variously referred to as *approach, world view* or *strategy* in the simulation literature (for example see Fishman, 1978). There are two general groups: those that are *event based* and those that are *process* (i.e. entity) *based.* This is depicted in Fig. 3.1, which further subdivides the event-based strategies into *event scheduling* (or *two phase*) and *three phase*, and names a single process-based strategy: *process interaction.*

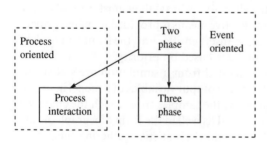

Figure 3.1 Classification of simulation strategies.

New customer   Queue   Checkout   Exit

Figure 3.2 A simple FIFO queue.

Despite the fact that we have a number of different approaches, there is a common thread that unites them. This is in their management of simulated time. All strategies employ asynchronous timing, in which the simulation clock is allowed to advance in steps which depend on the instantaneous system state. In other words, when the program has processed an event in the model, it proceeds to the next given in a *calendar* of those waiting to occur and the simulated time becomes equal to the occurrence time of the event. We will often refer to these advances of the simulation clock as 'clock ticks'; unlike normal clocks, though, these clock ticks usually have unequal intervals.

In order to explain the salient features of each of the approaches, an example model of a simple first in first out (FIFO) queuing system, such as may be found at a supermarket checkout, is used. This example is represented schematically in Fig. 3.2. Customers arrive and are either immediately served at the checkout when the checkout is free or have to wait in line at the service queue when the checkout is busy. When the checkout has finished with a customer, the customer leaves the store and the next waiting customer enters the checkout for service. If no customer is available the checkout becomes dormant.

In a real simulation we would be interested in obtaining output data such as waiting time or queue length, but for the purposes of this explanation such complications are deferred to later chapters.

We now look at each of these approaches in more detail.

3.3.1 Event scheduling

Time management in the event-scheduling approach is summarized in the algorithm of Fig. 3.3. We refer to the main activities of this approach as the *A phase* and the *B phase*. Conceptually, we have a *calendar* of scheduled events ordered by activation time which we refer to as *bound events* because they are associated together and made to occur at some time in the future. In the A phase, those events in the calendar which are the earliest bound events scheduled to occur are identified. This may involve more than one event if they are scheduled to occur together. The simulation clock is then advanced to their common occurrence time. In the B phase, each of the identified events is actioned by calling an associated *event routine*, which may result in the addition of further events to the calendar. If the calendar is not empty and the termination conditions for the simulation have not been reached, then the A and B phases are repeated again.

In this simplified example, the termination conditions for the simulation are embodied in the single Boolean-valued variable *RUNNING*, which is assumed to take the value *TRUE* while the simulation can continue and *FALSE* when it should cease. The normal condition for terminating the simulation is that the simulation clock has reached a predefined maximum value, but other conditions are possible. We may, for example, want to simulate for as long as it takes to process a given number of entities.

The execution of the event routine in the B phase may release resources required by other events, so event routines really have *two* jobs. The first is to model the effect of an event and the second is to see if the occurrence of this event has freed any resources which would allow other events to proceed. Hence, in most event routines, it is necessary to review the subset of activities that use

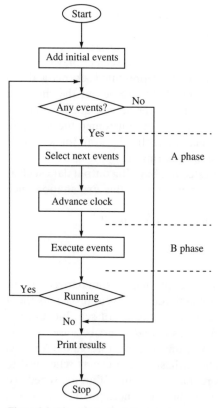

Figure 3.3 The event-scheduling strategy.

resources released by the event and, where possible, schedule future events using the newly available resources.

To illustrate the event scheduling approach consider the simple FIFO queue described above. Our familiarity with this situation allows us to identify two fairly obvious events, the *customer arrival* event and the *customer departure* event. The logic of the model can be described in terms of these events using a pseudocode that allows us to write in a structured form without worrying too much about the strict syntax of a programming language. Ignoring for the moment details such as the time between customer arrivals and the service completion times, we have the following pseudocode for the customer arrival event:

```
arrival()
{
  <<Create a new customer>>
  <<Schedule the next customers future arrival>>
  if <<The checkout is free>>
  {
    <<Make checkout busy>>
    <<Schedule a departure event for the current customer>>
  }
  else
  {
    <<Place this customer at the end of the queue>>
  }
}
```

Function *arrival( )* creates a new customer and then schedules itself to cause the arrival of the next customer some time later. Hence, the arrival of many customers is efficiently handled by daisy chaining. The first customer schedules the arrival of the second which schedules the arrival of the third and so on. The new customer is added to the queue if the checkout is busy, otherwise it acquires the checkout and schedules its own departure a short time later when the service has been completed.

The pseudocode for the departure routine is as follows:

```
departure()
{
  <<Remove this customer from the model>>
  if <<The queue is not empty>>
  {
    <<Take the next customer from front of the queue>>
    <<Schedule a customer departure event>>
  }
  else
  {
    <<Make the checkout free>>
  }
}
```

Function *departure( )* takes the customer being served and removes it from the model. If the queue is now non-empty, the next customer is selected and a departure event scheduled for it. Otherwise the checkout is flagged as free. In contrast to the arrival event, the customer departure event schedules a subsequent departure only if there are customers waiting to be served, otherwise it must be activated by the arrival of a new customer into an empty queue. In other words, the checkout is treated as a resource and when a departure takes place the events corresponding to subsequent customer arrivals must be reviewed to see if a customer is available which may now proceed to the checkout.

3.3.2 Three phase

The three-phase approach is a development of event scheduling and is outlined in the algorithm of Fig. 3.4. In the previous section we saw that the event-scheduling approach requires that each event routine explicitly identifies the subset of activities that use resources released by the event. In an initially complex model, or a model which has been progressively modified over a period of time, these relationships may be difficult to follow. The three-phase structure, on the other hand, tests all those events whose occurrence is conditional on the state of a queue or resource. These events are known as *conditional events* and they are scanned in a new phase of the simulation—the *C phase*.

In the three-phase approach, the A phase and B phase are functionally similar to their namesakes in the event-scheduling approach. The A phase is the recognition phase where all the bound events that have the same, earliest, activation time are selected. In the B phase the bound events are caused to occur and this is realized by calling the applicable event routine.

The C phase *conditional event routines* perform the second of the jobs performed by routines in the event-scheduling approach—they action activity which is dependent on the availability of resources. So, having selected and run the next bound events in the B phase, we see if any events that are waiting for the availability of resources can occur by scanning the conditional event routines. Frequently, when a conditional event routine is able to run it will result in the acquisition of resources and the scheduling of subsequent bound events to release them some time later.

As before, the simulation proceeds until the termination conditions are true, which is tested in the condition block labelled *RUNNING*, as for the event-scheduling approach described above.

The three-phase approach is modular because bound event routines do not need to identify conditional events which can run—we have decoupled them. On the minus side it has redundancy. The more events in the model that depend on queues and resources, the greater the degree of redundancy. This is due to the fact that at each scan of the conditional events only a small subset of them can run.

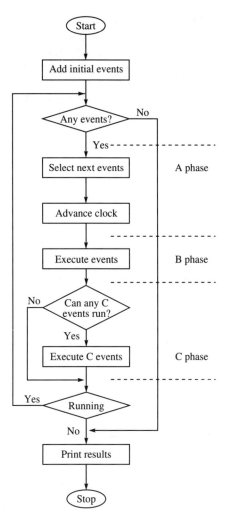

Figure 3.4 The three-phase strategy.

We do not know beforehand which of them this will include, so we must scan them all. In practice this is a small price to pay for the convenience of ignoring the model structure when determining the position of the tests. If the overhead is significant, tests can be optimized, or a mixed strategy can be adopted that moves events into and out of the set of conditional events as they are required.

Let us take our previous simple queue example and implement it using a three-phase approach. The two events that we have identified must be subdivided into those events that can be scheduled to occur and those whose occurrence is conditional on some state of the system. In this case the relevant state comprises the length of the queue and the status of the checkout. So we must separate the previous customer arrival event into two events; one which is scheduled (the actual customer arrival) and one which depends on the current system state (the commencement of service).

The new customer arrival event is represented in pseudocode below. The event creates a fresh customer, adds it to a queue and then reschedules itself to create the next customer some time later.

```
arrival()
{
  ⟨⟨Create a new customer⟩⟩
  ⟨⟨Add new customer to the queue⟩⟩
  ⟨⟨Schedule arrival of next customer⟩⟩
}
```

The corresponding service routine is function *start_service()*. This is a conditional event and so will be called at each tick of the simulation clock (i.e. after each set of bound events has been processed). The pseudocode is

```
start_service()
{
  if ⟨⟨Queue is non_empty and the checkout is free⟩⟩
  {
    ⟨⟨Take the customer from the front of the queue⟩⟩
    ⟨⟨Make the checkout busy⟩⟩
    ⟨⟨Schedule the departure event for this customer⟩⟩
  }
}
```

The purpose of *start_service()* is to take the first customer from the queue, make the checkout busy and then schedule the end of service by the activation of routine *departure()* after an appropriate delay. At that moment the customer releases the checkout, making it available for the next customer, and then leaves the model. The pseudocode for *departure()* is

```
departure()
{
  ⟨⟨Make the checkout free⟩⟩
  ⟨⟨Remove entity from the model⟩⟩
}
```

Notice in this example how the logic of the events is simplified in comparison to the event-scheduling approach and how customer arrival has been decoupled from service commencement. Now, arrival events only cause the arrival of a new customer and departure events only ever take the customer from the checkout and remove it from the simulation.

3.3.3 Process interaction

In the process view the event is replaced as the focal point by the sequence of events undertaken by an *entity*. Entities most naturally represent the existence of some *object* in the modelled system such as a customer. The 'processes' in the process interaction model correspond to classes (types) of entities in the modelled system. The function of the modeller is now to prepare for each entity class a life cycle showing which actions must occur at each point in the life of entities belonging to that class. The life cycle takes the form of an *entity routine* that combines all the events that can occur to a single entity class.

There are several ways in which to organize a process view of the simulation model. The quintessential process interaction model requires inter-process communication supported by a message-passing mechanism, a method of encapsulation which allows attributes to be declared private to the process and preserved between activations of the process, activation to be suspended and resumed at arbitrary points (reactivation points) within the process and inheritance, in which a process may take a set of base attributes and procedures from parent processes. Readers familiar with object-oriented techniques may recognize some of these characteristics and may not be surprised to hear that an early version of such a language, namely SIMULA, is also considered the forebear of modern object-oriented programming.

Unfortunately, this purist's view of the process interaction approach is not easily supported (in a portable form) in many procedure-oriented languages, so a slightly different implementation must be adopted. For example, communication can be implemented with shared variables and reactivation pointers can be implemented by splitting the entity routine into *phases* and selecting a particular phase via some sort of C *switch* statement. As regards inheritance, we can provide an entity routine that models the behaviour of the entity class and parameterize it so that each instance of the class can, if necessary, adopt different parameter values and behaviour. Since this deviation is clearly different from pure process interaction we will refer to it as *process-oriented*.

The algorithm we choose to adopt for time management is very similar to the three-phase approach and is summarized in Fig. 3.5. In the process-oriented approach we have a set of *bound entities* that are waiting until their activation time. In the A phase the next group of such entities is selected for activation. In the B phase the simulation clock is advanced to their common activation time and the selected entities are activated by calling the appropriate entity routine. Each entity routine can continue to execute as long as the entity is not blocked, which occurs when an entity either requires a resource that is not available, becomes scheduled for later activation or is terminated.

In the C phase, *conditional entities* which have been blocked because they require a resource which is currently unavailable are scanned. If any

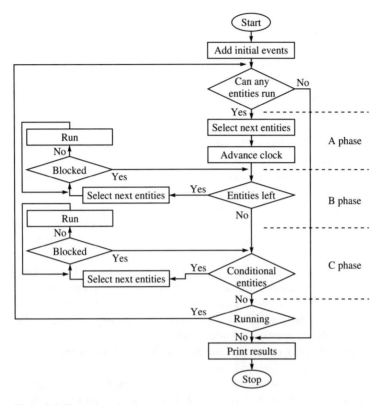

Figure 3.5 The process interaction strategy.

conditional entities can run they are allowed to do so until they become blocked again.

From Fig. 3.5 it is evident that the real difference between the three-phase and process-oriented approaches stems not so much from the way the time management algorithm is implemented, but from the way in which the event routines themselves are organized. We can appreciate this difference by turning again to the example of the simple queuing system. In this system we have a single active entity—the customer. The customer variously participates in the actions of arrival, queue entry, and departure. The checkout can be thought of as a passive resource that must be acquired by an entity in order to obtain service and that will block the entity if it is not available. The following pseudocode illustrates a model of the customer entity.

```
customer()
{
  while (ACTIVE) {
    switch (⟨⟨The phase of the customer⟩⟩)
    {
    case ARRIVAL:
      ⟨⟨Set phase to SERVICE⟩⟩
      ⟨⟨Add to list of conditional entities⟩⟩
      ⟨⟨Schedule the next customer (with phase arrival)⟩⟩
      break;
    case SERVICE:
      if ⟨⟨Checkout is free⟩⟩
      {
        ⟨⟨Make the checkout busy⟩⟩
        ⟨⟨Make phase DEPARTURE⟩⟩
        ⟨⟨Schedule the departure⟩⟩
      }
      else
        ⟨⟨Wait until checkout free (i.e. do nothing)⟩⟩
      break;
    case DEPARTURE:
      ⟨⟨Remove entity from the model⟩⟩
      ⟨⟨Make the checkout free⟩⟩
      break;
    }
  }
}
```

In the above pseudocode the customer entity is first activated with phase *ARRIVAL*. In this phase it schedules the next customer arrival, sets the phase to *SERVICE* and then enters the conditional entity list, where it waits for the checkout to become free. Because the entity is now blocked the value of *ACTIVE* is set to *FALSE*, so the loop is exited and the current processing for this entity is finished. After all the bound entities are processed we scan the list of conditional entities. When such an entity is scanned it will have a phase equal to *SERVICE*, and so the code in that branch of the switch statement will be executed. This consists of a conditional statement that tests the state of the checkout. If the checkout is free, the entity can enter the checkout straight away and schedule its departure some time later. If, however, another entity is ahead in the queue, then it will have already taken service and the condition will be *FALSE*, so the entity will remain suspended in the conditional entity list. Eventually all prior entities will have been served so the test will succeed, allowing the entity to obtain service and schedule its final departure from the system.

In terms of the three-phase approach then, the behaviour of the entity in the *SERVICE* phase is the dual of the *start_service( )* event routine. However, in the process-oriented approach we do not need to include a check in the conditional statement part of the *SERVICE* phase that there are entities in the queue awaiting service, because the fact that the condition is being tested at all is proof that at least one such entity exists.

The important point to note in this approach is that explicit queuing, found in the event-based approaches, is replaced by implicit queuing. We can think of the conditional entity list as a global queue of all those entities that are waiting for some resource in the model to become free. As a consequence, the modeller does not have to worry about assigning an entity to a queue. All he has to do is suspend activity at the appropriate point so that the entity enters the list of conditional entities. The result is less work for the modeller but the conditional entity list can become very large. Since it must also be scanned for every tick of the simulation clock there can be a severe degradation in performance.

A modification of this approach replaces implicit queuing with explicit queuing. The difference is illustrated in the following pseudocode.

```
customer()
{
  while (ACTIVE)
  {
    switch (⟨⟨The phase of the customer⟩⟩)
    {
    case ARRIVAL:
      ⟨⟨Set phase to SERVICE⟩⟩
      ⟨⟨Add to queue⟩⟩
      ⟨⟨Schedule the next customer (with phase arrival)⟩⟩
      break;
    case DEPARTURE:
      ⟨⟨Remove entity from the model⟩⟩
      ⟨⟨Make the checkout free⟩⟩
      break;
    }
  }
}

service()
{
  if ⟨⟨Queue is non_empty and the checkout is free⟩⟩
  {
    ⟨⟨Take the customer entity from the front of the queue⟩⟩
    ⟨⟨Make the checkout busy⟩⟩
    ⟨⟨Schedule the entity with phase DEPARTURE⟩⟩
  }
}
```

In this arrangement we have taken the *SERVICE* part of the customer entity and implemented it as a conditional entity, as we did in the three-phase approach. This alternative model retains some of the benefits of the process-oriented approach by grouping together events that apply to a particular entity (*ARRIVAL* and *DEPARTURE*). But, by separating out the conditional part, we make a new conditional entity that is exclusively concerned with taking the next customer entity from the queue and scheduling its departure from the system. The advantages as far as the simulation modeller is concerned are twofold. First of all, additional flexibility is provided by the use of explicit queues (e.g. the possibility of using a priority queue) and second, an improvement in efficiency is achieved since it is no longer necessary to scan all queued entities, it is only necessary to scan those that control access to a resource such as a queue server.

3.3.4 Comparison

All three strategies are widely used but the choice of a particular approach is often determined more by prejudice based on previous experience rather than any rational decision. In fact all have complementary strengths and weaknesses.

Event-scheduling models improve efficiency by placing the burden of deciding when conditional events should take place on to the modeller. They are thus more difficult to write and harder to maintain. For these reasons this approach is not recommended.

The three-phase approach is good for structuring larger models. In particular, this applies to those models that require complex assignments of resources based on logical conditions, since such detail can be localized to the conditional event routines. However, as the size of the model grows, the inefficiency becomes significant, but it is unlikely that the inefficiency will be so great that the use of the event-scheduling approach is justified.

The process interaction approach is useful when there are a few classes of entities, but they have quite complex behaviour involving queuing for resources. Generally such models will be easier to understand when structured with a process view. One reason for this is that the modeller does not have to be concerned about explicitly creating queues and adding entities to them, the scheduler does that automatically. The main drawback is that much time is wasted repeatedly scanning entities that cannot proceed. In larger models the penalty may be too large to ignore.

In addition, the process interaction approach is difficult to implement faithfully with procedure-oriented languages like C and Pascal. The process-oriented approach was introduced as a practical means of implementing process models in these situations. The way in which process-oriented models are implemented in the simulation library means that they can only be used where queuing is non-priority FIFO (although this limitation can be avoided with some additional complexity in the library). Such a limitation may preclude the use of this approach in some models. However, when this technique is used with explicit queuing, we have a cross between the three-phase and process-oriented approaches which offers some of the advantages of both views.

As far as the implementation described here is concerned the three-phase approach and the process-oriented approach in which explicit queuing is performed would seem to offer the best compromise between efficiency, flexibility and eloquence. In addition, it is probably true to say that the event-based approaches fit the mind set of most programmers better than the process-oriented approach, and that this may well influence the approach adopted. Bear in mind, of course, that such an opinion is not general, it simply reflects the implementation decisions made for this particular C simulation library.

3.4 SUMMARY

Simulation models can be implemented with either dedicated simulation packages, SPLs or GPLs. General-purpose languages can be used to build efficient models and can normally be ported relatively easily. With care they can also provide almost as convenient a modelling environment as special purpose languages.

Construction of simulation models with GPLs is simplified if a library of simulation routines is available that can be reused. Such a library should contain a scheduler and provide routines for handling random numbers, entities, resources, queues and simulation results.

There are three main strategies for discrete event simulation in use today:

- *Event scheduling* deals with the significant events existing in the system, and consists of an initial A phase which identifies the next bound events to activate followed by a B phase which consists of the actual event activation.
- *Three phase* is similar to event scheduling but has an additional phase known as the C phase. The C phase is responsible for scanning the set of conditional events whose activation depends on the state of the system and processing them.
- *Process interaction* focuses on the entities or objects in the model. The basic algorithm is similar to the three-phase approach except that each routine describes the behaviour of a class of entities in the model rather than an event. Hence the A phase identifies the next bound entities to execute, the B phase executes them and the C phase searches for blocked entities which are now free to execute after resources have been released.

3.5 EXERCISES

3.1 Identify and describe the principal events in the model of a packet switch node. The node has four bidirectional communication lines along which data packets are transmitted and received. When a packet is received, the node determines the output line on which the packet is to be transmitted, based on the intended packet destination.

3.2 Repeat Exercise 3.1 for the case of a process-based simulation so that the object classes and the events that affect them are identified.

3.3 Describe how the simple queue models used in this chapter may be modified to take into account n servers in parallel, all serviced by the same single waiting line.

4

SIMULATION IN C

In this chapter we focus on C as a vehicle for discrete event simulation. We start by looking at some of the benefits of the C language and then present a structure for models written in C, but which can be adapted to suit other general-purpose languages (GPLs) as well. A simple example model of the alternating bit protocol illustrates how this structure can be applied.

4.1 THE C PROGRAMMING LANGUAGE

There are a number of GPLs which support the necessary features for discrete event simulation that were listed in the previous chapter. Some versions of Pascal fall into this category, for example, as does Modula 2. However, C has two important advantages over many of these alternative languages, namely *portability* and *availability*.

Portability is important in all software development. As far as simulation is concerned it means that upgrading hardware if extra performance is required does not force us to abandon or rewrite the model. It should also not be too much trouble to port the model from one machine to another in, say, a different part of the same company.

C is one of the most widespread languages currently available. It is common on machines ranging from personal computers to large mainframes. This has resulted in a large market for C-oriented development tools. As a result there are now many excellent, low-cost compilers and they generally come bundled with good support utilities such as assemblers, run-time profilers, pretty printers and powerful interactive source-code debuggers. Another consequence of this large market is the availability of C-based utilities and a thriving C components industry where off-the-shelf libraries covering such areas as graphics, man-machine interfaces, numerical analysis and statistics are readily available both as marketed products and in the public domain.

This does not mean to say that C is perfect. One of its main drawbacks is that the typing mechanism is relatively weak. This makes it quite easy for a programmer to introduce errors which the compiler will not pick up but which will be left unnoticed until the run-time behaviour of the program is not as expected. However, ANSI C is much better in this respect than the older Kernigan and Richie version and so ANSI C is the version used in this text. Additionally source-code checkers such as UNIX *lint* can be employed which will pick up many of the potential problems before the executable is produced.

For a full description of C consult *The C Programming Language* by Brian Kernigan and Dennis Richie, the original and still the best reference work. The second edition (Kernigan and Richie, 1988) is especially recommended as it covers the ANSI version of the language.

4.2 SIMULATION MODEL STRUCTURE

The structure of a normal C application is indicated conceptually in Fig. 4.1(a), which can be compared with the simplified structure of a C simulation model in Fig. 4.1(b). In a normal C application a single *main( )* procedure can call user

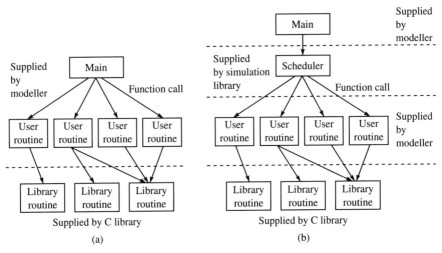

Figure 4.1 Structure of a simulation model.

routines and library routines which, in turn, can call other user routines and library routines as necessary. In contrast, the user routines in a model are essentially services called upon by a private scheduler function. The scheduler must be able to control the activation and termination of user routines because, as we shall see in Chapter 7, it alone has knowledge of the sequence of future events and the routines which must be called. User modules can, in turn, call upon other library routines and user routines as dictated by the logic of the model.

4.2.1 A template

Independently of the simulation approach chosen, the high-level structure of the simulation model can take the form shown in the following template. This shows normal C code along with English descriptions in double angle brackets acting as a place holder for source code to perform the indicated tasks.

```
/*standard include files */
#include ⟨stdio.h⟩
 :

/* simulation include files */
#include "sim_lib.h"
#include "resource.h"
 :

/* external declarations */
extern float sim_clock;
 :

/* function prototypes */
⟨⟨Event or process function prototypes⟩⟩
void print_results ( void );
void init ( void );
void reset_results ( void );
 :

/* global object declarations */
⟨⟨Queues⟩⟩
⟨⟨Resources⟩⟩
⟨⟨Statistics⟩⟩
 :

/* other global declarations */
 :

main (int argc, char *argv[])
{
```

```
  <<use command line arguments to set up simulation>>
  :

  init ();
  run_sim (duration+sim_clock , termination_count);
  print_results ();
  return 0;
}

/* Initialize the simulation. */
void init ( )
{
  init_sim();
  <<Initialize queues>>
  <<Initialize histograms>>
  <<Initialize statistics>>
  <<Initialize resources>>
  <<Initialize random number streams>>
  :
  /*run simulation for an initial transient period */
  run_sim (transient_duration , termination_count);
  reset_results();
  :
}

/* Output simulation results. */
void print_results ( )
{
  <<Print simulation results>>
  :
}

/* Reset results variables. */
void reset_results ( )
{
  <<Reset all results gathered after initial transient phase>>
  :
}

/* Routines representing the logic of the */
/* simulation model. */
:
```

The template consists of declarations and functions implementing the desired model. In this example we tacitly assume that the simulation program exists in one source file. In larger simulation models it will probably be necessary to modularize the program by splitting it across several files.

Function *main( )* must obviously be included as this is required by all executable C programs. In the general case the program will receive command line parameters via input arguments to *main( )*. These could be used to initialize random number generators or to set the values of key variables such as the length of the simulation run and so on. Of course, in a simple simulation, *main( )* may not have any parameters at all. Alternatively, the user may be prompted for model parameters or values read from a configuration file.

Function *init( )* is called to create the components of the model and perform any initialization. The simulation library is prepared first with the call to *init_sim( )*. Likely components for initialization include random number streams, resources, queues, results variables and so on, all of which must be created and set to some initial value. Also, initial event or entity routines normally have to be created and added to the calendar before the simulation is started.

Chapter 10 describes *transient* and *steady state* effects and how the start of the steady state phase can be detected. Often we will be interested only in the steady state phase, hence in function *init( )* the simulation is run for an initial transient period. In order to eliminate the effects of the transient phase from the final results, we must clear the results accumulated in the various statistical variables. This is the purpose of the call to *reset_results( )*. If results during the transient phase are of interest, then slightly different treatment is necessary, which will involve keeping and analysing some of them. This approach assumes that the *duration* of the transient phase is known beforehand. Section 10.3 demonstrates a slightly different treatment when we know only the number of samples required before the transient phase dies away.

The simulation proper takes place with the call to the library routine *run_sim( )* in the main function. Note that one of the arguments to *run_sim( )* is the time of the simulated clock when the simulation is to stop. Since this is an absolute value it must take into account the duration of the initial transient period. In the template shown this is done by adding the value of the simulation clock to the desired steady-state duration.

After the simulation has terminated we are able to print the results, possibly to a file, so that we can analyse them off-line, perhaps with the assistance of a standard statistical package.

The final comment heads a section that declares the active components of the model, simulating the occurrence of events or entities in the real system. The declaration for such routines is:

```
void function_name ( void );
```

in which we have used the ANSI form for function prototypes. The internal structure of the function itself obviously depends on the particular approach used and on the logic of the model. We will see some examples of this structure in the following section.

4.3 AN EXAMPLE—THE ALTERNATING BIT PROTOCOL

Let us turn now to the actual code of an example model using the three-phase and process-oriented approaches. Do not worry too much about following all the details of these examples at this juncture, the main objective is to give a more concrete idea of the structure discussed above.

The alternating bit protocol is a hypothetical data communications protocol described in Tanenbaum (1988). It allows unidirectional data transfer and can handle the loss or duplication of single frames. It can also be extended to allow bidirectional data transfer, but this extension will not be considered here.

Figure 4.2 shows the idea behind the protocol. A network layer prepares data buffers for transmission by the data-link layer. The data-link layer provides services such as error detection and uses the services of the physical layer for transmission. The physical layer transfers the actual sequence of 0s and 1s to the other end of the link. We are interested in the behaviour of the data-link layer.

The protocol works as follows. On the send side, the network layer delivers data buffers to the data-link layer to transmit. The transmit sequence number is added to the data buffer received from the network layer and the complete ensemble passed to the physical layer for transmission to the receiver. A timer is started by the data-link layer so that the sender can transmit the frame again if no acknowledgement is received within the timeout interval.

The receiver maintains a one-bit sequence number, being the sequence number it expects to be present on the next frame. If the sequence number of the received frame is the same as the one expected the data content of the frame is

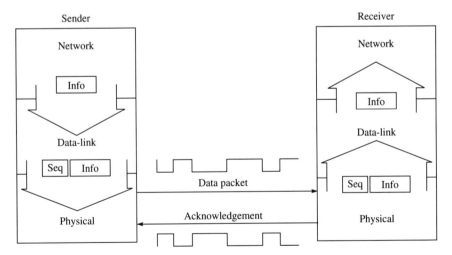

Figure 4.2 The alternating bit protocol.

passed to the network layer as it is assumed that reception has been successful. In the case of successful reception, an acknowledgement is passed to the sender giving the sequence number received, and then the sequence number is incremented modulo 2 (i.e. inverted).

If no acknowledgement is received by the sender, the timeout expires and the sender will retransmit the buffer, believing that the transmission failed.

The protocol behaviour can be summarized with the following pseudocode. For the transmitter we have:

```
sender()
{
      sequence_num tx_seq_num = 0;
      frame buffer;
      frame s;

      <<get next frame to send and store it in a buffer>>
      repeat
      {
            s.info = buffer;
            s.seq  = tx_seq_num;
            <<send s to physical layer>>
            <<start timer>>
            <<Pause here until some event occurs>>
            switch (event)
            {
            case FRAME_ARRIVAL:
                  <<cancel the timeout>>
                  <<get next frame to send and store in buffer>>
                  <<increment tx_seq_num modulo 2>>
                  break;
            case TIMEOUT:
                  <<send s to the physical layer again>>
                  <<start timeout>>
                  break;
            default:
                  break;
            }
      } until (forever);
}
```

and for the receiver we have:

```
receiver()
{
      sequence_num rx_seq_num = 0;
      frame r;
      repeat
      {
```

```
⟨⟨wait for an event⟩⟩
switch (event)
{
case FRAME_ARRIVAL:
    ⟨⟨get received frame and store in r⟩⟩
    if (r.seq == rx_seq_num)
    {
        ⟨⟨Deliver r.info to network layer⟩⟩
        ⟨⟨increment rx_seq_num modulo 2⟩⟩
    }
    break;
default:
    break;
}
⟨⟨send r to the physical layer to be transmitted as an ack⟩⟩
} until (forever);
}
```

A useful characteristic for communications protocols, and one of interest for this example, is throughput. Throughput in bits per second (bps) is defined as the amount of information that successfully gets sent from one end of the communications link to the other in unit time.

4.3.1 Library routines used

Many library routines will be introduced and their use explained in the following chapters. However, we provide here an overview of just those routines used in the alternating bit protocol models so that you may find it easier to follow the code. The nine functions used are:

- *add_event( )*. This library routine adds an event to the calendar. The routine to run when the event occurs is passed as an input argument along with the time period later at which the event is due to be activated.
- *delete_event( )*. This library routine removes an event from the simulation and the memory occupied by the data structure is reclaimed.
- *passivate( )*. This library routine removes an entity record from the calendar and makes it available to be manipulated by other library routines.
- *terminate( )*. This library routine removes an entity record from the simulation and frees up memory occupied by it.
- *init_sim( )*. This library routine is responsible for doing one time only initialization of the simulation library at the start of a simulation.
- *run_sim( )*. This library routine contains the main simulation loop. It repeatedly selects events or entities to process, calls the associated routines and then checks the termination conditions. If the simulation can continue, the loop is repeated again. If the simulation clock has reach the limiting value the simulation is ended and control returns to *main( )*.

- *make_stream( )*. This library routine dynamically creates a new data structure to be used for the generation of random numbers.
- *make_scheduled_entity( )*. This library routine creates an entity record which associates all the data required by the simulation library to handle entities and events. Its input arguments include the pointer to the routine to call when activated, data (i.e. attributes) which apply to this entity and the time delay after which the routine is to be called.
- *probability( )*. This library routine returns the value 1 with a probability of *p*, and the value 0 with a probability of $1 - p$. The probability is passed as an argument to the routine along with a *stream* data structure with which random numbers can be sampled.

4.3.2 Three-phase model

An example three-phase model is shown in Listings 4.1a–4.1c. In fact this model could equally be an event-scheduling model because no A phase event will ever free resources, so that we do not require procedures corresponding to conditional events.

In the first part of the model we find the required declarations and input the parameter *bit-error rate* (*ber*) which must be added as a command line argument by the user. The variable *P* represents the probability that the frame will reach the other end. It is (simplistically) related to the *ber* from the expression $1 - ber*N$, where *N* is the number of bits in the frame, which we assume is 1024. If *P* turns out to be less than or equal to 0.0 when we calculate it from the *ber*, we print an error message and stop the program.

From the system description at the beginning of this section we can identify the significant events as the transmission of a frame, the reception of a frame, the expiry of a timeout and the reception of an acknowledgement frame. Hence, for an event-oriented model we expect functions corresponding to these events. In the model these functions are *tx( )*, *rx( )*, *timeout( )* and *ack( )* declared at the beginning of Listing 4.1a and given in Listing 4.1c.

```
#include <stdio.h>
#include <stdlib.h>
#include "sim_lib.h"
#include "random.h"

#define DATA_SIZE  1024      /* The size of a frame */
#define ACK_SIZE   1024      /* The size of an acknowledgement frame */
#define LINE_SPEED 4096      /* The speed of the comms link */
#define DURATION   1000.0    /* The duration of the simulation (secs)*/
#define TD_DATA    0.25      /* The time taken to send a frame (size/speed) */
#define TD_ACK     0.25      /* The time taken to send an ack */
#define TO_VAL     0.52      /* The timeout value */
```

```
extern entity *current;
extern float  sim_clock;

stream      *rl ;                      /* The source of all random numbers */
entity      *time_out ;                /* The timeout */
float       data_rxd= 0.0,             /* Total amount of data received */
            P,                         /* Probability of frame error */
            ber;                       /* (b)it (e)rror (r)ate */
unsigned int       tx_seq_num = 0;     /* Transmit sequence number */

void tx( void );                       /* Transmit event */
void rx( void );                       /* Receive frame event */
void timeout( void );                  /* Timeout event */
void ack( void );                      /* Receive ack frame event */
void init( void );                     /* Initialize the model */
void print_results();                  /* Output model results */

main(int argc, char *argv[])
{
  if (argc != 2)
  {
    printf(" \nUsage: abp <ber> \n");
    exit(0);
  }
  /* Get the probability P that a frame */
  /* reaches the other side. */
  ber = atof(argv[1]);
  P = 1.0 - (ber * DATA_SIZE);
  if (P < 0.0) {
    printf("abp: ber too low \n");
    exit(0);
  }
  init();
  run_sim(DURATION, 0);
  print_results();
}
```

Listing 4.1a C code for alternating bit protocol—three-phase model.

The initialization provided by *init()* is very simple. First of all we must initialize the simulation library. We can then create a random number stream and add our first event to the calendar.

The *print_results()* routine is called at the completion of the simulation. It just prints the parameters of interest, namely the line speed, throughput (data received per second) and *ber* as shown in Listing 4.1b.

```
void init()
{
  init_sim ();
  rl = make_stream(1,0);
  /* Add an initial tx event */
  make_scheduled_entity ( tx, (void *)0, 0.0, 0, 0, 1, NULL);
}
```

```
void print_results()
{
  printf("line speed = %d, Bit Error Rate = %f, throughput = %f \n",
    LINE_SPEED,ber,data_rxd/DURATION);
}
```

Listing 4.1b C code for alternating bit protocol—three-phase model (*cont.*).

The event routines are shown in the final part of the listing, Listing 4.1c. The *tx( )* routine adds a timeout event and then creates a receive event with probability *P*, simulating the loss of data because of some noise or interference on the line. The variable *time_out* which includes a pointer to the *timeout( )* routine is defined as a global *entity* because it must be known to both *timeout( )* and *ack( )*. In the alternating bit protocol the transmit sequence number must be communicated to the receiver by the frame. We perform this in the model by using the attribute component of the entity record. This is actually a pointer to *void* but we use a cast to pass an *unsigned int*.

The *rx( )* routine implements the reception event at the distant end of the link. It compares the received sequence number and the expected sequence number. If they are the same an acknowledgement is returned to the sender. The rather unlikely scenario of a completely reliable communications path is assumed from receiver to sender for the purposes of this simple model. Obviously this can be extended to represent more complex protocol behaviour, should we be so inclined. If the receive sequence number is not as expected then we just discard the received frame. When the transmit side times out, the frame will be sent again.

The *timeout( )* routine is called via the scheduled *time_out* event when the acknowledgement frame does not reach the sender. This, not unexpectedly, simply results in the retransmission of the frame by repeating the call to *tx( )* without altering the transmit sequence number.

The *ack( )* routine simulates the receipt of an acknowledgement by the sender. This means that the sender can increment the transmit sequence number and send the next frame with a call to *tx( )*. To prevent spurious timeouts, *time_out* is removed from the calendar by the *passivate( )* library call and then terminated, i.e. removed from the simulation, with the call to *delete_event( )*.

Running the model produces the kind of output shown in Fig. 4.3, where user input is shown in italics, and model output is shown non-italicized. By repeating the simulation run with different values of *ber*, we collect the kind of results shown in Fig. 4.4.

We have not made any effort in this example to scrutinize the results and establish their statistical validity, which of course would be essential in any 'real' simulation. The purpose of the example is simply to illustrate the possible

```c
void tx()
{
  /* Add timeout */
  time_out = add_event ( timeout, TO_VAL );
  /* Add an Rx event with probability P */
  if (probability(r1,P)) {
    make_scheduled_entity ( rx , (void *)tx_seq_num , TD_DATA , 0 , 0, 1,
      NULL);
  }
}
void rx()
{
  static unsigned int rx_seq_num = 0;
  unsigned int sn;

  sn = (unsigned int)ATTRIBUTES(current);

  /* If sequence numbers agree, return an acknowledgement */
  if (rx_seq_num == sn) {
    rx_seq_num = !rx_seq_num;
    data_rxd += DATA_SIZE;
    current->event = ack;
    wait ( TD_ACK );
  }
  else
    /* Remove this entity */
    terminate(current);
}
void timeout()
{
  /* Get rid of this timeout */
  delete_event(current);

  /* No ack has been received so resend */
  tx();
}

void ack()
{
  /* Remove timeout */
  passivate ( time_out );       /* in calendar - so passivate */
  delete_event ( timeout );

  /* Remove ack */
  terminate(current);

  /* Send a new frame */
  tx_seq_num = !tx_seq_num;
  tx();
}
```

Listing 4.1c C code for alternating bit protocol—three-phase model.

```
abp 0.0001
Simulation started at 0.000000
Simulation stopped - end time reached at 1000.031616
Actual time taken - 10.000000 seconds
line speed = 4096, bit error rate = 0.000100, throughput = 1820.672000


abp 0.00001
Simulation started at 0.000000
Simulation stopped - end time reached at 1000.000244
Actual time taken - 11.000000 seconds
line speed = 4096, bit error rate = 0.000010, throughput = 2021.376000
```

Figure 4.3 Typical output from the alternating bit protocol model.

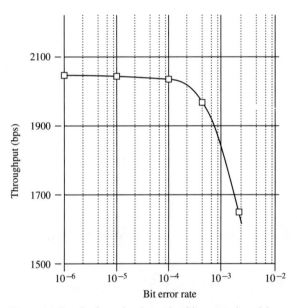

Figure 4.4 Results from the alternating bit protocol model.

structure of a model organized using the three-phase structure. Compare this with the following model of the same system structured using the process-oriented approach.

4.3.3 Process-oriented model

The code of Listing 4.2 illustrates how the alternating bit protocol model can be implemented in a process-oriented form.

The main difference between this version and the previous version is the presence of a function *frame( )* representing a generic frame class. The frame entity consists of three phases *TX, RX* and *ACK* representing a frame as it is transmitted, received and then echoed back to the sender as an acknowledgement. The actions performed in each of these phases match the actions performed in the corresponding events of the previous model. The timeout remains as before. A scheduled entity *time_out* is added to the calendar to become active at the end of the timeout period. If no frame is received, function *timeout( )* creates a repeat of the transmit event and then terminates itself. However, if a frame is received within the timeout period, then *time_out* is removed from the calendar with *passivate( )* and terminated.

```c
#include <stdio.h>
#include <stdlib.h>
#include "sim_lib.h"
#include "random.h"

#define DATA_SIZE   1024
#define ACK_SIZE    1024
#define LINE_SPEED  4096
#define DURATION    1000.0
#define TD_DATA     0.25
#define TD_ACK      0.25
#define TO_VAL      0.52
#define TX          1
#define RX          2
#define ACK         3

extern entity *current;
extern float  sim_clock;
extern int    active;

stream    *rl;
entity    *time_out;
float     data_rxd= 0.0, P, ber;
int       tx_seq_num = 0;
int       rx_seq_num = 0;

void frame( void );
void timeout( void );
void initialize( void );
void print_results( void );

main(int argc, char *argv[])
{
  if (argc != 2)
  {
      printf(" \nUsage abp <ber> \n");
      exit(0);
```

```
  }
  /* Get the probability P that a frame */
  /* reaches the other side. */
  ber = atof(argv[1]);
  P = 1.0 - (ber * DATA_SIZE);
  if (P < 0.0) {
    printf("abp: ber too low \n");
    exit(0);
  }
  initialize();
  run_sim(DURATION,0);
  print_results();
  return 0;
}

void initialize()
{
  init_sim ();
  r1 = make_stream(1,0);
  /* Add an initial tx event */
  make_scheduled_entity ( frame, (void *)0, 0.0,    TX, 0, 1, NULL);
}

void print_results()
{
  printf("line speed = %d, Bit Error Rate = %f, throughput = %f \n",
      LINE_SPEED,ber,data_rxd/DURATION);
}

void frame ()
{
  while (active)
  {
    switch (PHASE_OF(current))
      {
      case TX:
        /* Add timeout */
        time_out = add_event ( timeout , TO_VAL );
        /* Add an Rx event with probability P */
        if (probability(r1,P)) {
          PHASE_OF(current) = RX;
          wait (TD_DATA);
        }
        else
          terminate ( current);
        break;
      case RX:
        /* If sequence numbers agree, add acknowledge */
        if (rx_seq_num == tx_seq_num)
          {
```

```
            rx_seq_num = !rx_seq_num;
            data_rxd += DATA_SIZE;
            PHASE_OF(current) = ACK;
            wait ( TD_ACK );
          }
          else
            terminate ( current );
          break;
        case ACK:
          /* Remove timeout */
          passivate ( time_out );
          delete_event ( time_out );
          /* Send a new frame */
          tx_seq_num = !tx_seq_num;
          /* Next tx request */
          PHASE_OF(current) = TX;
        }
     }
 }

 void timeout()
 {
    /* No ack has been received so make new request */
    make_scheduled_entity ( frame , (void *)0 , 0.0 , TX , 0, 1, NULL);
    /* Get rid of this timeout */
    delete_event(current);
 }
```

Listing 4.2 C code for alternating bit protocol—process-oriented model.

We shall see in the following chapters some more models employing the three-phase and process-oriented views that will reinforce the ideas introduced here, add more diverse modelling constructs and describe the analysis which should be performed to the model outputs.

4.4 SUMMARY

The principal advantages of C as a means of implementing simulation models are portability and availability. Portability makes it quite straightforward to take a model written for one hardware platform and compile and run it on another. The availability of C means that there are also good, low-priced, development tools for most platforms and readily available C libraries many of which are in the public domain.

A C template was defined which can be used as the basis for a model. An example model of the alternating bit protocol was given to illustrate the basic structure in event-scheduling/three-phase and process interaction forms. Results

from some test runs were given which indicated the throughput performance of
the protocol.

4.5 EXERCISES

4.1 Compare the use of C as an implementation language for discrete event
simulation with Pascal and BASIC. What features of these languages might
be used and what particular problems does each language present?

4.2 How could the template be extended if we decided to perform several runs
from a single invocation of the model? Assume that we reset the simulation
to its start-up state at the beginning of each run and collect intermediate
results at the end of each run.

4.3 What debugging aids could be usefully incorporated into the simulation
library to help us trace errors in a model?

5

RANDOM NUMBERS

This chapter describes random numbers and their use in simulation. This is an important topic because reliable random numbers are essential to the success of any stochastic simulation. We begin by discussing the concept of randomness in general and how it can be synthesized. We then consider probability and probability distributions, focusing on some techniques for generating random numbers for particular distributions. A number of specific probability distributions are then covered along with the applicable generating functions from the simulation library.

5.1 RANDOMNESS

Random numbers are used in a discrete event simulation model to imitate those situations where some pattern of behaviour is discernible which seems intuitively predictable, but for which we can say only in approximate terms what will happen. This could be a result of a complex causal mechanism which makes exact analysis impossible, the lack of accurate data on which to base a judgement, or simply because there is some fundamental indeterminacy in the system. We say that such behaviour exhibits *randomness*.

Randomness is not rare, it exists all around us. Consider a coastline and waves breaking on a beach. Tide tables give the average height of the tide at any point in time and it is possible to predict how far a given tide will come in. But it is impossible to predict in exact terms how far the next breaker will roll up the beach, or the exact height of a point on the sea surface even one minute into the future. The physical processes involved are just too complex for us even to begin.

Randomness is also found in simpler processes such as the waiting line at a supermarket checkout, or the time between the arrival of buses. The factors determining these parameters involve complex interactions between a number of system variables and so the effect as experienced by a customer or passenger is unpredictable in detail. Although we may not be able to say with absolute certainty when the next bus will arrive we expect it to be predictable in some average sense or we probably would not wait for it!

5.1.1 Random variables

It is nearly always the case that the randomness of use in simulation work can take numerical values. A variable that takes random values is termed a *random variable* or *random variate*. There are two types of random variable: *discrete random variables* which could be used, for example, to represent the result of rolling a die and *continuous random variables* which could be used to represent the weight of a person.

Discrete random variables can only take values from a finite set or a special type of infinite set which has the property that its members can be arranged into a simple sequence (technically termed *enumerably infinite*). The set of positive integers for example is infinite, but it can be arranged into the familiar simple sequence 1, 2, 3, ..., etc.

Continuous random variables can, in principle at least, take on values from an infinitely large set even if the set has a finite maximum and minimum value. However, this set is not enumerable—that is, it is not possible to arrange all its values into a simple sequence—so that concepts such as 'the ith largest' are meaningless. Having said that, it must be realized that any implementation only approximates to a continuous random variable since computer arithmetic is always of finite precision.

5.1.2 Random number streams

A sequence of random numbers is called a *random number stream*. However, a true random number stream is not normally available on a computer system. It would require for instance, the digitization of a random noise source. Moreover, simulation modelling requires repeatability and the means to control key characteristics of the generator in order to apply some of the rich theory of mathematical statistics. For this reason, the random number generators we employ are purely deterministic mathematical functions. Starting with the same initial conditions, the generator will always produce the same stream of random numbers.

The normal conceptual view of a random number as something unpredictable as discussed above is clearly inadequate here, since our random number streams are completely deterministic and yet we still conjecture that they exhibit random characteristics! These characteristics are statistical in nature. For this reason, our new notion of randomness is normally termed *pseudo-random* but for clarity and brevity we shall simply use the term *random* with the understanding that we are actually referring to a deterministic process.

5.2 PROBABILITY

Closely connected with the idea of randomness is the concept of *probability*, which most of us are no doubt familiar with as something to do with the likelihood of an event such as the generation of a number in a particular range. This concept of probability is termed *statistical probability*. In more formal language it is the limiting value of the relative frequency with which the event occurs. Suppose that we have an experiment which can, in theory at least, be repeated indefinitely. If during this experiment the number of occurrences of event A is $A(n)$ after n repetitions, then the fraction $A(n)/n$ is clearly the proportion of the number of times that A has occurred, call it $p(n)$. As n increases, the value of $p(n)$ tends to fluctuate less and approaches some stable limiting value. This stable limiting value is the (statistical) probability of A and is denoted by $P[A]$.

As a more concrete example, consider the act of throwing a die a large number of times. We would expect that the number of 1s would be roughly 1/6 of the number of times the die was rolled. Counting the fraction of 1s as a function of the number of rolls we should not be surprised to see a graph like the one shown in Fig. 5.1. This shows that for an unbiased die, the value of $p(n)$ is tending towards the value $1/6 = 0.1667$ and so we can say that we believe it has a *statistical probability* of 0.1667 of occurring.

Statistical probability is a feature of the real world that can be proved or disproved only by experiment. We can believe that our die is fair and conjecture that there is a probability of 1/6 of obtaining a 1, but this belief can be proved or disproved only by repeatedly throwing the die and recording the outcome. It should be clear that from this that we can never be completely sure of the probability, since any experiment must always take a finite amount of time and yet an infinite amount of time is needed to get an exact answer.

There is a second notion of probability called *inductive probability* which refers to the belief we have that a certain event will happen. Here we appeal to what is essentially an exercise in mathematical logic. Given some evidence, various deductive rules can be used to determine our degree of faith in the likelihood of the outcome. If we obtain more evidence, we have a different set of conditions and therefore may have a different degree of faith in the various outcomes. Although this kind of reasoning may sound convoluted, it is common in everyday life. If we arrive at a regular morning bus stop only to find that there

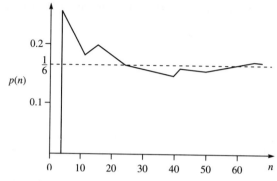

Figure 5.1 Proportion of 1s rolled.

is nobody queuing, we would place a high probability on the hypothesis that we have just missed a bus.

We see, then, that statistical probability is empirical, it is based on measurement, whereas inductive probability is based on logic. This poses problems when we want to express inductive probability numerically because it relies on subjective belief. There have been attempts to devise a method of quantifying inductive probability and one such effort is *Bayesian inference*. Although there are advocates strongly in favour of this approach it is of little use for simulation work, therefore we will only be concerned with statistical probability in this text.

5.2.1 Probability distributions

A random number stream represents samples drawn from a *probability density function* (usually abbreviated to pdf). The pdf gives the probability that a random variable will take particular values. For example, if X is the sum of the numbers on two unbiased dice, then

$$P[X = 2] = \frac{1}{36}$$

because we have only one way of getting a 2, by rolling two consecutive 1s, and

$$P[X = 3] = \frac{2}{36}$$

because we have two ways of getting a 3, a 1 followed by a 2 and a 2 followed by a 1. Enumerating all possible outcomes in this way allows us to determine the pdf displayed in Table 5.1.

Table 5.1 Probability density function associated with rolling two dice

Number	2	3	4	5	6
Probability	0.03	0.06	0.08	0.11	0.14

Number	7	8	9	10	11	12
Probability	0.17	0.14	0.11	0.08	0.06	0.03

An alternative presentation for this table is as a function such as

$$P[X = x] = \frac{6 - |x - 7|}{36}, \qquad x = 2, 3, ..., 12$$

where a new variable x has been introduced to represent a particular, but arbitrary, value that the random variable X can take. If the probability function is known, then once x is specified we can calculate the probability that X will take this value. In general then the *pdf* of X, denoted by $f_X(x)$, can be defined as

$$f_X(x) = P[X = x] \qquad (5.1)$$

For convenience, we sometimes drop the X suffix.

Most random number generators generate random variables distributed according to the normalized uniform distribution which has the pdf

$$\begin{aligned} f(x) &= 1 \quad \text{for} \quad 0 \leqslant x \leqslant 1 \\ &= 0 \quad \text{otherwise} \end{aligned} \qquad (5.2)$$

so that the sequence generated consists of random fractions between 0 and 1 which occur with equal probability. Sequences belonging to other distributions can then be obtained by manipulating this base sequence using techniques which will be considered later.

A related concept to the pdf is the *cumulative distribution function* (*cdf*), *probability distribution function* or just *distribution function*, which represents the probability that a random variable drawn from the distribution will take a value less than or equal to X. The cdf is conventionally represented as a capital letter, thus

$$F_X(x) = P[X \leqslant x] \qquad (5.3)$$

When we are dealing with continuous random variables the cdf can be derived from the pdf by the mathematical relationship

$$F_X(x) = \int_{-\infty}^{x} f(X)dX \qquad (5.4)$$

In other words, the cdf gives the area under the curve of the pdf up to some value x on the x-axis. Since the area of the pdf is 1 then we have the two further results

$$F(\infty) = 1 \qquad (5.5)$$

and

$$F(-\infty) = 0 \qquad (5.6)$$

In the discrete random variable case the integral can be replaced with a summation. The probabilities of all values less than or equal to x must be summed to get the discrete cdf so that

$$F_X(x) = P[X = 0] + P[X = 1] + \ldots P[X = x] = \sum_{u \leqslant x} P[X = u] \qquad (5.7)$$

Again, we often drop the X suffix.

Referring to the uniform distribution once more, from Eq. (5.4) we see that the cdf must be

$$
\begin{aligned}
F_X(x) &= \int_{-\infty}^{x} f_X(u)\, du \\
&= \int_{0}^{x} 1\, du = x \qquad \text{for } 0 \leqslant x \leqslant 1 \\
&= 0 \qquad \qquad \text{otherwise}
\end{aligned}
\qquad (5.8)
$$

where the name of the independent variable of $f(x)$ has been changed in order to avoid name conflicts.

5.2.2 Mean and variance

Two important statistical measures that are used extensively and that can be derived from the pdf are the *mean* (or *average value*) and the *variance*. The mean gives a measure of the location of a distribution and the variance gives a measure of the spread of a distribution.

In the simplest case, the mean of a set of samples is the sum of the set divided by the number of samples. For example, the mean of the set $\{12, 67, 34, 52, 8\}$ is $173/5$ which is 34.6. Hence we have the formula

$$\bar{x} = \frac{1}{n} \sum_{i=1}^{n} x_i \qquad (5.9)$$

for the mean $\bar{x}$ of a set consisting of n samples.

Equation (5.9) is fine when applied to a finite set of samples, but we need to generalize the concept somewhat when we are referring to the mean of a pdf. If we set $p(x) = n(x)/n$, representing the proportion of the number of times that sample x has occurred, then from Eq. (5.9), the formula for the mean is evidently equal to

$$\bar{x} = \sum_x xp(x) \tag{5.10}$$

This gives the mean as the sum of all possible values of x, where each value is multiplied by its relative frequency of occurrence. When dealing with discrete pdfs we can replace $p(x)$ by $P[x]$, the probability that a sample x will occur. If we now consider a continuous pdf $f(x)$ then the probability of occurrence of x, $P[x]$, must be replaced by an infinitesimal element of probability $f(x)dx$ and the sum replaced by an integral. So

$$\mu = \sum_x xP[x] \tag{5.11}$$

for the discrete case and

$$\mu = \int_{-\infty}^{\infty} xf(x)dx \tag{5.12}$$

for the continuous case. Notice that the symbol μ has been used for the true mean of the probability distribution $f(x)$ to which $\bar{x}$ tends as the number of samples taken from $f(x)$ increases. The value $\bar{x}$ is known as the *sample mean* and μ is known as the *population mean*. Clearly μ is the correct value. Since $\bar{x}$ is only based on a finite subset of the population, it is an approximation to μ.

The *variance* of a set of samples is the average of the squared deviations from the mean. So, given a set of samples $\{x_1, x_2, ..., x_n\}$ the variance is given by

$$
\begin{aligned}
s^2 &= \frac{1}{n} \sum_{i=1}^{n} (x_i - \bar{x})^2 \\
&= \frac{1}{n} \left(\sum_{i=1}^{n} x_i^2 - 2\bar{x} \sum_{i=1}^{n} x + \sum_{i=1}^{n} \bar{x}^2 \right) \\
&= \frac{1}{n} \sum_{i=1}^{n} x_i^2 - \frac{1}{n} 2n\bar{x}^2 + \frac{1}{n} n\bar{x}^2 \\
&= \frac{1}{n} \sum_{i=1}^{n} x_i^2 - \bar{x}^2
\end{aligned}
\tag{5.13}
$$

The final form is the most convenient for computational purposes and means that only the running sum of the samples and the running sum of the samples squared needs to be recorded in order to calculate s^2.

If the data is given in the form of a frequency distribution in which the value of x has occurred $n(x)$ times, then we may set $p[x] = n(x)/n$, representing the proportion of the number of times that sample x has occurred, then from Eq. (5.13), the formula for the variance is

$$s^2 = \sum_x (x - \bar{x})^2 p(x) \tag{5.14}$$

As the number of samples increases, the sample mean tends to the population mean μ and the proportions $p(x)$ tend to the probabilities $P[x]$, hence the sample variance s^2 will tend to the actual variance σ^2 given by

$$\sigma^2 = \sum_x (x - \mu)^2 P[x] \tag{5.15}$$

For a continuous pdf $f(x)$ the probability of occurrence of x, $P[x]$, must be replaced by an infinitesimal element of probability $f(x)dx$ and the sum replaced by an integral so that

$$\sigma^2 = \int_{-\infty}^{\infty} (x - \mu)^2 f(x)dx \tag{5.16}$$

Again notice the switch of symbol from s^2 to σ^2 when we are referring to the population (and hence the correct value) as opposed to an approximation to it based on a subset of the population obtained by sampling.

Another interesting quantity is the *standard deviation* which is the positive square root of the variance. It is useful because it transforms the variance to a form which is comparable to the original data set both in terms of magnitude and dimension. For instance, the variance of a set of samples which are in units of metres will be in units of metres squared, but the standard deviation will be in units of metres. From the earlier example of the set of samples {12, 67, 34, 52, 8} the standard deviation is $\sqrt{(409)}$ which is 20.2.

5.3 GENERATING RANDOM NUMBERS FROM THE UNIFORM DISTRIBUTION

In many simulation systems numbers drawn from a generator for the uniform pdf forms the basis for all random numbers drawn from all the distributions available in the system. So the use of a poor random number generator in this case can have dire results. Unfortunately random number generators are often taken purely on faith and so can unknowingly contribute to the failure of a simulation study. Therefore, when faced with a new simulation environment it is wise to ask the question: 'What evidence is there that the random number generators at my disposal are of sufficient quality.' By 'high quality' we mean that such generators should:

1. Provide numbers from as large a set of values as possible. Ideally, any value between 0 and 1 should be expressible but, on any realizable computer architecture, this is impossible because it must have a finite number representation. The standard ANSI C random number generator, for instance, guarantees a minimum of only 32 767 different values, which is insufficient even for small simulations.
2. Have a long cycle time. We will see in the next section an illustration of the fact that all pseudo-random number generators produce a repeating pattern and we require that this be as long as possible.
3. Exhibit small autocorrelation. Autocorrelation refers to the effect of the previous history of a sequence on its present behaviour. Such behaviour is undesirable from a statistical point of view as it adds a bias to the simulation results.
4. Have good statistical properties. Based on the assumption of randomness in a long random number stream, it is possible to predict the frequency of occurrence of numbers in different interval bands. As the length of the stream increases, our predictions should be closer and closer to the actual frequencies encountered.
5. Be portable. It is clearly advantageous to have simulation results independent of the particular environment in which they were obtained. It would give very little confidence in a model if results obtained with, say, two alternative C compilers produced statistically significant differences.
6. Be fast. In a large simulation a random number generator could be called thousands or even millions of times. Clearly, its speed could have a significant effect on the performance of the simulation as a whole.

To discover if the generator at hand is adequate we can either consult analysis performed by previous users or information from the supplier of the simulation package. In the absence of existing evidence, the tests described in Sec. 5.3.3 can be used to provide a sift of the worst offenders. If the quality of a generator is suspect then it can be replaced with your own code for producing a random number stream based on one of the established algorithms such as the one used in the simulation library and described in the next section, or those described in Dagpunar (1988) or Devroye (1986). It is not a good idea, however, to try and design your own from scratch. The design of random number generators is full of nasty surprises for the unwary and is best left to established experts.

5.3.1 The linear congruential generator

A number of methods for generating random numbers have been devised since the inception of simulation. Initially these methods were observational—

researchers measured a physical process and translated this into a sequence of random digits. These methods have significant drawbacks though for computer use, such as the length of time it takes to build a table of numbers and the size of any such table which must contain a million or more numbers to be useful. Attempts were made to devise alternative schemes to overcome these difficulties. Of these, the approach which has stood the test of time the best is the *linear congruential generator*, discovered by D.H. Lehmer, and described by him in a paper published in 1951 (Lehmer, 1951).

The linear congruential generator consists of the following four numbers:

m, the modulus	$m > 0$
a, the multiplier	$0 \leqslant a < m$
c, the increment	$0 \leqslant c < m$
X_0, the starting value (seed)	$0 \leqslant X_0 < m$

from which a sequence of random numbers $\langle X_n \rangle$, $n > 0$ ($\langle X \rangle_n$ denotes a sequence of random numbers indexed by n) can be generated by setting

$$X_n = aX_{n-1} + c(\bmod m) \qquad (5.17)$$

Example 5.1 The sequence obtained when $m = 11$, $a = 3$, $c = 2$, and $X_0 = 8$ is 8, 4, 3, 0, 2, 8, 4, 3, 0, 2, ...

Example 5.2 The sequence obtained when $m = 20$, $a = 5$, $c = 12$, and $X_0 = 17$ is 17, 17, 17, ...

As can be seen from the above examples one should not take the quality of such generators too much on faith—some are clearly better than others! The best period possible is a period of length m, which is termed a *maximal period*.

5.3.2 Selection of linear congruential generators

Although, as was mentioned above, we should never design our own generators (for serious use), it is useful to appreciate some of the applicable mathematical rules. Designing a suitable linear congruential generator boils down to selecting the best values for the parameters m, a and c. Fortunately, the rich field of number theory provides results which enable this selection to be performed reliably. As a first step, the period can be determined from the following theorem.

Theorem 5.1 If $\gcd(a,m) = 1$ (i.e. the largest integer which exactly divides both a and m is 1), then the period of the sequence generated by Eq. (5.17) is the smallest positive integer d for which

$$\rho_d((a - 1)X_0 + c) = 0(\text{mod } m) \tag{5.18}$$

where

$$\rho_d = 1 + a + a^2 + \cdots + a^{d-1} \tag{5.19}$$

Example 5.3 Applying this theorem to Example 5.1 in order to find the period, we need to find the smallest integer d such that $\rho_d(2X_0 + 2) = 0(\text{mod } 11)$. With $X_0 = 8$ this is the smallest d for which $(1 + 3 + 3^2 + \cdots + 3^d - 1)(18) = 0(\text{mod } 11)$ by trying values from 1 upwards, we find that the first such value is $d = 5$, which agrees with the period of the sequence generated in the example.

We can also discover when the period is maximal (i.e. the longest possible period and equal to m) from the following theorem.

Theorem 5.2 If $\gcd(a,m) = 1$, then the period of the sequence generated by equation 5.1 is maximal if, and only if, for each prime p that divides m we have the following:

1. $a = 1(\text{mod } p)$ for each prime $p > 2$
2. If 4 divides m, then $a = 1(\text{mod } 4)$
3. $\gcd(c,m) = 1$.

Lets us see how this theorem applies by looking at a realistic example.

Example 5.4 A generator recommended in Press *et al.* (1988), has $m = 714\,025$, $a = 4096$ and $c = 150\,889$. The factors of a are $\{1, 2, 4, 8, 16, 64, 4096\}$. Only 1 is also a factor of $714\,025$ which has a prime factorization* of $5^2 13^4$, so the condition for the theorem (i.e. $\gcd(a,m) = 1$) is met. The value of c is prime, hence condition 3 is satisfied. Also, m is odd so that condition 2 is satisfied. Finally, the prime factorization of a is 2^{12}, since all prime numbers greater than 2 are odd, there must be a difference of 1 between any such prime and a multiple of 2. Hence, condition 1 is satisfied and therefore the period of this congruential generator is $714\,025$, which is maximal.

5.3.3 Tests of randomness

Objective tests and assessment criteria are required to judge the quality of a random number stream. These tests should be capable of being applied mechanically and hence computerized. We describe here some suitable tests that could be used when we are faced with an unfamiliar random number stream and we wish to establish whether it is adequately random. There are, in fact, a large number of such tests, but they can all be classified as either *empirical* or

---

* A prime factorization is a factorization consisting of prime numbers only. Such a factorization exists uniquely for all integers greater than 1.

theoretical. The outcome of an empirical test is not known beforehand but a test statistic can be calculated that tells us whether the random number stream passes the test with some small, fixed, probability of error. With a theoretical test we know in advance how well the test will come out and we can say with confidence when the test has failed. Theoretical tests require deep insight into the mathematical properties of the generators and are in general more difficult to do than empirical tests.

Probably the seminal reference in this area is Knuth (1981), which should be consulted for further details on all of the following tests and many others.

Objective evaluation of test results As mentioned above, the objective evaluation of the outcome of an empirical test requires that we calculate a test statistic (a significance test) that tells us whether the test passed or failed with some small probability of error. This represents the probability that the random number generator will be wrongly classed as bad when in fact it is good. Hence the single failure of such a test is no proof that the generator is definitely bad since even good ones occasionally fail. To provide convincing evidence, the tests should be repeated many times with different seeds. If unfavourable results are repeated several times then we will be more justified in rejecting such a generator.

The statistic we will use to judge whether a test has passed or failed is based on the χ^2 (pronounced ki-squared) distribution. To perform the χ^2 test we define k *categories*. A sequence of n *independent* random numbers are then sampled and each assigned to one of the categories. If p_s is the probability that an observation falls into category s and the actual number in category s is Y_s then, expecting np_s in category s, the χ^2 statistic V can be formed from

$$V = \sum_{1 \leqslant s \leqslant k} \frac{(Y_s - np_s)^2}{np_s} \tag{5.20}$$

which, when coupled with the fact that

$$\sum_{1 \leqslant s \leqslant k} Y_s = n \tag{5.21}$$

and

$$\sum_{1 \leqslant s \leqslant k} p_s = 1 \tag{5.22}$$

gives an alternative form for V

$$V = \frac{1}{n} \sum_{1 \leqslant s \leqslant k} \left(\frac{Y_s^2}{p_s} \right) - n \tag{5.23}$$

which is more convenient for computation.

To answer the question 'What is a reasonable value for V?' we consult a table of values for the χ^2 distribution which gives us the probability that the value would occur if the sequence were actually random. Such a table is given in Appendix C. Down the leftmost column we have *degrees of freedom*. With k categories we have $k - 1$ degrees of freedom because the Y_s are related as shown by Eq. (5.21) which reduces the degrees of freedom by 1. So, taking the row corresponding to $k - 1$ we find the χ^2 distribution for different percentage points p. Each such value x tells us that for a random sample, V, would be greater than x with probability p if n were large enough. Notice that as x increases the probability decreases because if the hypothesis of randomness is true *small* values of V are to be expected. For example the row corresponding to 29 degrees of freedom gives 17.71 for the column headed 0.95. Hence, values of V can be expected to be greater than 17.71 with 95 per cent probability. However, we find 49.59 for the column headed 0.01. In other words, values greater than 49.59 can be expected with 1 per cent probability.

To apply the χ^2 test we take our test statistic V_0 and identify the approximate probability α that this value of V_0 would occur under the assumption that the sequence is random. If this probability is very low then V_0 must be large, so large in fact that randomness is unlikely. We can quantify this belief by noting that a probability of α per cent means that we may be wrong once every $100/\alpha$ occasions in the long run and so we say that this test is *significant* at the α per cent level. Obviously the lower this value the better. It is customary to use values of 1 per cent or 5 per cent signifying that we will be wrong (in this case that we will falsely classify a generator as non-random when in fact it is random) on average 1 time in 100 or 1 time in 20 respectively.

It is important to realize that the χ^2 distribution is only an approximation. The results are very sensitive to the number of observations in each category. For it to be accurate, each category must have at least five and preferably many more observations. In tests where this rule of thumb is violated it becomes necessary to combine some of the categories.

Example 5.5 Assume we do a test with 20 categories that results in a value of V_0 of 31.0. For $20 - 1 = 19$ degrees of freedom the table of values for the χ^2 distribution places $V_0 = 31.0$ above the value in the 0.05 column ($= 30.14$); it is therefore significant at the 5 per cent level. This value would occur in less than five tests in every hundred if the sequence were random. This low probability leads us to believe that the sequence is *not* random at the 5 per cent level.

Example 5.6 Suppose that in another test we have 28 categories and a value of V_0 of 16.0. For 27 degrees of freedom the table of values for the χ^2 distribution places $V_0 = 16$ in the 0.95 column ($= 16.15$), it is therefore not significant at the 5 per cent level. So this test statistic is entirely consistent with an assumption of randomness.

Empirical random number tests
Test 1. Uniformity test. In this test the interval[†] $[0, 1]$ is split into m equal intervals so that each is $1/m$ wide. The number of occurrences in each of the intervals is then counted. For randomness, we would expect the counts in each interval to be approximately equal. The χ^2 test can be used to judge the results with:

$$p_s = \frac{1}{m} \qquad 1 \leqslant s \leqslant m \tag{5.24}$$

Example 5.7 A uniformity test with 10 divisions has been performed on a random sequence and the following results obtained:

Division	1	2	3	4	5	6	7	8	9	10
Expected	20	20	20	20	20	20	20	20	20	20
count	21	19	17	24	17	25	22	21	16	18

$$V = \frac{1}{200} \sum_{1 \leqslant s \leqslant 10} \left(\frac{Y_s^2}{0.1} \right) - 200$$

$$= 0.005*40860 - 200$$

$$= 4.3$$

from tables of χ^2 with 9 degrees of freedom there is a 95 per cent chance that V will be greater than 3.33 on the assumption of randomness. Therefore the value obtained of 4.3 is not significant at the 5 per cent level and so we have no grounds for saying that the sequence is not random.

Test 2. Gap test. In this test an interval between a and b, $b > a$ is defined. Each random fraction is compared to the interval and replaced with 0 if outside and 1 if inside. A run of s 0s means that s consecutive random fractions are outside the interval, i.e. we have a gap of s. The number of occurrences of gaps between 0 and $k - 1$ are recorded as separate counts with a further single count of all gaps equal to or longer than k for some fixed k.

The probability of a gap of s is

$$p_s = p(1 - p)^s \tag{5.25}$$

for s in the range $0 \leqslant s \leqslant k - 1$ and

$$p_k = (1 - p)^k \tag{5.26}$$

when s is equal to or greater than k.

The gap test is often applied with intervals of $[0, 0.5]$, $[0.5, 1.0]$ and $[0.333, 0.667]$. In a sequence of 10 000 random fractions, we could build a table of

---

[†] The usual notation for intervals has open intervals (i.e. including the limit value) represented by parenthesis '(' and closed intervals (i.e. not including the limit value) represented by square brackets '[]'.

observed counts and expected counts for gap lengths 0 to 9 and above (i.e. $k = 10$) and then use a χ^2 test statistic.

Example 5.8 The gap test was applied to a random number stream using an interval of (0, 0.5). The following results were obtained when 512 gaps were observed:

Gap	0	1	2	3	4	5	6 +
Expected count	256	128	64	32	16	8	8
count	222	131	73	34	21	15	16

$$V = \frac{1}{512} \sum_{0 \leqslant s \leqslant 6} \left(\frac{Y_s^2}{p_s} \right) - 512$$

$$= 0.000195*273236 - 512$$

$$= 21.66$$

From χ^2 tables with 6 degrees of freedom, we would expect this value of V less than 5 times in 1000 if the sequence was random. The result is significant at the 5 per cent level and we therefore conclude that the test result does not support the hypothesis of randomness.

Test 3. Poker test. In this test we define a set of 10 equal intervals I_j in [0, 1] so that $I_1 = [0.0, 0.1)$, $I_2 = [0.1, 0.2)$, and so on. The sequence of random fractions is then replaced by a sequence of integers j ($1 \leqslant j \leqslant 10$). The sequence of such integers $j_1, j_2, j_3, \ldots$ is grouped into sequences of five consecutive integers $(j_1, j_2, j_3, j_4, j_5)$, $(j_6, j_7, j_8, j_9, j_{10})$, ... and the frequency of each of the following categories recorded:

Category 1: All the same or two different integers in a group.
Category 2: Three different integers in the group.
Category 3: Four different integers in the group.
Category 4: Five different integers in the group.

If we have a sequence of n random fractions, we have the following probabilities for each category:

$$p_1 = 0.0136$$
$$p_2 = 0.1800$$
$$p_3 = 0.5040$$
$$p_4 = 0.3024$$

The assumption of randomness can be tested with the χ^2 test.

Example 5.9 The following results were obtained when 1000 numbers were tested with the poker test:

Category	1	2	3	4
Expected	14	180	504	302
count	12	191	488	309

The test statistic is

$$V = \frac{1}{1000} \sum_{1 \leqslant s \leqslant 4} \left(\frac{Y_s^2}{P_s} \right) - 1000$$

$$= 0.001 * 1001512.44 - 1000$$

$$= 1.51$$

The χ^2 test statistic for 3 degrees of freedom is 1.213 with a probability of 75 per cent. Hence there is no evidence for rejecting this random number stream as non-random based on this evidence.

Test 4a. Coupon collectors test A. In this test the interval [0, 1] is divided into equal intervals [0.0, 0.2), [0.2, 0.4), [0.4, 0.6), [0.6, 0.8), [0.8, 1.0]. The number of random fractions needed to get at least a count of 1 in every interval is counted. This is the test statistic, call it Q. If the process is repeated with a long sequence we will find values of Q that range from 5 upwards (we obviously need at least 5 fractions, 1 for each interval). We define 16 categories which depend on the value of Q as follows:

Category 1: Sequence of 5.
Category 2: Sequence of 6.
and so on up to
Category 15: Sequence of 19.
Category 16: Sequence of 20 or more.

The following are the expected probabilities for each category:

$$p_1 = 0.03840000 \qquad p_9 = 0.07680000$$
$$p_2 = 0.09984000 \qquad p_{10} = 0.10752000$$
$$p_3 = 0.10450944 \qquad p_{11} = 0.09547776$$
$$p_4 = 0.08381645 \qquad p_{12} = 0.07163904$$
$$p_5 = 0.06011299 \qquad p_{13} = 0.04979157$$
$$p_6 = 0.04086200 \qquad p_{14} = 0.03331007$$
$$p_7 = 0.02702163 \qquad p_{15} = 0.02184196$$
$$p_8 = 0.01760857 \qquad p_{16} = 0.07144851$$

Test 4b. Coupon collectors test B. In this variant of test 4a, the interval [0, 1] is divided into equal intervals [0.0, 0.1), [0.1, 0.2), ... giving 10 intervals and the number of random fractions counted as before. We would expect a sequence of 10 or more fractions to be required. We define 6 categories depending on the value of Q as follows:

Category 1: Sequence of between 10 and 19 (inclusive).
Category 2: Sequence of between 20 and 23 (inclusive).
Category 3: Sequence of between 24 and 27 (inclusive).
Category 4: Sequence of between 28 and 32 (inclusive).
Category 5: Sequence of between 33 and 39 (inclusive).
Category 6: Sequence of 40 or more.

The following are the expected probabilities for each category:

$$p_1 = 0.17321155$$
$$p_2 = 0.17492380$$
$$p_3 = 0.17150818$$
$$p_4 = 0.17134210$$
$$p_5 = 0.15216056$$
$$p_6 = 0.15685380$$

Test 5. Run test. This is a rather powerful test that counts the runs up or down within a random number stream. A run is a sequence of decreasing or increasing value. Hence the sequence 0.26, 0.51, 0.54, 0.72, 0.3 contains an increasing run with a length of 4. The basic run test is complicated by the fact that the run lengths are correlated. If we are measuring say, increasing runs, then after a long run we will have a value near 1.0, call it v. The next random fraction must be between 0 and v. After a short run we will probably have a value less than this, call it u. Since on average u is less than v we expect a longer run starting at u than a run starting at v. The net result is that long runs tend to be followed by short runs and so the χ^2 test cannot be applied.

Fortunately, this problem can be solved quite neatly by discarding the fraction following a run. So that if we have a sequence, say, 0.22, 0.34, 0.30, 0.51, 0.50, 0.40, 0.92, we would record a run of length 2, throw away the 0.30, record a run of length 1, throw away the 0.50 and then record a run of length 2. The output from the run test is now *independent* and we can happily apply the χ^2 statistic.

The expected probability of a run of length s assuming randomness is

$$p_s = \frac{1}{s!} - \frac{1}{(s+1)!} \qquad 1 \leqslant s \tag{5.27}$$

Theoretical random number tests There are fewer theoretical tests available than empirical tests. Those that are available however are more conclusive than empirical tests, but they tend to apply to the sequence the entire period of the generator, unlike empirical tests which can sensibly be applied to subsequences.

We will look at one theoretical test which determines the autocorrelation of a linear congruential generator (see Chapter 10 for a description of auto correlation).

Test 1. Serial correlation test. The statistical correlation between consecutive numbers from a linear congruential generator is given by

$$\text{Corr}(U_i, U_{i+1}) = \frac{1}{a}\left[1 - \frac{6c}{m} + 6\left(\frac{c}{m}\right)^2 + \varepsilon \right] \tag{5.28}$$

with

$$|\varepsilon| \leqslant \frac{a + 6}{m} \tag{5.29}$$

We can treat as correlated any generator for which Eq. (5.28) is greater than 0.01 and Eq. (5.29) is less than 0.005.

Example 5.10. The generator described in Example 5.4 has

$$|\varepsilon| \leqslant \frac{4096 + 6}{714025} = 0.0057449$$

and

$$\text{Corr}(U_i, U_{i+1}) = \frac{1}{4096}\left[1 - \frac{905334}{714025} + 6\left(\frac{150889}{714025}\right)^2 + 0.0057 \right]$$
$$= 0.000132$$

So we can conclude that this generator exhibits adequately low autocorrelation.

Spectral test This is a good but rather complex test, often cited in the literature. It makes use of the observation that n-tuples from a generator lie on a small number of hyperplanes. A measure of the quality of the generator is given by the interplanar distance. The smaller this distance, the better the generator. We do not consider it in any more detail here because of its complexity, but a full treatment is given in Sec. 3.3.4 of Knuth (1981).

5.3.4 Implementation

The algorithm employed by the simulation library is based on congruential generator URN13 as recommended in Karian and Dudewicz (1991). The parameter values are $a = 663\,608\,941$, $c = 0$ and $m = 2^{32}$. The congruence is

$$X_{i+1} = X_i * 663\,608\,941 \ (\text{mod}\,2^{32}) \tag{5.30}$$

where the seed X_0 is an odd positive integer greater than 0. This linear congruential generator has a period of about 10^9.

The random number generator in the simulation library is function *uniform01()* with the following prototype:

```
float uniform01 (stream *rs);
```

which returns a floating point random fraction in the interval [0, 1]. This routine is the foundation of all random number generation in the library and, in common with the other random number functions, it receives a pointer to a *stream* as an argument. This makes it possible to declare and use many different and unconnected streams in different parts of the model but still only use a single fixed set of generation functions.

Function *uniform01( )* implements congruence (5.30) in one of two ways. If *unsigned long int*s have 32-bit precision, then we can simply multiply by 663 608 941 secure in the knowledge that in ANSI C unsigned integers obey the laws of arithmetic modulo 2^n, where n is the number of bits. Alternatively, when more than 32 bits are involved it is necessary to provide an explicit modulus operation. It is assumed that unsigned long integers always have at least 32 bits.

This generator satisfies our quality requirements (characteristics 1–6 in Sec. 5.3) for the following reasons:

- It has 16.7 million different values equally spaced in [0, 1) which is plenty for most simulation models.
- It has a period of 10^9.
- It has passed the statistical tests of Sec. 5.3.3 and many others into the bargain.
- Since it only uses standard C it is portable.
- Finally, at around 700 μs to generate a random variable on a 80386/DOS machine (without coprocessor), it is fast.

Most simulations will probably require several different and independent streams, the exact number of which varies from model to model. For this reason we make random number streams dynamically, using the *make_stream( )* function which has the prototype

```
stream *make_stream (int seed, unsigned int anthtc);
```

This returns a pointer to a *stream* data structure that comprises the information needed to generate an independent random number stream. The arguments to *make_stream( )* are a seed and a flag that indicates whether we require antithetic random variables (the idea behind antithetic random variables is covered in Chapter 10). The value of *seed* gives the starting value of the random number stream. Declaring *seed* as an unsigned integer means that there are around 65 000 different starting values.

The type *stream* is defined as

```
typedef struct {
        unsigned long int xi;
        unsigned int  antithc;
} stream;
```

where the *xi* component is the value of the last random number generated by function *uniform01( )* and the flag for antithetic random variables is stored in the *antithc* component.

5.4 GENERATING RANDOM NUMBERS FROM OTHER PROBABILITY DISTRIBUTIONS

In a typical simulation model we find that we do not just require uniformly distributed random variables, we also require random variables from other probability distributions to model various statistical phenomena. A good simulation environment, therefore, should provide a rich variety from which to choose. We will now look at the basic techniques that can be used for generating random numbers from probability distributions and then afterwards review the specific distributions provided by the simulation library.

5.4.1 Methods for generating random numbers from probability distributions

There are several methods which can be used to generate random values from probability distributions. We will discuss five of them here: inversion, rejection, composition, convolution and transformation.

Inversion The *inversion method* allows us to obtain probability distributions by drawing a number x in the range 0 to 1 from *uniform01( )* and then transforming with the inverse of the desired cdf. Given a desired cdf $F_X(x)$ and a uniform random number U in the interval $[0,1]$, the desired sample can be obtained by inverting the function to get $F^{-1}(U)$ since

$$P[F^{-1}(U) \leqslant x] = P[U \leqslant F_X(x)] = F_X(x) \qquad (5.31)$$

so all we need to do is find the inverse cdf to generate random variables from the distribution we want. Unfortunately, many cdfs are too complex to do this, but one distribution to which this method is universally applied is the exponential distribution.

Rejection The *rejection method* is a powerful and general method for generating exact random deviates whose pdf $p(x)$ is known and computable. It can be used to obtain probability distributions without having to calculate the inverse of the cdf which we saw was necessary for the inversion method.

The fundamental concept is that the area under a curve of a pdf $p(x)$ corresponding to some region $\alpha \leqslant x \leqslant b$ is the probability of generating an x in that region. Hence, if a random two-dimensional point is selected from the area under $p(x)$ with uniform probability in both dimensions, the x coordinate of that point would have the desired distribution.

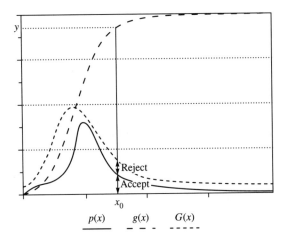

Figure 5.2 The rejection method.

Consider the graph of some probability function that we wish to generate from, call it $p(x)$. Suppose that we have a function $g(x)$ that is everywhere above $p(x)$ and for which the integral $G(x)$ and its inverse $G^{-1}(y)$ exist. Let the total area under the function $g(x)$ be A. The function $G^{-1}(y)$ gives x as a function of the area y to the left of x. Based on this observation, the following algorithm will generate a random variable with the desired distribution.

Step 1: Generate a uniform random deviate y, $0 \leqslant y \leqslant A$, corresponding to the area to the left of some point x.

Step 2: Calculate the corresponding point on the x-axis x_0 from $x_0 = G^{-1}(y)$.

Step 3: Generate a uniform random variable z, $0 \leqslant z \leqslant 1$.

Step 4: Calculate the ratio $r = p(x_0)/g(x_0)$.

Step 5: If $r < z$ then go to Step 1.

At the end of this process the required random variable ends up as x_0, although some of the steps, such as the selection of a random variable z at Step 3 and the ratio test at Step 5, are often found puzzling. The function of these steps may be understood by realizing that they are equivalent to generating a random variable y' in the interval $0 \leqslant y' \leqslant p(x_0)$ and so fixing a point $P(x_0, y')$ in two-dimensional space. P can then be accepted or rejected depending on whether it is underneath the curve of function $p(x)$ or not.

This algorithm is used for generating random variables with gamma, binomial and Poisson pdfs in the simulation library.

Composition If we have a set of efficient algorithms for obtaining probability distributions F_i, we may be able to combine the random variables generated from the known distributions to obtain another distribution F using *composition* if the following relationship holds:

$$F(x) = \sum_{i=1}^{n} p_i F_i(x) \tag{5.32}$$

where $F_i(x)$ are the cdfs for the component distributions and p_i is the probability of the random variable being generated from distribution i. To generate random variables using this technique we must generate an index j such that

$$P(i = j) = p_j \tag{5.33}$$

and then generate a random variable z from the jth cdf F_j. Such an algorithm is used in the simulation library by the *laplace( )* function.

Convolution If we can generate a random variable from a new distribution just by summing the random variables from several component distributions then we are employing a process of *convolution*. We use this approach in several library routines such as *erlang( )* and *chi_square( )*. In the case of the χ^2 distribution, we actually sum the squares of the random variables.

Transformation There are several ways in which random numbers from one distribution can be *transformed* to give numbers from a different distribution. When we are dealing with a distribution defined over a finite range, say $[a,b]$ with $a < b$, then *linear translation* can be used to give values over an arbitrary (real) range $[u,v]$. That is, a linear transformation is applied to each value X to give a value

$$Y = \frac{X(v - u)}{b - a} + u \tag{5.34}$$

This technique can be applied to the triangular and beta distributions described in the next section to obtain families of related distributions. The uniform distribution is also obtained in this way from the standard uniform distribution defined over $[0,1]$. However, since the uniform distribution tends to be used quite frequently, it is represented with a dedicated generating function in the simulation library.

Transformations are not confined to linear translations or to distribution functions with a finite range. We may find that, say, the logarithm or the square of the random variables from one distribution gives the necessary transformation.

Transformations are not necessarily simple functions either. One important, and quite complicated, transformation is the method of obtaining normal random variables devised by Box and Muller (1958). Their method generates exact normal variables based on the observation that if U_1 and U_2 are uniform random variables in the interval [0,1], then

$$X_s = \sqrt{-2\ln(U_1)}\sin(2\pi U_2) \tag{5.35}$$

and

$$X_c = \sqrt{-2\ln(U_1)}\cos(2\pi U_2) \tag{5.36}$$

are exactly normally distributed, independent, random variables with mean 1 and standard deviation 0.

The algorithm can be further simplified by replacing the sin and cos functions with the values

$$v_1 = 2U_1 - 1 \tag{5.37}$$

and

$$v_2 = 2U_2 - 1 \tag{5.38}$$

which are the coordinates of a point inside a unit circle, with radius $R = v_1^2 + v_2^2$. The normally distributed random variables in Eqs (5.37) and (5.38) are now replaced by

$$X_s = \sqrt{\frac{-2\ln(R)}{R}}v_1 \tag{5.39}$$

and

$$X_c = \sqrt{\frac{-2\ln(R)}{R}}v_2 \tag{5.40}$$

this substitution reduces the computational overhead since time-consuming trigonometric calculations are no longer required. Normally only one of the random variables, either X_s or X_c, would be used because independence could be compromised by imperfections in the uniform random number generators if both were used.

If a sequence of normally distributed random variables with mean μ and standard deviation σ different from 0 and 1 respectively are required, then we can use the following transformation

$$Y = \mu + \sigma X \tag{5.41}$$

where X has zero mean and unit standard deviation generated using the Box–Muller method.

Table 5.2 Characteristics of the uniform distribution

cdf	$\dfrac{x - x_{low}}{x_{high} - x_{low}}$,	for	$x_{high} \geqslant x \geqslant x_{low}$
pdf	$\dfrac{1}{x_{high} - x_{low}}$,	for	$x_{high} \geqslant x \geqslant x_{low}$
	0,	otherwise	
mean	$\dfrac{x_{low} + x_{high}}{2}$		
variance	$\dfrac{1}{12}(x_{high} - x_{low})^2$		

5.4.2 Distributions

We look here at the range of distributions available in the simulation library that have been implemented using the techniques discussed above. For each distribution the important characteristics are given and we outline the method of generation. To keep the presentation succinct no derivations are given but most good textbooks on probability theory provide these details. Some suggestions are given in the references.

The uniform distribution The *uniform distribution* represents the situation whereby a random number can take values within a finite range $[x_{low}, x_{high}]$ with equal probability. The important characteristics are shown in Table 5.2.

   The uniform distribution is illustrated in Fig. 5.3 for the case where x_{low} is 1 and x_{high} is 4.5.

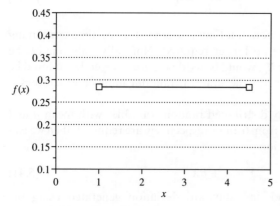

Figure 5.3 The uniform distribution.

Generating random variables from the uniform distribution can be done by simple linear translation of the standard uniform distribution as described in Sec. 4.4.1 with $u = x_{low}$, $v = x_{high}$, $a = 0$ and $b = 1$. This is performed by function *uniform( )* which has the prototype:

```
float uniform (stream*rs, float lower, float upper);
```

The triangular distribution The *triangular distribution* is a simple way to obtain random variables whose distribution functions exhibit various degrees of *skew* based on a mode parameter m, $0 \leqslant m \leqslant 1$. It has the principal characteristics shown in Table 5.3.

As can be seen from Fig. 5.4, the triangular distribution takes on various shapes depending on the value of m. As the m changes from 0 to 1, the skew of the distribution changes sides. At values less than 0.5 the distribution is skewed to the left and for values greater than 0.5 it is skewed to the right. When m equals 0.5 the skew is neutral since the distribution is symmetrical.

Random numbers for this distribution can be generated using the composition method. We generate a uniform random number, U_1 say, and use this to select the distribution we will sample from. If $0 \leqslant U_1 < m$ then we can select the first cdf, otherwise we select the second cdf. Having selected the cdf we sample another number U_2 and transform this by the applicable inverse cdf.

Table 5.3 Characteristics of the triangular distribution

cdf	$\dfrac{x^2}{m}$,	for	$0 \leqslant x < m < 1$
	$\dfrac{(x-1)^2}{(m-1)} + 1$,	for	$m \leqslant x \leqslant 1$
pdf	$\dfrac{2}{m}x$,	for	$0 \leqslant x < m < 1$
	$\dfrac{2}{1-m}(1-x)$,	for	$m \leqslant x \leqslant 1$
	0	otherwise	
mean	$\dfrac{1+m}{3}$		
variance	$\dfrac{1-m^3}{6(1-m)}$		

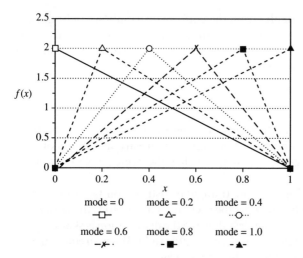

Figure 5.4 The triangular distribution.

This is the algorithm implemented in the simulation library by function *triang( )* which has prototype

```
float triang (stream *rs, float mode);
```

The exponential distribution The *exponential distribution* has a single non-negative parameter θ and the characteristics given in Table 5.4.

Figure 5.5 illustrates the graph of the pdf which decreases from 1 to near 0 as x increases from 0 to infinity. The distribution shown displays different curves for values of the parameter θ equal to 1, 0.4 and 0.22. It will be seen that the basic shape is always the same, the effect of changing θ is to scale the x-axis.

The inverse cdf can be obtained from the cdf directly as

$$F^{-1}(x) = -\theta \ln(1 - x) \tag{5.42}$$

Table 5.4 Characteristics of the exponential distribution

cdf	$1 - e^{-\frac{x}{\theta}},$	for $\quad x \geqslant 0$
pdf	$\frac{1}{\theta} e^{-\frac{x}{\theta}},$	for $\quad x \geqslant 0$
	$0,$	otherwise
mean	θ	
variance	θ^2	

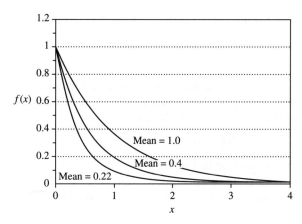

Figure 5.5 The exponential distribution.

so that given a uniformly distributed random fraction U in the interval [0,1] an exponentially distributed variable can be generated from

$$F^{-1}(U) = -\theta \ln(U) \qquad (5.43)$$

In the simulation library this distribution is provided by the function *exponential* which has the prototype:

```
float exponential (stream *rs);
```

and provides random variables with mean 1. Random variables with other means can be obtained by simply multiplying the sample returned by the required mean θ.

The gamma distribution The *gamma distribution* is a commonly utilized distribution that is also suitable as the basis for the generation of random variables for several other distributions. It is parameterized by two values α and β with $\alpha > 0$ and $\beta > 0$. The principal characteristics are shown in Table 5.5.

Table 5.5 Characteristics of the gamma distribution

pdf	$\dfrac{\beta^{\alpha} x^{\alpha-1} e^{-x\beta}}{\Gamma(\alpha)}$	for	$0 \leq x \leq \infty$
	0	otherwise	
mean	$\dfrac{\alpha}{\beta}$		
variance	$\dfrac{\alpha}{\beta^2}$		

In Table 5.5 $\Gamma(\alpha)$ is the gamma *function* of α which is defined by the integral

$$\Gamma(\alpha) = \int_0^\infty z^\alpha e^{-z} dz \qquad (5.44)$$

In fact the gamma function is a generalization of the common factorial and defined for all real values of its argument α. When α is a positive integer, the gamma function simplifies to the factorial, offset by one:

$$k! = \Gamma(k + 1) \qquad (5.45)$$

The gamma distribution is illustrated in Fig. 5.6.

In order to generate gamma distributed random variables the range of possible values for α must be subdivided. There are three cases to consider:

Case 1: $\alpha < 1$.
  - *Generate two uniformly distributed random numbers in $[0,1]$, call them u_1, u_2. Then calculate*

$$a = u_1^{1/(1-\alpha)} \qquad (5.46)$$
$$b = u_2^{1/\alpha} \qquad (5.47)$$

  - *if $a + b > 1$ then repeat the above steps.*
  - *Generate a random variable z from an exponential distribution.*
  - *The desired random variable is*

$$\frac{bz}{\beta(a + b)} \qquad (5.48)$$

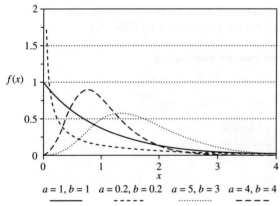

$a = 1, b = 1$ $a = 0.2, b = 0.2$ $a = 5, b = 3$ $a = 4, b = 4$

Figure 5.6 The gamma distribution.

Case 2: $\alpha = 1$.
  Use the exponential distribution with mean $1/\beta$.
Case 3: $\alpha > 1$.
  Use the rejection method. A convenient comparison function $g(x)$ to use is

$$g(x) = \frac{c_0}{1 + (x - x_0)^2/a_0^2} \tag{5.49}$$

which has inverse cdf $G^{-1}(y)$ given by the tangent function. Using the rejection method with this comparison function, a gamma distributed random variable x is given by

$$x = a_0 \tan(\pi U) + x_0 \tag{5.50}$$

where U is a uniform random variable in the interval $[0,1]$. It only remains to determine the coefficients a_0, c_0, x_0 in Eq. (5.49) so that the gamma distribution is everywhere covered by $g(x)$. This is done in Knuth (1981).

In the simulation library routine *gamma*() implements this algorithm. It has the prototype

```
float gamma (stream *rs, float alpha, float beta);
```

The beta distribution The *beta distribution* is useful when it is necessary to generate a continuous random variable between fixed bounds. The standard beta distribution is bounded in [0,1] but this can be scaled to an arbitrary $[u,v]$ by translating the random variable x using

$$\hat{x} = u + x*(v - u) \tag{5.51}$$

Table 5.6 Characteristics of the beta distribution

pdf	$\dfrac{\Gamma(\alpha + \beta)}{\Gamma(\alpha)\Gamma(\beta)} x^{\alpha-1}(1-x)^{\beta-1}$	for $\quad 0 \leqslant x \leqslant 1$
	0	otherwise
mean	$\dfrac{\alpha}{\alpha + \beta}$	
variance	$\dfrac{\alpha\beta}{(\alpha + \beta)^2(\alpha + \beta + 1)}$	

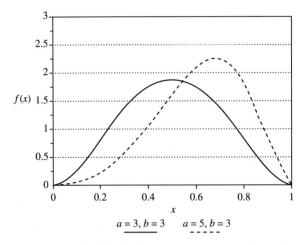

Figure 5.7 The beta distribution.

The beta distribution has two parameters, α, which affects the degree of skew and β, which affects the peakedness, where $\alpha > 0$, $\beta > 0$. The main characteristics are displayed in Table 5.6.

The beta distribution is displayed in Fig 5.7 for various values of α and β.

Beta distributed random numbers can be generated from the gamma distribution. If $\gamma(\alpha,\beta)$ generates gamma distributed random numbers then when

$$y = \gamma(1,\alpha) \tag{5.52}$$

and

$$z = \gamma\left(1, \frac{1}{\beta}\right) \tag{5.53}$$

$z/(y + z)$ will have a beta distribution with parameters α and β. This is the method used in the simulation library by routine *beta( )* for which we have the prototype

```
float beta (stream *rs, float a, float b);
```

The Erlang distribution The *Erlang distribution* of order r is the waiting time to the rth event in a so-called Poisson process (see Chapter 8). If the mean is fixed at 1, then the Erlang distribution can be thought of r exponentially distributed servers with a mean of $1/r$ connected in series. The result, for varying r, is that the mean remains the same but the variance reduces as $1/r$. The important characteristics are summarized in Table 5.7.

Table 5.7 Characteristics of the Erlang distribution

pdf	$\dfrac{\lambda(\lambda x)^{r-1}e^{-\lambda x}}{(r-1)!}$	for	$0 \leqslant x \leqslant \infty$
	$0,$	otherwise	
mean	$\dfrac{1}{\lambda}$		
variance	$\dfrac{1}{r\lambda}$		

The Erlang distribution is depicted in Fig. 5.8 for various values of r with $\lambda = 1$.

In order to generate Erlang distributed random variables with a mean of 1 either a direct method or the gamma distribution can be used since, if α is a positive integer, then $\Gamma(\alpha)$ becomes $(\alpha - 1)!$ and letting $\alpha = r$ and $\beta = \lambda$ in the pdf for the gamma distribution gives the pdf for the Erlang distribution. Thus we have the following algorithm:

Case 1: $r < 7$.
Sum r exponentially distributed random variables and divide the result by r to give a mean of 1.

Case 2: $r \geqslant 7$.
Calculate gamma($r,1$) and divide the value returned by r to give a mean of 1.

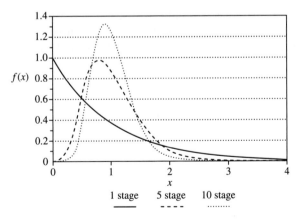

Figure 5.8 The Erlang distribution.

This technique is employed in the simulation library by function *erlang( )* with prototype

```
float erlang (stream *rs, unsigned int r);
```

which returns random variables with a mean of 1. Scaling by multiplying the value returned by the desired mean allows Erlang distributions with arbitrary mean to be catered for.

The binomial distribution A *Bernoulli trial* is an experiment that can have an outcome of *success* or *failure* with the probability of success p and the probability of failure $1 - p$. If n successive Bernoulli trials are conducted and the probability of success remains constant at p, then the probability of the number, X, of successes being x is given by the binomial distribution which has the principal characteristics given by Table 5.8.

The term $_n^xC$ is the binomial coefficient representing the number of ways x objects can be taken from a collection of n objects with replacement, so

$$_n^xC = \frac{n!}{x!(n - x)!} \tag{5.54}$$

We sometimes see $\binom{n}{x}$ written instead of $_n^xC$.

The binomial distribution is widely encountered in problems of sampling with replacement, i.e. an item is sampled and evaluated, then replaced before the next sample is taken, so that the probability of success or failure is constant from one sample to the next.

The binomial distribution identifies a family of distributions which are parameterized by p and n. The pdfs are defined only for non-negative integer arguments. This is shown in Fig. 5.9 for values of n of 10 and values of p of 0.1, 0.3, 0.5 and 0.8.

Table 5.8 Characteristics of the binomial distribution

pdf	$_n^xC \cdot p^x(1 - p)^{n-x}$	for	$x = 0, 1, ..., n$
	0	otherwise	
mean	np		
variance	$np(1 - p)$		

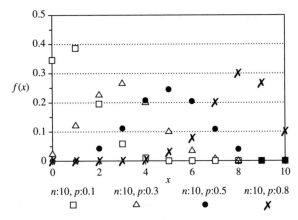

Figure 5.9 The binomial distribution.

In computing the binomial distribution three cases can be distinguished depending on the number of trials n and the probability of success p:

Case 1: $n < 25$
  Use the direct method by sampling n random numbers between 0 and 1 and count the number greater than p. This is the random variable required.
Case 2: $n < 1/p$.
  In this case fewer than 1 success is expected in n trials so that the Poisson distribution is an accurate approximation and can therefore be used directly.
Case 3: *For all other values of n the rejection method can be used with a function for g(x) similar to the one used in the gamma distribution.*

In the simulation library, routine *binomial( )* uses this algorithm to generate binomially distributed random variables. It has the prototype

```
float binomial (stream *rs, int n, float p);
```

The geometric distribution The *geometric distribution* represents the number of trials that occur in a sequence of Bernoulli trials until the first success is encountered. In the sequence of trials the probability of success is kept fixed and equal to p, $0 \leqslant p \leqslant 1$, and the trials are all independent. The characteristics of the geometric distribution are given in Table 5.9.

The geometric distribution is shown in Fig. 5.10 for various values of p.

Table 5.9 Characteristics of the geometric distribution

pdf	$(1 - p)^{x-1}p$	for	$x = 0, 1, ..., \infty$
	0	otherwise	
mean	$\dfrac{1}{p}$		
variance	$\dfrac{1-p}{p^2}$		

Fortunately it is quite easy to obtain the inverse transformation for the geometric distribution, so that the expression

$$F^{-1}(p) = \text{ceil}\left(\frac{\ln(U)}{\ln(1-p)}\right)$$
(5.55)

where U is uniformly distributed in the range 0 to 1, can be used directly to generate the required random variables.[‡]

In the simulation library, routine *geometric( )* uses this expression to generate geometrically distributed random variables. It has the prototype

```
float geometric (stream *rs, float p);
```

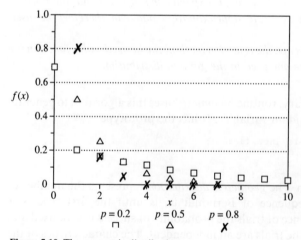

Figure 5.10 The geometric distribution.

‡ The function *ceil* returns the smallest integer greater than or equal to its argument.

Table 5.10 Characteristics of the negative binomial distribution

pdf	$\dfrac{r-1}{r+x-1}C p^r(1-p)^x$	for $\quad x \geqslant 0$
	0	otherwise
mean	$\dfrac{r}{p}$	
variance	$\dfrac{r(1-p)}{p^2}$	

The negative binomial distribution The *negative binomial distribution* is a generalization of the geometric distribution. The latter distribution gives us the number of trials to the first success. In contrast, the negative binomial distribution gives us the number of failures before the rth success, where the probability of success is fixed at p and the probability of failure is $1 - p$, $0 \leqslant p \leqslant 1$. The principal characteristics are given in Table 5.10. The term $_{r+x-1}^{r-1}C$ is the familiar binomial coefficient giving the number of ways $r - 1$ objects can be taken from a collection of $r + x - 1$ with replacement.

The negative binomial distribution is illustrated in Fig. 5.11 for various values of r and p.

In order to generate negative binomially distributed random variables we can use the fact that a gamma distributed random variable with parameters $\alpha = r$ and $\beta = (1 - p)/p$ when passed as the argument to the generator for the Poisson distribution generates random numbers with a negative binomial distribution. This method allows for both integer and non-integer values of x. The resulting pdf is a generalization of the pdf in Table 5.10 with gamma functions in place of factorials and the analytical form

$$\frac{\Gamma(r+x)}{\Gamma(r)\Gamma(x)} p^r (1-p)^x \qquad (5.56)$$

This function is also shown for various values of r and p in Fig. 5.11.

This relationship is exploited in the simulation library in function *neg_binomial( )* which has the prototype

```
float neg_binomial (stream *rs, float p, unsigned int r);
```

The Poisson distribution The *Poisson distribution* can be considered as the limiting case of the binomial distribution. If the probability of success, p, of a Bernoulli trial is reduced to zero, then we approach the case where Poisson events are studied over an infinitesimal period of time, so that there is an infinitesimal

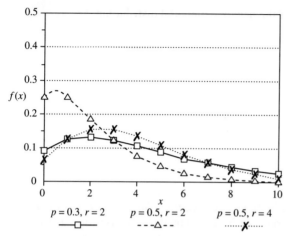

Figure 5.11 The negative binomial distribution.

probability of one event occurring in one time period and a negligible chance of more than one event. The principal characteristics of a Poisson distribution are shown in Table 5.11.

There is a close association between the Poisson distribution and the exponential distribution. If the time between events is considered, then the probability that there will be a time difference of no more than 1 time unit between two events is given by

$$P[t \leqslant 1] = 1 - P[t > 1]$$

$$= 1 - P[0 \text{ events} \in \text{unit time}] \tag{5.57}$$

The number of events in unit time is Poisson distributed with parameter μ so that

$$P[t \leqslant 1] = \frac{1 - \lambda^0 e^{-\mu}}{0!} = 1 - e^{-\mu} \tag{5.58}$$

Table 5.11 Characteristics of the Poisson distribution

pdf	$\dfrac{\mu^x}{x!} e^{-\mu}$	for	$x = 0, 1, ..., \infty$
	0	otherwise	
mean	μ		
variance	μ		

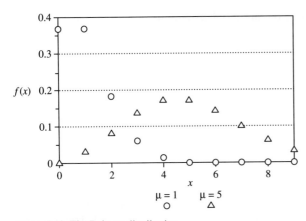

Figure 5.12 The Poisson distribution.

which is the cdf for the exponential distribution with mean μ. Differentiation gives the exponential pdf illustrated in Fig. 5.5.

We can generate Poisson distributed random variables as follows:

Case 1: $\mu < 12$.

Add exponentially distributed random variables together. When the sum exceeds μ then the number of Poisson events in a period of μ is known and this value less one is the required Poisson distributed random variable.

Case 2: $\mu \geqslant 12$.

Use the rejection method. There is a problem in using the rejection method though because the Poisson distribution, when viewed as a continuous pdf, is zero everywhere except when x is a positive integer. At these points it has finite area but is infinitely tall and infinitely thin and so no comparison function can actually cover this. However, what we can do is spread the area over a finite interval from x to x + 1 so that the height becomes finite. The comparison function§ is then

$$g_m(x) = \frac{m^{\text{floor}(x)}}{\text{floor}(x)!} e^{-m} \tag{5.59}$$

This approach is used in the simulation library in the implementation of function *poisson( )*, which has prototype

```
float poisson (stream *rs, float mn);
```

where the argument is the mean of the required Poisson distribution.

---

§ The function *floor* returns the largest integer less than or equal to its argument.

Table 5.12 Characteristics of the normal distribution

pdf	$\dfrac{1}{\sqrt{2\pi}\sigma}e^{-(x-\mu)^2/2\sigma^2}$	for $\quad -\infty \leqslant x \leqslant \infty$
	0	otherwise
mean	μ	
variance	σ^2	

The normal distribution The *normal distribution* is used extensively in statistics because it is tractable and useful for describing many statistical processes. It is parameterized by two values μ and σ, $-\infty \leqslant \mu \leqslant \infty$ and $\sigma > 0$. The principal characteristics are given in Table 5.12.

The pdf is shown in Fig. 5.13 for the case $\mu = 0$ and $\sigma^2 = 1$; this is the so-called *standard normal distribution*.

In the simulation library this distribution is provided with function *normal( )*, which has the prototype:

```
float normal (stream *rs, float mean, float std_dev);
```

The Box–Muller transformation method discussed in Sec. 5.4.1 is used to generate random variables for this distribution.

The lognormal distribution If a variable x is normally distributed with mean μ and variance σ^2 then the *lognormal* variable y is found from the transformation

$$y = e^x \tag{5.60}$$

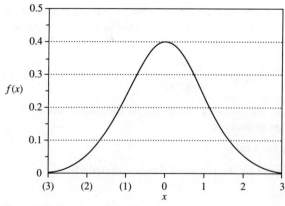

Figure 5.13 The normal distribution.

Table 5.13 Characteristics of the lognormal distribution

pdf	$\dfrac{1}{\sigma x\sqrt{2\pi}}e^{-(\ln x - \mu)^2/2\sigma^2}$	for	$0 \leqslant x \leqslant \infty$
	0		otherwise
mean	$e^{\mu + \sigma^2/2}$		
variance	$e^{2\mu + \sigma^2}(e^{\sigma^2} - 1)$		

so that

$$\ln y = x \qquad (5.61)$$

which is normally distributed. The product of a large number of positive random variables tends to have a lognormal distribution so this distribution is often used to model errors that are a product of a large number of factors. The principal characteristics are given in Table 5.13.

The lognormal distribution is illustrated in Fig. 5.14 for the case $\mu = 0$ and $\sigma = 1$. To generate random variables with other values for the mean and variance we can simply take a normally distributed random variable X with mean μ and variance σ^2 and return e^X.

In the simulation library this distribution is provided with function *lognormal( )*, which has the prototype

```
float lognormal (stream *rs, float mean, float std_dev);
```

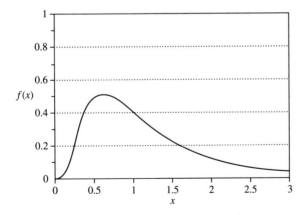

Figure 5.14 The lognormal distribution.

Table 5.14 Characteristics of the Weibull distribution

pdf	$\dfrac{\gamma}{\theta} x^{\gamma-1} e^{-x^{\gamma}/\theta}$	for $\quad x > 0$
	0	otherwise
mean	$\theta^{1/\gamma} \Gamma\left(1 + \dfrac{1}{\gamma}\right)$	
variance	$\theta^{2/\gamma} \left\{ \Gamma\left(1 + \dfrac{2}{\gamma}\right) - \left[\Gamma\left(1 + \dfrac{1}{\gamma}\right)\right]^{2} \right\}$	

The Weibull distribution The *Weibull distribution* is often used for modelling the failure rate function for components of a system. It is parameterized by two values θ and γ, where $\theta > 0$ and $\gamma > 0$. If $\gamma < 1$, the Weibull distribution gives a failure rate increasing with time. If $\gamma > 1$ the failure rates decrease with time. If $\gamma = 1$ the failure rates are constant and component lifetimes are simple exponential distributions with mean θ. The characteristics are shown in Table 5.14.

The Weibull pdf is shown in Figure 5.15.

Samples from the Weibull distribution can be generated from the exponential distribution since, if X is exponentially distributed with mean θ, Y is Weibull distributed when $Y = X^{1/\gamma}$. Hence only a simple transformation of the exponential deviate is needed.

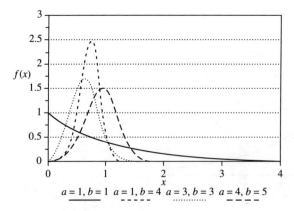

Figure 5.15 The Weibull distribution.

Table 5.15 Characteristics of the Laplace distribution

pdf	$\dfrac{1}{2\lambda}e^{-|x|/\lambda}$ for $-\infty \leqslant x \leqslant \infty$
mean	0
variance	$\dfrac{1}{\lambda^2}$

In the simulation library this distribution is provided with function *weibull( )*, which has the prototype

```
float weibull (stream *rs, float theta, float gamma);
```

The Laplace distribution The *Laplace distribution* looks like an exponential distribution with a mirror image in the y-axis as shown in Fig. 5.16. The principal characteristics are shown in Table 5.15.

Random values from this distribution can be obtained by using two functions g and h, where g is the exponential function and h is a function returning $+1$ with probability 0.5 and -1 with probability 0.5. Then gh is the desired distribution—in other words, an exponentially distributed random variable with a random sign.

In the simulation library function *laplace( )* generates Laplace distributed random variables, it has the prototype

```
float laplace (stream *rs);
```

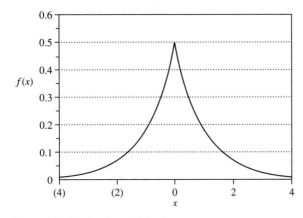

Figure 5.16 The Laplace distribution.

Table 5.16 Characteristics of the χ^2 distribution

pdf	$\dfrac{x^{(n/2)-1}e^{-x/2}}{2^{n/2}\Gamma(n/2)}$	for	$x \geqslant 0$
	0	otherwise	
mean	n		
variance	$2n$		

The variables returned have a mean of zero. To generate variables with an arbitrary mean θ simply add θ to the returned value. This has the effect of shifting the distribution along the x-axis.

The χ^2 distribution The χ^2 or *chi-squared* distribution with n degrees of freedom is the sum of n independent standard normal deviates squared. That is to say

$$Y = X_1^2 + X_2^2 + \cdots + X_n^2 \tag{5.62}$$

where each X_i is independent of all the others and has mean zero and standard deviation unity. The principal characteristics are given in Table 5.16.

The pdf is shown in Fig. 5.17. The χ^2 distribution becomes more spread out along the x-axis and flatter with increasing n (the degrees of freedom). For instance, the peak value at $n = 20$ is less than half that of the peak value at $n = 6$.

Random variables could be generated according to the χ^2 distribution from the sum of n independent normal distributions squared. However, a more efficient method is to use the fact that the χ^2 distribution is a special case of the

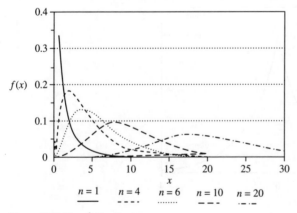

Figure 5.17 The χ^2 distribution.

Table 5.17 Characteristics of Student's *t* distribution

pdf	$\dfrac{\Gamma(n+1/2)}{\sqrt{n\pi}\,\Gamma(n/2)}\dfrac{1}{(1+x^2/n)^{(n+1)/2}},$	$-\infty \leqslant x \leqslant \infty$	
mean	0	for	$n > 1$
variance	$\dfrac{n}{n-2}$	for	$n > 2$

gamma distribution with $\alpha = n/2$ and $\beta = 0.5$. This latter approach is used for the simulation library routine *chi_square( )*, having the prototype

```
float chi_square (stream*rs, unsigned int n);
```

Student's *t* distribution *Student's t distribution* (or just the *t* distribution) is often used for defining confidence intervals as described in Chapter 10. It has the principal characteristics given in Table 5.17.

The pdf of Student's *t* distribution is shown in Fig. 5.18 and, as can be seen, it resembles the normal distribution. In fact, for infinite *n*, Student's *t* distribution simplifies to the normal distribution with zero mean and unit standard deviation. Even for finite (large) values of *n* the Student's *t* distribution can be approximated by the standard normal distribution. However, when *n* is less than 30 this approximation is too inaccurate.

We can generate random variables from Student's *t* distribution with *n* degrees of freedom by using the relationship

$$X = \frac{Y}{\sqrt{Z/n}} \tag{5.63}$$

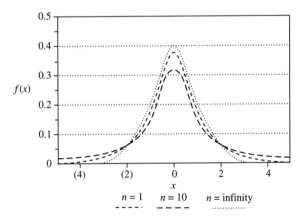

Figure 5.18 Student's *t* distribution.

Table 5.18 Characteristics of the F distribution

pdf	$\dfrac{\Gamma\left(\dfrac{n+m}{2}\right)\left(\dfrac{n}{m}\right)^{n/2}}{\Gamma\left(\dfrac{n}{2}\right)\Gamma\left(\dfrac{m}{2}\right)} x^{(m/2)-1}\left(1+\dfrac{nx}{m}\right)^{-(n+m)/2}$	for	$x > 0$
	0		otherwise
mean	$\dfrac{m}{m-2},$	for	$m > 2$
variance	$\dfrac{2m^2(n+m-2)}{n(m-2)^2(m-4)},$	for	$m > 4$

where Y is normally distributed with zero mean and unit variance, Z is χ^2 distributed with n degrees of freedom and Y is independent of Z. This relationship is employed in the simulation library routine *student_t( )*, which has the prototype

```
float student_t (stream *rs, unsigned int n);
```

The F distribution The *F or variance ratio distribution* is often used for testing variances, as will be demonstrated in Chapter 11. It takes two arguments m and n, both positive integers, defining the degrees of freedom of the variances being tested. The principal characteristics of this distribution are given in Table 5.18.

Figure 5.19 shows the pdf of the *F* distribution for various values of n and m. As n and m increase, the pdf gets closer and closer to a single spike centred at $x = 1$.

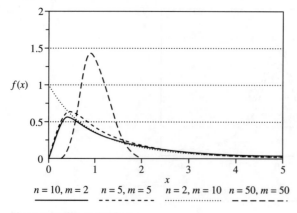

Figure 5.19 The *F* distribution.

In order to generate random variables from an F distribution use can be made of the fact that

$$X = \frac{Y_1 m}{Y_2 n} \qquad (5.64)$$

is F-distributed when Y_1 and Y_2 are independent χ^2 distributed random variables with m and n degrees of freedom respectively. This is the method used to generate F-distributed random variables from the simulation library routine $f\_distr()$, which has the prototype

```
float f \distr (stream *rs, unsigned int n, unsigned int m);
```

Empirical distributions If a set of samples does not fit one of the standard statistical distributions described above, then an *empirical distribution* can be derived from the samples themselves. To construct an empirical distribution a set of contiguous interval classes is defined that completely covers all the samples. Just how many intervals to choose is a compromise. Accuracy will clearly be better with more intervals. However, if there are too many, then accuracy may be adversely affected because there will only be a few samples in some classes (compare with the need to maintain at least 5 samples per class in the χ^2 test). There will also be additional memory requirements for the larger data structures and resulting performance penalties. In practice, somewhere between 5 and 10 interval classes should suffice.

The total range of values covered also needs careful consideration. In the tails of the distribution few observations will be logged but we should make sure that the range still covers all possible values. Suppose, for example, that the service time of a queue is measured and the range of measurements is found to be between 4.7 and 117.1 seconds. If it is known that the lowest possible value is 0 seconds and the highest possible value is 120 seconds, then it is necessary to make sure the intervals cover these outlying values even though they are not represented in the data set. Thus the lowest interval might span 0 to 30 seconds and the highest 90 to 120 seconds.

Data for empirical distributions is sometimes only available in a graphical or tabular histogram format; the source data may be missing or destroyed. If this is the case then any open-ended limits must be replaced by sensible values. For example, hypothetical job response times may be classified as having a lower class interval of '1 second or less' and an upper class interval of '5 minutes or more'. These must be replaced by, say, 0 seconds for the lower bound and 15 minutes for the upper bound.

Once all the intervals have been defined the samples can be assigned to them. The total number of samples assigned to a class is the frequency for that class. This could be translated very easily into a *frequency histogram* of course, but in a computerized setting the data is actually processed in a tabular form although it is often useful to view the histogram representation as well.

Table 5.19 Inter-arrival times

Interval	Frequency
0–0.1	54
0.1–0.2	75
0.2–0.3	88
0.3–0.4	56
0.4–0.5	21
0.5–0.6	27
0.6–0.7	21
0.7–0.8	11
0.8–0.9	7
0.9–1.0	4
1.0–5.0	8

An example set of data of the observed inter-arrival time of customers into a queuing system is given in Table 5.19. This table of values illustrates that all intervals do not have to be the same size. In the example most of them are 0.1 minutes, but the last interval is 4 minutes. The reason for making such uneven intervals is to ensure that there is a reasonable number of samples logged in each class. When displayed as a histogram, this table produces the graph shown in Fig. 5.20.

Section 5.4.1 showed how the inverse of the cdf is required in order to draw samples from a probability distribution. To sample from histograms the dual of the cdf is required, the *cumulative relative frequency histogram*. The cumulative relative frequency histogram is obtained by adding together the columns of a

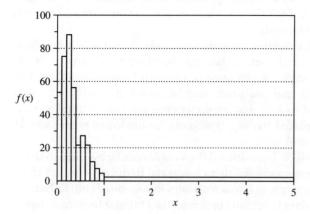

Figure 5.20 An example histogram based on Table 5.19.

frequency histogram to give a cumulative histogram which is then normalized. The normalizing constant S is the sum of all the histogram columns:

$$S = \sum_{i=1}^{n} y_i \qquad (5.65)$$

where y_i is the column height and the columns are indexed from 1 to n. The interval width of the ith column of the cumulative relative frequency histogram is the same as the ith column of the original histogram but its height is now $\hat{y}_k\{1 \leqslant k \leqslant n\}$, where

$$\hat{y}_k = \frac{1}{S} \sum_{i=1}^{k} y_i \qquad (5.66)$$

That is, to calculate the height of histogram column k all the values of histogram columns to the left of and including the kth interval are added together and then divided by the normalizing constant S.

The cumulative frequency histogram corresponding to Table 5.19 is illustrated in Fig. 5.21. From Table 5.19 the normalizing constant for this histogram is found to be 372.

Having obtained the data in the form of cumulative statistics, explicit generation of the inverse of the cdf can be avoided by sampling along the y-axis and finding a matching value on the x-axis. This is simplified by the knowledge that the y-axis must, by definition of the cdf, be defined over the interval [0,1]. Therefore, a uniformly distributed random variable U can be generated and this used to select a column from which to sample.

Sampling within a column can be performed in one of two ways. Either a

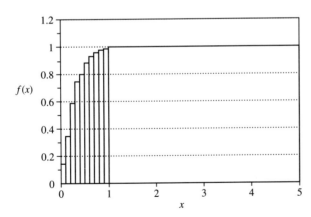

Figure 5.21 Cumulative relative frequency histogram.

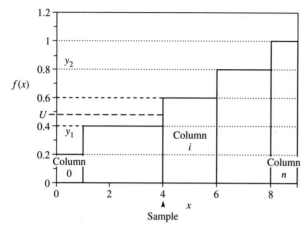

Figure 5.22 Discrete sampling.

discrete random variable can be generated or else linear interpolation between neighbouring columns can be performed in order to obtain a continuous random variable. Sampling for discrete random variables is summarized in the following algorithm:

Step 1: Generate a uniform random number U in the interval [0, 1].

Step 2: Identify two points y_1 and y_2 corresponding to the incremental height of the ith histogram column such that $y_2 \geqslant U \geqslant y_1$ as shown in Fig. 5.22.

Step 3: Take the random variable x_i to be the lower class limit of the ith column which in the figure is 4.

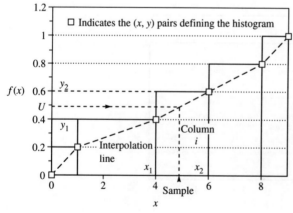

Figure 5.23 Continuous sampling.

and in the following algorithm for the continuous case:

Step 1: *Generate a uniform random number U in the interval [0, 1].*
Step 2: *Identify two points y_1 and y_2 corresponding to the incremental height of the ith histogram column such that $y_2 \geqslant U \geqslant y_1$ as shown in Fig. 5.23.*
Step 3: *Identify the end points of the interpolation which are*
  (a) the upper right corner of the $(i-1)$th and ith columns if $2 \leqslant i \leqslant n$, where n is the number of columns, and
  (b) the bottom left corner and top right corner of the first column for $i = 1$.
Step 4: *Calculate the sample from*

$$x_1 + (U - y_1)\left(\frac{x_2 - x_1}{y_2 - y_1}\right) \tag{5.67}$$

These samples are returned by a call to the simulation library routines *draw_discrete( )* and *draw_continuous( )*, with prototypes

```
float draw_discrete (stream *rs, table *t);
```

for obtaining discrete samples and

```
float draw_continuous (stream *rs, table *t);
```

for obtaining continuous samples.

The second argument to each of these functions are pointers to a *table* data structure created with the library function *make_table( )*, which has the prototype

```
table *make_table (int number, float *x_axis, float *y_axis);
```

This function creates a data structure containing the x and y coordinates of the pairs of points which define the histogram of the distribution. The pointers *x_axis* and *y_axis* passed as arguments are arrays which must be static since the *make_table( )* function does not copy values into locally created arrays, it only records the pointers given. In addition, the value of *number* must be the number of x and y pairs, which is of course one more than the number of columns. The data must also adhere to the following rules:

1. The first point in the y array is 0.0.
2. The last point in the y array is 1.0.
3. All x values are increasing.
4. All y values are non-decreasing.

which ensures that the arrays defining the histogram satisfy the principal characteristics of a cdf.

5.5 GOODNESS OF FIT

Goodness of fit tests allow us to assess whether a set of data could possibly have been generated from a given probability distribution. For example, we may have a set of waiting times and wish to know if the waiting times could have been generated by an exponentially distributed random variable with an appropriate mean.

We present here two such tests, the χ^2 test for discrete distributions and the Kolmogorov-Smirnov test for continuous distributions.

5.5.1 The χ^2 test

The χ^2 test has already been used in this chapter to establish whether the results from random number tests are significant or not. In effect what we were doing then was testing the *goodness of fit* between a distribution formed by the test results and a theoretical distribution based on the assumption of randomness. This method can, in fact, be used for discrete distributions in general. Consider the following example.

Example 5.11 The number of customers arriving at a queue in 200 one-minute measurement periods was recorded and the results are given below:

Arrvl	0	1	2	3	4	5	6	7	8	9
$p(s)$	0.0498	0.1494	0.2241	0.2241	0.168	0.101	0.05	0.022	0.0081	0.0027
Count	8	38	34	48	34	24	6	6	0	2

The number of arrivals are given in the first row. Beneath each number is given the corresponding expected proportion based on the Poisson pdf with μ, the mean, taking the value 3 and x taking the values 0, 1, 2, ..., 9. The actual counts are given in the third row. Notice that the last two count values are less than 5 and they must therefore be combined with the third from last count so that the observed value in each interval is greater than 5. We are left then with 8 counts and the last count is for the interval 7 to 9. We now wish to examine the hypothesis that the customer arrival pattern is described by a Poisson distribution with a mean of 3. The χ^2 statistic is

$$V = \frac{1}{200} \sum_{0 \leqslant s \leqslant 7} \left(\frac{Y_s^2}{p(s)} \right) - 200$$

$$= 0.005*41645 - 200$$

$$= 8.2$$

By consulting the χ^2 table in Appendix C we see that with 7 degrees of freedom a value of 8.2 can be expected somewhere between 50 per cent and 75 per cent of the time. So 8.2 is not significant at the 5 per cent level and therefore there is no basis for rejecting the hypothesis that the arrival process is Poisson with mean 3.

Often the distributions being tested have unknown parameters that must be estimated from the data. In such cases one degree of freedom must be deducted for each parameter so estimated. For example, if the mean in Example 5.11 was unknown, then it would be necessary to use the estimated value of 2.94 and redo the calculation for 6 degrees of freedom. The probabilities for counts in each class then become

Arrvl	0	1	2	3	4	5	6	7	8	9
$p(s)$	0.0529	0.1555	0.2286	0.2241	0.1647	0.0968	0.0474	0.020	0.0073	0.0024

and that the test statistic is now

$$V = \frac{1}{200} \sum_{0 \leqslant s \leqslant 7} \left(\frac{Y_s^2}{p(s)} \right) - 200$$

$$= 0.005*41717 - 200$$

$$= 8.6$$

With 6 degrees of freedom, 8.6 is not significant at the 5 per cent level and so there is insufficient evidence to reject the hypothesis that the data follows a Poisson distribution when the true mean is unknown and must be estimated.

5.5.2 The Kolmogorov–Smirnov test

The *Kolmogorov–Smirnov* (K–S) test is used to test whether a set of samples could have been obtained from a given continuous pdf $f(x)$ which has a continuous cdf $F(x)$ (i.e. that contains no jumps). To perform the test the empirical cdf $F_n(x)$ is first calculated where

$$F_n(x) = \frac{\text{number of samples } x_i \leqslant x}{n} \tag{5.68}$$

in which n is the number of interval classes. $F_n(x)$ is a step function and its value changes suddenly at values of $x = x_i$. The K–S test is based upon the observation that if the samples really did come from $F(x)$ then there should be little difference between $F(x)$ and $F_n(x)$. This comparison can be viewed graphically as shown in Figs 5.24 and 5.25. Figure 5.24 shows a poor match between $F(x)$ and $F_n(x)$. The more extensive this mismatch, the more improbable it is that the sample data is

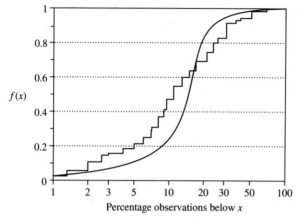

Figure 5.24 Empirical distribution showing a poor match.

consistent with the cdf $F(x)$. Figure 5.25 on the other hand, shows a much better match since the step curve more closely approximates to the continuous curve.

To make the test two values are derived from the data:

$$K_n^+ = \sqrt{n} \max_{-\infty < x < \infty} (F_n(x) - F(x)) \qquad (5.69)$$

and

$$K_n^- = \sqrt{n} \max_{-\infty < x < \infty} (F(x) - F_n(x)) \qquad (5.70)$$

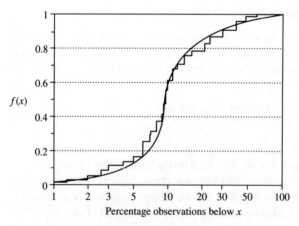

Figure 5.25 Empirical distribution showing a good match.

where K_n^+ represents the largest deviation when F_n is greater than F and K_n^- represents the largest deviation when F_n is less than F. The values of K_n^+ and K_n^- are looked up in a table of percentage points of the distributions for K_n^+ and K_n^- to see if they are significantly high or low. This table is given in Appendix C.

The K–S test has the useful property that the distributions for K_n^+ and K_n^- are exact for all values of n. There are, however, other considerations that must be taken into account in determining n. On the one hand, a large value is necessary to show conclusively that a set of data does not belong to the supposed distribution $F(x)$. On the other hand, large values of n tend to mask local deviations and are therefore undesirable. Knuth (1981) suggests that n be moderately large, say 1000, and that a large number of calculations of K_{1000}^+ and K_{1000}^- be made on different sections of the sequence deriving a subsequence of

$$K_{1000}^+(1), K_{1000}^+(2), ..., K_{1000}^+(r) \qquad (5.71)$$

and the K–S test applied to this derived sequence using an $F(x)$ which approximates to

$$F(x) = 1 - e^{-2x^2} \qquad \text{for} \qquad x > 0 \qquad (5.72)$$

A similar test being performed on the K_n^-. This approach will tend to detect both local and global deviations.

5.6 SELECTING A DISTRIBUTION

Sampling distributions model physical processes in the system under study such as the waiting time in a queue, the inter-arrival time between customers or the service time at a checkout. Therefore, to ensure that the model is accurate a close match must be established between the sampling distribution used and the physical process it models. There are four possible ways in which a suitable distribution can be selected which, in order of desirability, are:

1. Fit a standard distribution to samples taken from the modelled system (if it exists).
2. Sample from a histogram derived from measurements of the modelled system.
3. Make a guess based on experience or theory of which standard distribution and parameters to use.
4. Take measurements of the modelled system and then use these measurements directly, removing the requirement to select a distribution completely.

We will consider each of these strategies in turn.

5.6.1 Fitting a distribution to sample data

Fitting a distribution to sample data taken from a system is the preferred method of obtaining appropriately distributed random variables. The steps involved in using this approach are as follows:

Step 1: Generate a frequency histogram from the sample data.
Step 2: Select a standard distribution which looks something like the frequency histogram.
Step 3: Calculate the first and second moments of the sample data.
Step 4: Use the moments to calculate the parameters of the standard distribution (i.e. match the moments).
Step 5: Perform a goodness of fit test to assess the accuracy of the match using the standard tests described in Sec. 5.5.

If a standard distribution that fits the original data cannot be found, then it may be possible to transform it some way. To do this a new set of samples Y_i is obtained from the original data X_i as $Y_i = g(X_i)$, where $g(x)$ is a transformation function. The above steps are then re-applied, and hopefully a standard distribution is identified that now matches the transformed data Y_i. In selecting $g(x)$ it is advisable to use simple functions such as linear translations, logarithms or powers. Some pointers about which functions to use may be gleaned from comparing the histogram of the data to the available distributions but to get anything like a reasonable match will probably take considerable trial and error.

An altogether more systematic variant of this method is described in Karian and Dudewicz (1991) which involves fitting the sample data to a member of the family of *generalized lambda distributions*. To use this method it is necessary to calculate the first four moments from the sample data and then to select the parameters of the generalized lambda distribution which best match the moments from a set of tables.

5.6.2 Sampling from a histogram

It is sometimes the case that the sample data is only available in the form of a histogram, the actual observations made are not available. In such circumstances samples can be taken from the histogram directly using the method described in the section on empirical distributions. This method works well when the histograms are derived from a large number of samples and they have many interval classes.

Alternatively, we can try and fit a distribution to the histogram by proceeding from step 2 of the algorithm in the previous section.

5.6.3 Selection based on theory

On occasions there is no existing data at all on which to base the selection of a sampling distribution. This is often the case when modelling a hypothetical system. In such circumstances it may be necessary to resort to previous experience, reports of similar systems, reviews of relevant research material or theoretical analysis to select an appropriate distribution. Some of the better statistical texts may also provide useful information on which distributions are applicable in certain circumstances. The following, for example, are some often quoted uses of a selection of the probability distributions we looked at earlier:

1. *Exponential distribution.* Used to model purely 'random' events such as the time between failures or the time between arrivals of a customer. Often used in the absence of any clues as to which distribution to select.
2. *Beta distribution.* Used to model random proportions such as the fraction of packets requiring retransmission in a data communication link.
3. *Erlang distribution.* Used to model service times. In a queuing system that has *m* servers, each with exponentially distributed service times, then the overall service time is given by the Erlang distribution.
4. *Binomial distribution.* Used to model the number of successes in a sequence of *n* independent Bernoulli trials. For example, the number of bits in a packet not corrupted by noise.
5. *Geometric distribution.* Used to model the number of occurrences between significant events such as the number of error-free bits between two corrupted bits in a data packet or the number of enquiries to a local database between enquiries to a remote database.
6. *Negative binomial distribution.* Used to model the number of failures before the *m*th success such as the number of retransmissions of a file consisting of *m* packets or the number of queries to a local database before the *m*th remote query.
7. *Poisson distribution.* Used to model the number of occurrences over a given period such as the number of component failures in unit time or the number of queries to a database in *t* seconds.
8. *Normal distribution.* Used for modelling the additive effect of several independent sources such as measurement errors.
9. *Weibull distribution.* Used for reliability measures such as the lifetime of components.

In general be prepared to change the sampling distribution and judge the effects on the model. The aim here is to identify those areas of the model most sensitive to the selection of the distribution function and pay special attention to them.

5.6.4 Using historic data

It can be tempting to obtain *historic data* and use this directly in a simulation. We could, for example, sample from such a set of data $\{x_1, ..., x_n\}$ by generating a uniform random number i in the range 1 to n and use this as an index to select a particular sample x_i. Alternatively the historic data could be used directly. The first sample would be x_1, the second x_2 and so on. This approach would seem to guarantee that the stream produced has the desired probability distribution and so, on the face of it, it appears to be a sound proposition. There are, however, several drawbacks:

1. In most simulations a large number of samples are required. The number needed is inflated by the common requirement to repeat simulation runs with different data in order to increase our confidence in the results. Often the necessary volume of data is simply not available.
2. The historic data may have hidden biases, may not represent the current conditions or be otherwise impaired in such a way that it leads to erroneous results.
3. We often want to vary the characteristics of the sampled distribution to look at the effects of, say, a doubling in the offered load. Clearly this is not possible using historic data.
4. We may be unable to predict future behaviour based on historic data if the future distribution changes.

In view of these problems this method should be used with care, if at all. In practice one of the other methods described above is preferable.

5.7 SUMMARY

Random numbers are essential for stochastic modelling. They can be generated from simple linear expressions with carefully chosen parameters. Such expressions are termed linear congruential random number generators. To be useful, the sequence or stream of numbers produced must

- be from as large a set of values as possible
- have a long cycle time
- exhibit small autocorrelation and have good statistical properties
- be portable and efficient.

Numerous tests exist for verifying the randomness or otherwise of random number streams. These can be classified as either empirical or theoretical tests. Empirical tests are based on measurement and have an associated probability of error. Theoretical tests are precise, but are difficult to do.

In a simulation we often need random numbers generated from different probability distributions. Five popular methods for generating numbers for probability distributions are

- the inversion method, which requires the inversion of the cdf of the distribution

- the rejection method, which uses a secondary function which covers the cdf
- the composition method, which involves the combination of random variables from simpler distributions to produce the desired distribution
- the convolution method, in which the random variables from several component distributions are added together
- the transformation method, which involves the use of a function to translate variables from one distribution to obtain another.

The match between a distribution and data can be expressed quantitatively. The χ^2 test can be used for discrete distributions and the Kolmogorov–Smirnov test can be used for continuous distributions. Both of these tests generate a test statistic that allows us to accept or reject a random number stream with some small, fixed, level of significance such as 5 per cent or 1 per cent. These tests work only when the test data is independent.

It is very often necessary to choose a suitable probability distribution to model some aspect of system behaviour. If measurements are available from the real system then we may be able to use a standard distribution. The samples should be displayed as a histogram and the first couple of moments calculated. A similar looking distribution can be selected by inspection and the parameters determined so that the distribution is a best fit to the measurements. Alternatively, the histogram itself can be directly sampled from. If no measurements are available then it may be possible, based on theory or experience, to make a reasonable guess as to what the distribution should be. A final option is to take measurements of the system and use these measurements directly.

5.8 EXERCISES

5.1 Add a function *translate( )* to the simulation library that takes a random variable, its range, and the range of the translated variable as input and returns the translated value as a floating point number.

5.2 Write a program that tests the quality of a random number generator using the methods described in Sec. 5.3.3. Your program should read a file containing the random numbers to be tested and print out the result of each of the empirical tests.

5.3 Compare the quality of your standard C library random number generator with the one described in Sec. 5.3.4 and implemented in the simulation library. Use the test program developed in Exercise 5.2 to compare the quality of the generators.

5.4 Look at the effect on the simple queue in Chapter 3 of changing the probability distributions. Change the inter-arrival times to normally distributed with mean as before and standard deviation equal to half the mean. Change the service time to be uniformly distributed with the same mean but with upper and lower limits given by $\pm 0.33*$mean.

5.5 Using the χ^2 test with a level of significance of 5 per cent, examine whether the following results from the Coupons Collectors Test (test 4a) applied to 1000 numbers indicate randomness:

Category	Count	Category	Count
1	31	9	63
2	112	10	97
3	131	11	89
4	92	12	103
5	57	13	76
6	36	14	31
7	31	15	19
8	20	16	9

5.6 Use the K–S test to examine whether the following data has a normal distribution with mean 0 and variance 2.5 with a level of significance of 1 per cent.

1.549 422	2.444 344	− 1.356 287	− 1.158 468	1.986 288
− 1.317 650	1.203 433	− 2.405 187	− 0.983 101	− 0.942 457
2.627 202	2.295 194	0.253 501	− 0.256 372	− 1.221 426
− 2.819 277	2.729 291	1.374 238	− 0.028 606	0.940 219
− 1.100 076	− 2.032 944	− 1.105 679	1.694 956	0.019 935

6

ENTITIES AND RESOURCES

In this chapter we look at how objects in the real system can be modelled in terms of entities and resources and the facilities provided by the simulation library to handle them.

6.1 ENTITIES

Entities are the representation in the model of active objects in the system such as customers or processors. Because entities are active they have a close affiliation with events. An entity responds to events in the model and it may cause additional future events to be scheduled. We saw in the model of the simple queue in Chapter 3, for example, that a departure event caused a new customer entity to leave the queue to obtain service and then create a scheduled event corresponding to its own departure from the system.

An entity can also have characteristics that represent important information relevant to the behaviour of the entity in the context of the model. This information normally allows us to distinguish between individuals of the same sort. For instance, in a model of the X.25 packet switch protocol (see Hewlett-Packard, 1985) there must be entities representing *packets*. The behaviour of a packet is involved with events such as *transmit, receive* and *retransmit*. Additionally, packets have properties such as size (number of bits), transmit sequence number, receive sequence number, logical channel number and so on. If this level of detail is pertinent, then these properties are important in the way they influence the behaviour of a packet and so must be represented as attributes of the entity that denotes a packet in the model.

These two ideas of characterization by a set of attributes and behaviour in terms of significant events can be integrated in a data structure called an *entity record* which has the following, incomplete, declaration

```
typedef struct {
    :
    void *attr;
    int   phase;
    void (event *)();
    :
} entity;
```

Here *attr* is a pointer to some data that has significance within the model but is irrelevant as far as the simulation library is concerned. It should be as general as possible so that it does not constrain the structure of the model. For this reason *attr* is declared as a pointer to the C data type *void* which allows an arbitrary data structure to be created dynamically and accessed using the C cast mechanism. The result is a reasonable compromise between generality and memory efficiency. If the entity does not possess any attributes only the memory allocated to a single pointer is wasted.

Event is a pointer to a function that simulates the occurrence of an event. In the event-based approaches the function implements the event and we sometimes refer to it as the *event routine*. In the process-oriented approach the function is the collection of events that describe the life-cycle of an entity and we refer to this as an *entity routine*.

In the event-scheduling approach, the entity record binds an event, represented by the *event* component, to an entity, represented by the *attr* component. In effect this makes a temporary association between the event and the entity. There is an extra set of events in the three-phase approach, the conditional events, which are scanned at each advance of the simulation clock. However, a conditional event is often unconnected to any particular entity in the model. For example, a queue service event involves the selection of different entities from the waiting queue. Hence, the *attr* component of the entity record in this case is frequently ignored.

In the process-oriented approach the events that apply to the same entity class are grouped together in a single routine. In this case, the *entity* data structure requires an extra component *phase* to act as a reactivation pointer to determine which of the primitive events apply at a given epoch in the existence of the entity. These primitive events are normally C *switch* alternatives in the routine pointed to by the *event* field. Conceptually, the entity routine can be thought of as the active part of the description of a class of entities and the *attr* component can be thought of as defining the characteristics of an individual of the class. Normally, the value of the *event* component does not change as the simulation progresses; rather the *phase* and *attr* components change as the life of the entity evolves.

6.1.1 Entity states

Entities are involved in several different activities, such as queuing or waiting for an event to occur, during the course of a simulation. Generally speaking, these activities are mutually exclusive. It makes little sense, for example, to enable an entity that is currently waiting in a queue to be scheduled for later activation. If this is allowed to happen then the data structure representing the queue will be corrupted if the removal is performed naively without updating all the necessary pointers. Hence, it would be advantageous to incorporate in an entity record information that describes the current activity and to ensure that functions which operate on the entity observe the rules about what is permissible for each activity.

The information required forms an *entity state*. The effect of the entity state can be expressed by a *state-transition diagram* (std). The std contains a node for each state and arrows labelled with the name of a function. This gives the function calls which are legal in each state and the effect that they have in determining the new state. Such an std in shown in Fig. 6.1. The possible entity states are as follows

- *PASSIVE*, indicating that the entity is currently not available for any processing.

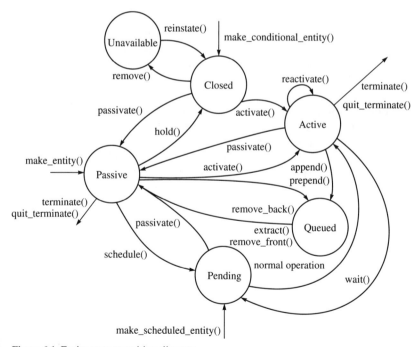

Figure 6.1 Entity state-transition diagram.

- *ACTIVE*, indicating that this is the entity currently being processed.
- *QUEUED*, indicating that the entity is currently in a queue.
- *PENDING*, indicating that the entity is currently in the calendar.
- *CONDITIONAL*, indicating that the entity is part of the set of entities that are conditional on some state of the model.
- *CLOSED*, indicating that the entity is part of the set of entities that are conditional on some state of the model but that it is currently unavailable.
- *TERMINATED*, indicating that this entity has been terminated and the memory occupied by it deallocated. This state is represented explicitly because it can aid the debugging of errant models.

Thus, the std conveniently shows the possible transitions between entity states and the functions that cause them. No other transitions are possible, unless of course this mechanism is circumvented by modifying the state directly, but this is not recommended. So, for example, it is not possible to delay an entity that is already in a queue. Instead, it must first of all be removed with a call to *passivate( )*, changing its state from *QUEUED* to *PASSIVE*. It can then be scheduled with function *schedule( )*, changing its state from *PASSIVE* to *PENDING*. In summary, the library functions available for operating on entities are:

- *Passivate( )*, which takes an entity in state *CONDITIONAL, PENDING or ACTIVE* and makes it *PASSIVE*. This takes an entity out of the simulation but does not destroy it. It is left to the logic of the model to manage the resulting entity record. This provides a useful mechanism to delay an activity for an *unknown* period.
- *Hold( )*, which takes a passive entity and adds it to the linked list of conditional entities, changing its state to *CONDITIONAL*. *Hold( )* is used when it is necessary to wait for some state of the model to occur at some unpredictable time in the future.
- *Schedule( )*, which takes a currently passive entity and delays it by a known (but possibly random) period, changing its state to *PENDING*.
- *Wait( )*, which does the same as *schedule( )* but for the *current* entity which will be in the *ACTIVE* state. *Schedule( ) and wait( )* are used when it is necessary to perform some action at a defined time in the future.
- *Activate( )*, which takes a passive or conditional entity and schedules it for activation at the current simulated time (i.e. delays by zero). In this case there is a temporary *PENDING* state but the scheduler activates the entity at the current simulated time and the state then becomes *ACTIVE*. A typical use of *activate( )* is to bring forward the occurrence of an event from when it was scheduled to occur to the present time.
- *Reactivate( )*, which takes the *current* entity, if in the *ACTIVE* state, and schedules it for activation again at the current simulated time. *Reactivate( )* is

ordinarily used to repeat some entity behaviour, possibly with different attributes.

- *Terminate( )* and *quit_terminate( )*, which take an entity out of the simulation when in the *ACTIVE* or *PASSIVE* state. *Quit_terminate( )* can also end the simulation if the number of entities processed exceeds the threshold established when *run_sim( )* was called.
- *Append( )* and *prepend( )*, which add passive and active entities to a queue and change their states to *QUEUED*.
- *Extract( )*, *remove_front( )* and *remove_back( )*, which obtain entities from a queue and make them *PASSIVE*.
- *Queue_front( )* and *queue_back( )*, which return the current entities at the front or back of a queue but do not affect any changes.
- *Withdraw( )*, which disables an entity that is currently conditional, making it unavailable to the model by changing its state to *CLOSED*.
- *Reinstate( )*, which takes an entity that is currently in the state *CLOSED* and so unavailable, and adds it back to the set of conditional entities. The state then becomes *CONDITIONAL*.

These last two functions perhaps need a little more elaboration. They are based on the idea of *cellular simulation* (see Spinelli de Carvalho, 1976). The idea of this is that not all conditional entity or event routines will be able to run at each tick of the simulation clock. In fact, it may be that for some period it is known that a subset cannot possibly run. If this is the case then the routines in question can be blocked from being called during the scan of the conditional entities in order to reduce execution time. They can then be enabled later on when it is known that they will be needed. Care should, however, be exercised when using this technique to ensure that the conditional entities are really not required when disabled and that enough of them are enabled and disabled *en bloc* to offer some performance benefit.

6.1.2 Using entities

When an entity changes from one state to another it must often adopt different behaviour in the new state. For instance, when the *current* entity has been delayed with a call to *wait( )* it may be necessary to activate it with a different priority or phase, or for a different event routine to be called. In the model all that has to be done is to assign the new component to the entity record. For instance, if an entity must be made *CONDITIONAL* in order to wait for a specific condition to occur at some unknown time in the future then, in an event-based model, we could code this as

```
/* A function to wait for the occurrence of a condition */
    void wait_for_condition ( void );
```

```
void some_event_routine ()
{
    :
    current->event = wait_for_condition;
    hold(current)
}
```

where the function to be executed during the C phase is set to *wait_for_
condition()* prior to the call to *hold()*. Alternatively, in a process-oriented model
we could use

```
/* Phase in which an entity waits for the occurrence of a condition */
  #define WAIT_FOR_CONDITION 99

void some_entity_routine ()
{

    :
    current->phase = WAIT_FOR_CONDITION;
    hold(current)
    :
  case WAIT_FOR_CONDITION:
    :

}
```

The current state of an entity is something that might be useful to know in a
simulation model. For this reason seven macros are provided of the general form
IS_x(entity) where *x* is one of the states mentioned above. Each macro takes an
entity as an argument and returns *TRUE* if the entity is in the tested state. The
macros can be used wherever a Boolean expression is valid, such as the
conditional expression part of an *if* statement, as in

```
    if ( IS_PENDING ( e ) ) {
    :
    /* Do something to entity e that is in the calendar. */
    :
    }
```

to test if an entity record *e* is in the calendar. This is both succinct and readable.
The macros, together with the definitions of *state*, are provided in the header file
sim_lib.h.

6.1.3 Creating entities

Entities may be created with the *make_conditional_entity()*, *make_entity()* or *make_scheduled_entity( )* library function calls. These library functions have the following arguments in common (some of which have already been mentioned):

- *void (*event)( )* is a pointer to an event or entity routine.
- *void *at* is a pointer to attribute data associated with an entity.
- *int phase* is normally only used in a process-oriented model. It is used to establish the phase that the entity will execute with.
- *int priority* assigns an integer priority to an entity which is used when the entity is added to a queue.
- *void (*destroy)(void *attr)* is a pointer to a function that frees the attribute component of the entity when the entity is terminated.

The first of the creation functions, *make_conditional_entity( )*, creates a new entity record dynamically and adds it to the current set of conditional entities. These are maintained in a linked list so that they may be easily scanned. The new entity record added has the initial state of *CONDITIONAL*. The function prototype is

```
entity* make_conditional_entity ( void (*event)(), void *at, int phase,
            int priority, void (* destroy)(void *attr) );
```

Make_entity( ) also creates a new entity record dynamically but with an initial state of *PASSIVE*. It has the prototype

```
entity *make_entity ( void (*event)( ), void *at, int phase, int priority,
            void (*destroy)(void *attr) );
```

A new entity created by *make_entity( )* is not added to any of the entity sets like the calendar or the list of conditional entities which are maintained by the simulation library. Instead the returned pointer must be handled explicitly within the model.

Another function which is convenient to have allows entity records to be created and added directly into the set of entities scheduled to occur at some future time. This set is called the calendar and is described in the next chapter. The function in question is *make_scheduled_entity( )* and it has the prototype

```
entity* make_scheduled_entity ( void (*event)(), void *at, float t,
            int phase, int priority, int number,
            void (*destroy)(void *attr));
```

The parameter *t* defines the time after the current simulated time at which the entity is to be activated. The argument *number* indicates exactly how many entities with the given parameters will be added to the calendar. If this is less than one then an error message is printed and the simulation abandoned. The initial state of all entities so added will be *PENDING*.

6.1.4 Entity attributes

We have already seen the need for modelling the attributes of an entity. Attributes may be simple data types such as *int*s or *char*s which can be cast to a pointer and so require no additional memory allocation. However, if the data structure is more complex it can be created dynamically and the pointer maintained as the *attr* component of the entity record.

When the attribute data must be referenced in a model the convenience macro *ATTRIBUTES*, declared in *sim_lib.h*, can be used. This takes an entity as an argument and returns the attributes data structure. For instance, in a model of a communications protocol we might model the attributes of a packet entity by the compound data structure *packet* which has a component *packet_size*. Then we could use

```
if ((packet *)ATTRIBUTES(current)->packet_size >= buffer_space) {
    :
}
```

to test if there is enough buffer space available for the current packet.

6.1.5 Destroying entities

In most models entities must be destroyed as the simulation progresses. This can be done with a call to *terminate( )*. The result will be the release of the dynamic memory occupied by the entity record. If the *attr* component is non-NULL and a non-NULL pointer to a *destroy( )* function is available in the entity record, then a call to the routine *(*destroy)( )* will be made with the entity attribute pointer as an argument. This procedure must arrange appropriate release of the memory by calling the standard C function *free( )* as required for the particular data structure used. It is not possible to do this transparently within the simulation library because no knowledge of this data type is available. The prototype of *terminate( )* is

```
int terminate ( entity *e );
```

Terminate( ) will only succeed if the entity is in the *PASSIVE* or *ACTIVE* states. All other states cause the routine to fail and no termination will take place. A return value of *False* indicates this situation.

A related function to *terminate( )* is *quit_terminate( )*. This behaves in the same way as *terminate( )* with the additional ability to stop the simulation if the termination count, which is decremented by each call to *quit_terminate( )*, becomes 0. This allows the duration of the simulation to be based on the number of entities processed rather than on elapsed simulated time. The initial value of the termination count is established when the call to *run_sim( )* is made.

6.1.6 Time stamps

A common requirement in a simulation model is to measure the time interval between certain states of an entity or between significant events. For instance, if we were interested in the total time spent queuing then we would measure the simulated time between the entry of an entity into a queue and its exit from the queue after receiving some service. The *interval* component of an entity record can be used for this purpose. The *interval* component records values of the simulation clock. The current value of the clock is assigned to *interval* by the function *stamp( )* which has the prototype

```
void stamp ( entity *e );
```

The value of the simulation clock can be recorded by the currently active entity by using the function

```
void stamp_current ( void );
```

We can access the value of *interval* by using the macro *TIME_SPENT*, declared in header file *sim_lib.h*. *TIME_SPENT* takes an entity as an argument and returns the difference between the time stamp of the entity and the current simulated time that is stored in the floating point variable *sim_clock*. For example, suppose we wanted to add waiting time statistics to the simple queue described in Chapter 3. Taking the three-phase model, the arrival and departure events could be modified as follows:

```
arrival ()
{
  <<create a new customer>>
  <<add new customer to the queue>>
  stamp_current();
  <<schedule arrival of next customer>>
}

departure()
{
  <<make the checkout free>>
  print("Time in system = %f \n",TIME_SPENT(current));
  <<remove entity from the model>>
}
```

In this example a time stamp has been added when the entity enters the queue and the difference between the time stamp and the current simulated time has been printed out when the entity leaves the checkout. This is the total time in the system.

6.1.7 Competing conditional entities

It may be that conditional entities can affect each other. For example, if there are two conditional entities say *A* and *B*, and entity *A* is scanned first but entity *B* releases a resource required by entity *A*, then entity *A* may never run despite the fact that the resource is available after the scan. What we require in this case is that the C-phase be structured as follows:

```
do {
    at_least_one_executed = False;
    〈〈Go to first conditional entity〉〉
    while (〈〈Not end of list〉〉) do
    {
        〈〈Try and execute conditional entity〉〉
        〈〈Get next conditional entity〉〉
    }
} while (at_least_one_executed) ;
```

Here we repeatedly scan through the list of conditional entities, trying to execute each of them, until none can run. To indicate when a conditional entity is able to proceed the global flag *at_least_one_executed* must be set to *True* as in the following skeletal conditional entity routine:

```
void a_conditional_entity ()
{
    :
    if (〈〈The entity can proceed〉〉)
    {
        at_least_one_executed = True;

        / *Do something */
        :
    }
    :
}
```

There is certainly a performance penalty in structuring the model like this. It also forces extra discipline on to the modeller since the variable must be set in each conditional routine. For these reasons, coupled with the likelihood that such situations are the exception rather than the rule, the simulation library uses the simpler structure

```
do {
    〈〈Try and execute next conditional entity〉〉
} while (Not last entity) ;
```

This forces dependencies between conditional entities to be recognized beforehand and explicitly coded by the modeller in each applicable routine. However, if there are many dependencies between conditional entities, events and resources then the simulation library may be modified to incorporate the more elaborate scheme above.

6.2 RESOURCES

A *resource* in the real-world system is usually some form of reusable asset such as the amount of free storage in a computer system or a checkout in a supermarket. The principal characteristic that both of these examples have in common is limited capacity. In the case of free storage the processes and data that can reside in memory without being swapped out to disk are restricted. In the case of the checkout the ability of a customer to receive service is dependent on whether the checkout is currently busy or not.

The most useful parameter of a resource is how much of it is currently available. Another convenient parameter is how much resource we started off with. This latter information is necessary, for example, to reset a resource to its value at the beginning of the simulation and for calculating how much has been consumed. Therefore, we can define a *resource record* as

```
typedef struct {
  float initial_amount;
  float amount_left;
} resource;
```

For reasons already outlined resources are created dynamically. The library function for this is

```
resource *make_resource ( float a );
```

which returns a pointer to a new resource object. The value of *a* is normally the initial amount of the resource that is available when the simulation started. Creating a resource with an argument *a* causes the components *initial_amount* and *amount_left* to be both initialized to *a*. Future acquisition and release of a resource affects only the *amount_left* component. The *initial_amount* component is unmodified.

The convenience macro *IS_AVAILABLE*, defined in *resource.h*, is a logical expression that can be used to test if the current amount of a resource exceeds some value, as in

```
resource *mem;
   :
   :
/* mem initially has 256 k free */
mem = make_resource ( 256.0 );
   :
/* If more than 25 k of memory is free then do something... */
if (IS_AVAILABLE(mem, 25)) {
   :
}
```

Resources are normally acquired and released by many entities in a model and so there are library routines *acquire( )* and *release( )* to do just this. Function *acquire( )* has the prototype

```
void acquire ( resource *res , float a );
```

As a result of a call to this function, the value of *res-> amount_left* is decremented by *a*. It is usually not sensible to have a negative amount of a resource, so a warning message is printed by the simulation library if *a* is greater than *res-> amount_left*. Function *release( )* has the prototype

```
void release ( resource *res , float a );
```

and, as can be expected, the result of a call to *release( )* is that the value of *res-> amount_left* is increased by *a*. Most models use these library functions together. A call to *acquire( )* is balanced by a subsequent call to *release( )* some time later in the course of the simulation.

If conditions regarding the value of *amount_left* in relation to the *initial_ amount* of the resource are to be enforced, then they must be explicitly added to the model. We could use something like the following code fragment to do this:

```
if (AMOUNT_USED(res) >= a)) {
  release(res , a);
}
else {
  /* Error - attempt to release too much of resource res */
  :
}
```

Here use has been made of the convenience macro *AMOUNT_USED*, which returns the value of *res-> initial_amount − res-> amount_left* for the resource passed as a parameter. Other useful macros are *AMOUNT_LEFT*, which provides the value of the *amount_left* component of the resource, *IS_FULL*, which gives a value of *True* if *amount_left* and *initial_amount* are equal and *False* otherwise and *IS_EMPTY* which gives a value of *True* if the amount of resource *res* remaining is zero. In all cases the resource pointer *res* is a parameter passed to the macro.

All macros, type definitions and functions related to resources are declared in *resource.h* and the source is in *resource.c*.

6.3 AN EXAMPLE—THE DINING PHILOSOPHERS

The ideas in this chapter can be illustrated by a model of the so-called *dining philosophers problem*. This is a hypothetical problem that expresses some of the issues involved in resource sharing, such as how to control access to a resource when there are several competing users. It was originally developed by

E.J. Dijkstra, and has appeared in numerous technical publications in various guises since then.

There are five philosophers seated around a table in (this version of) the dining philosophers problem. Situated between each philosopher is a chopstick. So keen are these philosophers in the intellectual challenge of philosophy that all they do for a week is either eat or discuss philosophy. To eat some rice a philosopher must obtain both his left and right chopstick. If his neighbour is currently eating at least one of the chopsticks will not be available and so the philosopher will have to wait for them to be put down. While waiting for a chopstick to become available a philosopher does not enter into the intellectual deliberations and so this period of time is effectively wasted.

We need to know the amount of useful thinking time, i.e. the time not spent eating or waiting for chopsticks to become available. Two types of model will be shown to obtain this information, the first a three-phase model and the second a process-oriented model.

6.3.1 Three-phase model

A three-phase model for this system is shown in Listing 6.1. It contains three routines corresponding to the significant events *start to eat*, *start to think* and *start waiting*. The start waiting event is modelled by *await( )*. It attempts to acquire the two chopsticks. If the chopsticks are not available, the event is made conditional so that after each bound event occurs, the availability of the chopsticks can be rechecked. When a pair of chopsticks has been obtained with a call to the *acquire( )* function, the entity record is taken out of the conditional events list and eating commences as modelled by *eat( )*. Eating is scheduled to last for an average of two hours (exponentially distributed) at which time the think event is activated again.

The *think( )* event is somewhat simpler than the *await( )* event. All that has to be done in this event is to make the chopsticks available again with the call to *release( )*, add the amount of think time to the running total and then schedule a new meal on average five hours in the future, again exponentially distributed.

```
#include <stdio.h>
#include "sim_lib.h"
#include "random.h"
#include "results.h"
#include "resource.h"

#define NUM_OF_PHILOS 5
#define SIM_TIME      (24.0*7)      /* One week ! */
#define THINK_TIME    5            /* Five hours */
#define EAT_TIME      2            /* Two hours */
#define LEFT_CHOPSTICK(x)      chp_stk[x]
#define RIGHT_CHOPSTICK(x)     chp_stk[(x+1)%NUM_OF_PHILOS]
```

```
stream       *rsl;
float        x[NUM_OF_PHILOS];
resource     *chp_stk[NUM_OF_PHILOS];     /* To record the times */

extern entity *current;
extern float   sim_clock;
void eat( void );
void think( void );
void await( void );
void init( void );
void print_results( void );

main ()
{
    init();
    run_sim (SIM_TIME , 1);
    print_results();
    return 0;
}

void init()
{
    int   i;
    float t;
    init_sim ();
    rsl    = make_stream(1, 0);
    for (i = 0;i < NUM_OF_PHILOS;i++) {
        chp_stk[i] = make_resource(1.0);
        /* Create a philosopher (given by i) to start eating at t */
        t = exponential(rsl) * THINK_TIME;
        x[i]      = t;
        make_scheduled_entity ( eat , (void *)i , t, 0, 0, 1, NULL);
    }
}

void print_results()
{
    int i;
    printf(" \n \nPercentage think time (max = %f) \n \n",
        100.0*THINK_TIME/(THINK_TIME+EAT_TIME));
    for (i = 0;i < NUM_OF_PHILOS;i++) {
        printf("Philosopher %d : %f (abs = %f) \n",i+1,100.0*x[i]
            /sim_clock,x[i]);
    }
}

void eat ()
{
    float t;

    t = exponential(rsl) * EAT_TIME;
    current->event = think;
    wait (t);
```

```
}

void think ()
{
    float t;
    int this_philo;

    /* Get philosopher number */
    this_philo = (int)ATTRIBUTES(current);
    release(LEFT_CHOPSTICK(this_philo), 1.0);
    release(RIGHT_CHOPSTICK(this_philo), 1.0);
    current->event = await;
    t = exponential(rs1) * THINK_TIME;
    x[this_philo] += t;
    wait(t);
}

void await()
{
    int this_philo;

    this_philo = (int)ATTRIBUTES(current);
    if (IS_AVAILABLE(LEFT_CHOPSTICK(this_philo), 1.0) &&
        IS_AVAILABLE(RIGHT_CHOPSTICK(this_philo), 1.0) )
    {
        /* Could be conditional so make active - */
        /* no longer waiting for chop sticks */
        acquire(LEFT_CHOPSTICK(this_philo), 1.0);
        acquire(RIGHT_CHOPSTICK(this_philo), 1.0);
        current->event = eat;
        activate(current);
    }
    /* Chopsticks not available so wait indefinitely for them */
    else if (!IS_CONDITIONAL(current))
    {
        /* Make this event conditional */
        passivate(current);
        hold (current);
    }
}
```

Listing 6.1 The dining philosophers.

Output from the model gives the percentage amount of time each philosopher actually spends thinking and the maximum possible time that could be spent thinking if there was no queuing. This is printed with the call to *print_ results( )*. Since the results are the same for both models they will only be given for the following process-oriented version of the same model.

6.3.2 Process-oriented model

Listing 6.2 shows the same model, this time implemented using the process-oriented structure in which the event routines have been lumped into one place and phases *THINKING, EATING and WAITING* have been defined. This makes it clearer that the events are related to the same entity—a philosopher. The result is that this alternative structure seems to be easier to follow. Judge for yourself by comparing the models.

The actions performed in each phase of the life cycle of a philosopher map directly on to the event routines in the three-phase model. There is some additional simplicity in this approach though. Here the identity of the entity does not have to been obtained with each new event; instead for the same activation of an entity we need only get it once and store it in variable *this_philo*.

```c
#include <stdio.h>
#include "sim_lib.h"
#include "random.h"
#include "results.h"
#include "resource.h"

#define NUM_OF_PHILOS 5
#define SIM_TIME (24.0*7)               /* One week ! */
#define EATING          0
#define THINKING        1
#define WAITING         2
#define EAT_TIME        2.0             /* Two hours */
#define THINK_TIME      5.0             /* Five hours */
#define LEFT_CHOPSTICK(x)    chp_stk[x]
#define RIGHT_CHOPSTICK(x)   chp_stk[(x+1)%NUM_OF_PHILOS]

stream   *rsl ;
resource *chp_stk[NUM_OF_PHILOS];
float    x[NUM_OF_PHILOS];              /* To record the times */

extern entity *current;
extern float   sim_clock;
extern int     active;

void philos();
void init();
void print_results();


main()
{
    init();
    run_sim (SIM_TIME, 0);
    print_results();
```

```
        return 0;
}


void init()
{
    int   i;
    float t;

    init_sim ();
    rsl   = make_stream(1, 0);
    for (i = 0;i < NUM_OF_PHILOS;i++) {
        chp_stk[i] = make_resource(1.0);
        t = exponential(rsl) * THINK_TIME;
        /* Create a philosopher (given by i) to start eating at t */
        x[i]      = t;
        make_scheduled_entity ( philos, (void *)i , t, EATING, 0, 1, NULL);
    }
}


void print_results()
{
    int i;
    printf(" \n \nPercentage think time (Max : %f)\n \n",
        100.0*THINK_TIME/(THINK_TIME+EAT_TIME));
    for (i = 0;i < NUM_OF_PHILOS;i++) {
        printf("Philosopher %d : %f (abs = %f) \n",i+1,
               100.0*x[i]/sim_clock,x[i]);
    }
}


void philos()
{
    float t;
    int this_philo;

    this_philo = (int)ATTRIBUTES(current);
    while (active)
    {
        switch ( PHASE_OF(current) )
        {
        case EATING:
            t = exponential(rsl) * EAT_TIME;
            current->phase = THINKING;
            wait(t);
            break;
        case THINKING:
            release(LEFT_CHOPSTICK(this_philo),1.0);
            release(RIGHT_CHOPSTICK(this_philo),1.0);
            t = exponential(rsl) * THINK_TIME;
```

```
            x[this_philo] += t;
            current->phase = WAITING;
            wait(t);
            break;
        case WAITING:
            if (IS_AVAILABLE(LEFT_CHOPSTICK(this_philo),1.0) &&
                IS_AVAILABLE(RIGHT_CHOPSTICK(this_philo),1.0) )
            {
                activate(current);
                acquire(LEFT_CHOPSTICK(this_philo),1.0);
                acquire(RIGHT_CHOPSTICK(this_philo),1.0);
                current->phase = EATING ;
            }
            else if (!IS_CONDITIONAL(current))
            {
                passivate(current);
                hold(current);
            }
            else
                active = 0;
            break;
        }
    }
} /* philos */
```

Listing 6.2 The dining philosophers revisited.

The output obtained is shown in Fig. 6.2. The differences between the thinking time of the five philosophers is due to the statistical nature of the random eating and thinking times. For a serious simulation additional runs would be performed and they would be subject to statistical analysis in order to reduce variability and calculate the accuracy or reliability of the simulation. These aspects are covered in Chapters 9 and 10.

```
Simulation started at 0.000000
Simulation stopped — end time reached at 168.530045
Actual time taken — 1.000000 seconds

Percentage think time (max = 71.428571)
Philosopher 1 : 57.755633 (abs = 97.335594)
Philosopher 2 : 69.446354 (abs = 117.037971)
Philosopher 3 : 53.972748 (abs = 90.960297)
Philosopher 4 : 53.092690 (abs = 89.477135)
Philosopher 5 : 62.536446 (abs = 105.392700)
```

Figure 6.2 Output of the dining philosophers model.

6.4 SUMMARY

Entities and resources model objects in the real world. Entities are active and often have only a temporary existence. Resources constrain the behaviour of entities and are generally permanent.

Entities are modelled with entity records. An entity record has several components, including the following:

- attributes, which enable the entity to be parameterized so that important features of real objects can be modelled
- an event, which is a pointer to a C routine which is to be executed in response to the occurrence of the event
- phase, which acts as a reactivation pointer for process-oriented models
- a state, which is introduced to reduce the chance that the simulation library is misused by limiting the operations that affect an entity record in each state.

Resources are simpler than entities. They have only a current value and an initial value.

Several functions and macros are provided by the simulation library to facilitate the use of entities and resources in models. For entities this includes functions for queue processing and scheduling. For resources this involves functions for acquiring and releasing various-sized amounts of the resource.

6.5 EXERCISES

6.1 Add an additional output statistic to the dining philosophers model. Use the library routine *stamp( )* to find the total amount of time spent waiting for chopsticks and output this value for each philosopher with the *print_ results( )* function.

6.2 Generalize the dining philosophers model so that the thinking time can be input as a parameter to the model on the command line. Using the modification of Exercise 6.1 run the model for values of think time between 0.5 and 10 hours and plot the variation in the percentage time spent waiting.

6.3 In a data acquisition system, a processor polls a sensor every 5 seconds ±3 seconds. The sensor measures external events that occur with an interval given by an exponential distribution with mean 2.4 seconds and queues the measurements internally. When polled, the sensor delivers all sensor data to the processor in a negligible amount of time. Simulate this system for 20 minutes' operation.

6.4 Simulate the following computer system in which jobs arrive at a cpu with an inter-arrival time that is normally distributed, with a mean of 4 seconds and variance 2 seconds. When a job is submitted it joins a queue. The cpu processes each job in the queue on an FCFS basis. Processing consists of a calculation lasting an exponentially distributed amount of time with a mean of 0.1 seconds, after which the job leaves the system with a probability of p or rejoins the end of the job queue with probability $1 - p$. Run the model with a probability p of 0.1, 0.5 and 0.9.

THE SCHEDULER

In this chapter we look at that part of the simulation system known as the scheduler. Two scheduling algorithms are explored and the relative merits of each of them assessed.

7.1 THE JOB OF THE SCHEDULER

The *executive*, or *scheduler*, is responsible for activating the different components of the simulation model in the correct order and for maintaining the simulation clock. Information about which piece of code can be executed in response to the occurrence of a particular event is held in a data structure consisting of entity records which, conceptually at least, is a *list* because it is ordered by activation time. However, a particular implementation is free to choose any of the well-known tree, array or linked data structures as long as the essential order is maintained. We will call this data structure the *calendar*.

As we saw in Chapter 3, there are three basic approaches to the organization of the simulation model, event scheduling, three-phase and process interaction. However, the operation of the scheduler is the same in each. To reiterate, the set of entity records with the same activation time that can occur next are identified. Next, the simulation clock is updated to their common activation time. The scheduler then activates each of them in turn. After this, in the two-phase approach, the next set of entity records is identified and the cycle repeated. In the other approaches the conditional components of the model are executed before repeating the cycle.

The above cycle must be repeated a large number of times in the course of a simulation run, certainly many hundreds and possibly very many thousands. Hence, in order to minimize execution times it should operate with the minimum of overhead. This becomes increasingly important as the model gets bigger. In general it is acceptable to trade off performance for small models if larger models can run significantly faster.

7.2 TYPES OF ALGORITHM

Scheduler algorithms can be classified according to the data structures they use. Two broad categories exist: static and dynamic. Memory for static data structures is declared at compile time and allocated as part of the program initialization when the compiled code is executed. If this kind of data structure is employed the calendar is implemented as an array. Therefore, either the maximum number of scheduled events must be known beforehand, or else a large safety factor must be taken into account so that overflows are avoided. In contrast, memory for dynamic data structures is assigned as required when the program is executing. Providing there is enough memory available the calendar can always be extended but a small run-time performance penalty is incurred in doing so.

The advantage of a dynamic approach is that it is unnecessary to dimension the simulation. This makes the task of constructing the model easier and also allows for a more abstract modelling interface. Another benefit is that when all data objects are created dynamically the unnecessary limitations of a static solution are avoided. The only factor limiting the structure of the model is the total amount of available memory, we are free to use it as necessary on a model-by-model basis. For example, one model may require a large number of queues but few random number streams, whereas another model may need many entities and many random number streams but only a few queues. Dynamic data structures and associated algorithms are therefore far more suited to the implementation of simulation models and it is to these that we turn now.

7.3 DYNAMIC ALGORITHMS

Two popular methods of representing a varying-sized group of data items are *linked lists* and *binary trees*. We discuss here the use of these two approaches as the basis for the calendar, and since in simulation modelling we are concerned about run-time efficiency, a comparison is made of their relative performance.

7.3.1 Linked list

The first data structure to be considered is the linked list described in detail in Aho *et al.* (1974). A linked list is a chain of records whose length (number of links in the chain) can vary dynamically. Each element in the list contains a time, being the time of occurrence, and a pointer to the successor. The time value defines an ordering relation such that each entity record in the list must have an occurrence time before or simultaneous with its successor.

In the simplest case there is a single pointer to the head of the list which, in terms of scheduled events, is the event to be activated next. Entries are made into the list by scanning the list in the direction of increasing time, starting at the head, until the activation time of the entity record to be inserted is before the activation time of the entity record being scanned. The new entity record is then inserted in front of the scanned entity record. This is illustrated in Fig. 7.1, where the numbers in the circles indicate activation time.

The complexity of the linked list insertion algorithm is $O(n)$, i.e. on average it takes $nk + c$ time units to insert an entity record into a list which is n elements long, where k and c are two finite numbers. From this expression it is apparent that linked list management becomes time consuming as the length of the list increases. There are, however, ways in which the naive implementation can be improved. For example, if a pointer is also kept which points to the last entity record inserted there are two insertion points. If, in addition, the list is doubly linked (i.e. has pointers from last to first as well as from first to last) and a pointer to the end of the list is kept, there are now three insertion points. To insert an entity record in such a list an insertion point is first selected and then the list is scanned sequentially from this point. Marsden (1984) reports that this approach can decrease the insertion time for large n by up to 60 per cent.

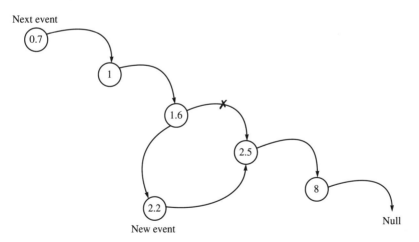

Figure 7.1 Adding to the calendar-linked list.

7.3.2 Binary tree

The second data structure is the binary tree. The binary tree is familiar to most programmers and is described in depth in most good texts on algorithms (such as Sedgewick, 1988 and Cormen *et al.*, 1989). A binary tree consists of nodes, each of which has pointers to two children, *left* and *right*. Each node except the root has a parent, and all nodes except leaf nodes have children. Figure 7.2 shows a binary tree schematically.

For use in a scheduler, the tree must be ordered by time of activation of the corresponding entity record so that if an arbitrary node *n* is selected in a completely time-ordered tree, *left* (if present) will occur before *n* and right will occur later or at the same time as *n*. By ensuring that only one path can be taken in the case where the times are the same we avoid ambiguity in the sequencing of simultaneous events. For a well-formed tree we have the obvious rules that the earliest scheduled entity record in the tree cannot itself have a *left* and the latest entity record in the tree cannot have a *right*.

Binary trees and their access operations are simple to implement and yet are reasonably efficient. For a complete binary tree with *n* nodes, the complexity of the insert and delete operations is $O(log(n))$. For a tree built randomly, the depth of the tree is $O(log(n))$ deep. However, this behaviour cannot be guaranteed. In the worst case, the tree resembles a linked list if all the entities are added in time order or reverse order. To ensure that this never occurs the trees can be balanced. The difference between an unbalanced and a balanced tree is illustrated in Fig. 7.3. To add and delete from these modified trees, algorithms like those described in Sedgewick (1988) must be employed.

In practice, however, trees are usually built randomly. For randomly produced trees the reduction in tree depth obtained by balancing the tree

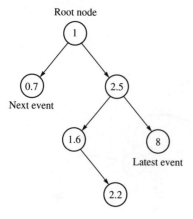

Figure 7.2 An example binary tree.

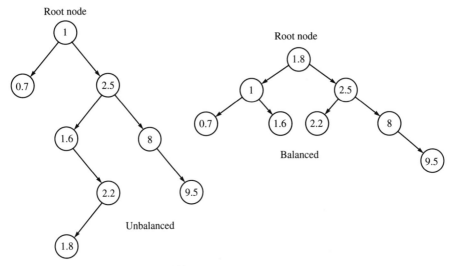

Figure 7.3 Balanced and unbalanced binary trees.

becomes less significant as the number of insertions increases. Frost and Peterson (1982) report that the gain in efficiency is only about 20 per cent with 64 entries. Therefore, the saving in keeping the tree balanced is likely to be outweighed by the overhead incurred, and so this additional complexity is not incorporated in the functions provided in the simulation library.

7.4 PERFORMANCE COMPARISON

The performance of the two types of algorithm outlined above are compared in this section. There are several scenarios that could be used for comparison. The one described here is simple but quite representative of a typical simulation. The test consists of inserting and retrieving entity records into and out of a calendar of a given size. Entity records will in general be submitted to the scheduler in random order, but in normal operation they will be withdrawn earliest first. So in this test we have a cycle consisting of the insertion of an entity into a calendar of a given size with uniform randomly selected insertion time, followed by the removal of the earliest entity. In outline, the test consists of the following:

```
test ( int n )
{
    <<Add n entities into the calendar with random times>>
    start_clock ();
    /* Do 1000 insertion and extractions */
    for (i = 0;i < 1000;i++) {
```

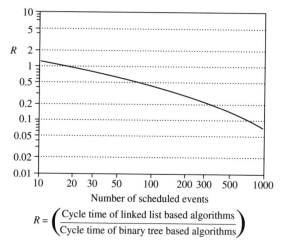

$$R = \left(\frac{\text{Cycle time of linked list based algorithms}}{\text{Cycle time of binary tree based algorithms}} \right)$$

Figure 7.4 Performance comparison of linked list and binary tree.

```
        ⟨⟨Extract earliest entity record, call it e⟩⟩
        ⟨⟨Calculate a random insertion time for e⟩⟩
        ⟨⟨Add e back to the calendar⟩⟩
    }
    stop_clock();
    print_elapsed_time();
}
```

The parameter n is the size of the calendar into which insertions and extractions are made. The results are displayed in Fig. 7.4 for values of n between 10 and 1000 in order to assess performance for both small and large model conditions.

The graph gives the ratio of processing times for binary tree related algorithms to linked list related algorithms. The results suggest that algorithms using the binary-tree-based data structure are faster for all but the smallest models. In practice, the performance of most models benefit greatly when tree-based algorithms are employed. They are therefore the preferred implementation and have been used in the simulation library.

7.5 IMPLEMENTATION

We now describe the details of a binary-tree-based scheduler. Recall from Chapter 3 that the three-phase and event-scheduling approaches identify all the events that are scheduled to occur at the same instant in simulated time. The set of entity records is then actioned and after this, in the case of the three-phase

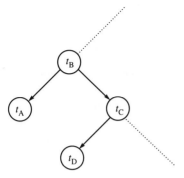

Figure 7.5 Binary tree after insertion of entity records *A*, *B*, *C* and *D*.

approach, the conditional events are scanned. However, there can be problems if such a mechanism is executed with the tree data structure described above. Consider a calendar into which entity records *A*, *B*, *C* and *D* are inserted in this order at simulated times t_A, t_B, t_C and t_D respectively. If t_A had the same value as t_D but less than both t_B and t_C, the resulting binary tree would resemble Fig. 7.5. Since $t_A = t_D$ entity records *A* and *D* should be activated together, but their position in the tree makes this difficult.

One way around this problem is to employ a tertiary tree. Such a tree has, in addition to left and right pointers, a pointer *middle* that points to a doubly linked

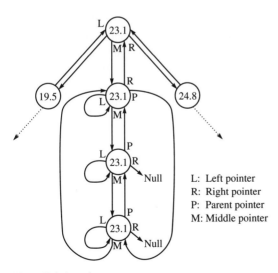

L: Left pointer
R: Right pointer
P: Parent pointer
M: Middle pointer

Figure 7.6 A tertiary tree.

list forming a ring of entity records, all of which have the same activation time. The right pointer is now reserved for entities that have a later activation time. Since those entities with equal activation time are doubly linked, additions to both the beginning and end can be made efficiently. This is an important consideration when the algorithm is reused with queues, since additions to queues are typically made to the back.

The processing necessary to add entity records to the tertiary tree depends on whether they are to go in a list (i.e. there are already others with the same activation time) or the tree itself. The *left* pointer can be used to differentiate between these two cases. This is shown in Fig. 7.6 which illustrates a tertiary tree in which each node has its time of activation shown. If the entity record is to go into a list, the left pointer is not required and so can be set to the address of the entity record. In all other cases the left pointer will either point to a left subtree or else be NULL if there are no left subtrees. The code on the accompanying disk can be consulted for all further details of the implementation.

7.6 SIMULTANEOUS EVENTS

In the real-world events can occur simultaneously, but in the calendar they are always sequenced. In the absence of any other ordering relation the sequence of simultaneous events is unpredictable. This can cause problems when there are mutual dependencies between events because the order of activation may influence the results. This is known as a *race condition*. In the real system this situation may be resolved by some additional priority mechanism. Alternatively, there may actually be a race condition in the system which produces an unpredictable event sequence. Depending on the level of detail involved, these effects may need to be simulated in the model. However, the simulation library as it stands provides no facilities to do this and so it must be modelled explicitly. For example, to simulate *priority scheduling* we might be able to adjust the time that an event is added to the calendar. If we have events A and B that occur together, but A takes priority over B, then we can make event A occur at time t and event B occur at time $t + \Delta t$ where Δt is small enough so as to have negligible effect on the logic of the simulation. Alternatively, in those (rare) cases where priority scheduling is very significant, the simulation library may be modified to take it into account. Another parameter may be added to an entity record, say of type *int*, call it *sched_priority* for example, and the calendar modified so that it takes this priority into account when scheduling events. Similar algorithms as used for queue manipulation, described in the next chapter, could be employed for this purpose. However, we will, as a result, suffer a performance degradation which may or may not be significant for a particular model.

To simulate a race condition between a set of events, each of which have an equal probability p of occurring, something like the following could be implemented

```
void an_event () ;
{
    :
    if (!probability ( rs, p ) )
        /* Don't activate the event */
        reactivate () ;
    else
    {
        /* This event has won the race! */
        ⟨⟨Action the event⟩⟩
        :
    }
}
```

In this example the event returns to the top of the calendar (i.e. is not activated) with probability $1 - p$ and is activated with probability p. Suppose a set of n such events are identified in the A-phase. Each event routine will be executed and the result will be that, on average, pn of them are activated and $(1 - p)n$ of them are returned to the calendar. The next cycle of the scheduler will then identify $(1 - p)n$ of these events in the A-phase and again a fraction of these will be activated and a fraction returned to the calendar. Eventually all the events will have been activated and the simulation clock will be advanced to the next set of events. If p must be a function of the number of events that are competing then this number has to be determined, possibly by counting the simultaneous events during the A-phase. If a function, *num_concurrent( )*, was added to the simulation library to do just this, then a suitable value of p is given by

```
p = 1.0 / (float)num_concurrent () ;
```

There are also occasions when it is necessary to perform some conditional activity between simultaneous events, perhaps to see if some resource has been released. There are two choices: either we include the code to check for the condition within the event or entity routine or else we scan the conditional entity record list after each bound event has occurred (assuming of course we are not using the pure event scheduling strategy in which case there would be no choice). The disadvantage of the former approach is that the event or entity routine is complicated by including checks that could be part of a separate conditional entity routine. The obvious disadvantage of the second approach is performance impairment.

The simulation library provides for both alternatives. The default mode at the beginning of a simulation, after *init_sim( )* has been called, is to process all concurrent activities before scanning conditional entities. However, this can be overridden with a call to *scan_always( )* which has the prototype

```
void scan_always ( int yes );
```

If the flag *yes* has a positive value then the conditional entity list is scanned after every bound event or entity routine has been actioned, irrespective of whether there are others with the same activation time. If the flag is not positive, then the default mode is taken, in which the scan is only done after all events which can occur together have been actioned.

7.7 SUMMARY

The scheduler is responsible for activating the different parts of the simulation model at the prescribed instants in simulated time. Because the scheduler is run many times during the course of a simulation it must use efficient algorithms. Two commonly used algorithms for implementing the scheduler are based on linked lists and binary trees. The binary tree based algorithms are significantly more efficient as the size of the model increases and so are preferable.

The simulation library uses a variant of the binary tree called a tertiary tree, in which all entity records which have the same activation time are linked together in a list and only one of them is directly linked into the tree. This makes it easy to schedule the activation of all those entity records that should occur together.

Events which occur together in the system being modelled are always sequenced in the calendar. This may produce undesirable effects when there are dependencies between them which can give rise to race conditions or may reveal some form of priority mechanism in the system being modelled. If the effects are significant, then they must be explicitly included in the model.

It may be necessary to check conditions in the model between activations of concurrent entities. This can be done by coding the extra checking logic in the event or entity routines themselves or by forcing the scheduler to scan the list of conditional entities after each bound entity has executed.

7.8 EXERCISES

7.1 As mentioned in Sec. 7.3.1, it is possible to employ doubly linked lists in the scheduler. A doubly linked list contains a pointer to the head as well as the tail of the list and each node in the list has pointers to the node before and the node after. Such lists are sometimes cyclic, in that a pointer to the predecessor of the first node (i.e. the last node) is present as well as a pointer to the successor to the last node (i.e. the first node). Provide an alternative scheduler that uses doubly linked lists.

7.2 Rerun the simple queue model from Chapter 3 using the modified scheduler of Exercise 7.1 and compare its performance with the scheduler used in the simulation library. See how the performance changes as the number of scheduled entity records changes and plot this as a graph like the one in Fig. 7.4.

7.3 Investigate alternative algorithms for the scheduler. Implement them and compare their performance. Some possible candidates are the various forms of balanced trees (Aho *et al.*, 1974 and Sedgewick, 1988) and partitioner trees (Ogilvie, 1990).

7.4 A company hiring out building equipment has six mechanical diggers that are in high demand. Customers hire the diggers for three days at a time. Assume that customers arrive with an exponentially distributed inter-arrival time of mean six hours. If a customer arrives and all the diggers are on hire he takes his custom to a competitor. Simulate this system for a month and estimate the percentage of lost custom. Assume that the company is open for business 24 hours a day.

7.5 Redo Example 7.4 with the following changes. First of all assume that the company is only available to do business eight hours a day and that the inter-arrival time is six *business* hours. Further assume that on Saturdays the arrival rate of customers for diggers is exponentially distributed with a mean of three hours and that the company is closed on Sundays. Simulate this system for three months' operations.

7.6 Introduce a function *num_concurrent( )* to the simulation library that returns the number of events that have the same current execution time as described in Sect. 7.6.

8

QUEUES

In this chapter we introduce the concept of queues and consider their use in simulation models. First of all we look at them from a theoretical perspective and consider how they can be characterized mathematically. We then look at the implementation of a queue in a general simulation context and the facilities available in the simulation library.

8.1 THE STRUCTURE OF A QUEUING SYSTEM

The notion of a *queue* as a waiting line in front of a *service facility* is a familiar one to most of us. Many activities in modern-day life involve some form of queuing, so it should be no surprise that queues are an essential part of nearly all simulation models. Queues occur wherever an imbalance occurs between requests for a limited resource and the ability of a service facility to provide that resource. The size of the queue depends on the amount of the resource available and the demand for it by customers. The decision as to how much resource to make available is normally made on the basis of cost, a trade-off between the cost of providing more of the resource and the cost of allowing larger queues to form. Decisions like this are common in engineering and commerce. Examples are the size of telephone switch to install in an exchange or the number of checkouts to provide in a supermarket.

Two important components of a queuing system then are *resources* and *customers* that wish to use the resource. Another necessary component is the *server* which controls access to the resource, and associated with the server is a *policy* to allocate all or part of the resource to the customer.

Queuing systems also have an *arrival pattern* which describes the sequence of customers arriving in the queue. It is characterized by a *population size* and an *arrival process*. The population is the set from which customers are drawn and may be finite, or infinite. In terms of tractability, the choice is of little consequence as far as a simulation model is concerned. However, the choice of an infinite population makes analytical solution far easier. The arrival process is the statistical process which extracts customers from the population. It may be thought, intuitively, that a process which generates customers at regular intervals is the most basic. Again, from a simulation point of view it is not particularly significant. But, analytically, the regular process is difficult to handle. The easiest by far is the completely random process, termed a *Poisson process* because it is based on the Poisson distribution with exponential inter-arrival times, that was described in Chapter 5.

The *service demand* refers to the amount of resource required. The time that the resource is allocated is sampled from a *service distribution*. The same comments apply to the service distribution as to the arrival distribution. The simplest to handle analytically is the *exponential* distribution, but from a simulation point of view any service distribution can be used.

The arrival process and the service demand determine the *average inter-arrival time* and the *average service interval*. The average inter-arrival time is the average time between arrivals of customers into the system, and the average service interval is the average time between arrivals of customers to the server. If it takes on average t seconds to serve a customer, then it might be thought that the average service interval is t seconds also. This is not true, however, because it does not take into account the time that the server is idle. In fact, for a well-behaved queue in the steady state the average service interval must be the same as the average inter-arrival time, as we shall discover in Sec. 8.2.4.

The *queue discipline* or *service policy* is the algorithm used to select customers from the queue. The most common service discipline in real life is the so called first in first out (FIFO) or first come first served (FCFS) discipline where new customers are inserted into the queue at the back and removed from the front. This is the customary type of queue and one that is normally associated with waiting lines. Other service disciplines are described below.

Queues can also be prioritized. In a *priority queue* the position that a customer takes in a queue is based on the customer priority. The result is that high-priority customers are inserted in front of lower-priority customers but, for a series of customers of the same priority, the queue behaves as a FIFO queue.

8.2 BASIC QUEUING THEORY

The mathematical analysis of queues is a branch of probability theory. It has built up into an extensive field of mathematics and provides analytical methods for solving a large number of queuing problems. Although this material is not covered in depth here, it is useful to understand the basics because simple queuing models can often be used to benchmark a simulation model. They can also, sometimes, make the model simpler by collapsing part of a simulation submodel into an analytical form. Over and above that, understanding queue behaviour, even at a conceptual level, provides useful insights into the behaviour of many systems.

8.2.1 Stochastic processes

A *stochastic process* describes the statistical behaviour of a system as a function of time (see Cox and Miller, 1965). Of particular interest is a special case of stochastic processes called *Markov processes* which are applicable to queuing theory. A Markov process consists of *states*. The concept of state as it is applied here refers to the set of values assumed by all the system variables. The set of states and the transitions between them are referred to as a *Markov chain*, and if the transitions are independent of time we have a *stationary Markov chain*.

Many systems of importance can take a number of states and through their lifetime change from one state to another, with particular probabilities associated with the state transitions. This is true for queues, whose state can be taken to be the number of customers in the queue. The queue changes state by customers entering or leaving. In real life, behaviour in queues can be quite complex. People queuing, for instance, are likely to be influenced by the history of the queue. If it is moving slowly they are likely to get fed up and leave. This makes analytic analysis rather difficult. Fortunately, this sort of behaviour is rare in most systems and the probability of any state transition is usually independent of any prior states, depending only on the starting and finishing states and possibly on time. This allows such systems to be considered Markovian and makes them amenable to relatively straightforward analysis. To calculate the probability of a state transition in a Markov system the only information required is the current state. For this reason the term *memoryless* is often applied.

The case of particular interest to us is when the timing of the transitions is itself a random variable. If the timings are also memoryless, so that the amount of time spent in a state depends only on the current state, then the transitions are Markovian. If, however, the time spent in a state can be drawn from an arbitrary distribution, so that to determine the amount of time left in a state we may need to know how long we have already been in the state, then we have a *semi-Markov process*.

8.2.2 Birth–death processes

A queue is one example of a *birth–death process*. A birth–death process is a special case of a Markov process in which state transitions can take place

Figure 8.1 A birth–death process.

between neighbouring states only. If a birth–death system is observed at two times, then as the interval between the observations decreases to zero, the probability of the state's having changed by more than one step becomes negligible. Hence, the probability of a state j at time t varies with time according to the differential difference equation:

$$\frac{d}{dt}P_j(t) = \lambda_{j-1} P_{j-1}(t) + \mu_{j+1}P_{j+1}(t) - \lambda_j P_j(t) - \mu_j P_j(t) \qquad (8.1)$$

where
λ_j is the birth rate, assuming the system is in state j,
μ_j is the death rate assuming the system is in state j.

Equation (8.1) can be stated in words as the sum of the rate at which births occur in state $j - 1$ and the rate at which deaths occur in state $j + 1$ minus the rate at which births and deaths occur in state j. The result is the rate at which the probability of finding the system in state j is changing. This can be represented schematically as shown in Fig. 8.1.

As a special case, it is possible to have a *pure birth system*, for which the death rates are zero. If the birth rate is constant at λ, then:

$$P_j(t) = \frac{(\lambda t)^j}{j!}e^{-\lambda t} \qquad (8.2)$$

which is the Poisson distribution introduced in Chapter 5.

Another important example is the *pure death system*, where the death rate is proportional to the population size. In other words, for any individual the probability of death is constant and equal to that for any other individual. In this case $\mu_j = j.\mu$ and

$$P_j(t) = {}^j_n C(e^{-ut})^j(1 - e^{-ut})^{n-j} \qquad (8.3)$$

which is the binomial distribution of Chapter 5 with $p = e^{-ut}$.

8.2.3 Naming convention for queues

A generally understood naming convention has evolved for queues. A queue is said to be of type $A/B/C/D/E/F$, where A represents the customer arrival pattern,

B represents the service pattern, *C* represents the number of servers, *D* is the service policy, *E* is the maximum number of customers allowed in the system and *F* is the population size. The latter three parameters are regularly left out, in which case *D* defaults to FIFO and *E* and *F* default to infinite. Alternatively, the parameter *E* may be included in a four-parameter representation $A/B/C/E$.

The *A* and *B* parameters defining the statistical distributions used can have the following values:

- *M*: Markov, where samples are drawn from a negative exponential distribution
- *D*: Deterministic, where samples are fixed
- E_R: R-stage Erlangian, where *r* exponential distributions are sampled in series
- *G*: General for an arbitrary distribution with fixed mean and variance
- Γ: For a gamma distribution
- H_R: R-stage hyperexponential, where *r* exponential distributions are sampled in parallel (see Kleinrock, 1975).

The possible service policies are as follows:

- *FIFO*: first in first out as mentioned above
- *FCFS*: first come first served, same as FIFO
- *SIRO*: service in random order where the selection is arbitrary
- *LIFO*: last in first out, where the most recent entity inserted into the queue is removed first (an example of which is the ubiquitous *stack*)
- *GD*: general service policy, something other than the previous three policies.

Example 8.1 A queue described as M/M/1 has an exponential inter-arrival time distribution, an exponential service time distribution and a single server.

Example 8.2 A queue described as G/G/N/M has general inter-arrival and service time distributions, *N* servers and a maximum of *M* customers in the system including both those receiving service and those queuing.

Example 8.3 A queue described as M/G/1/GD/M/P has exponential inter-arrival and general service time distributions, one server, a general service policy, at most *M* customers in the system and a population size of *P*.

8.2.4 Queues in the steady state

The solution of any queue can, in principle, be obtained by solution of the differential difference equation for birth–death systems. There are a number of cases which are relatively straightforward to solve analytically to obtain the distribution of waiting times, mean queue length, etc. In other cases the parameters required may not be calculable, or the service policies may make analysis difficult or impossible. In such cases simulation is the only recourse.

One condition that will facilitate analysis is if the queue is studied in its steady state. The steady state is described in detail in Chapter 10, but the essential point is that when the queue has reached steady state the queue may fluctuate in length, but there will be no long-term tendency for it to grow or shrink. The queue can exist in this state indefinitely and so the long-term behaviour of the queue is generally taken to be its behaviour in the steady state.

Birth-death process in the steady state Assuming a steady state is equivalent to setting a constant probability for each rate of change of state in the birth–death equation (Eq. 8.1). Setting the rates of change equal to zero in the differential difference equations for a birth–death system leads to a series of equations as follows:

$$0 = P_1\mu_1 - P_0\lambda_0$$

or

$$P_1\mu_1 = P_0\lambda_0 \tag{8.4}$$

and in general we find that

$$P_{n+1}\mu_{n+1} = P_n\lambda_n \tag{8.5}$$

which can be used to find the probabilities that the system is in the different states in any steady-state birth–death system, given the birth and death rates and that the sum of the probabilities over all states is one. This information can then be used to find the mean number in the system. The easiest queuing system to analyse in this way is the M/M/1 queue, for which

$$N_t = \frac{\rho}{1 - \rho} \tag{8.6}$$

the derivation of which is given in full in Kleinrock (1975).

It is interesting to note that the service policy does not alter the above result provided that service times are not taken into account when selecting the customer from the queue to service. For example, an LCFS policy would produce exactly the same expression for the mean number in the system.

Little's result This interesting result, first proved by J.D. Little in 1961 (Little, 1961), relates averaged parameters of a queue in the steady state. It is especially useful because it makes no assumptions about the arrival pattern or service time distribution. It is also independent of the service policy and number of servers. In words it can be stated as *the average number of customers is equal to the arrival rate multiplied by the average time resident*. Notice that the boundary defining where this rule applies has not been given. This is because it can be applied equally well to the queuing system as a whole (queue plus server) or just the queue by itself. Hence we have the two algebraic forms

$$N_t = \lambda W \tag{8.7}$$

for the queue and server together, where $W = T_s + T_q$ and

$$N_q = \lambda T_q \tag{8.8}$$

for the queue by itself.

Metrics Queues can be characterized by metrics which summarize their performance in the steady state. These metrics often form part of the set of output data generated by a simulation. In general, the following relationships defining the metrics only work with average values when the queue is in the steady state:

- *Waiting time* refers to the total amount of time spent queuing and obtaining service. Hence

$$waiting\ time = time\ in\ system$$
$$= queuing\ time + service\ time \tag{8.9}$$

- *Traffic intensity* in a queuing system reflects the capacity of a server to cope with customers. It provides a measure of how many servers are on average occupied. The unit of traffic intensity is the *Erlang*. Traffic intensity can be determined from

$$traffic\ intensity = \frac{mean\ service\ time}{mean\ inter\text{-}arrival\ time}$$
$$= \frac{mean\ arrival\ rate}{mean\ service\ rate} \tag{8.10}$$

- *Utilization factor* is related to the traffic intensity. A low traffic intensity implies that the server is lightly loaded and therefore has a low utilization factor. Utilization factor can be calculated from

$$utilisation = \frac{traffic\ intensity}{number\ of\ servers} \tag{8.11}$$

Obviously, a server cannot be utilized more than 100 per cent of the time, so utilization factor is at most 1. For many systems the utilization factor is less than 1. It is because servers are not fully utilized that makes the arrival and departure rates the same.

- *Throughput* is a measure of the amount of work done in some interval of time, typically the duration of the simulation. It is given by

$$throughput = \frac{number\ of\ customers\ served}{interval} \tag{8.12}$$

- *Mean queue size* is defined as the number of customers in front of a service facility averaged over a period which is long compared to the inter-arrival time. If the traffic intensity is less than 1 then the queue size will have a well-defined mean value. If the traffic intensity is always greater than 1 the queue size never settles down to a steady-state value but continues to grow as the simulation proceeds.

$$\text{mean queue size} = \text{mean number in system} - \text{traffic intensity} \quad (8.13)$$

These metrics are now applied to the M/M/1 queue discussed above. With an arrival rate of λ customers per second and a service rate of μ customers per second, then

1. $$\text{utilization} = \text{traffic intensity}$$

$$= \rho = \frac{\lambda}{\mu} \quad (8.14)$$

since there is only a single server and the system has random arrivals from a Poisson process.

2. $$\text{throughput} = \lambda \quad (8.15)$$

because in the steady state the number of customers entering the queuing system is a constant average rate of λ customers/second which must be the same as the number leaving.

3. $$\text{mean queue size} = \bar{L} = N_t - \rho$$

from Eq. (8.6) this is equal to

$$\frac{\rho}{1 - \rho} - \rho = \frac{\rho^2}{1 - \rho} \quad (8.16)$$

4. The mean time in the system is

$$W = N_t / \lambda$$

$$= \frac{1/\mu}{1 - \rho} \quad (8.17)$$

5. The mean time spent queuing is

$$T_q = \frac{\bar{L}}{\lambda}$$

$$= \frac{\rho/\mu}{1 - \rho} \quad (8.18)$$

Most of the more useful results above involve a denominator of the form $1 - \rho$. When $\lambda = \mu$ an interesting thing happens: the denominator becomes zero and the metric in question becomes infinite! This is a common effect in queuing

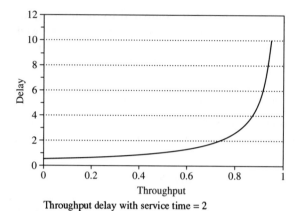

Throughput delay with service time = 2

Figure 8.2 Variation of delay with throughput.

systems and represents the maximum rate at which the server can work. At this point the server is 100 per cent utilized. Let us investigate how these parameters vary, and in particular what happens as this limit is approached, by displaying the above results in graphical form assuming a normalized arrival rate of one customer per second.

The first graph is throughput versus delay. These kinds of graphs are frequently quoted in relation to the performance of systems such as communications protocols. The delay/throughput performance for the M/M/1 queue is derived from Eq. (8.17) and shown in Fig. 8.2. As can be seen, it stays at a low value until the throughput exceeds 0.7, at which point it starts to grow rapidly.

A similar variation is demonstrated by the graph of queue size against utilization for the M/M/1 queue derived from Eq. (8.16) and shown in Fig. 8.3. A sharp increase is seen as the utilization increases beyond 0.7.

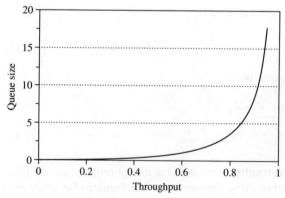

Figure 8.3 Variation of queue size with utilization.

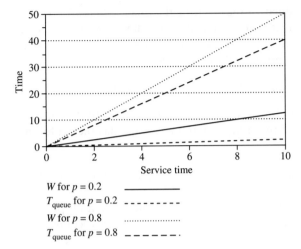

W for $p = 0.2$ ————

T_{queue} for $p = 0.2$ ---------

W for $p = 0.8$ ....

T_{queue} for $p = 0.8$ — — — — — .

Figure 8.4 Variation of total system time and queuing time with service time.

Finally, Fig. 8.4 shows the variation of total system time (W) and queuing time (T_q) with service time ($T_s = 1/\mu$) derived from Eqs (8.17) and (8.18) for two different values of utilization. These latter two relationships are linear.

8.3 THE IMPLEMENTATION OF QUEUES

As with the scheduler that we looked at in Chapter 7, the tree and the linked list are two common methods of implementing queues. Similar arguments apply to queues as were discussed in relation to the scheduler. The argument in favour of using a tree structure for queue implementation is particularly strong in large simulations involving priority queues. For this reason, the tree implementation is adopted in the simulation library.

The ordering of entities in a priority queue is based on an integer-valued attribute, the *priority*. Entity records are added to the queue so that all entities in a left subtree of a node are of a higher priority and all entities in the right subtree of a node are of a lower priority than the node. All entities with the same priority as the node are arranged in a list with the node at the head. This is the same data structure used by the scheduler.

Conceptually, a priority queue with entities e_i, where i represents a priority ranging from 0 to m, would look like this:

$$\text{front->} \; e_m...e_m e_{m-1}...e_{m-1}...e_1...e_1 e_0...e_0 \; \text{<-back}$$

If an entity e_p is inserted into the queue its position in the queue depends on whether it was added to the front or the back. Adding in priority order implies that if the entity is being added to the front of the queue, then all preceding entities must have priority greater than p and all proceeding entities must have a value equal to or less than p. So with our previous conceptual picture an entity e_p would enter the queue at the position shown in bold:

$$\text{front-} > e_m...e_m...\textbf{e}_p e_p...e_p...e_0...e_0 <\text{-back}$$

In the simulation library function *prepend( )* adds entities to the front of a queue. It takes the queue and the entity as parameters and has the prototype

```
int prepend ( queue *q, entity *e );
```

The return value indicates success or failure. The function will fail if either the queue or the entity record is NULL.

If the entity is being added to the back of the queue, then all preceding entities must have a priority equal to or greater than p and all proceeding entities must have a priority less than p. Our conceptual queue would look like this after insertion:

$$\text{front-} > e_m...e_m...e_p...\textbf{e}_p e_p...e_0...e_0 <\text{-back}$$

Insertion to the back of a queue is performed using function *append( )* which, like *prepend( )*, has parameters giving the queue and the entity to insert:

```
int append ( queue *q, entity *e );
```

It is also necessary to be able to extract an entity from an arbitrary position in the queue. Function *extract( )* performs this in a similar manner to comparable operations on the calendar. The main difference is that at most one entity is withdrawn from a queue, whereas the scheduler can withdraw *all* entities with the same activation time from the calendar during the *A*-phase. *Extract( )* has the prototype

```
int extract ( queue *q, entity *mbr );
```

Other useful functions are as follows:

- *remove_front( )*, which returns the first entry of the queue and adjusts the queue accordingly
- *remove_back( )*, which returns the last entry of a queue and adjusts the queue accordingly
- *queue_front( )*, which returns the first entry of the queue but does not adjust the queue. The entity returned remains in the queue and its state is unchanged.
- *queue_back( )*, which returns the last entry of the queue but does not adjust the queue or modify the state of the entity.

Each of these routines take a queue pointer as an argument.

In the simulation library, function *make_queue( )* returns a pointer to a *queue* data structure. The structure of a queue is defined as

```
typedef struct {
        entity *root;
        int size;
} queue;
```

root points to the root of the tertiary tree representing the queue. The *size* component gives the number of entries in the queue. On creation, the length of the queue is zero and the root is a *NULL* pointer.

It is necessary sometimes to remove all entries from a queue in a single operation. This is performed by operation *clear_queue( )* which also terminates all the queue members and frees any attributes they might have. It has the prototype

```
void clear_queue ( queue *q );
```

Such an operation is useful when a simulation run is to be repeated several times under different conditions, in which case the model must be reset to its state on invocation.

8.4 QUEUE BEHAVIOUR

We will look at some queue behaviour in this section with the goal of providing some examples of how more complex scenarios involving queues can be modelled. These ideas can then be reused in your own models. The types of behaviour covered are as follows:

- *queue swapping*, where customers move between queues
- *balking*, when a customer decides not to queue
- *reneging*, when a customer decides to give up waiting for service
- *service pre-emption*, in which customers being served can be interrupted
- *time dependency*, in which the arrival rate or service rate fluctuates with time.

8.4.1 Queue swapping

This phenomenon occurs when a member of a queue leaves in preference for an alternative queue. It can be witnessed when a person has a choice of queues and moves from one to the other when it looks as if the other queue is being served faster. If this behaviour is prominent in the system being analysed then it must normally be incorporated into the model. Failure to do so will result in overestimated queuing times and underestimated service utilization.

Implicit in this form of behaviour is the detection of a state which triggers swapping. Since the occurrence of such a state is normally unpredictable a conditional event routine is required to detect it. Suppose we have a model in which the conditions for swapping are detected by a function *test_swap( )* which returns pointers to the entity to swap, the source queue, the destination queue and a value of 1 when swapping can occur or a value of 0 when swapping is not possible. Then in the model we might have

```
        :
    int test_swap( queue **from_queue, queue **to_queue, entity **e );
    void swap ( void ); /* The conditional event routine to perform swapping */


        :
    void swap()
    {
        entity *e;
        queue *src, *dest;
        :
        if (test_swap (&src, &dest, &e) )
        {
            extract ( src, e );
            append ( dest, e );
            :
        }
        :
```

where *swap( )* is a conditional event routine. Alternatively, global variables could be used to communicate between *test_swap( )* and *swap( )* if the run-time performance is a problem.

In practice, some care has to be exercised as to exactly how this phenomenon is modelled. If potentially each customer in a queue could swap and there are a large number of customers and/or queues, then a large amount of time is wasted testing all the possible conditions. If such detail is not essential, then it may be possible to select only a subset of the conditions to test. For example, it may be decided that in the real system only the last customer is likely to swap, in which case significant simplifications can be made to the model and the performance improved.

8.4.2 Balking

If a queue is too long then it usually deters further additions. Again this mode of behaviour is prevalent when people have to queue but it also results from systems with bounded queues in which a queue has a maximum size and additions which would make the queue length longer than the maximum are forbidden. A packet switching node, for example, may simply discard packets when there is no output buffer space left leaving it up to higher-level protocols to maintain end-to-end integrity.

Modelling this situation is straightforward because the decision to queue or not is made before the customer has entered into the queue. A balking situation can be modelled by simply testing for the queuing condition before queue entry. The following code fragment could be used:

```
queue *op_buffer;
:
void some_event ()
{
    :
    if (QSIZE(op_buffer) < MAX_SIZE)
    {
        /* There is room in the op_buffer */
        append(op_buffer, current);
    }
    else
    {
        /* Do something else because the queue has no room */
        :
    }
    :
```

In this example the current entity is added to the queue *op_buffer* only if there is room for it.

8.4.3 Reneging

Reneging is the premature departure of a customer from a queue before it has had chance to receive any service. This is normally triggered when the waiting time has exceeded some upper limit.

To model this kind of situation an event must be added to remove the queuing entity prematurely when it has timed out. A removal of the entity cannot be scheduled directly using function *schedule( )* because the entity would already be in the queue and so its state would prevent addition to the calendar. Instead the *add_event( )* library function can be used to create a dummy entity record which has a pointer to the entity to remove. If the entity does reach the server, then the corresponding removal event must be deleted. If, however, the removal event matures first, then the selected entity is removed from the queue.

Reneging is demonstrated in the following event-oriented code fragment.

```
    :
void       renege_ev ();
void       add_to_queue ();
void       service ();
entity     *renent, *renev;
```

```
    :
    :

void add_to_queue ()
{
    :
    /* add a new entity to a queue */
    append ( q, current );

    /* add an event to renege in t time units */
    renent = current;
    renev = add_event( renege_ev , t );
}

/* Event to prematurely remove the entity from the queue */
void renege_ev ()
{
    /* Extract from queue */
    extract ( q, renent );
    /* Do something with the entity extracted */
    :
}

/* Event for normal service */
void service ()
{
    /* Don't want the renege event now */
    passivate ( renev );
    delete_event ( renev );

    /* start of service for this entity */
    :
}
```

In this example the event routine *add_to_queue( )* is responsible for adding the entity to the queue and for scheduling a renege event modelled by *renege_ ev( )*. If the entity is serviced via function *service( )* the renege event will not be required and so can be removed using the pointer *renev* before continuing with normal queue servicing. If, on the other hand, the entity stays in the queue too long, the renege event must remove it using the *renent* pointer and then proceed with whatever subsequent processing is required.

8.4.4 Service pre-emption

Pre-emption occurs when a customer being serviced is abandoned by the server in favour of a new customer that has a higher priority. The interrupted customer can wait to complete its service, wait to be served again from afresh or simply leave the system. The interrupting customer takes the place of the interrupted customer and stays in service for a defined interval unless it, too, is interrupted by yet another higher-priority customer.

This mode of behaviour is often found in multi-tasking operating systems. A process can get pre-empted when another process which is waiting for cpu time has a higher priority. In many operating systems the allocation of priority is not static but dynamic—it increases the longer the process is kept waiting.

Consider the following extract of a process-oriented simulation model for a queue that exhibits pre-emption

```
        :
        :
queue        *q1, *interrupt_q;
resource     *checkout;
entity       *in_service;
        :
        :
        :
        :
void customer ( ) ;
void server ( ) ;
void old_customer ();
void new_customer ();
void select_highest ();
void check_priorities ();
        :
        :
void customer()
{
    switch(PHASE_OF(current))
    {
    case ARRIVAL:
        /* calc inter-arrival time ... */
        make_scheduled_entity(customer, (void *)0, inter_arrival_time,
            ARRIVAL, priority_of_next_entity, 1, NULL);
        append ( q1 , current );
        break;
    case DEPARTURE:
        release(checkout , 1.0);
        terminate ( current );
        break;
    }
}
void server ()
{
    if ( !ISEMPTY(q1) && !ISEMPTY(interrupt_q)) {
        if ( ISAVAILABLE(checkout, 1.0) )
            select_highest();
        else
            check_priorities ();
```

```
    }
    else if ( !ISEMPTY(q1) )
    {
        if (ISAVAILABLE(checkout , 1.0) )
            new_customer();
        else
            check_priorities ();
    }
    else if ( !ISEMPTY(interrupt_q) && ISAVAILABLE(checkout , 1.0) )
        old_customer();
}

void select_highest ( )
{
    if (queue_front(q1)->priority > queue_front(interrupt_q)->priority )
        new_customer();
    else
        old_customer ();
}

void check_priorities ()
{
    if (queue_front(q1)->priority > in_service->priority )
    {
        passivate ( in_service );
        in_service->time = in_service->time - sim_clock;
        append ( interrupt_q, in_service );
        release ( checkout, 1.0 );
        new_customer ();
    }
}

void new_customer()
{
    float time_in_service;
    time_in_service=...;
    acquire ( checkout, 1.0 );
    in_service = remove_front(q1);
    in_service->phase = DEPARTURE;
    :
    schedule ( in_service , time_in_service );
}

void old_customer()
{
    acquire ( checkout, 1.0);
    in_service = remove_front( interrupt_q );
    schedule ( in_service, in_service->time );
}
    :
    :
```

Here a function *customer( )* generates new entities and a function *server( )* simulates the behaviour of a pre-emptable server. When an entity is generated it enters queue *q1* in priority order. A second queue, *interrupt_q*, also exists which keeps all those customers whose service has been interrupted by a higher-priority customer. The server, modelled as a conditional entity with function *server( )*, scans the available customers and selects one to service from the normal queue *q1*, the interrupt queue *interrupt_q* or the current entity already receiving service.

Function *server( )* checks the state of the queues. If both queues are not empty and the server is free, then the entity with the highest priority is selected with function *select_highest( )*. If the server is busy, then the entity from the normal queue may interrupt if it is of higher priority, but the entity from the interrupt queue cannot interrupt because it can have equal priority at most. This is implemented with function *check_priorities( )*, which also records the amount of service time the interrupted entity has left and then adds the interrupted entity to *interrupt_q*. The new entity can then receive service.

If only *q1* contains an entity and the server is busy, the in-service entity may be interrupted if the priority levels permit it, otherwise the customers wait as normal. However, if the server is free then the first entity from the normal queue can take service straight away.

If *interrupt_q* is the only queue that is not empty, then it can supply an entity to the server, provided the server is free. If the server is busy, then the priority levels prevent pre-emption and no action can be taken. Note that if an entity from *interrupt_q* receives service it is assumed that the service time is equal to the outstanding time remaining at the instant of interruption. Other service policies can be incorporated. For example, the service time could be sampled afresh or it could be sampled from a special 'interrupt' distribution. In these cases a completely new service time is generated.

8.4.5 Time dependencies

In the queues considered so far the arrival rate and service rate have been assumed to be constant for the duration of the simulation. However, this is not always a realistic scenario. The arrival rate of customers at a barber shop, for instance, may show a noticeable peak around midday and early evening. Assuming a constant arrival rate in this case would probably underestimate the worst-case queue size, so the arrival rate must vary with time. There are two basic ways that a time dependency may be incorporated into the model. Either a scheduled event can be added to adjust the rate in a series of steps or else the arrival rate can be adjusted as each new customer is scheduled, which can produce a gradual change. The effect of these two approaches on the mean arrival rate is shown in Fig. 8.5.

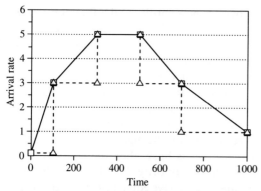

Figure 8.5 Time-dependent arrival rates.

The step approximation can be implemented by scheduling a rate recalculation event at each recalculation instant. This is illustrated in the following code, which simulates the step curve shown in Fig. 8.5:

```
float arrival_rate[5][2] = {{0.0, 0.1}, {100.0, 3.0}, {300.0, 5.0}, {500.0,
                            3.0}, {700.0, 1.0}};
float rate; /* The arrival rate */

    :

void init ()
{
    :
    make_scheduled_entity( recalc, NULL, 0.0, 0, 0, 0, 1, NULL );
    :
}

void recalc ()
{
    int index;

    /* Get the index */
    if (sim_clock >= arrival_rate[4][0])
        index = 4;
    elsif (sim_clock >= arrival_rate[3][0])
        index = 3;
    elsif (sim_clock >= arrival_rate[2][0])
        index = 2;
    elsif (sim_clock >= arrival_rate[1][0])
        index = 1;
    else
        index = 0;

    rate = arrival_rate [index][1];
```

```
    /* Schedule the next rate change */
    if (index < 4)
        wait (arrival_rate[index+1][0] - sim_clock)
    else
        terminate_current();
}

float next_time ( )
{
    return (expenential (rs) / rate);
}
```

In this example, a function *recalc( )* is responsible for setting the arrival rate, which is stored in the global variable *rate*. The arrival rate is used by function *next_time( )* to generate exponentially distributed inter-arrival times. After each rate recalculation event, the event reschedules itself in preparation for the next one. When the last rate recalculation has been actioned the entity record is discarded because the event is no longer required. Thereafter, the arrival rate remains constant at one customer per time unit.

The approach which adjusts the arrival rate at each sample can approximate the variation in a piecewise linear manner which is continuous (i.e. contains no steps). The following function performs this adjustment, and the resulting change in arrival rate simulates the piecewise linear curve shown in Fig. 8.5:

```
float arrival_rate[5][2] = {{0.0, 0.1}, {100.0, 3.0}, {300.0, 5.0}, {500.0,
                            3.0}, {700.0, 1.0}};

    :

/* Calculate the next arrival time */
float next_time ( )
{
    float rate;
    float calc_rate ( int high, int low );

    if (sim_clock >= arrival_rate[4][0])
        rate = arrival_rate[4][1];
    elsif (sim_clock >= arrival_rate[3][0])
        rate = calc_rate ( 4, 3 );
    elsif (sim_clock >= arrival_rate[2][0])
        rate = calc_rate ( 3, 2 );
    elsif (sim_clock >= arrival_rate[1][0])
        rate = calc_rate ( 2, 1 );
    else
        rate = calc_rate ( 1, 0 );

    return (exponential (rs) / rate);
}
```

```
/* Perform linear interpolation between points */
float calc_rate ( int high, int low )
{
    float x1, y1;

    x1 = arrival_rate[low][0];
    y1 = arrival_rate[low][1];

    return ((sim_clock-x1) * (arrival_rate[high][1]-y1) /
            (arrival_rate[high][0]-x1) + y1);
}
```

At each call to *next_time( )* to determine the next arrival time, the instantaneous mean arrival rate is determined by function *calc_rate( )* using interpolation between the points defined in the array *arrival_rate[ ][ ]*. An exponentially distributed random number is then returned which has this arrival rate as mean.

A variant of this approach is known as *thinning*, in which a process that generates arrivals at the maximum rate is scaled down according to the required continuous function. Thinning is demonstrated in the following code:

```
float arrival_rate[5][2] = {{0.0, 0.1}, {100.0, 3.0}, {300.0, 5.0}, {500.0,
                            3.0}, {700.0, 1.0}};

float max_rate = 5.0;
 :

/* Calculate the next arrival time. */
float next_time ( )
{
    float t;
    float ratio ( float t );

    t = sim_clock;
    /* Drop events with probability equal to 1-ratio(t) */
    do
        /* Calculate the next event at the maximum rate */
        t += exponential ( rs ) / max_rate ;
    until ( probability ( rs ) < ratio ( t ) );
    return ( t - sim_clock );
}

/* Calculate the ratio of the instantaneous arrival rate to the */
/* maximum arrival rate. */
float ratio ( float t )
{
    float rate;
    float calc_rate ( float t, int high, int low );

    if (t >= arrival_rate[4][0])
        rate = arrival_rate[4][1];
```

```
    elsif (t )= arrival_rate[3][0])
        rate = calc_rate ( t, 4, 3 );
    elsif (t )= arrival_rate[2][0])
        rate = calc_rate ( t, 3, 2 );
    elsif (t )= arrival_rate[1][0])
        rate = calc_rate ( t, 2, 1 );
    else
        rate = calc_rate ( t, 1, 0 );

    return rate / max_rate;
}

/* Perform linear interpolation between sample points. */
float calc_rate ( float t, int high, int low )
{
    float x1, y1;

    x1 = arrival_rate[low][0];
    y1 = arrival_rate[low][1];

    return ((t - x1) * (arrival_rate[high][1] - y1) /
            (arrival_rate[high][0] - x1) + y1);
}
```

In this scheme the ratio of the continuous piecewise linear function to the maximum arrival rate is calculated by *ratio( )*. This function determines the instantaneous (future) arrival rate at time *t* and then divides it by *max*. The value returned by *ratio( )* is employed in function *next_time( )* to determine the probability with which a Poisson event is allowed to proceed. The closer this ratio is to 1.0 the fewer Poisson events that are discarded and so the closer the actual rate becomes to the maximum rate.

The main difference between this method and the previous one is that with this method the arrival rate for time *t* is effectively determined at time *t*, whereas, with the previous method, the arrival rate for time *t* was calculated during the previous arrival event. Thus, this method may be more accurate, especially when there is a large difference between the maximum and minimum rates. On the other hand, there is an additional unavoidable overhead because of the need to take more samples because of those events that get dropped.

8.5 AN EXAMPLE—A BATCH COMPUTER SYSTEM

This example illustrates the use of priority queues in a simple simulation of a batch computer system. A batch computer system is one where a central computer resource is shared by customers that submit complete jobs for processing and receive some form of output such as weekly payslips. Typically

Table 8.1 Parameters for job submissions

Type of job	Mean	Standard deviation	Percentage of total
A	0.56	0.16	21
B	2.14	0.22	57
C	13.65	1.83	22

the cost to the customer in using this service is based on the amount of cpu time required to process the particular job. In this example, a company offering such batch computer facilities has decided to update its existing single grade of service. In future the customer will be able to select from four grades of service and a premium will be paid for a higher grade of service because higher priority jobs will always go in front of lower priority jobs when queuing for cpu time.

Based on the existing job load, we require to know what the effect will be on job waiting time if customers use the grade of service they have indicated they would prefer in a recent poll.

Each grade of service has an associated job priority. The grade of service and job priority are defined as being either 0, 1, 2 or 3 with 3 being the highest and 0 the lowest.

Existing measurements of the traffic load have indicated that job submissions basically fall into three classes of cpu usage which are independent of grade of service (in other words each type of job will have the same mix of grades of service). Job submissions follow a normal distribution with the parameters shown in Table 8.1. It is anticipated that this will be a reasonable approximation for the new services.

The analysis of the customer poll has suggested that the traffic character-

Table 8.2 Traffic characteristics

Grade of service	Distribution	Mean time between jobs (seconds)
0	Exponential	19.8
1	Exponential	13.6
2	Exponential	11.2
3	Exponential	27.5

istics (inter-arrival time of jobs) shown in Table 8.2 apply in the busy hour to the jobs submitted for the new services.

The three-phase model in Listing 8.1 can be used to simulate this system and estimate the waiting time for each type of job. It consists of the scheduled event routines *arrival( )* and *finish_job( )* and the conditional event routine *seize_cpu( )*.

```
#include <stdio.h>
#include "sim_lib.h"
#include "random.h"
#include "resource.h"
#include "results.h"

#define    NUM_JOB_TYPES 3
#define    NUM_GOS 4

/* Traffic load groups — assume time unit seconds */
float    mean[NUM_JOB_TYPES] = {0.56, 2.14, 13.65};
float    std_dev[NUM_JOB_TYPES] = {0.16, 0.22, 1.83};
float    prob_job[NUM_JOB_TYPES] = {0.21, 0.57, 0.22};

/* The mean time between jobs for each grade of service */
float    arrival_rate[NUM_GOS] = {19.8, 13.6, 11.2, 27.5};
void     init ( void );
void     arrival ( void );
void     finish_job ( void );
void     seize_cpu ( void );
void     print_results( void );
int      get_type_of_job( void );

stream   *sl;
queue    *cpu_queue;
resource *cpu;
summary  *st[NUM_GOS];
extern   entity *current;
extern   float  sim_clock;

main ()
{
    int i;

    init();
    run_sim (10000.0, 1);
    print_results();
    return (0);
}

void arrival ()
{
```

```
    int     priority;
    entity  *job;

    priority = PRIORITY_OF(current);
    job = make_entity( NULL, (void *)0, 0, priority, NULL);
    /* Queue up for cpu resource */
    append(cpu_queue, job);
    /* to calculate waiting time */
    stamp(job);
    /* Calculate the next arrival for a job with this priority */
    wait ( exponential(s1)*arrival_rate[priority] );
}

void seize_cpu()
{
    entity *this_job;
    int     type_of_job;
    int     priority;

    if (IS_AVAILABLE(cpu, 1.0) && !QEMPTY(cpu_queue))
    {
        this_job = remove_front( cpu_queue );
        priority = PRIORITY_OF(this_job);
        /* Record the time spent queuing by each type of job */
        add_sdata(st[priority],TIME_SPENT(this_job));
        /* Get the cpu */
        acquire(cpu, 1.0);
        /* Determine the type of job which determines */
        /* the amount of cpu resource obtained */
        type_of_job = get_type_of_job();
        this_job->event = finish_job;
        schedule(this_job, normal(s1, mean[type_of_job],
            std_dev[type_of_job]));
    }
}

void finish_job ()
{
    release(cpu,1.0);
    terminate(current);
}

void init()
{
    init_sim ();
    s1 = make_stream ( 1, 0);
    cpu_queue = make_queue ();
    /* can only have one job at a time */
    cpu = make_resource ( 1.0 );
    make_conditional_entity(seize_cpu, (void *)0, 0, 0, NULL);
    {
```

```
        int i;
        for (i = 0;i < NUM_GOS;i++)
        {
            /* schedule arrival of jobs */
            make_scheduled_entity(arrival, (void *)0,
                exponential(s1)*arrival_rate[i], 0, i, 1, NULL);
            /* Results collection */
            st[i] = make_summary();
        }
    }
}

void print_results()
{
    print_summary(stdout, st[0], "Waiting time for priority 0 jobs.");
    print_summary(stdout, st[1], "Waiting time for priority 1 jobs.");
    print_summary(stdout, st[2], "Waiting time for priority 2 jobs.");
    print_summary(stdout, st[3], "Waiting time for priority 3 jobs.");
}

int get_type_of_job ()
{
    float p;

    /* Generate a random probability */
    p = uniform01(s1);
    /* Return the type of job based on the probability */
    if (p < prob_job[0])
        return 0;
    if (p < (prob_job[0]+prob_job[1]))
        return 1;
    return 2;
}
```

Listing 8.1 Model for the batch computer system simulation.

There is a scheduled event created for each grade of job since the arrival of jobs of each priority level is independent. The actual arrival of a job is simulated by function *arrival( )*. It results in the creation of an entity record *job* which is inserted into the queue of jobs awaiting processor time. The priority of the arrival is assigned to the priority of the job created, which determines its position in the queue. Higher-priority jobs will go towards the front of the queue, lower-priority jobs will go towards the end of the queue.

The conditional event *seize_cpu( )* assigns the first free job from the queue to the cpu, making the cpu unavailable for other jobs until the job has completed. Job completion is performed by *finish_job( )*, which is scheduled to occur a time *t* later, where *t* is determined from the parameters for that type of job.

Job type is obtained by generating a discrete sample from *get_type_of_job( )*

Table 8.3 Waiting-time parameters

Grade of service	Mean	Standard deviation
0	1038.7	546.38
1	58.4	55.18
2	14.3	16.29
3	6.1	5.43

which returns either 0, 1 or 2 with the desired probability. The type of job determines the mean and standard deviation of the normal distribution from which t is sampled.

Results are collected in the model using a *summary* data structure, the use of which is described in the next chapter. The mean and standard deviation of the waiting times obtained from this model are shown in Table 8.3. This clearly indicates that the higher the grade of service, the shorter the waiting time. The highest grade of service has job waiting times of about 6 seconds, while the lowest grade of service has waiting times of around 16 minutes.

8.6 SUMMARY

Queues are an indispensable part of a simulation model and are provided as part of the simulation library using tree-based algorithms.

A queuing system consists of a resource that customers are queuing for and a server that controls access to the resource. The supply of customers into the queue is described by an arrival pattern. This is characterized by a population size and an arrival process. The service demand refers to the amount of the resource requested by the customer. The length of time the resource is required for is sampled from a service distribution. Customers are selected to receive service according to a selection policy, the most common of which is FCFS.

Queues can be classified according to a standard scheme that defines the arrival distribution, the service distribution, the customer population, the number of servers, the service policy and number of customers allowed in the system.

There is a significant body of analytical theory and results which can be applied to queuing systems. The simplest queue to analyse using this theory is the M/M/1 queue—Poisson arrivals with exponential service times and a single server. When this queue is analysed it displays a characteristic throughput limit when the arrival rate equals the service rate. This is the rate at which the server is fully utilized. A higher rate results in an unstable system because the server can never satisfy customer demand and so the queue length increases indefinitely.

Some common patterns of behaviour of a queuing system are queue swapping, balking, reneging, service pre-emption and time-varying arrival and service rates. In queue swapping, customers switch between queues. In balking, a customer refuses to join a queue, normally because it is too big. Customers that renege leave a queue before receiving service. Service pre-emption takes place when a customer receiving service is rejected in favour of another customer of a higher priority. Finally, we may have arrival or service rates that vary with time, simulating, for instance, a morning or evening rush hour.

8.7 EXERCISES

8.1   Run the simple queuing model from Chapter 3. Compare the output obtained with that expected from theory.

8.2   Calculate the mean time in the system, the mean time queuing and the mean number in the system for an M/M/1 queue which has a mean inter-arrival time of 5.4 seconds and a mean service time of 4.2 seconds.

8.3   Add a new type of modelling primitive to the simulation library. This new primitive is to be called a *service facility*. It is an extension of a queue that is to transparently handle service pre-emption as described in Sec. 8.4.4. It consists of two queues. One queue is the normal queue where customers receive service. The other queue is the interrupt queue where interrupted customers temporarily reside until their service is resumed. Design and implement the necessary data structures and support functions and add them to the simulation library.

8.4   Students queue to use a single computer terminal. They come to use the terminal every 15 ± 5 minutes (uniformly distributed) and occupy it for an exponentially distributed amount of time with mean 37 minutes. If the queue is more than three long new arrivals do not join it but return 22 ± 8 minutes (uniformly distributed) later. They either join the queue within three attempts or else give up completely. Simulate this system for eight simulated hours of operation and obtain the percentage of users who receive no service.

8.5   An operating system employs the following scheduling mechanism. Incoming jobs arrive every 11 ± 7 seconds and are placed in a queue. Each second the scheduler interrupts the job being serviced and places it to the back of the queue and takes the next available job for processing. New jobs require a normally distributed amount of cpu time with mean four seconds and variance three seconds but no new job requires less than 0.1 seconds cpu time. Jobs that have been pre-empted only require the amount of cpu time that was outstanding when the scheduler interrupted them. Simulate this system and find the mean time to process a job.

8.6 Repeat Exercise 8.4 but assume that students also leave a queue if they have waited more than 30 minutes. In this situation they behave exactly as if they had not bothered to queue because the queue was too long.

8.7 A car wash service is provided by an automobile service station. To obtain a car wash a driver must go to the attendant, purchase a token and then drive round to the car wash which takes one minute. At the car wash they either wait if the car wash is busy or enter it if it is free. A car wash takes three minutes to complete. Assume that car wash customers must queue with normal customers to get their token. Normal customers arrive with a uniformly distributed inter-arrival time between one and ten minutes. Car wash customers arrive with an exponentially distributed inter-arrival time with mean ten minutes. Assume that service time for normal customers is normally distributed with mean three minutes and standard deviation ten seconds and that service time for car wash customers is normally distributed with mean two minutes and standard deviation 15 seconds. Simulate this system for six simulated hours of operation.

8.8 A supermarket has 19 checkouts. Customers paying for their goods select the checkout with the smallest queue. Once in a queue they may move to another queue up to two queues away if that queue is smaller by three or more customers. A survey has shown that customers have N goods, where N is drawn from a normal distribution with mean 35 and standard deviation 5. The time taken to serve a customer depends on the number of goods and is roughly $2N+30$ seconds on average. Assuming that customer arrival is a Poisson process with an average rate in the busy hour of one per second. Collect queue length statistics for the busy hour.

8.9 The supermarket of Exercise 8.8 wants to convert one of its normal checkouts into an express checkout. The express checkout will be restricted to customers with seven items or less to pay for. The server on the express checkout can serve customers in $1.4N+21$ seconds, where N is the number of items to check. Analysis at stores that have already introduced this scheme has shown that a customer with seven items or less decides whether or not to go into the express checkout queue based on the number of items customers in other queues have. If it is estimated that the total number of items of customers in the express queue is less than any of the normal queues then it will be chosen, otherwise the shortest of the normal queues will be chosen. Collect queue statistics on this system and see if it offers any improvement in customer waiting time.

9

GATHERING RESULTS

A discrete event simulation model must produce some quantitative results if it is to be of any use. In this chapter we discuss some of the mechanisms by which results may be obtained from the simulation library.

9.1 HISTOGRAMS

Chapter 5 looked at *histograms* as a source of sampling data. We can also use them as a convenient means to display results data. Showing data in this way often helps in analysing the behaviour of random variables, because of the human preference for pictorial rather than textual information. The histograms provided by the simulation library can be divided into

- *frequency histograms*, for the distribution of output variables frequency data
- *time series histograms*, for displaying data varying over time (trend data).

9.1.1 Frequency histograms

When we wish to display simulation results given in terms of pairs of values, as a histogram, we partition the range of samples into a series of smaller subranges called *classes or class intervals*. Let a range of samples from x_{min} to x_{max} be divided into n class intervals defined by boundary points $x_0, x_1, x_2, ..., x_n$. Let the ith class be the interval $(x_{i-1}, x_i]$, $1 \leqslant i \leqslant n$, and let the sum of the samples falling in the ith interval be t_i. A graph with the x-axis divided into intervals each of which contains a column whose height is proportional to t_i, is known as a *frequency histogram*.

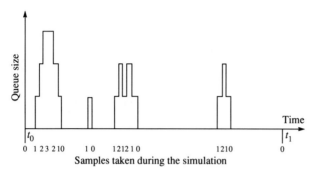

Samples taken during the simulation

Figure 9.1 Variation in queue length over time.

If the total value of all the intervals is t, then the fraction

$$f_i = \frac{t_i}{t} \tag{9.1}$$

is the *relative frequency* of the ith interval. A graph consisting of rectangular areas equal to f_i is known as a *relative frequency histogram*. This is a discrete analogy of the pdf.

There are two basic types of frequency histogram, *unweighted* and *weighted*. The distinction depends on whether or not each sample recorded by the histogram is modified to take into account the amount of time that it has persisted in the model. Consider the fluctuation in queue length depicted in Fig. 9.1. The y-axis gives the number of customers in the queue and the x-axis gives time. The sequence of digits running underneath the x-axis gives l, the number of customers that were found in the queue after the entry or departure of a customer. This is the instant when the queue length is sampled.

An unweighted histogram of queue size in which the data has been sampled as shown in Fig. 9.1 could be constructed by establishing four class intervals from -0.5 to 0.5, 0.5 to 1.5, 1.5 to 2.5 and 2.5 to 3.5. Each interval contains a single possible value of queue size. Samples consist of (x,y) pairs. The x component selects the interval and the y component is the value to be recorded. In this case the x component is l, the queue length, and the y component is 1 (i.e. one sample of this queue length). To record this value the class interval to which l belongs is first identified and then 1 is added to the total in that class. The result is shown in the histogram depicted in Fig. 9.2. In this histogram we see, for example, that the queue was found to have a single occupant on the arrival or departure of a customer on eight separate occasions. This can be confirmed by counting the number of 1s in the sequence of digits running underneath the x-axis of the graph in Fig. 9.1.

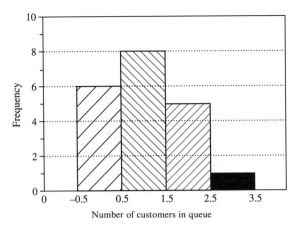

Figure 9.2 Unweighted histogram of queue length.

Alternatively, the time difference between entry and departure can be taken into account by recording $1.t_d = t_d$ instead of 1 in the class interval for l, where t_d is the difference between the value of the simulated clock when the previous sample was recorded and the current value. Incorporating the length of time that each sample has persisted gives the histogram of Fig. 9.3. In this histogram we see that for about 72 per cent of the time the queue was empty and for about 15 per cent of the time the queue had a single customer.

There is an obvious difference between Figs 9.2 and 9.3, so it is clear that the use of an appropriate type of histogram is important when presenting results. The applicable histogram for recording times such as waiting time in a queue or service time at a checkout is a time-weighted histogram. However, an unweighted

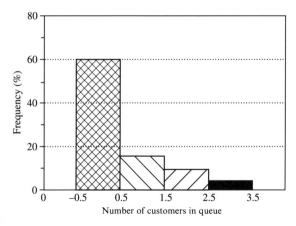

Figure 9.3 Weighted histogram of queue length.

histogram must be used when the statistics of interest are not related to time, such as the number of customers found already queuing by a newly arrived customer.

9.1.2 Cumulative frequency histograms

It can also be interesting to construct the *cumulative frequency histogram*. The cumulative frequency histogram is less sensitive to variations in class length than the frequency histogram. This is because the accumulation is essentially equivalent to integration along the *x*-axis, which filters out chance variations. Figure 9.5 shows a cumulative histogram corresponding to the hypothetical frequency histogram of Fig. 9.4.

Values for the area of each of the columns of the cumulative frequency histogram can be determined from the corresponding relative frequency histogram as follows. Let the sum of the samples in intervals up to the *i*th interval be $H(i)$. Then

$$H(i) = 0 \qquad \text{for } i < 0$$
$$= \sum_{j=1}^{i} t_j \qquad \text{for } 0 \leqslant i \leqslant n$$
$$= t \qquad \text{for } i > n \qquad (9.2)$$

is the value of the required area. Note that the maximum value of the histogram is *t* and that it is monotonically non-decreasing (i.e. columns never decrease in area with increasing *x* value).

The *relative cumulative frequency histogram* can also be generated. This is the discrete analogy of the cdf. To build this histogram, the areas of the columns are normalized by dividing by *t*, the total of all columns, as represented by

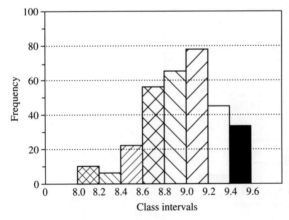

Figure 9.4 Frequency histogram of service time.

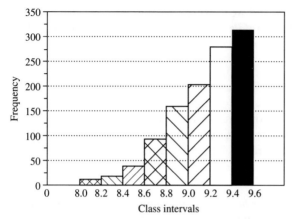

Figure 9.5 Cumulative frequency histogram of service time.

Eq. (9.1). The maximum value of the relative cumulative frequency histogram is now 1.0. The net result is a rescaling of the y-axis. So the histogram in Fig. 9.4 would have its y-axis rescaled giving the height of the largest column as $80/320 = 0.25$ and the corresponding cumulative frequency histogram shown in Fig. 9.5 would have its y-axis rescaled so that the height of the largest column was equal to $320/320 = 1.0$.

9.1.3 Time series histograms

A *time series histogram* shows the fluctuation of a variable as a function of time. The x-axis represents time and it normally runs from the start of the simulation, after any initial run-in period, to the end. The y-axis gives the value of the variable. Figure 9.1 is an example of a time series histogram.

In order to generate a time series histogram the x-axis is divided into n equal width intervals between points $x_0, x_1, \ldots x_n, x_0 \leqslant x_1 \leqslant \ldots \leqslant x_n$. If the width of each interval is w, the current simulation clock time is t_k and the value of the variable being logged is y_k then y_k will be added to the set of histogram columns indexed by i, where i takes values

$$
\left\{ \text{floor}\left(\frac{t_{k-1}}{w} + 1\right) \ldots \text{floor}\left(\frac{t_k}{w}\right) \right\}, \qquad \text{if floor}\left(\frac{t_k}{w}\right) > \text{floor}\left(\frac{t_{k-1}}{w}\right)
$$

$$
\left\{ \text{floor}\left(\frac{t_k}{w}\right) \right\}, \qquad\qquad\qquad \text{otherwise} \qquad\qquad (9.3)
$$

As an example, consider a time series histogram running from $t = 0$ to $t = 100.0$ which has 20 intervals each 5 time units wide. If the last time at which a sample was recorded was 12.5, and we make a recording of $y = 1.0$ at $t = 23.4$, then we will have to add 1.0 to the totals of the third ($=$ floor($12.5/5 + 1$)) and the fourth ($=$ floor($23.4/5$)) class interval.

9.2 RECORDING RESULTS

The simulation library provides the data structures and functions necessary to record results in several different ways. We will now look briefly at the data structures and functions which are available to record data values.

9.2.1 Results data structures

File *results.h* defines two data types *histogram* and *summary*. The *histogram* data structure has the following type definition:

```
typedef struct
{
        float     *data;
        int       first;
        float     sum_f;
        float     sum_xf;
        float     width;
        int       num_columns;
        float     start;
        float     sum_xxf;
        float     total;
        float     sum_squares;
        float     min_val;
        float     max_val;
        float     time_last_recording;
        histogram_t kind;
} histogram ;
```

The component *data* is used to hold the value of each histogram column. It is an array of *float*s which span *num_columns* beginning at *start*. Each histogram column is *width* units wide. The highest and lowest sample values are stored in *max_val* and *min_val* respectively. By using Eq. (5.13) the variance can be determined from the sum of all the samples, recorded in *sum_xf*, and the sum of the samples squared, recorded in *sum_xxf*, along with the number of samples which is recorded in *sum_f*. The mean can be obtained from *sum_f* and *sum_xf*. The time of the simulated clock when the last sample was made is kept in *time_last_recording*. The type of histogram is stored in *kind*, which takes one of the three values defined for the type of histogram, namely *UNWEIGHTED*, *WEIGHTED* and *SERIES*. The component *first* is used to flag the first call to *add_hdata( )*, so that the initial values of *max_val* and *min_val* can be set at this time.

As can be seen, the histogram data structure is quite large, typically occupying some several hundred bytes. However, it is not always necessary or desirable to maintain all of this information. Significant savings in memory usage can be obtained by using the simpler *summary* data structure along with its associated handling functions. A summary data structure has the type definition

```
typedef struct
{
    int    zero;
    float  sum_xf;
    float  sum_xxf;
    int    sum_f;
} summary;
```

The *zero* component is used to record the number of zero entries made, *sum_ f*, *sum_xf* and *sum_xxf* are used in the same way as their namesakes in *histogram*.

9.2.2 Recording samples

We require variables in the model to maintain data from which the model outputs are obtained. Creation of these results variables should be done during the initialization phase using the functions *make_histogram( )* and *make_ summary( )*.

Function *make_histogram( )* takes arguments *start* defining the lower limit of the first histogram column (i.e. the base), *width* giving the width of each column, a count *num_columns* giving the number of columns and *kind* specifying the type of histogram required. A pointer to a histogram data structure is returned. The prototype is

```
histogram *make_histogram (float start, float width, int num_columns,
                histogram_t kind);
```

Function *add_hdata( )* is used to add the sample to a histogram data structure. The prototype is

```
void add_hdata ( histogram *h, float x, float y ) ;
```

the actual value to be added is determined as follows:

- *Unweighted.* A call to *add_hdata( )* with the arguments *h*, *x*, *y* updates the value of the data maintained for histogram *h*. The applicable class range is selected by the *x* argument, and its content increased by *y*. (Often, the value of *y* will be 1.0.)
- *Weighted.* As we saw above, in a time-weighted histogram, not only are we interested in the amount of some measurement, but also in the length of simulated time that it has persisted. When *add_hdata* is called with the arguments *h*, *x*, *y*, the applicable class range is selected by the *x* argument as before, but the value added is actually

```
y * (current_time-h->time_last_recording)
```

and the value of *h-> time_last_recording* is updated.

- *Time series*. In a time-series histogram, the indexes are identified as described in Sec. 9.1.3 and the value of *y* added to each column indexed. The *x* value is ignored.

The function *make_summary( )* takes no arguments and returns a pointer to an initialized *summary* data structure. The prototype is

```
summary *make_summary ( void ) ;
```

Function *add_sdata( )* is used to add a sample to a summary data structure. The prototype is

```
void add_sdata ( summary *s, float v ) ;
```

which will add the sample *v* to summary data structure *s*.

It is sometimes necessary to reset the results accumulated at some point in the simulation. This may be necessary when the effect of the initial system transient has to be discounted (see Chapter 10). To accomplish this we can use functions *clear_histogram( )* and *clear_summary( )* which have the prototypes

```
void clear_histogram ( histogram *h );
```

and

```
void clear_summary ( summary *s );
```

These two functions take appropriate pointers and reset the results accumulated. No result is returned.

9.3 MEASUREMENTS

There are frequently very many variables that could be monitored in a simulation model. The more variables measured the harder it is to analyse the results and the longer the simulation will take to run. On the other hand, if we forget to measure some variables or decide later that the results are not quite the ones required, then we are forced to re-run the simulation. It is therefore essential to be selective and carefully identify those variables for which results are likely to be needed and incorporate suitable measurements for them into the model. However, it is not always that easy to decide exactly which of them are necessary from the outset and it probably works out cheaper in the long run if we err on the side of too much rather than too little.

Exactly what value to measure depends on the goals of the simulation. We looked at some useful metrics related to queues in the previous chapter. In addition, the following have also been found useful:

- *Response time*. The occurrence of a significant event frequently gives rise to subsequent dependent events; the first event can be thought of as a form of trigger. In these situations the interval between the first event and one of the dependent events may be an interesting quantity. For instance, a user at a remote terminal might send commands one line at a time to a central computer, which performs some action and then returns one or more lines of text to the user. The response time here is the time between sending the command and receiving the reply.

$$response\ time = time\ of\ trigger\ event - time\ of\ dependent\ event \qquad (9.4)$$

● *Idle time.* The *idle time* is the time that a resource or server remains unused. It represents unused spare capacity. This may be because the system itself is not operating to its full potential or because another part of the system is restricting the total throughput.

$$idle\ time = available\ time - time\ occupied \qquad (9.5)$$

● *System throughput.* The system being modelled may consist of several queues connected together in some way. In this situation the throughput of the system as a whole cannot normally be determined by a consideration of the throughput of individual queues in isolation. Instead it is determined by the first queue to reach saturation, which occurs when utilization becomes 1 or at least very close to 1.

● *Efficiency.* The efficiency refers to the amount of usable capacity that is actually employed over some interval. It can be expressed as

$$efficiency = \frac{capacity\ used}{total\ available\ capacity} \qquad (9.6)$$

which must be less than or equal to 1.

We can choose to record these values in either a weighted or unweighted form. The decision to use one form or the other should be based on whether time-averaged values or the number of instances are of interest. Measurements related to parameters of a queue such as length should be recorded in a weighted form, or else at regular intervals so that the weighting is implicit in the interval size. When time-weighted values are recorded it is important to note the value at each instant that it changes in order that unbiased results are obtained. For example, if the queue length is recorded with a call to *add_hdata( )* just before the addition of a new customer to the queue but the matching call just before the customer was removed from the queue is omitted, then the queue length statistics will be grossly inaccurate and biased on the low side. This situation is illustrated in Fig. 9.6, which is based on the graph of Fig. 9.1. This compares the effect of taking measurements at the appropriate points to that when only the measurement for the customer arrival is made.

If data is recorded at regular sampling intervals, then the intervals must be chosen so that accuracy is maintained. This means that intervals must be

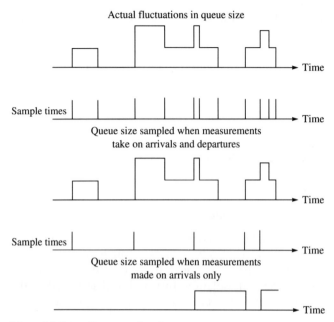

Figure 9.6 Recording queue length.

sufficiently small so that significant variations of the variable being sampled are caught. However, if the interval is too small, then we waste time taking unnecessary samples.

9.4 OUTPUTTING RESULTS

The simulation library can handle the output of data in the form of histograms, tables or as summary statistical data. It can also support output to a variety of media such as disk files and physical devices like line printers, using the same output routines. This flexibility allows results to be stored in a convenient form for input to further statistical analysis packages or for inclusion in reports. It is achieved by passing a file pointer as one of the arguments to the various output functions. The standard console stream *stdout*, defined in *stdio.h*, being used when output is required on the terminal.

9.4.1 Frequency histograms

Histogram data is output using the library function *print_histogram( )* which has the prototype

```
void print_histogram ( FILE *fp, histogram *h, char *title );
```

Each type of histogram consists of the following elements:

- *Title*. This is optional, and is passed as an argument to *print_histogram*. If present, the title is printed on the first line of output.
- *Mean*. This is the mean calculated from the samples recorded in the histogram.
- *Variance*. This is the variance for the data represented in the histogram. If insufficient data has been recorded, 'UNDEFINED' is printed instead of a numerical value.
- *Standard deviation*. This is the positive square root of the variance. If insufficient data has been recorded, 'UNDEFINED' is printed instead of a numerical value.
- *Minimum value*. This is the lowest numerical value recorded.
- *Maximum value*. This is the highest numerical value recorded.
- *Sum of frequencies*. This represents the number of times that *add_hdata( )* was called.

The histogram is then printed, running down the page instead of across the page to make best use of the output format. The abscissa is printed in the first column from the left margin. The numerical value of the ordinate is printed in the second column from the left margin. The width of the line represents the value recorded (that is, the height of the histogram column), and is printed as a sequence of left-aligned '#' symbols. The output function automatically scales the display so that there is always room to show the widest line.

If alternative symbols are required for the histogram columns then they can be set by calling the *set_fill_char( )* function, defined in *results.h*, with the prototype

```
void set_fill_char ( char fc );
```

where the argument is the new character required.

The first and last lines are not always printed in the histogram as they represent gutters. A gutter mops up any observations that 'spill' over the range defined by the histogram. When gutter lines are displayed this indicates that the results are outside of the expected range and, if the values recorded in the gutter lines are significant, the simulation should be re-run with more and/or wider histogram columns.

Example 9.1 The above library routines were used to obtain some results from the simple queue of Chapter 3. The output results are illustrated in Fig. 9.7 for a utilization factor of 0.8. The top histogram gives the number of customers in the system (those queuing and those being served). The mean of the number of customers in the system is 4.792 and the variance is 44.586. The upper gutter has been printed, indicating that some observations have fallen outside of the defined range. The value outside the range though, only 57.91, may be considered unimportant. The second histogram gives the total waiting time for customers. It can be seen to have a significant gutter, which implies that the tail is longer than expected. This may lead to a repetition of the simulation with a higher upper range.

```
-------------------------------------------------------------------
NUMBER OF CUSTOMERS IN SYSTEM

mean     =        4.792, variance =     44.586, std dev =       6.677
sum of frequencies              = 1000
min val =        0.000    max val =     33.000

   0.00    314.41################################################################
   1.00     94.64##################
   2.00     99.95###################
   3.00     75.60##############
   4.00     64.49############
   5.00     55.94##########
   6.00     56.61##########
   7.00     41.51########
   8.00     34.58######
   9.00     22.93####
  10.00     15.44###
  11.00     13.22##
  12.00      9.10#
  13.00      7.49#
  14.00      5.09
  15.00      2.24
  16.00      4.66
  17.00      7.05#
  18.00      8.22#
  19.00      8.91#
over         57.91##########
-------------------------------------------------------------------
TOTAL WAITING TIME STATISTICS

mean     =        5.549, variance =     42.261, std dev =       6.501
sum of frequencies              = 1006
min val =        0.003    max val =     32.547

   0.00    112.00##################################################
   0.05     79.00###################################
   1.00     66.00#############################
   1.50     64.00############################
   2.00     60.00###########################
   2.50     59.00##########################
   3.00     61.00###########################
   3.50     59.00##########################
   4.00     45.00####################
   4.50     45.00####################
   5.00     37.00#################
   5.50     26.00###########
   6.00     26.00###########
   6.50     23.00##########
   7.00     30.00#############
   7.50     19.00########
   8.00     20.00#########
   8.50     19.00########
   9.00     13.00######
   9.50     10.00####
over        133.00############################################################
```

Figure 9.7 Example histogram output.

9.4.2 Cumulative frequency histograms

Cumulative histogram data is printed using the library function *print_cumulative()* which has the prototype

```
void print_cumulative ( FILE *fp, histogram *h, char *title );
```

The file pointer *fp* is any open file stream or device to which the data accumulated by histogram *h* will be printed with a first line banner of *title*, as for the *print_histogram()* function.

Example 9.2 An example of the sort of output that can be obtained is illustrated in Fig. 9.8. The cumulative histogram displayed is derived from the same source data as the frequency histograms in Fig. 9.7 so that the mean, variance and other statistical measures have the same value.

9.4.3 Tables
It is sometimes necessary to obtain histogram data in the form of tables, possibly to use in an alternative type of graph or for off-line analysis. Histogram data can be output in a tabular form using the *print_table()* library function which has the prototype

```
void print_table ( FILE *fp, histogram *h, char *title );
```

Tabular output consists of five columns of data. The columns are

- *Range.* This gives the interval to which the data values on a row belong.
- *Observed frequency.* This gives the value recorded for that interval.
- *Percentage of total.* This gives the percentage that the value in column 2 contributes to the total.
- *Cumulative percentage.* This gives the cumulative percentage of the total that this row and all rows above contribute to the total. The last row will always have a value of 100.0 in this column.
- *Cumulative remainder.* This gives the value of (100 − CUMULATIVE PERCENTAGE), giving a measure of the outstanding samples. The last row will always have a value of zero.

Also printed with the tabulated data are the mean, variance, standard deviation, sum of frequencies and maximum and minimum values as for the histogram output in Sec. 9.4.2. In addition, after the last row containing data has been printed, the message 'remaining frequencies all zero' is output if there are further class intervals that are empty.

Example 9.3 An example of the sort of output that can be obtained is illustrated in Fig. 9.9, which is the tabular equivalent of the frequency histograms in Fig. 9.7.

```
--------------------------------------------------------------------
NUMBER OF CUSTOMERS IN SYSTEM

mean     =      4.792, variance =     44.586, std dev =      6.677
sum of frequencies            = 1000
min val =       0.000   max val =     33.000

    0.00   314.41###################
    1.00   409.05#######################
    2.00   509.00##############################
    3.00   584.60#################################
    4.00   649.09#####################################
    5.00   705.03#########################################
    6.00   761.64############################################
    7.00   803.15###############################################
    8.00   837.73#################################################
    9.00   860.66###################################################
   10.00   876.10####################################################
   11.00   889.32#####################################################
   12.00   898.43######################################################
   13.00   905.92######################################################
   14.00   911.01#######################################################
   15.00   913.25#######################################################
   16.00   917.91#######################################################
   17.00   924.96########################################################
   18.00   933.18#########################################################
   19.00   942.09#########################################################
over      1000.00###########################################################
--------------------------------------------------------------------
WAITING TIME STATISTICS

mean     =      5.549, variance =     42.261, std dev =      6.501
sum of frequencies            = 1000
min val =       0.003   max val =     32.547

    0.00   112.00#####
    0.05   191.00##########
    1.00   257.00##############
    1.50   321.00##################
    2.00   381.00#####################
    2.50   440.00########################
    3.00   501.00###########################
    3.50   560.00###############################
    4.00   605.00#################################
    4.50   650.00###################################
    5.00   687.00#####################################
    5.50   713.00#######################################
    6.00   739.00########################################
    6.50   762.00##########################################
    7.00   792.00###########################################
    7.50   811.00############################################
    8.00   831.00#############################################
    8.50   850.00##############################################
    9.00   863.00###############################################
    9.50   873.00###############################################
over      1006.00##################################################
```

Figure 9.8 Example cumulative histogram output.

```
--------------------------------------------------------------------
NUMBER OF CUSTOMERS IN SYSTEM

mean     =     4.792, variance =     44.586, std dev =      6.677
sum of frequencies             = 1000
min val =       0.000   max val =    33.000
```

Range		observed value	per cent of total	cumulative percentage	cumulative remainder
0.00 ->	1.00	0.00	0.00	31.44	68.56
1.00 ->	2.00	314.41	31.44	40.90	59.10
2.00 ->	3.00	94.64	9.46	50.90	49.10
3.00 ->	4.00	99.95	10.00	58.46	41.54
4.00 ->	5.00	75.60	7.56	64.91	35.09
5.00 ->	6.00	64.49	6.45	70.50	29.50
6.00 ->	7.00	55.94	5.59	76.16	23.84
7.00 ->	8.00	56.61	5.66	80.32	19.68
8.00 ->	9.00	41.51	4.15	83.77	16.23
9.00 ->	10.00	34.58	3.46	86.07	13.93
10.00 ->	11.00	22.93	2.29	87.61	12.39
11.00 ->	12.00	15.44	1.54	88.93	11.07
12.00 ->	13.00	13.22	1.32	89.84	10.16
13.00 ->	14.00	9.10	0.91	90.59	9.41
14.00 ->	15.00	7.49	0.75	91.10	8.90
15.00 ->	16.00	5.09	0.51	91.32	8.68
16.00 ->	17.00	2.24	0.22	91.79	8.21
17.00 ->	18.00	4.66	0.47	92.50	7.50
18.00 ->	19.00	7.05	0.71	93.32	6.68
19.00 ->	20.00	8.22	0.82	94.21	5.79
21.00 ->		57.91	5.79	100.00	0.00

```
--------------------------------------------------------------------
WAITING TIME STATISTICS

mean     =     5.549, variance =     42.261, std dev =      6.501
sum of frequencies             = 1006
min val =       0.003   max val =    32.547
```

Range		observed value	per cent of total	cumlative percentage	cumlative remainder
0.00 ->	0.50	0.00	0.00	11.13	88.87
0.50 ->	1.00	112.00	11.13	18.99	81.01
1.00 ->	1.50	79.00	7.85	25.55	74.45
1.50 ->	2.00	66.00	6.56	31.91	68.09
2.00 ->	2.50	64.00	6.36	37.87	62.13
2.50 ->	3.00	60.00	5.96	43.74	56.26
3.00 ->	3.50	59.00	5.86	49.80	50.20
3.50 ->	4.00	61.00	6.06	55.67	44.33
4.00 ->	4.50	59.00	5.86	60.14	39.86
4.50 ->	5.00	45.00	4.47	64.61	35.39
5.00 ->	5.50	45.00	4.47	68.29	31.71
5.50 ->	6.00	37.00	3.68	70.87	29.13
6.00 ->	6.50	26.00	2.58	73.46	26.54
6.50 ->	7.00	26.00	2.58	75.75	24.25
7.00 ->	7.50	23.00	2.29	78.73	21.27
7.50 ->	8.00	30.00	2.98	80.62	19.38
8.00 ->	8.50	19.00	1.89	82.60	17.40
8.50 ->	9.00	20.00	1.99	84.49	15.51
9.00 ->	9.50	19.00	1.89	85.79	14.21
9.50 ->	10.00	13.00	1.29	86.78	13.22
10.50 ->		133.00	13.22	100.00	0.00

Figure 9.9 Example table output.

The table format gives us a convenient way of answering particular questions about the results obtained. The columns of figures headed 'Cumulative percentage' are useful for answering questions related to the number or percentage below a certain threshold. In this example it could be used to discover the probability of there being 7 or less customers in the system which we would find by reading the value for the row corresponding to the '6.00-> 7.00' class interval in the first table. This gives us a probability of around 0.76 (76 per cent). Or, if we wanted to know how many customers waited up to 4 seconds, we would read 56 per cent from the second table. The 'Cumulative remainder' permits the converse question to be answered simply. For example, if we asked 'How many waited longer than 4 seconds?' then we would look up the same row in the second table and read off 44 per cent.

9.4.4 Statistics summary

Output of summary information is achieved via the *print_summary()* library function which has the prototype

```
void print_summary ( FILE *fp, summary *s, char *title) ;
```

The output generated consists of the mean, variance and standard deviation as for histogram results. It also contains a count of the number of times *add_sdata()* was called—i.e. the number of samples taken. An additional value 'number of zero entries' gives the number of times the *add_sdata()* function was called with a sample value of zero.

Example 9.4 An example of the sort of output that can be obtained is illustrated in Fig. 9.10.

```
--------------------------------------------------------------------
NUMBER OF CUSTOMERS IN SYSTEM
mean =       1.109, variance =     2.458, std dev =     1.568
number of zero entries    = 49
total number of entries   = 101
--------------------------------------------------------------------
WAITING TIME STATISTICS
mean =       0.974, variance =     1.452, std dev =     1.205
number of zero entries    = 0
total number of entries   = 990
```

Figure 9.10 Example summary statistics output.

9.5 SUMMARY

It is often beneficial to present information from simulation runs in pictorial form such as histograms. There are three kinds of histogram supported by the simulation library:

- Unweighted frequency histograms add the data value to the total for the applicable class interval.
- Weighted frequency histograms scale the data value sampled by the length of time it has persisted.
- Time series histograms record the variation of data over time.

Histograms can be printed to files or physical devices such as printers in the form of a frequency histogram or as a cumulative frequency histogram and the same information can be output in a tabular form.

Another facility provided by the simulation library for data collection involves *summary* statistical information, which uses a smaller set of statistics. The benefit is that less memory space is taken up and it takes less time to process.

9.6 EXERCISES

9.1 Write a program to generate random numbers from the following distributions and output a plot of them in a suitable histogram.

Normal: with a mean of 3.5 and a standard deviation of 5.8.
Gamma: with $\alpha=0.3$ and $\beta=4.0$,
with $\alpha=3.3$ and $\beta=4.0$.
Binomial: with $n=35$ and $p=0.1$.
Poisson: with mean $= 4.2$.
Weibull: with $\theta=2.33$ and $\gamma=0.45$,
with $\theta=5.0$ and $\gamma=3.1$.

9.2 Simulate an office building with 10 floors (not including the ground floor) and three lifts during the peak morning period. Each lift can take up to six people. Employee inter-arrival time is exponentially distributed; the mean varies as shown in the following table which gives the hourly arrival rate as a function of time:

Period (mins)	0–15	15–30	30–45	45–60	60–75	75–∞
Rate (emp/hour)	100.0	200.0	300.0	220.0	140.0	50.0

Assume a total of 200 employees are uniformly distributed between the ten floors (nobody works on the ground floor). Assume also that the lift doors take 1 second to open or close, that the lift takes 1.2 seconds to move between floors and that it takes 0.4 seconds per person to enter the lift. Simulate this system during the peak morning period until all the employees have arrived and generate a histogram showing the waiting time for lifts.

9.3 The Aloha protocol was developed to allow several users to share a single data channel (see Tanenbaum, 1988). Each user is allowed to transmit at any time. Transmission takes $W = N/S$ seconds where N is the number of bits and S is the speed of the channel. By listening to the channel after the message has been sent a user can determine whether the transmission was successful. When two or more transmissions overlap a *collision* occurs, in which case the message is garbled and must be abandoned. If the worst case propagation delay is t seconds then a user must listen to the channel $T = 2t + W$ seconds after the start of the transmission of data to determine if the transmission was successful.

Simulate this protocol when used in a satellite system in which $t = 135$ milliseconds and $W = 50$ milliseconds. Present your results in terms of throughput (number of successful messages) against normalized offered load in which the number of messages is averaged over T seconds.

9.4 A barber shop with two barbers is open from 09:00 to 17:30. Customer arrival is exponentially distributed with a mean of 15 minutes from 09:00 to 14:00 and from 16:00 to 17:30. From 14:00 to 16:00 the mean decreases to 10 minutes. The length of time for a haircut is normally distributed with mean 25 minutes and standard deviation three minutes. The barbers take a lunch break from 12:00 to 13:00 and during this time new customers are turned away, but any existing customers are served. Model this system and generate a time-series histogram showing the number of customers waiting as a function of time.

9.5 A trunked radio system is a mobile radio system that assigns radio channels to mobile subscribers on a demand basis. It consists of a central control computer which sends messages on a control channel and a set of users equipped with mobile radio units. Each user is allocated to a group and users in a group can talk to each other but not to users outside of the group. A user who wishes to speak waits until no one else in the group is talking and then presses a Push To Talk (PTT) button that sends a data message to the central controller. The central controller responds immediately by allocating a free channel to the group if one is available, or by informing the requester that all channels are busy and refusing the request. The mobile units will not transmit if the control channel is busy, in which case the user gives up and tries again a time t_w later, where t_w is uniformly distributed between 60 and 600 seconds.

Two alternative control channel schemes are available. In scheme A, a high-speed (4800 bps) dedicated control channel is used. In scheme B, low speed (350 bps) signalling is used on one of the voice channels (i.e. a channel that can also be used for user communication). Assume the following:

- A 64-bit message must be sent to the central controller for each transmission request to obtain a channel assignment.
- A 32-bit reply message is returned, telling the group which channel to move to or else informing the group that no channel is yet available.
- A group consists of ten users.
- The duration of each transmission can be approximated by a normal distribution with mean 10 seconds and standard deviation 2 seconds.
- Individual users make transmission requests at intervals described by an exponential distribution with mean 10 minutes.

Evaluate the performance of the two systems operating with 2, 6 and 12 channels under various levels of traffic load. Vary the number of groups from 2 to 30 to obtain the different load levels.

9.6 The owner of the service station in Exercise 8.7 wants to get rid of the token system and allow drivers to use coins directly. Assume in this new arrangement that 80 per cent of all car wash customers have change and that 20 per cent must obtain change in which case the service time distributions for car wash customers apply (see Exercise 8.7). Simulate this new system and generate data in tabular form showing the waiting time for normal customers and for car wash customers.

9.7 Extend the data structures and functions related to *histograms* in the simulation library to print the third and fourth moments along with the other data from a set of samples. The third moment is given by

$$\frac{1}{n}\sum_{i=1}^{n}x_i^3 - \frac{3\bar{x}}{n}\sum_{i=1}^{n}x_i^2 + 2\bar{x}^3 \tag{9.7}$$

and the fourth moment is given by

$$\frac{1}{n}\sum_{i=1}^{n}x_i^4 - \frac{4\bar{x}}{n}\sum_{i=1}^{n}x_i^3 + \frac{6\bar{x}^2}{n}\sum_{i=1}^{n}x_i^2 - 3\bar{x}^4 \tag{9.8}$$

10

RESULTS ANALYSIS

After the results from a simulation model have been obtained we need to evaluate them and derive conclusions. This is the purpose of results analysis and the topic of this chapter. We start by discussing the general behaviour of simulation models and then look at some applicable statistical analysis techniques.

10.1 THE DYNAMIC BEHAVIOUR OF SIMULATION MODELS

Samples taken during a simulation run should be expected to fluctuate because of the stochastic nature of the model. In some models we may find wild fluctuations or fluctuations that increase with time, while in others we may find that fluctuations decrease with time. Such variations can be broadly classified into one of the three following categories of dynamic behaviour:

- *steady-state behaviour*, in which the average fluctuation tends to remain essentially constant
- *transient behaviour*, in which the average fluctuations do not settle down to a single value
- *regenerative behaviour*, which is cyclic.

In addition to the above categories we find that a model may either *terminate* or continue indefinitely. If the model *terminates*, then at some point the output variables will assume an idle value (possibly, but not necessarily, zero) and stay like that from then on. Alternatively the model may soldier on for as long as we care to run the simulation. This sort of behaviour is called *non-terminating*.

The main reason for making this distinction is that the analysis techniques that can be applied to the model outputs depend on which category of behaviour is involved. The distinction is made even more important by the fact that a model ordinarily displays several types of behaviour, so we must know when each type of behaviour starts or becomes dominant and adjust the treatment accordingly. We will now consider classes of behaviour in more detail.

10.1.1 Steady-state behaviour

In *steady-state behaviour* the probability distributions are *stationary*. This means that the characteristics of the distribution (mean, variance, etc.) remain constant. Hence the mean value of random variables can be expected to converge to a fixed value as the number of samples increases. Most (but not all) simulation models will be of interest to us only in the steady state. The onset of the steady state, though, will not be a sudden system-wide phenomenon. What normally happens is that transient behaviour ripples through the system from the source of a disturbance and gradually dies away. This is the case with the class of systems known as *queuing systems*. A queuing system consists of a network of interconnected queues, and each queue has its own local transient and steady-state behaviour. Therefore, the system as a whole attains steady state only when all the queues in the system are in the steady state.

When samples in the steady state are displayed in a times-series fashion they often resemble the graph illustrated in Fig. 10.1. In this graph the response is shown as a jagged line which is approximately horizontal, indicating that the mean value averaged over the many small perturbations will be essentially constant.

Steady-state behaviour is normally considered to last indefinitely. However, a system will sometimes display steady-state behaviour between transient phases. In this case, each new steady state may exist at a different level and be of dissimilar duration to previous steady states.

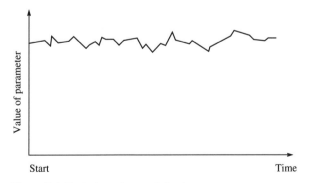

Figure 10.1 Typical steady-state behaviour.

Sampling in the steady state Suppose that $\{x_1, x_2, ..., x_n\}$ is a set of n independent samples taken in the steady state from a probability distribution with a mean μ and variance σ^2. The sample mean of the set, namely $\bar{x}$, can be calculated using Eq. (5.9). In the parlance of estimation theory we say that $\bar{x}$ is an *unbiased estimate* of μ, the true mean of the distribution from which the samples are drawn. An unbiased estimate is one that can be relied upon to get closer and closer to the true value as more samples are taken. So, in the long run, $\bar{x}$ should get closer to μ.

Suppose that a second set of samples is taken from the same distribution and that their mean $\bar{x}$ is calculated. This mean will be similar to the mean from the previous set because the samples are drawn from the same distribution, but it is unlikely to be the same. In fact, because the samples are independent, the second set of samples is totally unaffected by whatever samples have been chosen for the first set. If this process is repeated several times, then we obtain a set of means, each of which has been derived from a different set of samples. This set of means looks, to all intents and purposes, like a set of random values, and so has a distribution which is called the *sampling distribution for the mean*.

Using Eq. (5.13) the variance of the set of sample means can be calculated. As the number of sample means in the set increases, the mean of the sample means becomes closer and closer to the true mean. It should be expected, then, that the variance of the sample means decreases as the number of them increases. This seems intuitively reasonable because the mean of the sample means $\bar{\bar{x}}$ is becoming closer and closer to the actual population mean μ and so the 'uncertainty' of $\bar{\bar{x}}$ as expressed by the standard deviation or variance must be decreasing.

This behaviour of sampling distributions, illustrated in Fig. 10.2, is a mathematically provable fact. What is also mathematically verifiable is that any set of sample means $\{\bar{x}_j\}$, each of which is calculated from a different set of samples from a fixed, but arbitrary, probability distribution, behaves as if it were based on samples from the same probability distribution. This somewhat surprising result is *completely independent of the distribution of the original population*, it is a fundamental rule of mathematical statistics known as the *central limit theorem*, which can be stated as:

Theorem 10.1 (The central limit theorem). If a random sample of size n taken in the steady state is drawn from a population with fixed mean μ and variance σ^2, then the sample mean $\bar{x}$ has approximately a normal distribution with mean μ and variance σ^2/n.

From theorem 10.1 the distribution function of $(\bar{x} - \mu)/(\sigma/\sqrt{n})$ is approximately a standard normal distribution. The approximation gets better as the sample size increases.

We can perform a similar exercise for the variance. We obtain a set of sample

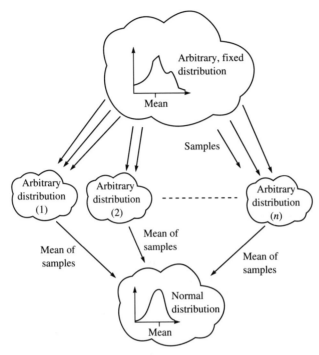

Figure 10.2 The central limit theorem.

variances s_i^2, where each variance has been calculated from a different sample set. The mean of these variances should get closer to the true population variance as more sample variances are included. However, the variance of random samples tends to have less variability than the distribution they come from. This should not be surprising since a few samples from a distribution will not exhibit the extreme values of the distribution. Instead of using Eq. (5.13) then, in order to estimate the value of the variance, it is better to use a larger value which is obtained by reducing the denominator by 1 to give

$$s^2 = \frac{1}{n-1} \sum_{i=1}^{n} (x_i - \bar{x})^2 \tag{10.1}$$

Now s^2 is an unbiased estimate of σ^2. The set of these estimates exhibits a *sampling distribution for the variance* and its own variance decreases as more sample variances are added to it.

10.1.2 Transient behaviour

In *transient behaviour* the probability distributions are not stationary, so we find

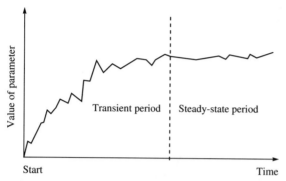

Figure 10.3 Typical transient behaviour.

divergence from, not convergence to, a mean value. Transient behaviour can be thought of as a reaction by the system to being 'kicked' which typically manifests itself as extreme fluctuations in the magnitude of the samples taken.

As a rule transient states do not exist permanently in a model because, more often than not, they are unstable. Instead they gradually die away and leave stable steady-state conditions. However, there are some notable exceptions to this rule. A model of a nation's economy, for instance, is unlikely to exhibit any long-term, steady-state behaviour.

Transient behaviour in the form of an *initial transient* is nearly always present when a simulation starts. As was remarked earlier, we may also see transient behaviour when some sudden change takes place while the system is running, which will eventually give rise to a new steady state. An instance of this latter sort of behaviour is exhibited by a fault-tolerant communications network in which, immediately after the detection of the failure, an initial transient period consisting of reconfiguration takes place. This is then followed by a new steady state in the fall-back mode.

Typical transient behaviour is illustrated in Fig. 10.3. It consists of erratic variations that gradually die down in magnitude, leaving the system in a (possibly new) steady state.

10.1.3 Regenerative behaviour

Behaviour is said to be *regenerative* if there exists a particular system state, called a *regenerative state*, such that whenever the system returns to that state the past history of states of the system has no influence on the future of the system. The point at which the system returns to the regenerative state is called a *regenerative* or *renewal point*, and the time between the kth and $(k+1)$th renewal point is called the kth *cycle*. If the time between renewal points is always finite, then observations made in one cycle are independent of observations made in any other.

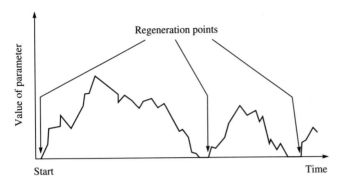

Figure 10.4 Typical regenerative behaviour.

Regenerative behaviour is illustrated in Fig. 10.4. Repeating cycles are seen to start at regeneration points where the system parameter is zero, although this is not a general requirement.

A queuing system can be thought of as a regenerative system if the regeneration points are defined as those instants when there are no customers in the waiting line and none being served. Clearly, at this time, the past history of the system has no effect on its future behaviour. In general, regenerative behaviour may be visible when a microscopic view is taken of a system which is ostensibly in the steady state. For, as we have just remarked, a queuing system which is less than 100 per cent utilized will have a steady state, yet it can also be considered regenerative.

10.1.4 Terminating and non-terminating simulations

Each of the above types of behaviour can exist in terminating and non-terminating modes. A *terminating* system can be thought of as a special case of a system displaying regenerative behaviour, in which the life of the system consists of a finite number of cycles. Typically, each cycle consists of an initial transient period possibly followed by a steady-state period of finite duration and then followed by another transient period in which the system returns to the regenerative state. Ultimately, however, the system assumes a completely dormant state from which it never recovers.

A *non-terminating* system continues indefinitely and the long-term behaviour is usually steady state and therefore predictable. Even so, we may not be able to treat the short-term behaviour as steady state. It could, instead, continuously oscillate between a number of states. Such a system is the subject of the case study in Chapter 12. In this system, over the short term, mean values do not converge. Instead, there appears to be a permanent transient state. However, the transient state is cyclic and when viewed over the long term, averaged over many cycles, we obtain converging mean values.

10.2 TRANSIENT EFFECTS

Transient effects can mislead the analyst looking for long-term, steady-state conditions because the system behaviour is quite different during transient and steady-state periods. If steady-state behaviour is sought, then ignoring the effect of the initial system transient introduces a bias to the simulation results. Eliminating this bias is essential if the steady-state results are to be accepted as accurate. This can be done in one of two ways:

1. *Ignore the transient phase.* In this approach we commence the simulation properly when the steady state is detected, which implies that the end of the transient state can be detected. At this point, all results that have been collected so far are discarded, but the model itself is otherwise unchanged. The steady state can be assumed to start from here and subsequent results kept. The main drawback of this strategy is that it takes time and computer resources to reach the steady state, and these resources do not directly contribute to the results.

2. *Pre-load a steady state.* In this approach the simulation starts off in a state that approximates to the steady state. This has the advantage that it does not significantly worsen the running time. On the negative side it introduces correlation which may add bias. Also, the assignment of a reasonable steady state can be quite difficult to do. In effect it requires a detailed knowledge of the system which may not always be available. One efficient method of assigning an initial state is to use the output of the previous run as the starting conditions for the next run by splitting one long run into a series of shorter subruns connected back to back. Another possibility is to take measurements from the real-world system, when feasible, and use these as the starting conditions in the model.

10.3 DETECTION OF THE STEADY STATE

Since, in most simulations, it is steady-state behaviour that is of interest, it is obviously important, from the point of view of efficiency, that its onset is detected as soon as possible. Underestimating the duration of the transient phase introduces unnecessary error, but being too conservative extends the running time more than is necessary. An initial series of runs should therefore be conducted to estimate the length of the transient phase. Methods for doing this are described later.

Measurements must be carefully made if a reliable estimate of the transient duration is to be obtained. For those models that consist of a network of queues, for example, the transient phase will be evident longer for those queues at the end of the network. Hence, if a system contains three queues *A*, *B* and *C* in tandem, such that queue *A* feeds queue *B*, the output of which feeds queue *C*, then it should be queue *C* that is monitored for the steady state, not queue *A* or *B*. Additional complexity is added because the transient duration varies with each set of model parameters. Generally, as the utilization and throughput increases, the length of the transient phase increases. Either the worst case (which maximizes utilization) should be evaluated or else separate evaluations must be done with each set of parameter values.

The duration of the transient phase can be specified in one of two ways. Either it can be specified in terms of simulated time or else it can be specified in terms of the number of samples to be taken. If the former method is adopted then we know, before the simulation has started, how long the transient phase will be, and we can therefore use the model structure given in Chapter 4. If, however, the latter method is used, then in our model we need to count the number of samples and terminate the simulation in preparation for data collection when the limit, that is the number of samples expected until the steady state, has been reached. This would require the following outline changes to the template already presented:

```
#define A_VERY_LONG_TIME      999999999.0

int    in_transient_phase         = 1;
int    num_results         = 0;
int    num_to_ss;
:
:
/* Initialize the simulation. */
void init ( )
{

        /* Initialize num_to_ss to be the number of samples */
        /* until the steady state phase */
        num_to_ss = ...;
        :
        run_sim (A_VERY_LONG_TIME, termination_count);
        reset_results();
        :

}


:
void some_event ( )
{
```

```
         :
      record_some_result ( .... );
      if (in_transient_phase)
      {
          if (num_results < num_to_ss) {
              num_results++;
          else {
              in_transient_phase = 0;
              quit();
          }
      }
         :
  }
      :
```

As can be seen, this latter approach confuses the model structure but it has the benefit that it is easier to obtain the estimate in the first place.

We will look at two techniques for obtaining estimates of transient duration. The first monitors the standard deviation of the sample mean and the second calculates a moving average. The techniques will be demonstrated with some example models that measure the duration in terms of the number of samples taken. However, it is quite easy to translate the principles so that they work with simulated time and we will see an example of this in the case study in Chapter 12.

10.3.1 Monitoring the standard deviation of the sample mean

Based on the central limit theorem the distribution of the sample mean follows a normal distribution with mean value μ and standard deviation $s = \sigma/\sqrt{n}$ where μ and σ are the true mean and standard deviation of the distribution being sampled from. Since the central limit theorem applies only when the distribution is stationary, it can be used to test for the onset of the steady state. This is done by plotting a graph of the logarithm of the standard deviation against the logarithm of n. If the standard deviation for the population distribution σ has logarithm equal to k ($k = log(\sigma)$) then the linear relationship $log(s) = -0.5*log(n) + k$ exists between s and n. Hence the graph will show an overall decrease with a slope of about -0.5. The assumption we make here of course is that there are enough samples to make the distribution for the sample mean close to a normal distribution. This is generally accepted as requiring at least 30 samples. We should be conservative and obtain at least 50.

Several runs must be made to apply this method. Starting from the idle state, a suitable statistic such as the total time that a customer spends in the system must be recorded. Each run must also be statistically independent, so random number streams must be seeded with different initial values. Assume that m runs are made and that a run is indexed by j where $1 \leqslant j \leqslant m$. Within each run assume that the samples are indexed by i and that there are the same number n in each run, so that $1 \leqslant i \leqslant n$. We end up with the following set of samples $\{x_{ij}\}$

run 1	run 2	...	run m		mean
x_{11}	x_{12}	...	x_{1m}	$=>$	y_1
x_{21}	x_{22}	...	x_{2m}	$=>$	y_2
$\vdots$	$\vdots$		$\vdots$		$\vdots$
$\vdots$	$\vdots$		$\vdots$		$\vdots$
x_{n1}	x_{n2}	...	x_{nm}	$=>$	y_n

If the value of m is large enough the set of samples y_i, where

$$y_i = \frac{1}{m} \sum_{j=1}^{m} x_{ij} \tag{10.2}$$

are independent normally distributed random variables, in which case the standard deviation s_n can be calculated as a function of n, the number of samples made, using (10.1):

$$s_n = \sqrt{\frac{1}{n-1} \sum_{i=1}^{n} (y_i - \bar{x}_n)^2} \tag{10.3}$$

Which, using the simplification introduced in Chapter 5, Eq. (5.13), becomes

$$s_n = \sqrt{\frac{1}{n-1} \left(\sum_{i=1}^{n} y_i^2 - n\bar{x}_n^2 \right)} \tag{10.4}$$

where $\bar{x}_n$ is the overall mean (i.e. the means of the mean y_i). With this expression we can construct the required graph of $\log(s_n)$ against $\log(n)$.

Let us see how this technique can be applied by considering the simple queue introduced in Example 3.2. The program code in Listing 10.1 implements this method for the queue and generates the necessary graph data. The simulation is repeated several times for each utilization factor and each run results in $num\_samples$ (i.e. n) samples being made. The $step\_size$ parameter defines how many samples are skipped before a value of x_{ij} is recorded. This is necessitated by the volume of data. Command line parameters establish the number of runs, the number of samples per run, the utilization factor and the step size.

The listing shows a process-oriented model of the simple queue, with the test statistic printed at the end of all the runs. In general, it is not necessary to record all the output data (i.e. take samples of all the output variables), we can just concentrate on the one being used to generate the test standard deviations. This reduces the running time. At the end of each individual run the model is reset to the idle state by resetting the random number streams, resources and queues, removing all scheduled and conditional entities, and resetting the clock. The model is then in the same state as when first activated. Most of this initialization is done with a single call to *clear_sim( )*. In addition, the sample index *this_sample* must be reset to 0 and the initial set of new scheduled and conditional entities must be added. The simulation is then set to run until it collects all *num_samples* samples. The end of a run is detected by the *if* statement at the end of function *customer( )* and a call to the library function *quit( )* prematurely aborts the run before the scheduled completion time.

The statistics collected are added to the array *sumx[ ]*. After run *j*, the value of *sumx[i]* is the sum of the *i*th sample from the previous *j* runs. At the end of the last run the logarithm of the standard deviation is calculated as a function of the number of samples and printed out.

```c
#include <stdio.h>
#include <stdlib.h>
#include <string.h>
#include <math.h>
#include "sim_lib.h"
#include "resource.h"
#include "random.h"

#define    ARRIVAL    0
#define    DEPARTURE  1

queue      *q1;
stream     *rs1;
resource   *checkout;
int        seed;
float      util, *sumx, running_square, running_total;
unsigned   int      num_samples, num_runs;

unsigned   int      this_run, this_sample, skip;
extern     entity *current ;
extern     int running, active ;
extern     float clock ;

void       collect_data ( float x );
float      variance ( int i );
void       init ( void ) ;
void       clear ( void ) ;
void       customer ( void ) ;
void       add_entities ();
void       server ( void ) ;
void       print_results ( void ) ;

main( int argc, char *argv[] )
{
```

```
    if (argc != 5)
    {
        printf("%s: [utilization] [skip] [num_samples]
                    [num_runs]",argv[0]);
        exit(0);

    }
    util        = atof(argv[1]);  /* Utilization for queue */
    skip        = atoi(argv[2]);  /* Calc std-dev every skip samples */

    num_samples = atoi(argv[3]);
    /* Need at least two samples! */
    if (num_samples < 2)
    {
        printf("Too few samples \n");
         exit(0);
    }

    num_runs = atoi(argv[4]);
    /* Need at least two runs! */
    if (num_runs < 2)
    {
        printf("Too few runs \n");
        exit(0);
    }
    init();
    while (this_run < num_runs )
    {
        /* run will be stoped when we have num_samples samples */
        run_sim ( 999999.0, 0);
        this_run++;
        clear ();
        printf("Completed run %d \n",this_run);
    }
    print_results();
}

void init()
{
    int n;
    float w;

    init_sim ();
    q1 = make_queue();
    checkout = make_resource ( 1.0 );
    add_entities ();
    sumx = (float *)malloc(size of(float )*num_samples);
    for(n = 0;n < num_samples;n++)
        sumx[n] =  0.0;
    running_total = 0.0;
    running_square = 0.0;
```

```
          this_run    = 0;
          this_sample = 0;
          rs1 = make_stream(this_run+1,0);
    }


    /* Reset simulation to the state on invocation */
    void clear ()
    {
          clear_sim ();
          reset_resource ( checkout );
          clear_queue ( q1 );
          /* Seed each run differently */
          reset_stream ( rs1, this_run+1 );
          add_entities ();
          this_sample = 0;
    }


    /* Pre load entities into simulation */
    void add_entities ()
    {
          make_scheduled_entity(customer , (void *)0 , 0.0 , 0 , 0, 1, NULL);
          make_conditional_entity ( server , (void *)0 , 0 , 0, NULL);
    }


    void customer()
    {
          switch ( PHASE_OF(current) )

          {
          case ARRIVAL:
                make_scheduled_entity(customer, (void *)0, exponential(rs1), 0,
                                         0, 1, NULL);
                stamp_current();
                append ( q1 , current );
                break;
          case DEPARTURE:
                collect_data(TIME_SPENT(current));
                release(checkout , 1.0);
                terminate ( current );
                break;
          }
          /* Terminate simulation when we have enough samples */
          if (this_sample >= num_samples)
                quit();
    }


    /* Collect the sums of sample from each run */
    void collect_data ( float x )
    {
          sumx[this_sample] += x;           /* The running sum of samples */
          this_sample++;                    /* Increment index for next sample */
```

```
}

void server ()
{
      entity *sr;

      /* Get waiting customers and serve them */
      while ( !QEMPTY ( q1 ) && IS_AVAILABLE ( checkout , 1.0 ) )
      {
            sr = remove_front( q1 );
            acquire ( checkout, 1.0);
            sr->phase = DEPARTURE;
            schedule ( sr, util*exponential (rs1));
      }
}

/* Print the variation in standard deviation */
void print_results ()
{
      static float oldlogn, oldlogstdd;
      static int   first_time = 1;
      float  logn, logstdd;
      int    i;
      for (i = 0;i < num_samples;i += skip) {
            sumx[i] = sumx[i]/num_runs;          /* Get average */
            running_total  += sumx[i];
            running_square += (sumx[i]*sumx[i]); /* sum of squares */
            logn    = log((float )(i+1));        /* log(num samples) */
            logstdd = 0.5*log(variance(i));      /* log(standard deviation)*/
            if (first_time) {
                  first_time = 0;
                  printf(" \nLOG N    LOG STD    SLOPE \n");
                  printf("%f   %f \n",logn,logstdd);
            }
            else {
            printf("%f   %f   %f \n",
            logn,logstdd,(logstdd-oldlogstdd)/(logn-oldlogn));
            }
         oldlogn    = logn;
         oldlogstdd = logstdd;
      }
   }
}

float variance (int i)
{
      float mean;

      if (i > 0) {
```

```
        mean = running_total/(float)(i+1);
        /* running_total equals (i+1)*mean */
        return ((running_square—mean*running_total)/(float)i);
    }
    else return 0.0001;        /* some arbitray low value */
}
```

Listing 10.1 Determination of the steady state for the simple queue using the standard deviation.

The graph generated by the output of the above program is shown in Fig. 10.5 for utilization factors of 0.4 and 0.6. It can be seen from the graph that the slope is initially positive, but that it eventually changes sign. In the utilization $= 0.4$ case the change in sign of the slope of the graph is quite marked, but in the utilization $= 0.6$ the change from a positive slope to a negative slope is more gradual. The higher utilization case also demonstrates the general rule that the higher the utilization the longer it will take to establish steady-state conditions.

From the graph we can estimate that for a utilization factor of 0.4 the steady state occurs when $\log(n) = 2.83$, which gives the number of samples as $e^{2.83}$ or 17 and for a utilization factor of 0.6 we have steady state after $e^{4.88}$ or 132 samples.

10.3.2 Moving average

The second common method of detecting the steady state is the use of *moving averages*. Moving averages are samples averaged over the last n values. As each new sample is included the oldest is dropped, thus keeping the number of observations making up the sample constant. In the steady state the sample

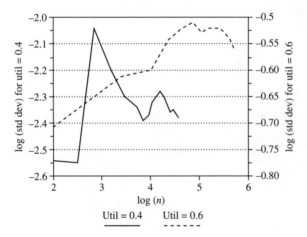

Figure 10.5 Graph of standard deviation against sample index.

distribution should be stationary and therefore the average value should fluctuate less and less. The point at which the levelling off occurs suggests where the steady-state phase starts.

A method of implementing this approach uses a ring buffer. A ring buffer can be implemented by an array which is indexed by an incrementing value i modulo the size of the buffer. If the buffer is n units long, adding a value to the $(m.n+k)$th element modulo n is equivalent to adding to the kth for any value of k less than n since $k=k+n.m$ (mod n). The reason that such a data structure is useful in this instance is that it is necessary to deduct the effect of the oldest sample and add the effect of the newest sample in its place to get the moving average.

The following example function *add( )* takes a sample and adds it to the current moving average using a ring buffer:

```
void add ( float x )
{
        unsigned int index;

        index = this_sample % sample_size;
        mov_avg -= buffer[index];
        buffer[index] = x/sample_size;
        mov_avg += buffer[index];
        this_sample++;
}
```

We first of all subtract the oldest sample from the moving average. This is then overwritten with the new sample being recorded divided by the sample size. Dividing by the sample size allows the moving average to be updated by simply adding the new sample.

An alternative approach records all the samples first and when the simulation has finished works out the moving averages. This algorithm is expressed in Listing 10.2, which again uses the model of the simple queue to illustrate the approach.

```
#include <stdio.h>
#include <stdlib.h>
#include <string.h>
#include <math.h>

#include "sim_lib.h"
#include "resource.h"
#include "random.h"
#define    ARRIVAL    0
#define    DEPARTURE 1

queue      *q1;
stream     *rsl;
resource   *checkout;
```

```
int       seed;
float     util, *sumx, *buffer;
unsigned int    num_samples, num_runs, skip;
unsigned int    this_run, this_sample, sample_size;

extern    entity *current ;
extern    int running, active ;
extern    float clock ;

void      collect_data ( float x );
void      init ( void ) ;
void      clear ( void ) ;
void      customer ( void ) ;
void      add_entities ();
void      server ( void ) ;
void      print_results ( void ) ;

main( int argc, char *argv[] )
{
     if (argc != 6)
     {
         printf("smplq_pi [utilization] [sample_size] [skip]
                   [num_samples] [num_runs]");
         exit(0);
     }

     util        = atof(argv[1]);
     sample_size = atoi(argv[2]);
     skip        = atoi(argv[3]);
     num_samples = atoi(argv[4]);
     /* Make sure we have enough samples */
     if (num_samples < 2)

     {
         printf("Too few samples \n");
         exit(0);
     }

     /* Make sure we have enough samples */
     num_runs   = atoi(argv[5]);
     if (num_runs < 2)
     {
         printf("Too few runs \n");
         exit(0);
     }
     init();
     while (this_run < num_runs ) {
         run_sim ( 999999.0, 0);
         this_run++;
         clear ();
```

```
            printf("Completed run %d\n",this_run);
        }
        print_results();
}

void init()
{
        int n;
        float w;

        init_sim ();
        ql = make_queue();
        checkout = make_resource ( 1.0 );
        add_entities ();
        sumx = (float *)malloc(sizeof(float )*num_samples);
        buffer= (float *)malloc(sizeof(float )*sample_size);
        for(n = 0;n < num_samples;n++) {
            sumx[n] = 0.0;
        }
        for(n = 0;n < sample_size;n++) {
            buffer[n] = 0.0;
        }
        this_run    = 0;
        this_sample = 0;
        rs1 = make_stream(this_run+1,0);
}
      :
!!! SAME AS LISTING 10.1 !!!
      :

void print_results ()
{
        int   first_time = 1;
        float mov_avg;
        int   i;

        for (this_sample = 0; this_sample < num_samples;this_sample += skip)
        {
            i = this_sample % sample_size;
            mov_avg -= buffer[i];
            buffer[i] = sumx[this_sample]/num_runs/sample_size;
            mov_avg += buffer[i];
            if (first_time) {
                first_time = 0;
                printf("N          MEAN\n");
            }
            printf("%-6d %f\n",this_sample+1,mov_avg);
        }
}
```

Listing 10.2 Determination of the steady state for the simple queue using moving averages.

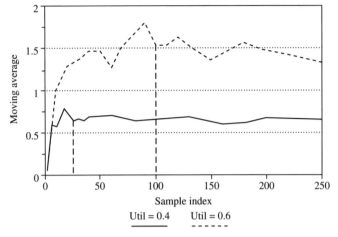

Figure 10.6 Graph of moving average against sample index.

Listing 10.2 illustrates some additional considerations which are necessary as a result of repeating the runs. Between each run we reset the simulation with *clear( )* so as to give a new initial transient condition. Then at the end of each run, with the results accumulated in the array *sumx[ ]*, the moving average is generated and the results printed.

The results of this technique, generated from the program in listing 10.2, are displayed in the graph of Fig. 10.6. Two levels of utilization were investigated, 0.4 and 0.6. The results were averaged over 50 runs, with a moving average consisting of 5 samples when utilization was 0.4 and 10 samples when utilization was 0.6. In both cases the moving average can be seen to increase from a value near zero and then, after some erratic changes in magnitude, settle down to more modest fluctuations. A figure of 20 samples when the utilization factor is 0.4 and 100 samples when the utilization factor is 0.6 seem reasonable estimates for the duration of the transient phase based on this evidence.

The above results for the same system and operating conditions show a difference of around 30 per cent between the two approaches. Part of the reason for this discrepancy is that the assessment is subjective and based on a graph of the numerical results. It is prudent, therefore, to include a good safety margin of, say, 50 per cent when the transient duration is estimated.

10.4 ESTIMATING ACCURACY

An important feature of statistical methods is that they never permit anything to be *proved*. What statistics can do, however, is provide a value for the likelihood of error in any statement or the confidence that can be placed in any measured value. After some consideration, this should seem entirely reasonable. There is no *proof*, for instance, that the sun will rise tomorrow morning. However, since this has happened at least since the beginning of recorded history and knowing something of the physics involved, we are content to believe that such will be the outcome. Similarly for the simulator, statistics will not allow absolute proof to be established concerning the results of a simulation. There will always be some residual degree of doubt about reliability. However, the application of statistical methods permits the likelihood of error to be determined and the degree of trust to be quantified. For example, if it is necessary to show the existence or not of some behaviour, it is possible to estimate just how frequently or infrequently such results would arise based solely on the existence of chance fluctuations. We can then use this to justify our belief that the particular behaviour is or is not present.

More frequently, not only is the presence of certain behaviour of interest but also the degree of its effect. Here again statistics will help in assessing the accuracy of the results. Not only can the size of the effect be estimated but it is possible to find limits within which the true value is almost certain to lie. None the less, it is still not possible to specify the range of values within which the effect will *definitely* lie, except by including all possible values. Instead we must be content with specifying a range of values within which the true value will lie with some fixed, high degree of probability.

Significance testing is the name commonly given to the determination of this experimental error. The significance test procedure gives the probability that the hypothesis under test will be rejected even if it is correct. The hypothesis under test is called the *null hypothesis* and denoted by H_0. Any other hypothesis is called the *alternative hypothesis* and denoted by H_1. For example, the null hypothesis could be that the true mean of some distribution is the estimated mean $\bar{x}$ and the alternative hypothesis that the true mean is significantly different from $\bar{x}$.

In practice, deciding exactly what constitutes the null hypothesis can be difficult. The main point is that the null hypothesis must be assumed to be true until proved otherwise by evidence. Hence, the analysis focuses on deviations from the null hypothesis rather than the alternative hypothesis.

To perform significance testing all possible results must be considered and divided into two sets, the accept set and the reject set. Those in the accept set are considered to support the null hypothesis, those in the reject set do not seem to support the null hypothesis and lead us to reject it. The probability of obtaining a result in the reject set when the null hypothesis is true is equal to some small pre-assigned value, normally shown as α. The value of α is called the *level of significance*. The value of $1 - \alpha$ is termed the *level of confidence*.

It should be obvious that, to be useful, the level of significance must be low. Typical values are 5 per cent and 1 per cent. The smaller the level of significance, the more confidence we can have that the null hypothesis is actually false when we reject it. Making the level of significance too small, however, increases the time necessary to run a simulation model and makes it more difficult to reject the null hypothesis when it is actually false.

It is important to realize that stating a level of confidence for some statistics such as the mean requires that measurements are taken in the steady state since the distributions must be stationary for the confidence interval to make sense. Hence, in the following analysis we deal with samples where observations in the initial transient phase have been removed.

10.4.1 One-tailed and two-tailed tests

We saw in the previous section that significance testing looks for statistical evidence to reject the null hypothesis. The set of results which allows us to reject the null hypothesis is called the *rejection region*. The significance test selected determines the particular rejection region. For maximum efficiency the test must be as powerful as possible, that is to say it must be able to reject the null hypothesis when it is false subject to some fixed, low probability α of rejecting it when it is true.

Normally there are several alternative hypotheses, and a particular test may be more powerful than a substitute test over one range of alternative hypotheses but not necessarily over another. A one-sided range of alternative hypotheses favours a *one-tailed test*, which considers departures from the null hypothesis in only one direction. If, however, alternative hypotheses are two-sided, then a *two-tailed test*, which considers departures in both directions, is appropriate.

Example 10.1 A simulation is conducted to estimate the mean utilization of a certain resource. The estimate obtained for the mean is 5.3. The null hypothesis is therefore

$$H_0 : \mu = 5.3$$

and one alternative hypothesis is

$$H_1 : \mu \neq 5.3$$

But if, somehow, it is known for sure that the sample mean cannot possibly be more than the true mean then a different alternative hypothesis may be employed:

$$H_1 : \mu > 5.3$$

which allows a smaller bound to be placed on the possible values of μ.

10.4.2 Confidence interval of mean

We can use the fact that the form of a sampling distribution is known in order to establish the band of values within which the true mean or standard deviation is likely to lie. The situation can be pictured as shown in Fig. 10.7, which depicts some distributions of the sample mean from which the true mean of a rather awkward-looking population distribution is estimated.

The figure shows that the more spread out the distribution the less reliably it predicts the mean. It is the variance or standard deviation that measures the 'spread' of a distribution and so these quantities should make good indicators of the probable error in estimation. We can say that the lower the variance or standard deviation, the more accurately the sample mean can be expected to predict the true mean. The literature also sometimes refers to a *standard error* as a measure of the relative accuracy of an estimation of a mean value. In fact this is just another name for the standard deviation, which emphasizes its use in this role.

In the following sections two variants of this form of analysis are considered in more detail. In the first, the source distribution has a known variance and in the second the variance is unknown and so has to be estimated from the samples.

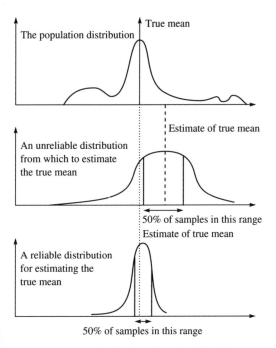

Figure 10.7 Some distributions for estimating the mean.

Known variance Suppose we are interested in estimating the population mean μ. We select *independent* samples $\{x_1, x_2, ..., x_n\}$ and calculate $\bar{x}$ as an estimator of μ using Eq. (5.9). If n is large, say greater than 30, and there is a *known* finite variance σ^2, then $\bar{x}$ has approximately a normal distribution with mean μ and variance

$$\bar{\sigma}^2 = \frac{\sigma^2}{n} \tag{10.5}$$

so that the sample z generated from

$$\frac{\bar{x} - \mu}{\sigma/\sqrt{n}} \tag{10.6}$$

is normally distributed with mean 0 and standard deviation 1. A table for the integral of this function $f(z)$, known as the *standard normal*, is given in Appendix C. The table gives us the value of the integral from 0 to v, as illustrated in Fig. 10.8 with a level of significance of 5 per cent.

In practice, two-tailed tests are normally used because we typically want to establish a *band* of values both above and below the sample mean within which the true mean lies. We can hypothesize that μ lies within this band with a stated level of confidence $1 - \alpha$, and so we are looking for the value v along the x-axis at which the integral from $-v$ to $+v$ is $1 - \alpha$, as shown in Fig. 10.9.

From the tables we can find for the level of significance α a value $z_{\alpha/2}$ (i.e. $v = \alpha/2$) such that

$$P[-z_{\alpha/2} \leqslant Z \leqslant z_{\alpha/2}] = 1 - \alpha \tag{10.7}$$

By substituting (10.6) into (10.7), after a little rearranging we get

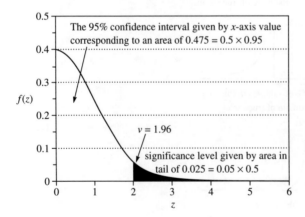

Figure 10.8 The standard normal distribution.

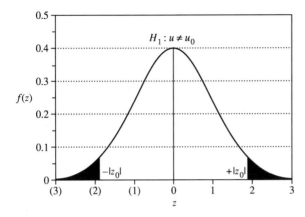

Figure 10.9 A two-tailed test of significance.

$$1 - \alpha = P\left[-z_{\alpha/} \leqslant \frac{\bar{x} - \mu}{\sigma/\sqrt{n}} \leqslant z_{\alpha/2} \right]$$

$$= P\left[\bar{x} - z_{\alpha/2}\frac{\sigma}{\sqrt{n}} \leqslant \mu \leqslant \bar{x} + z_{\alpha/2}\frac{\sigma}{\sqrt{n}} \right] \tag{10.8}$$

and so the approximate *large sample confidence interval* for μ with confidence level $1 - \alpha$ is

$$\bar{x} \pm \frac{\sigma}{\sqrt{n}} z_{\alpha/2} \tag{10.9}$$

which is valid for any stationary probability distribution provided we take enough samples (say greater than 30) and the variance is known. It is also valid if the distribution we are sampling from is normally distributed and the variance is known, in which case we can relax the requirement that n is large since the interval given by (10.9) is then valid for any $n > 0$.

Obviously, we want to make the estimate as accurate as possible and so the $1 - \alpha$ confidence levels should be close to 1.0. Typical values are 0.99, 0.95 and 0.90, which equate to confidence intervals of $\bar{x} \pm 2.58\sigma/\sqrt{n}$, $\bar{x} \pm 1.96\sigma/\sqrt{n}$ and $\bar{x} \pm 1.64\sigma/\sqrt{n}$ respectively. Notice how the interval decreases as the level of confidence decreases. In effect we are saying that with a smaller interval we are less sure that the true mean actually lies within it.

Example 10.2 A simulation was performed to estimate the mean waiting time of requests to obtain access to a computer system resource, for which the variance

Table 10.1 Means of waiting time

1.293642	5.209084	3.281298	10.696447	0.117547	3.442843	1.100627
5.113029	8.795870	0.735100	2.451475	0.332223	1.965079	2.359324
4.421183	4.966392	16.057766	14.386731	2.310999	1.009865	5.072875
4.324078	6.788266	15.455770	4.831755	7.110760	1.851678	2.847445
4.017943	11.436593	2.842126	3.129228	1.857041	2.253068	0.073448
2.485021	1.969834	3.432792	5.453597	1.306880	1.952523	0.765950
3.311110	3.634677	6.163199	15.905082	4.480319	0.068979	1.720580
5.096395						

was known to be 21.16. The means of the 50 sets of samples taken are given in Table 10.1.

Assume we require the 90 per cent and 95 per cent confidence intervals for the mean. We have a total of $n = 50$ samples, so we can safely apply the results for the large sample confidence interval. Now

$$\sum_i \bar{x}_i = 221.69$$

and

$$\sum_i \bar{x}_i^2 = 829.19$$

therefore the estimated mean is $221.69/50 = 4.434$. We can now calculate the 95 per cent confidence interval from Eq. (10.9) as

$$4.434 \pm 1.96*\frac{4.6}{\sqrt{50}} = 4.434 \pm 1.27$$

and the 90 per cent confidence interval is

$$4.434 \pm 1.69*\frac{4.6}{\sqrt{50}} = 4.434 \pm 1.10$$

In the simulation library, the confidence limit $(\sigma/\sqrt{n})z_{\alpha/2}$ is returned by the function *large_sample_conf_int( )*, which has the prototype

```
float large_sample_conf_int ( confidence_level cl, float std_dev, int n );
```

where the confidence level required is given by the argument *cl*, the standard deviation is given by *std_dev* and *n* gives the number of samples. Two values of confidence interval are defined, *PERCENT_99* and *PERCENT_95*, which are declared in *stats.h*. The confidence interval spans *mean − large_sample_conf_int( )* to *mean + large_sample_conf_int( )*.

Unknown variance Often the exact variance σ^2 is unknown. In these situations it can be replaced by an estimate s^2 as given by Eq. (10.4). Unfortunately, estimates of population mean are not normally distributed when we have to estimate the variance. Instead, they exhibit a Student's t distribution with $n - 1$ degrees of freedom. As we saw in Chapter 5, with small sample size the Student t distribution is considerably more spread out than the normal distribution, but as sample size increases, the Student t distribution approaches the normal distribution. So if enough samples are available we can proceed as if the variance were known.

If there are less than 30 samples, then the distribution is not a close enough fit to a normal distribution. We can, however, still apply the same basic approach by substituting the value $t(n)_{\alpha/2}$ from the tables of Student's t distribution given in Appendix C for the value $z_{\alpha/2}$ used in (10.8). The confidence interval for μ with confidence level $1 - \alpha$ is now

$$\bar{x} \pm \frac{s}{\sqrt{n}} t(n)_{\alpha/2} \tag{10.10}$$

which is an exact confidence interval if the distribution is normal. The confidence interval given by Eq. (10.10) is the so-called *small sample confidence interval*.

Example 10.3 The results of some measurements from a normal distribution with unknown mean and variance are given in Table 10.2.

Since there are only 25 samples the large sample confidence interval is not appropriate. We must use the small sample confidence interval given by Eq. (10.10). From the data in Table 10.2 we have

$$\sum_i x_i = 161.5$$

so that the estimated mean is $161.5/25 = 6.46$ and

$$\sum_i (x_i - \bar{x})^2 = 409.78$$

so that the estimated variance is $409.78/24 = 17.07$ and the standard deviation is

Table 10.2 Samples from an unknown normal distribution

12.278493	6.029903	0.601983	5.181922	8.483477
-1.225689	6.440870	7.271668	3.348386	4.510723
11.596211	15.163772	5.401721	2.454876	4.681327
13.254743	5.452853	1.734972	10.767482	8.589791
9.469012	6.076673	4.181540	8.553529	1.107449

4.13. Assuming we require the 99 per cent confidence interval then, for 24 degrees of freedom,

$$t_{0.005}(24) = 2.797$$

so the 99 per cent confidence interval is

$$6.46 \pm 2.797 * \frac{4.13}{\sqrt{25}} = 6.46 \pm 2.31$$

Function *small_sample_conf_int()* in the simulation library can be used to calculate the confidence limit $(\sigma/\sqrt{n})t_{\alpha/2}$. It has the prototype

```
float small_sample_conf_int ( confidence_level cl, float std_dev, int dof );
```

where the confidence level required is given by the argument *cl*, the standard deviation is given by *std_dev* and *dof* gives the degrees of freedom. The two levels of confidence defined are *PERCENT_99* and *PERCENT_95* which are the same as in the large sample case. The actual confidence interval then spans *mean − small_sample_conf_int()* to *mean + small_sample_conf_int()*.

10.4.3 Confidence interval of variance

In some simulations we may need to place a confidence interval on the estimate of the variance. Assuming that the sample $\{x_1, x_2, ... x_n\}$ comes from a normal distribution, then $(n-1)s^2/\sigma^2$ has a χ^2 distribution with $n-1$ degrees of freedom. From tables of the χ^2 distribution given in Appendix C we can find quantities $\chi^2_{\alpha/2}(n-1)$ and $\chi^2_{1-\alpha/2}(n-1)$ such that

$$P\left[\chi^2_{1-\alpha/2}(n-1) \leqslant \frac{(n-1)s^2}{\sigma^2} \leqslant \chi^2_{\alpha/2}(n-1)\right] = \alpha \qquad (10.11)$$

and so the exact confidence interval for σ^2 with confidence level $1 - \alpha$ is

$$\left(\frac{(n-1)s^2}{\chi^2_{\alpha/2}(n-1)}, \frac{(n-1)s^2}{\chi^2_{1-\alpha/2}(n-1)}\right) \qquad (10.12)$$

which is valid only if the distribution is normal.

Example 10.4 The 95 per cent confidence interval for the variance of the data in Example 10.3 is

$$\left(\frac{24*17.07}{\chi^2_{\alpha/2}(n-1)}, \frac{24*17.07}{\chi^2_{1-\alpha/2}(n-1)}\right) \qquad (10.13)$$

From Appendix C, we have $\chi^2_{0.975}(24) = 10.86$ and $\chi^2_{0.025}(24) = 39.36$ so that the confidence interval is

$$17.07 - 6.67 \text{ to } 17.07 + 20.65 = 10.40 \text{ to } 37.72$$

10.4.4 Confidence interval for the difference of means

We saw in Chapter 1 that one possible objective of simulation is the comparison of alternatives. When performing comparisons we need to be able to quantify our belief that the difference witnessed in a measured output parameter is in fact significant. We can do this by running a simulation model under the two operating conditions and obtain two sets of results. We then test the hypothesis that the means of the two sets are the same against the alternative hypothesis that the means are different. If there are more than two alternatives we can compare them in pairs.

Before we look at the details we will emphasize again that the approach applies only if the sets of results are independent. If the models used to obtain the results had *matched* random number streams, then independence can no longer be assured. One way around this dilemma is to take samples in pairs and form the difference $d_i = x_i - y_i$. This should then have a mean of zero if the null hypothesis is true, which can be tested using the method of Sec. 10.4.2. The implication here is that both sets of results consist of the same number of samples, but this is not normally a major deterrent.

Known variance We first consider the case when the distributions for the data sets A and B are *independent* and the variance is *known*. Suppose that the two populations of interest have, respectively, means given by μ_A and μ_B with $\mu_A - \mu_B$ the parameter to be estimated and a common variance σ^2. Also suppose that we have n_A samples from A and n_B samples from B. If the *expected value** $E(\bar{x}_A - \bar{x}_B)$ is used to estimate $\mu_A - \mu_B$, then

$$E(\bar{x}_A - \bar{x}_B) = \mu_A - \mu_B \tag{10.14}$$

because the estimator is unbiased and

$$Var(X_A - X_B) = Var(X_A) + Var(X_B)$$
$$= \frac{\sigma^2}{n_A} + \frac{\sigma^2}{n_B}$$

---

* The expected value of a function of a random variable X is the value which we could expect to obtain if we took a large number of samples $x_1, x_2, ..., x_n$, calculated $y_i = f(x_i)$ for each of them, and then calculated the average of the y_i. The expected value of a variable X is written $E[X]$ and is equal to the mean.

because the data is independent. The differences between the data sets $X_A - X_B$ will have approximately a normal distribution if there are enough samples (more than the magic 30). Thus we can construct a confidence interval for $\mu_A - \mu_B$ as we did in Eq. (10.8). Then

$$(\bar{x}_A - \bar{x}_B) \pm z_{\alpha/2}\sigma\sqrt{\frac{1}{n_A} + \frac{1}{n_B}} \tag{10.15}$$

is a large sample confidence interval for $\mu_A - \mu_B$ with level of confidence approximately $(1 - \alpha)$. Hence for testing $H_0: \mu_A = \mu_B$ versus $H_1: \mu_A \neq \mu_B$ we can use the test statistic

$$z = \frac{(\bar{x}_A - \bar{x}_B)}{\sigma\sqrt{\frac{1}{n_A} + \frac{1}{n_B}}} \tag{10.16}$$

rejecting H_0 for $|z| \geq z_{\alpha/2}$, for a specified α.

Example 10.5 Two alternative software architectures were evaluated to determine which was the most responsive. The results were as follows:

Architecture A	Architecture B
# samples = 50	# samples = 75
$\bar{x}_A = 2.5$	$\bar{x}_B = 1.9$
$\sigma^2 = 9$	$\sigma^2 = 9$

We require to know if the results provide evidence to suggest that there is a difference in the performance under the two architectures with a level of confidence of 95 per cent. Since we are testing a difference in either direction, we want to test the null hypothesis $H_0: \mu_A - \mu_B = 0$ against the alternative hypotheses $H_1: \mu_A - \mu_B \neq 0$. A two-tail test is applicable and the test statistic is

$$z = \frac{(2.5 - 1.9)}{3\sqrt{\frac{1}{50} + \frac{1}{75}}} = 0.912$$

where we have used the known variance $\sigma^2 = 9$

In other words, the difference between the sample means is z standard deviations from the hypothesized zero difference. Now, $z_{0.025} = 1.96$, and since $|z| < 1.96$, we accept H_0 with a level of confidence of 95 per cent. It does not appear that the two architectures differ significantly in performance.

Unknown variance We now consider the more typical case in which the distribution has an unknown variance. If the means are as before but we now replace the known variance with estimates s_A^2 and s_B^2 where

$$s_A^2 = \frac{1}{n_A - 1} \sum_{i=1}^{n_A} (x_{iA} - \bar{x}_A)^2 \tag{10.17}$$

and

$$s_B^2 = \frac{1}{n_B - 1} \sum_{i=1}^{n_B} (x_{iB} - \bar{x}_B)^2 \tag{10.18}$$

then the combined unbiased estimate is given by

$$s^2 = \frac{(n_A - 1)s_A^2 + (n_B - 1)s_B^2}{n_A + n_B - 2}$$

$$= \frac{\Sigma(x_{Ai} - \bar{x}_A)^2 + \Sigma(x_{Bi} - \bar{x}_B)^2}{n_A + n_B - 2} \tag{10.19}$$

the denominator $(n_A + n_B - 2)$ is the number of degrees of freedom of the estimate of the variance which is equal to the number of degrees of freedom of the estimate s_A^2 plus the number of degrees of freedom of the estimate s_B^2. If the hypothesis is true then the test statistic

$$t = \frac{\bar{x}_A - \bar{x}_B}{s\sqrt{\left(\frac{1}{n_A} + \frac{1}{n_B}\right)}} \tag{10.20}$$

follows a t distribution with $(n_A + n_B - 2)$ degrees of freedom. Hence for testing $H_0: \mu_A = \mu_B$ versus $H_1: \mu_A \neq \mu_B$ we calculate t and reject H_0 when $|t| \geq t(n_A + n_B - 2)_{\alpha/2}$ for a specified α. We also have the large sample confidence interval for $\mu_A - \mu_B$ which is

$$(\bar{x}_A - \bar{x}_B) \pm t_{\alpha/2}\, s \sqrt{\frac{1}{n_A} + \frac{1}{n_B}} \tag{10.21}$$

for a level of confidence of approximately $(1 - \alpha)$ when the variance is unknown.

Example 10.6 Let us repeat Example 10.5 assuming an unknown variance. The combined estimate of the common variance s^2 is given by

$$s^2 = \frac{49*8.7 + 74*7.5}{50 + 75 - 2} = 7.97$$

226 DISCRETE EVENT SIMULATION IN C

so that the t statistic is given by $0.6/(2.82*0.18) = 1.17$. Now, at the 5 per cent level we find that for 123 degrees of freedom (i.e. infinity) we have in the 0.025 column $t(123)_{0.025} = 1.96$. Since $t(123)_{0.025} > 1.17$ we can confidently accept the null hypothesis that the means are the same.

10.5 REALIZING ACCURACY GOALS

In the previous section we obtained estimates for the accuracy of the mean and variance in the form of confidence intervals. It is also useful to know how to achieve a stated accuracy so that the goals of the simulation study can be met as economically as possible. In this section we will look at some techniques for doing this.

10.5.1 Controlling the run length

It seems intuitively obvious that by increasing the duration of a simulation and obtaining more samples our results become, in some sense, more reliable. This gut feeling is supported by our previous analysis in which Eq. (10.9) implies that by taking more observations we can improve our precision since, as n increases, the confidence interval reduces. By reordering Eq. (10.9) and fixing the confidence interval as $\pm d$, we have

$$n = \left(\frac{z_{\alpha/2}\sigma}{d}\right)^2 \tag{10.22}$$

which gives us the number of independent samples required, after the initial transient phase has been discarded, to obtain a result with the stated confidence interval d. The catch with Eq. (10.22), however, is that the variance of the distribution must be known. We cannot use Eq. (10.1) to obtain an estimate, s^2, of the variance and then rewrite it to obtain a value for n in terms of s^2 because s, the estimate of σ, is a random variable and as a result n will also be random. Help is at hand, fortunately, in the form of the following procedure described in Karian and Dudewicz (1991). It assumes we require an estimate of μ within d corresponding to a level of confidence l. The algorithm is as follows:

Step 1: Set $n_0 > 1$. Set $w = t^{-1}_{n_0-1}((1 + l)/2)/d$
Step 2: Record the samples $x_1, ..., x_{n_0}$.
Step 3: Calculate

$$\bar{x}(n_0) = \frac{x_1 + \cdots + x_{n_0}}{n_0}$$

$$s^2 = \frac{1}{n_0 - 1}\sum_{i=1}^{n_0}(x_i - \bar{x}(n_0))^2$$

Table 10.3 Values of n_0 and w for two levels of confidence

Level of confidence (per cent)	$n_0 = 2$	$n_0 = 5$	$n_0 = 15$	$n_0 = 60$	∞
95	$w = 12.706$	$w = 2.776$	$w = 2.145$	$w = 2.00$	$w = 1.96$
99	$w = 31.821$	$w = 3.747$	$w = 2.602$	$w = 2.390$	$w = 2.326$

Step 4: Set

$$n = \max\{n_0 + 1, \ \mathrm{ceil}(w^2 s^2)\}$$

where ceil(x) is the largest integer less than or equal to x
Step 5: Record the samples $x_{n_0+1}, \ ..., \ x_n$.
Step 6: Calculate a new variable $\bar{\bar{x}}$ where

$$\bar{\bar{x}} = \frac{x_1 + ... + x_{n_0} + x_{n_0+1} + ... + x_n}{n}$$

*Step 7: Claim with 100*l per cent confidence that*

$$\bar{\bar{x}} - d \leqslant \mu \leqslant \bar{\bar{x}} + d$$

This algorithm fixes the value of two integers n and n_0 such that the desired confidence interval d is obtained. In determining d in Step 1 we need to select an initial value for n_0. This can be obtained from Table 10.3, which lists some values of the Student-t distribution. The table assumes d has the value 1.0, for any other value w must be scaled by dividing by d. A good value of n_0 to choose is 15, which makes the estimate s^2 of σ^2 quite accurate and so keeps n down to a reasonable value.

Example 10.7 Assume we want to know the number of samples to give a confidence level of 99 per cent and a confidence interval for the mean of 2.0. If we select n_0 as 15, then Table 10.3 gives $w = 2.60/d = 1.30$. Assume the first 15 samples of Table 10.2 are used to calculate $\bar{x}(n_0)$ then

$$\bar{x}(n_0) = 6.915$$
$$s^2 = 20.81$$

and

$$n = \max\{16, \ \mathrm{floor}\,(1.3*1.3*20.45)\} = \max\,(16,35) = 35$$

so that we need another $35 - 15 = 20$ additional samples. The estimate of the mean is then

$$\bar{\bar{x}} = \frac{x_1 + x_2 + \cdots + x_{34} + x_{35}}{35}$$

and the 99 per cent confidence interval is

$$\bar{\bar{x}} - 2.0 \leqslant \mu \leqslant \bar{\bar{x}} + 2.0$$

10.5.2 Correlation, covariance and autocorrelation

The preceding analysis has all assumed that the random variables involved are *independent*. This condition allows us to perform statistical analyses relatively easily, but it is sometimes not entirely realistic. If variables are not independent, i.e. if a variable x does indeed have an effect on the value of another variable y, then the variables are said to be *correlated*. If, when x increases or decreases y tends to increase or decrease in sympathy we have an example of *positive correlation*. If the contrary is true, i.e. when x increases or decreases then y tends to move in the opposite direction, then we have *negative correlation*.

The effect of correlation on the results of a simulation study can be considerable. If it is ignored either deliberately or accidentally, then our results can be dangerously misleading. Thus, we need to be able to do things. First of all we must be able to detect correlation if present and, secondly, we must be able to adjust our analysis of the results to take it into account.

To analyse correlation we need to introduce the concept of *covariance*. The covariance of a pair of random variables is defined as the expected value of the product of their deviations from their means, so the covariance can be written

$$\text{Cov}(X,Y) = E[(X - \mu_x)(Y - \mu_y)] \tag{10.23}$$

If the variables are independent, the covariance is zero since

$$E[(X - \mu_x)(Y - \mu_y)] = E[X - \mu_x]E[Y - \mu_y] \tag{10.24}$$

and both $E[(X - \mu_x)]$ and $E[(Y - \mu_y)]$ are zero. If the variables are dependent, the expression for the covariance of x and y becomes

$$\text{Cov}(X,Y) = \frac{1}{n}\sum_{i=1}^{n}(x_i - \bar{x})(y_i - \bar{y}) \tag{10.25}$$

We can now define the correlation coefficient. The *correlation coefficient* gives a numeric value to the degree of correlation between x and y. It can be expressed analytically as

$$\rho(X,Y) = \frac{\text{Cov}(X,Y)}{\sqrt{\sigma^2(X)\sigma^2(Y))}} \tag{10.26}$$

Substituting for $\text{Cov}(X, Y)$ from Eq. (10.25) into Eq. (10.26) we can rewrite the correlation coefficient as

$$\rho(X, Y) = \frac{\displaystyle\sum_{i=1}^{n}(x_i - \bar{x})(y_i - \bar{y})/n}{\dfrac{\displaystyle\sum_{i=1}^{n}(x_i - \bar{x})^2}{n} \dfrac{\displaystyle\sum_{j=1}^{n}(y_j - \bar{y})^2}{n}}$$

$$= \frac{\displaystyle\sum_{i=1}^{n}(x_i - \bar{x})(y_i - \bar{y})}{\sqrt{\displaystyle\sum_{i=1}^{n}(x_i - \bar{x})^2 \sum_{j=1}^{n}(y_i - \bar{y})^2}} \qquad (10.27)$$

When we are dealing with the correlation between samples of a single variable we require the *autocorrelation*. This gives the internal correlation of a series of samples of the *same* variable X, displaced in time. In our case we are dealing with time in a discrete sense rather than as a continuous value, so that we can write for the autocorrelation

$$\rho(p) = E[(x_i - \mu)(x_{i+p} - \mu)]$$

$$= \frac{1}{n-p} \sum_{i=1}^{n-p}(x_i - \bar{x})(x_{i+p} - \bar{x}) \quad \text{for} \quad 0 \leqslant p \leqslant n-1 \qquad (10.28)$$

which simplifies to the expression for the variance given by Eq. (5.13) when $p = 0$. The use of autocorrelation is demonstrated in the following example.

Table 10.4 Source data for autocorrelation analysis

1-> 10	11-> 20	21-> 30	31-> 40	41-> 50
0.218501	0.444697	0.701577	1.001084	1.219383
0.218312	0.553668	0.666899	1.565942	0.804416
0.220829	0.630419	0.380489	1.254715	0.262942
0.274271	0.661106	0.282059	1.400572	3.038916
0.329219	0.595610	0.326209	2.138810	3.321426
0.298853	0.482787	0.375335	0.941400	0.888211
0.271657	0.457108	0.187959	1.061289	0.757615
0.303960	0.468222	0.378181	0.779333	1.304893
0.502657	0.385798	0.569491	1.088069	2.284498
0.484846	0.434096	0.804096	2.936324	0.567961

Table 10.5 Autocorrelation of data in Table 10.4 for various values of p

$p=0$ to 9	$p=10$ to 19	$p=20$ to 29	$p=30$ to 39	$p=40$ to 48
0.537986	0.129970	−0.089758	−0.222765	−0.297875
0.260463	0.063018	−0.112459	−0.219331	−0.367040
0.084616	0.075361	−0.089694	−0.245775	−0.430675
0.135494	0.071218	−0.060744	−0.276107	−0.533613
0.318352	0.073530	−0.105359	−0.268967	−0.394753
0.311044	−0.001171	−0.146247	−0.209126	−0.191406
0.066778	−0.025261	−0.145823	−0.260807	−0.246553
0.075779	−0.039321	−0.156522	−0.337251	−0.340127
0.107323	−0.052875	−0.197362	−0.384153	−0.364560
0.191343	−0.047548	−0.236287	−0.379759	

Example 10.8 Table 10.4 gives 50 samples of a random variable which has a mean of 0.83. Table 10.5 gives the corresponding autocorrelation for various values of the offset p calculated using Eq. (10.28). As can be seen the data starts off with a strong positive correlation which decreases to near zero at an offset of about 15 and becomes strongly negative for offsets greater than about 30.

In the following sections we incorporate the effects of correlation in our results analysis and see how it can be used to improve the accuracy of a simulation.

10.5.3 Repetition

From what has already been discussed it should be clear that the more samples we take as the basis for statistical measures such as mean and variance, the greater the expected accuracy. One way in which more samples can be obtained is by repeating a run. Instead of having a single run and basing statistical analysis on that, we can have several runs and combine the results from them all. The drawback with repetition is that for each run we have an initial transient period for which results cannot normally be used even if they are available. Hence this method can be wasteful of computer resources. On the other hand it is quite straightforward to apply and does not complicate the logic of the model. We will now look at how it can be used with and without autocorrelation.

Repetition with no autocorrelation For the moment, assume that each variable sampled during a repetition has no autocorrelation, that repetitions are uncorrelated and that all repetitions consist of n samples. If k repetitions are made, then we can generate a sample of k estimates $y_j 1 \leqslant j \leqslant k$ of the sample mean of each repetition:

$$y_j = \frac{1}{n} \sum_{i=1}^{n} x_{i,j} \qquad (10.29)$$

in which $x_{i,j}$ is the ith sample of the jth repetition, $1 \leqslant i \leqslant n$ and $1 \leqslant j \leqslant k$.

The overall mean is the 'mean of the means', which is

$$\bar{x} = \frac{1}{k} \sum_{j=1}^{k} y_j \qquad (10.30)$$

and the estimated variance of the sample means from the overall mean is

$$s^2(n) = \frac{1}{k-1} \sum_{j=1}^{k} (y_j - \bar{x})^2 \qquad (10.31)$$

The accuracy of the mean in predicting the true mean of the distribution is, as we saw from Eq. (10.5), related to the variance of the sample mean, which is given by

$$\bar{\sigma}^2 = \frac{s^2(n)}{k} \qquad (10.32)$$

When there is correlation between repetitions the distribution of the sample mean is affected. Considering the simple case of *two* repetitions, the correlation between repetitions results in a mean of

$$\bar{x} = \frac{1}{2n} \sum_{i=1}^{2} \sum_{j=1}^{n} x_{i,j} \qquad (10.33)$$

which is of course obtained from Eqs (10.29) and (10.30) for the case $k = 2$. But now the variance of the sample mean is

$$\bar{\sigma}^2 = \frac{s^2(n)}{2}(1 + \rho) \qquad (10.34)$$

where ρ is the coefficient of correlation.

If the two repetitions are completely independent the coefficient of correlation is 0 and the variance is just the variance of $2n$ samples, which would be the same as if we had taken all the samples in a single run (ignoring the effect of the transient phase). However, the coefficient of correlation is made negative, the variance becomes even smaller. A method of obtaining negative correlation using *antithetic variates* is covered in Sec. 10.5.6.

Repetition with autocorrelation If we believe that autocorrelation is present between the variables, then it can be estimated directly based on the available data and taken into account when estimating the mean and variance. To do this we must record the sample data for off-line analysis. In this analysis we perform the following tasks:

- Use Eq. (10.28) to estimate the autocorrelation as a function of p.
- Calculate s^2, the estimate of the variance, using Eq. (10.1) and calculate the mean $\bar{x}$ using Eq. (5.9).
- Use the value of $\rho(p)$ to modify the variance using the expression

$$\bar{\sigma}^2 = \frac{s^2}{n}\left[1 + 2\sum_{p=1}^{n-1}\left(1 - \frac{p}{n}\right)\rho(p)\right] \qquad (10.35)$$

which, if $\rho(p) = 0$ for all p, reduces to Eq. (10.5).

10.5.4 Batch means

Another common technique for obtaining higher accuracy is to split a run into *batches* so that each run has more than one batch. In other words, a long run is treated as several shorter subruns. Each subrun produces a separate *batch mean*. The estimated value of the variable being measured is then the mean of the batch means.

Using batch means The method of batch means is effectively the same as repetition where the starting conditions of the ith run is exactly the finishing conditions of the $(i - 1)$th run. This obviously introduces autocorrelation, but can be taken into account by making each batch sufficiently large so that the autocorrelation between batches becomes insignificant. The net result is identical to the result obtained without batches. However, the assumption of independence and the application of the central limit theorem allows the sample of batch means to be treated as if it were normally distributed, even in the presence of significant autocorrelation within batches. The usual formulas (Sec. 10.4.2) can then be applied to estimate the confidence interval.

Assume that there are b batches and that the output of batch t is the starting conditions of batch $t + 1$. If a run consists of n autocorrelated samples $x_1, x_2, ..., x_n (n = wb)$ we can group the samples into the b batches so that each batch consists of w samples arranged like this:

...	x_1	...,	x_w,	x_{w+1},	...,	x_{2w},	...	$x_{(j-1)w+1}$,	...,	x_{jw}
<-transient->		<--batch 1-->			<--batch 2-->		...		<--batch j-->	

Then for each batch j we generate a batch mean y_j, where

$$y_j = \frac{1}{w}\sum_{i=(j-1)w+1}^{jw} x_i \qquad (10.36)$$

The mean of the total sample can now be calculated as

$$\bar{x} = \frac{1}{b} \sum_{j=1}^{b} y_j \qquad (10.37)$$

and the variance of the sample means can be calculated as

$$\bar{\sigma}^2 = \frac{\sigma_y^2}{b} \qquad (10.38)$$

Selecting the batch size The requirement for the batch size is that successive batches appear uncorrelated. If a model is cyclic with a defined period, such as a working day, then we may be able to treat each cycle as a single batch and not have to worry too much about correlation between batches. We can argue from the point of view of the system behaviour that correlation during each cycle will not spill over into subsequent cycles. In the case of a model which attains a single steady state the situation is more complicated. We could do either of the following:

1. Make an educated guess. A reasonable guess would be the size of the initial transient phase that was discarded at the beginning of the simulation.
2. Obtain a more rigorous figure based on the examination of the autocorrelation function $\rho(p)$. The autocorrelation function should decrease with p and when the rolling average falls to less than, say, 1 per cent of its initial value, it should be safe to assume that the autocorrelation is effectively zero. This then fixes the batch size.

10.5.5 Comparison between repetition and batch means

Both the repetition and batch methods provide a means to handle autocorrelation and increase accuracy, but the choice of which to use is not an easy one to make. Briefly, the pros and cons are as follows.

Method of repetitions The advantages are

1. Produces a minimum variance estimate in a minimum number of samples.
2. The variance is generally smaller for a given number of samples than the method of batches.

The disadvantage is

1. Requires considerable computer time to calculate the autocorrelation function, but this is tempered by the fact that such information can be reused.

Method of batches The advantages are

1. Can be done as the simulation proceeds, without having to record all the sample data for analysis after the run has completed.
2. No initial transient phase to discount for each batch, just one at the beginning of the run.

The disadvantage is

1. Loss of efficiency due to aggregating the samples in each batch.

In general it is probably true to say that the cost of using the batch method is less when the desired accuracy of the estimate is low. As the desired accuracy increases, the method of explicitly calculating the autocorrelation becomes increasingly attractive, eventually becoming the least cost method at some high level of accuracy. The availability of off-line statistics analysis packages makes this approach even more attractive.

10.5.6 Variance reduction

We have seen in Secs 10.5.3 and 10.5.4 two methods of reducing the variance of estimates that involves increasing the number of samples made. We discuss here some additional techniques used for variance reduction which do not affect the number of samples, they only affect the way the samples are handled.

Control variates The method of *control variates* is a technique for reducing the variance of model results and therefore of achieving a desired level of accuracy more efficiently. It involves calculating the difference between the measured average values and the theoretical average values of certain model variables, called control variates, which are correlated with an output variable. This difference is then applied to the mean of the output variable in order to adjust its value in line with the correlation. The net result is a reduction in sample variance.

To understand the basis of this method imagine an arrival process that generates customers for a queuing system. Interesting questions for this system may be 'What is the mean time a customer spends in the system for a given arrival rate?' To answer this question a model can be written that has as an input parameter, a, the mean value of an exponential distribution from which the inter-arrival times are sampled and, as an output, t, the mean time in the system. This defines a pair of input–output variables (a, t). Suppose the model is then run with an inter-arrival time of 4.0 seconds and it produces a mean time in the system of 12.9 seconds. This gives us our first input–output data pair of (4.0, 12.9). However, the arrival rate is a random variable and, although we have defined a mean value for it, the *actual* mean value is almost certainly a little different. We may find for instance, that an assumed mean of 4.0 seconds turns out to be 4.5

seconds when measured. Therefore the inter-arrival time could be selected as the control variate and used to make an adjustment to the measured output variable. This would reduce its value, making it more in line with an input of 4.0.

So much for the principle, how do we actually go about it? The most difficult problem appears to be determining exactly how much the output variable should be adjusted for a given difference in control variate. To calculate this let us assume

- The control variate is V_c and it has a true mean M_c.
- The sample mean of the control variate, measured over n repetitions or batches is $\bar{v}_c$.
- The variance of the control variate is $\sigma_{v_c}^2$.
- The output variable is X and it has a true mean μ_x.
- The output variable has a sample mean $\bar{x}$ (averaged over the same repetitions or batches as $\bar{v}_c$).
- The variance of the output variable is σ_x^2.

We want to find a better estimate of μ_x than $\bar{x}$. Let this be $\hat{x}$ where

$$\hat{x} = \bar{x} + k(\bar{v}_c - \mu_c) \tag{10.39}$$

We must choose k so that the variance of X is as small as possible. Taking variances of Eq. (10.39) we have

$$\sigma_{\hat{x}}^2 = \sigma_{\bar{x}}^2 + k^2 \sigma_{\bar{v}_c}^2 - 2k \operatorname{Cov}(\bar{v}_c, \bar{x}) \tag{10.40}$$

the derivation of which is given in most good statistics books.

To reduce the variance of $\hat{x}$ the product of k and the covariance must be positive. Hence if the covariance is negative, k must be negative, and if the covariance is positive, k must be positive. In practice it is advisable to only use control variates that have a large value of k, since the whole process is stochastic and small values of k may actually have the wrong sign.

A minimum value for $\sigma_{\hat{x}}^2$ can be determined by differentiation with respect to k as follows:

$$\frac{d\sigma_{\hat{x}}^2}{dk} = 2k\sigma_{\bar{v}_c}^2 - 2\operatorname{Cov}(\bar{v}_c, \bar{x}) = 0 \tag{10.41}$$

which we can solve for k to get

$$k = \frac{\operatorname{Cov}(\bar{v}_c, \bar{x})}{\sigma_{\bar{v}_c}^2}$$

$$= \frac{\rho\sqrt{\sigma_{\bar{v}_c}^2\sigma_{\bar{x}}^2}}{\sigma_{\bar{v}_c}^2}$$

$$= \rho\frac{\sigma_{\bar{x}}}{\sigma_{\bar{v}_c}} \tag{10.42}$$

where ρ is the correlation between $\bar{v}_c$ and $\bar{x}$ and can be determined from Eq. (10.27).

Substituting the value of k from Eq. (10.42) into Eq. (10.40) we find that

$$\sigma_{\bar{x}}^2 = \sigma_{\bar{x}}^2 + \frac{(\text{Cov}(\bar{v}_c, \bar{x}))^2}{\sigma_{\bar{v}_c}^2} - \frac{2(\text{Cov}(\bar{v}_c, \bar{x}))^2}{\sigma_{\bar{v}_c}^2} \qquad (10.43)$$

which can be rearranged to give us the variance reduction

$$\sigma_{\bar{x}}^2 - \sigma_{\bar{x}}^2 = \frac{(\text{Cov}(\bar{v}_c, \bar{x}))^2}{\sigma_{\bar{v}_c}^2}$$

$$= \rho^2 \sigma_{\bar{x}}^2 \qquad (10.44)$$

The use of control variates often entails a lot of additional work because of the need to calculate correlation coefficients. If the samples are averaged over n replications then several sets of n replications will be required to estimate k accurately and each of these replications should have different random number seeds to ensure independence.

Example 10.9 Let us see this method in action by applying it to the batch computer system that was modelled in Chapter 8. If we apply the arrival rate as a control variate to the waiting time for priority three jobs then we need to add to the original model a measurement of the inter-arrival time. We will also have to make, say, 15 runs of the model and, to ensure independence, we should add separate random number streams for the inter-arrival time of each priority of job, each type of job and the selection of job type. We must also repeat the runs several times to estimate k. Table 10.6 gives the result of 10 sets of such repetitions.

The first thing to do is work out the correlation between the arrival rate and the waiting time for priority three jobs. From Eq. (10.27) we have

$$\rho = \frac{-0.006628}{10*0.05426*0.02035}$$

$$= -0.60026$$

and so the value of k is

$$k = -0.6003*0.02035/0.05426$$
$$= -0.2251$$

which gives a variance reduction of

$$\sigma_{\bar{x}}^2 - \sigma_{\bar{x}}^2 = 0.6003*0.6003*0.143$$
$$= 0.051$$

From Example 10.9 it is clear that the control variates method really becomes useful only when we are dealing with simulations that need to be run several times under changing assumptions because the control variates will

Table 10.6 Table of mean and standard deviations

	Arrival rate:			Waiting time:	
Set	Specified mean	Measured mean	Measured standard deviation	Measured mean	Measured standard deviation
1	27.5	27.34074	1.84360	5.97468	0.42556
2	27.5	27.36866	1.85424	5.99387	0.42656
3	27.5	27.48608	1.77978	5.98449	0.40356
4	27.5	27.41463	1.70519	5.99375	0.40280
5	27.5	27.38339	1.62512	6.01824	0.41273
6	27.5	27.37112	1.58076	6.02115	0.42099
7	27.5	27.32122	1.58240	6.03153	0.40688
8	27.5	27.27428	1.55996	6.02907	0.40996
9	27.5	27.33325	1.55380	6.02927	0.40432
10	27.5	27.33928	1.52058	6.02842	0.40040
Overall	27.5	27.36327	0.05426	6.01045	0.02035

normally not have to be recalculated. The example also illustrates the fact that choosing an effective control variate is not always easy. In this case the variance reduction hardly seems worth all the effort.

Antithetic variates The method of *antithetic variates* is a means of introducing negative correlation between simulation runs which, as we saw in Eq. (10.34), reduces the variance of the sample mean. In theory, if we use a uniform random number stream $\langle X \rangle$ in one run and it produces estimates that are too high, say, then in a second run we can use the stream $\langle 1 - X \rangle$ which should produce estimates which are too low. When calculating the mean of the runs the average error will tend to cancel out to some extent and we will have therefore reduced the variance.

Antithetic variates are useful when the simulation is repeated but the parameters of the model are kept the same. However, for maximum benefit random number streams should be common. Also the method is really only satisfactory for small and relatively simple models. When model complexity increases, the effect of branching and feedback within the model tends to confuse the effectiveness of the supposed negative correlation.

Since in the simulation library (in common with nearly all such systems) random number distributions such as *gamma( )* and *normal( )* are derived from the same uniform random number generator *uniform01( )*, we can introduce antithetic properties to all generated variates very easily. Antithetic variates are specified when a random number stream is created. Recall from Chapter 5 that there is an argument *antithc* passed to the *make_stream( )* function. If *antithc* is zero then *uniform01( )* returns random numbers from the stream $\langle X \rangle$. However, if *antithc* is non-zero then random numbers from the stream $\langle 1-X \rangle$ will be returned.

10.5.7 Using positive correlation

We sometimes conduct a simulation study for the purpose of performing a comparative analysis of two sets of alternative strategies, say A and B. The goal of this exercise is to identify the best alternative. There are two ways we can go about this:

1. We can perform several runs of the model configured for strategy A and then several runs of the model configured for strategy B. All runs are completely independent and in fact can be different length. We then analyse the samples made during the steady-state phase, obtaining a mean and variance for strategy A, and a mean and variance for strategy B. Comparing the means and variance using the techniques of Sec. 10.4.4 allows the best alternative to be identified.

2. We can perform runs in pairs. For each *pair* of runs we ensure that the only difference in the samples is due to the different strategies adopted. We introduce strong positive correlation and maintain synchronization by using the same random number streams for both runs in a pair. Ensuring synchronization of a pair of runs means that the parameters being compared between runs A and B must use random number streams unconnected with the rest of the model so that they have no effect on the conditions of the comparison.

   We are interested in the *difference* of the means between pairs of runs based on their behaviour in the steady state. Depending on the value of the difference we can identify the optimum strategy.

The second approach is generally to be preferred because it is more efficient in terms of the number of runs required to select the best with a given confidence interval. This is due to the use of positive correlation, which reduces the variance associated with the comparison of alternatives. To see why this is so, assume that we have estimates for the mean and variance for two alternatives A and B and we must decide which of them is best. The mean of the difference between runs is

$$\bar{\mu}_D = \bar{\mu}_A - \bar{\mu}_B \tag{10.45}$$

and the variance of the difference between runs is

$$\sigma_D^2 = \sigma_A^2 + \sigma_B^2 - 2\rho\sigma_A\sigma_B \tag{10.46}$$

The significance test on the value of $\bar{\mu}_D$ depends on σ as we saw in Eq. (10.9). If ρ is zero we simply have that

$$\sigma_D^2 = \sigma_A^2 + \sigma_B^2 \tag{10.47}$$

However, Eq. (10.46) shows that if ρ is positive we can reduce σ_D. This is why the *same* random number streams are used for both runs and why the two runs must stay synchronized. To appreciate the importance of maintaining synchronization consider a model of a simple queuing system under two different service arrangements. We want to see the effect of changing the number of servers *only*. If we sample from a single distribution, then the first few arrivals will occur at the same time because the same random numbers are used in both cases. After a short while, however, there will be a customer who has to wait for service in one case but can obtain immediate service in the other. From there on the random numbers for the inter-arrival times get increasingly out of step and very quickly lose the positive correlation we sought. Therefore, we must use different random number streams for inter-arrival times and service times.

This procedure can be quite easily generalized for n alternatives rather than two. We end up with m sets of n positively correlated runs. Equations (10.45) and (10.46) can be used to select the optimum by comparing the n alternatives in pairs. We take alternatives 1 and 2, select the best and compare that with 3 and so on.

10.6 ANALYSIS OF TRANSIENT BEHAVIOUR

Although we have stressed in the analysis performed so far that the transient effects are to be removed, there may be times when it is precisely this behaviour that we are interested in. There are two main situations where this may be so:

1. when the system does not actually have a steady state phase
2. when we are interested in the effect of a sudden change in the operating conditions or in the initial system transient.

Transient behaviour presents very different problems for analysis from steady-state behaviour. In analysing steady-state behaviour we used the fact that probability distributions were stationary to calculate expected values and obtain confidence intervals. Moreover, we are able to run the simulations longer, using various techniques, in an effort to improve accuracy. Unfortunately, these devices all fail with transient phenomena because we are typically concerned with very short intervals. The only solution normally available is to (artificially) replicate the transient conditions, either by restarting the model or by applying some sort of periodic impulse.

The type of information required in the transient phase is also quite different from that required in the steady-state phase. When we are looking at transients we are invariably interested in extremes of system behaviour rather than in means or variances. For instance, we may be looking for the *largest* or *smallest* value during the transient period, or the number of times level X was exceeded, and so on. Sometimes the extremes we are interested in are very rare phenomena, in which case we must perform many replications in order to obtain any results.

Although transient effects may appear to be unpredictable when viewed as a time series they may actually be composed of regular components which vary with time in a predictable manner. It is sometimes useful to try and discover this underlying pattern of behaviour and to do this we can employ the technique of *spectral analysis*. Due to the complexity of this method of analysis we will not pursue it here, but details may be found in Fishman and Kiviat (1967).

10.7 SUMMARY

A simulation model may exhibit three types of dynamic behaviour:

- steady-state behaviour, in which the probability distributions are stationary and mean values converge as more samples are taken
- transient behaviour, which is normally a temporary state and decays away leaving the system in a steady state
- regenerative behaviour, which is cyclic and consists of periods of activity interspersed with a regenerative phase at which all previous history of the system has no effect on future behaviour.

A model may also be terminating or non-terminating. Terminating systems have a finite lifetime, non-terminating systems, on the other hand, can proceed indefinitely.

If the steady state is of primary interest, the transient state must be detected and the results accumulated for it discarded. Detection of the onset of the steady state can be accomplished by observing the variation of the standard deviation with the number of samples taken or by calculating the moving average.

It is important to present steady-state simulation results with confidence intervals so as to indicate how reliable the results are. A confidence interval for the mean can be calculated from the variance of the sampling distribution for the mean. A confidence interval for the variance can be obtained from an estimate of the variance of the population distribution if it is normally distributed.

In order to estimate the variance of the sampling distribution for the mean we need independent estimates of the mean. This can be done by replicating the run using different random number streams. Another approach is to split a long run into batches that are long enough to be considered independent.

If the value of one random variable affects another they are correlated. When the value of a single random variable is affected by its previous value, then autocorrelation is present. If these effects exist between the output variables of a model, then the analysis must take it into account or else the accuracy of the results could be severely impaired.

The variance of the means of repeated runs can be reduced by using the technique of control variates, in which the difference between the measured values and the known values of input variables is used to adjust the mean of output variables.

Another technique for reducing the variance of model results is to deliberately introduce negative correlation between pairs of runs by using the technique of antithetic variates. This entails the use of complementary random number streams $\langle X \rangle$ and $\langle 1 - X \rangle$ such that if one should have a tendency to increase the other should tend to decrease and vice versa. The combined effect is a reduction in the overall variability.

An effective technique for comparing alternatives is to introduce strong positive correlation between pairs of runs. Only the strategies being compared should differ. The rest of the model should maintain a high degree of synchronization so that the same random numbers are used to set the conditions of the comparison. This reduces the variance of the difference between the means.

10.8 EXERCISES

10.1 Calculate a 95 per cent confidence interval for the mean of the data in the following table assuming the distribution is normal

7.418	5.200	−3.828	10.696	0.157	3.443	−1.127
−0.078	4.969	16.066	−2.475	0.333	−1.979	2.354
2.943	6.788	15.455	4.755	−2.310	1.865	5.677
−2.509	11.436	2.416	3.928	1.857	1.878	−2.845
3.311	−1.969	3.392	−5.597	1.300	1.953	0.765
5.095	3.634	6.169	15.052	4.419	0.068	1.720

10.2 Calculate a 95 per cent confidence interval for the difference between the means of the following data, which is assumed not to be normally distributed:

Data A:

6.1017	4.1644	5.1217	2.4237	3.1371	3.7121
4.2757	5.2215	1.1184	4.5490	4.2749	4.0301
8.4564	8.4723	2.3434	5.2139	4.1596	7.1535
7.4764	2.7157	2.1381	6.1835	1.9111	7.1608
5.4114	3.6361	6.2485	1.6125	6.1364	7.5483

Data B:

3.7161	13.1537	13.1611	8.1211	17.2111	13.9115
1.2224	1.1999	16.3241	1.6531	1.1064	1.5089

10.3 Calculate the autocorrelation function for the following samples and tabulate it.

1-> 7	8-> 14	15-> 21	22-> 28	29-> 35	36-> 42
3.0137	2.4425	1.3617	1.2237	2.5471	3.0508
3.3366	2.3558	2.3584	2.5440	3.3012	2.7031
3.7576	1.2425	2.5393	1.2369	4.2099	3.3011
1.4715	2.1813	1.1304	2.7835	3.1236	2.4535
2.5604	1.7733	1.3486	2.4535	4.0914	1.1218
3.7164	3.1537	3.7171	1.1218	3.9161	3.0185
1.2224	1.1999	2.3044	1.6531	1.1064	1.5089

10.4 Re-implement the model of the dining philosophers presented in Chapter 6 using separate random number streams for thinking time and eating time for each philosopher. Estimate the transient period for this model.

10.5 Perform the following experimentation in the steady state with the model developed in Exercise 10.4:

(a) 30 replications with different random number seeds.

(b) 15 pairs of replications using the method of antithetic variates.

Determine the 99 per cent confidence intervals in both cases.

10.6 A networked database server receives remote SQL queries with inter-arrival time described by an exponential distribution with mean 25 seconds. Each query requires the searching of a database using a binary search algorithm that takes $0.7 \times log(n)$ seconds, where n is the size of the database in terms of number of records. There are 20 users on local terminals connected to the server. Assume that ten of the users have a workload cycle which consists of three read requests followed by a write request resulting in an increase in the size of the database by one record. Assume the other ten users have a workload cycle which consists of a single read request followed by a delete request which reduces the size of the database by one record. Requests are log-normally distributed with mean 57 seconds and standard deviation three seconds. Simulate this system until 1000 requests have been received, assuming that the database initially has 10 000 records.

10.7 *Carrier sense multiple access* (CSMA) protocols are used when a number of users must share a single channel for the transmission of fixed size messages (see Tanenbaum, 1988). Transmitting a message takes $W = N/S$ seconds, where N is the number of bits (assume 64 bits) and S is the speed of the channel (assumed to be 4800 bps). Each user is assumed to be able to monitor the state of the channel *before* transmission. In 1 — *persistent CSMA*, if an existing transmission is detected, the sender waits until the channel is free and then tries to transmit. If when transmitting the sender detects a collision because another party has transmitted, then the message is retransmitted a random time later. Assume that the random delays are exponentially distributed with a mean of *30*W* seconds. Design a simulation model to investigate the performance of this protocol, presenting the results in the form of a graph of throughput (number of messages) against normalized offered load, in which K messages per second is represented as WK attempts per message time.

10.8 Another variant of the CSMA protocol of Example 10.7 is *p-persistent CSMA*. In this scheme, the channel is divided into slots each W seconds wide, where $W = N/S$, N being the number of bits (assume 64) and S the speed of the channel (assume 4800 bps). The sender senses the channel before transmitting. If it is sensed idle the message is transmitted with probability p and deferred until the next slot with probability $q = 1 - p$. If the next slot is idle, it again transmits or defers with probability p and q. This is repeated until the message has been transmitted or until another station has broadcast on the channel. If the latter case is true then it is treated as a collision, a random time is waited and then the above procedure tried again. If the channel was initially sensed busy, then the above procedure is started from the first slot that is sensed idle. Assume that the random delay is geometrically distributed with a mean of 30 slot times.

Perform a simulation to analyse the performance of this protocol, presenting the results in the form of a graph of throughput (number of messages) against normalized offered load, in which K messages per second is represented as WK attempts per message time.

10.9 Compare the results of the CSMA protocols of Examples 10.7 and 10.8 and the Aloha protocols of Example 9.3. Which gives the best performance?

11

EXPERIMENTAL DESIGN AND REGRESSION ANALYSIS

The previous chapters have focused on the mechanics of model development and methods of results analysis. In this chapter we concentrate on the statistical design and analysis of the experiments performed with the model. We begin by introducing the terms that will be used throughout this chapter. This is followed by a discussion of experimental design. Details of some specific types of experiment are given along with appropriate methods of analysis. We then introduce the main ideas behind regression analysis.

11.1 INTRODUCTION

The two main topics of this chapter, namely experimental design and regression analysis, allow results to be obtained from simulation models (and sampling in general) efficiently. This capability is particularly desirable with optimization type problems. This is because with these types of problems we know at the outset the kind of result wanted (i.e. a minimum or maximum); what we are really trying to do is find the corresponding set of input values that give it. For example, suppose we have an optimization problem for which a simulation model has been developed. After running the model with a given set of input values a set of outputs, or samples, is obtained. The question to be answered is whether this represents the desired maximum or minimum. Obviously, there is no way of knowing unless the experiment is repeated with different inputs and the corresponding outputs compared. In the naive approach the entire input state space must be covered, that is, an experiment must be performed for every possible value and combination of the input variables. This is an enormous undertaking and simply not practical in most cases.

THE DESIGN OF EXPERIMENTS **245**

Compare the above process to, say, simulation studies oriented more towards analysis. Here we have a set of input variables and we wish to know how their value affects the output. The important point to note is that we are not searching for any particular output value. So only those input values that are, for one reason or another, of interest need be selected to run the model with. Optimization problems, therefore, present unique difficulties and it is these difficulties that experimental design and regression help to address. Using these techniques we only have to deal with a relatively few input values instead of having to search through all possible values. The problem therefore becomes tractable and so feasible for simulation analysis.

The benefits of experimental design and regression analysis that have been referred to above, become increasingly significant as the size of the problem space increases. The more input variables there are, the more inefficient naive experimentation is to perform. Such is the advantage of experimental design and regression analysis for optimization type problems that there is hardly any situation in which the naive approach, or any variant of it, is justified.

These techniques are also extremely useful for parameter estimation in which system parameters must be determined from measurements made on a real system. Rather than take naive measurements, a plan can be developed for gathering data in which a suitable experimental design is selected and appropriate analysis techniques employed. This will enable the parameters to be determined quickly and with the smallest possible error.

11.2 TERMINOLOGY

In line with most textbooks on statistical design we introduce here the term *treatment* to indicate the set of input variables and the value they have been assigned during a single execution of the experiment. This single execution of the experiment is termed a *trial*. An experiment will consist of several such trials. The trial generates samples or observations from each of the output variables. It is easier all round if there is only a single output variable. Where this is not true it is necessary to repeat the experiments for each variable concerned.

An *experimental unit* can be thought of as the environment or configuration of the experiment. In a simulation of a computer network, for example, it could encompass the number of workstations connected or the distribution of servers. In some experiments there may be a different experimental unit for each trial and in this situation it is necessary to decide how to assign treatments to experimental units. Alternatively, several trials may be made on the same experimental unit. In this case the trials must be made serially and the order in which they are carried out must be determined.

11.3 THE ANALYSIS OF VARIANCE

We saw in Chapter 10 a technique for comparing the equivalence of two means. It is often necessary to employ a more general technique that allows an arbitrary number of means to be compared. This new technique is called the *analysis of variance* (commonly abbreviated to ANOVA) since it partitions the variation in any series of samples into components due to ascribable causes, such as treatment effects or differences between groups of the treatment material, and a component unassignable to any individual cause—a *residual* or *error* component.

ANOVA allows us to state whether the means μ_1 ... μ_k from normal populations which equal variances, are all the same. The null hypothesis is thus

$$H_0: \mu_1 = \mu_2 = \cdots = \mu_k \tag{11.1}$$

against the alternative hypothesis that two or more means are different.

The test commonly used in the ANOVA is the *variance-ratio test* (the F test), carried out by calculating variances and using the ratios of each mean square to the error mean square. Tables of the F distribution (see Appendix C) can be used to decide when such ratios are significant. For instance, reference to the table of the F distribution in Appendix C shows that the ratio of two variances based on 3 and 12 degrees of freedom would exceed the value of 3.49 by pure chance in only 5 per cent of cases and the value 5.95 by pure chance in only 1 per cent of cases. A higher value would certainly indicate the existence of significant differences between the treatments, i.e. that the factors that differed in the treatments resulted in real differences in the output variable.

11.4 SOME TYPES OF EXPERIMENT

In its most limited form an experiment may consist of a number of samples taken from a system under a single set of conditions. An example of this is the evaluation of a communications system in which a single, fixed, topology and protocol configuration is considered under a steady traffic load. In such an experiment the variations in the results of system performance analysis can be attributed solely to uncontrollable random effects. This is the *unifactor* type of experiment.

More extensive is an experiment which varies some of the conditions assumed fixed in the unifactor type of experiment. For example, a number of network configurations and routing algorithms may be examined. The effect of different topologies and protocols could then be estimated at the same time as the system performance. This is a *factorial* type of experiment.

Still more general results can be obtained from unifactor or factorial experiments under variable conditions. In the example above, this may involve diurnal or seasonal variations in traffic patterns. The average effect of the traffic pattern may then be determined under these varying conditions. Obviously, a series of experiments must be carried out in order to do this.

These brief descriptions illustrate that a particular experiment may be organized or designed in several different ways. We will just concentrate on three important types of design from the many that have been developed over the years, to illustrate the central ideas involved. The designs that will be covered are:

- *completely randomized designs*, in which the aim is to remove systematic bias
- *randomized block designs*, in which stratification is used to improve efficiency
- *factorial designs*, in which the interdependences between system variables are analysed.

The treatment given in this subsection should be detailed enough to allow the techniques described to be applied to your own simulations. For a more comprehensive coverage encompassing many more designs refer to a specialist text such as Cochran and Cox (1957).

11.4.1 Completely randomized design

The errors present in most sampling experiments are rarely uncorrelated. It seems intuitively obvious that several measurements, taken in a short interval, will normally resemble each other more than measurements spread over a much longer period. There is clear evidence of correlation at work here. Such related measurements provide a poor basis for (global) inferences. Coupled with this is a natural tendency to be over-confident in the answer obtained because the results are so consistent. From a sampling viewpoint, a subpopulation has been selected which is more homogeneous than the population as a whole, so the expected random errors are actually unseen *systematic errors* or *bias*.

The problem of bias can be minimized with a procedure called *randomization*. The principles of randomization can be stated as follows:

1. Allocate treatments in random order to experimental units so that every treatment will have an equal chance of being assigned to each experimental unit.
2. Randomize the sequence in which treatments are applied so that the effect of uncontrolled variables that vary slowly with time are not confused with the effects of the controlled variables.

An experiment following along these lines is said to be *completely randomized*. The consequence is that the bias appears to be scrambled, making it appear more like a random error, and hence amenable to statistical treatment.

In order to analyse such an experiment the simplest version of the ANOVA procedure, called the *one-way ANOVA*, can be used. In this version there are k sets of samples, each one from a different population. Set i comprises n_i samples, there are $n = \Sigma n_i$ samples in total and the sum of all of them is T. The different populations involve variation in one controlled variable only. For instance, we might have results from a simulation concerning the performance of an operating system for several different scheduling algorithms all run under the same conditions. The jth observation from the ith population is labelled x_{ij}. The x_{ij} are assumed to be mutually independent and normally distributed and the true means μ_i and variance σ^2 from each population are unknown.

The ANOVA is laid out as a table. The normal method of presentation is to compute the sample totals, means and variances for each treatment as shown in Table 11.1.

We now compute various *sums of squares* (denoted by SS). There are three squares of interest in the one-way ANOVA. The first is the *total sum of squares*, the second is the *sum of squares due to treatments* or the *among populations sum of squares* and the third is the *sum of squares due to error* or *within population sum of squares*.

For the *total sum of squares* (TSS) we have

$$TSS = SS_x - \frac{T^2}{n} \tag{11.2}$$

where the sum of squares of all the samples is denoted by SS_x and given by

$$SS_x = \sum_{i=1}^{k} \sum_{j=1}^{s} x_{ij}^2 \tag{11.3}$$

Table 11.1 Data for the one-way analysis of variance

	Treatment 1	...	Treatment k
	x_{11}		x_{k1}
	x_{12}		x_{k2}
	$\vdots$		$\vdots$
	x_{1n_1}		x_{kn_k}
Column totals	$T_1 = \sum_{j=1}^{n_1} x_{1j}$		$T_k = \sum_{j=1}^{n_k} x_{kj}$
Sample means	$\bar{x}_1 = \dfrac{1}{n_1} \sum_{j=1}^{n_1} x_{1j}$		$\bar{x}_k = \dfrac{1}{n_k} \sum_{j=1}^{n_k} x_{kj}$

The sum of squares due to treatments (SS_T) is given by

$$SS_T = \sum_{i=1}^{k} \frac{T_i^2}{n_i} - \frac{T^2}{n} \tag{11.4}$$

and the sum of squares due to error (SS_E) is given by

$$SS_E = TSS - SS_T = \sum_{i=1}^{k} (n_i - 1)s_i^2 \tag{11.5}$$

where the s_i^2 are the sample variances.

The *mean squares* (MS) can now be calculated. These are the sums of squares which have been normalized by their degrees of freedom. For the mean square due to error we have

$$MS_E = \frac{SS_E}{n - k} \tag{11.6}$$

and for the mean square due to treatments we have

$$MS_T = \frac{SS_T}{k - 1} \tag{11.7}$$

The ratio F can now be computed from

$$F = \frac{MS_T}{MS_E} \tag{11.8}$$

The value of F can be used to judge whether the relative variation in the error term is sufficient to reject the null hypothesis with some fixed, pre-assigned level of confidence. As was mentioned above, the applicable test statistic is chosen from the F distribution since it can be shown that SS_T/σ^2 and SS_E/σ^2 each have χ^2 distributions with $k - 1$ and $n - k$ degrees of freedom respectively. Hence, the ratio F has an F distribution with $(k - 1, n - k)$ degrees of freedom irrespective of the value of σ^2 and the assumed common value of the μ_i. If some small fixed probability α such as 0.05 or 0.01 is selected, then a value d can be determined from

$$d = F_{k-1, n-k, \alpha} \tag{11.9}$$

and, from the table in Appendix C, the null hypothesis can be rejected when $F > d$ with a level of confidence of $1 - \alpha$.

Using the approach of Sec. 10.4 we can also ascribe a confidence interval to the treatment means. Since the random error is assumed to be normally distributed the standard deviation (or standard error) of the sample mean is

$$s = \sqrt{\left(\frac{MS_E}{n}\right)} \tag{11.10}$$

while the standard deviation of the difference between means of n and m samples is

$$\sqrt{\left[MS_E\left(\frac{1}{n}+\frac{1}{m}\right)\right]} \tag{11.11}$$

Example 11.1 The data in Table 11.2 consists of five sets of eight samples along with the corresponding sample means and variances. We now wish to perform an ANOVA on this data.

The first thing to do is determine the overall mean. This is the mean of the sample means, i.e.

$$\bar{x} = (62.6 + 65.4 + 64.2 + 63.4 + 70.9)/5 = 65.3$$

The overall total is

$$T = (500.7 + 523.4 + 514.0 + 506.8 + 567.0) = 2611.9$$

From (11.2) and (11.3) the total sum of squares is

$$TSS = (57.0^2 + 64.8^2 + \cdots + 54.4^2) - 2611.9^2/40 = 7584.1$$

From (11.4) treatment sum of squares is

$$SS_T = (500.7^2 + 523.4^2 + 514.0^2 + 506.8^2 + 567.0^2)/8 - 2611.9^2/40 = 346.9$$

and from (11.5) the error sum of squares is

$$SS_E = 7584.1 - 346.9 = 7237.2$$

The *ANOVA table* can now be constructed (Table 11.3).

Table 11.2 Data for Example 11.1

	Treatment 1	Treatment 2	Treatment 3	Treatment 4	Treatment 5
	57.0	64.8	70.7	68.3	76.0
	55.0	66.6	59.4	67.1	74.5
	62.1	69.5	64.5	69.1	76.5
	74.5	61.1	74.0	72.7	86.6
	86.7	91.8	78.5	90.6	94.7
	42.0	51.8	55.8	44.3	43.2
	71.9	69.2	63.0	53.8	61.1
	51.5	48.6	48.1	40.9	54.4
Column totals	500.7	523.4	514.0	506.8	567.0
Sample means	62.6	65.4	64.2	63.4	70.9

Table 11.3 An analysis of variance table for Example 11.1

Source of variation	Degrees of freedom	Sum of squares	Mean square	Ratio	F test
Treatments	4	346.9	86.7	0.42	$F_{4,35,0.05} = 2.63$
Error	35	7237.2	206.7		

From Table 11.3, it can be concluded that there is no evidence to reject the hypothesis that the population means are the same at the 5 per cent level. In other words the effect of each of the treatments is essentially the same, there is no apparent difference.

Confidence intervals for the means can also be deduced. Taking a 95 per cent confidence interval then, from tables of the Student's t distribution in Appendix C for $\alpha = 0.025$ and 7 degrees of freedom, we have

$$\pm 2.365 * \sqrt{206.7/8} = \pm 12.0$$

for the confidence interval of a treatment mean and

$$\pm 2.365 * \sqrt{206.7\left(\frac{1}{8} + \frac{1}{8}\right)} = \pm 17.0$$

for the confidence interval between treatment means.

11.4.2 Randomized block design

The previous section showed how randomization can be used to avoid bias even if nothing is known about the pattern of uncontrolled variables. Eliminating bias, though, is only part of our quest; we also want to be able to achieve some stated degree of accuracy. This implies that multiple samples must be taken. In many systems we will have some knowledge of the relationships between the system variables. This can be used to good effect in a technique called *stratification* or *stratified sampling*, in which experimental units are combined into blocks such that the grouped units resemble each other with respect to the uncontrolled variables, more so than the experimental units in other blocks. For example, suppose an experiment concerning two treatments called A and B is performed which extends over several hours. Further suppose that there exist uncontrolled variables fluctuating at an hourly rate. Then samples taken in the same ten minute interval will show better agreement than samples separated by an hour or more. This effect can introduce bias into the results if ignored. The danger can be minimized by taking equal samples from both A and B which are close together in time, say five minutes. This kind of design is termed a *randomized block design* and is far more effective in increasing precision than a completely randomized design.

In a randomized block design all comparisons are made within a block and not from block to block. In order to analyse such an arrangement the same ANOVA can be used as in the previous design, except that we also take into account the fact that x_{aw}, the wth observation in block a, is related to the x_{bw}, the wth observation in block b. This means that each treatment must have the same number of samples s. In comparison to the previous section, this method of analysis of variance is called the *two-way ANOVA*.

The standard way in which the data is laid out in the randomized block is shown in Table 11.4. Treatments are represented in columns and the blocks are represented as rows and there are $n = sk$ samples in total.

The overall sample mean is given by the mean of sample means:

$$\bar{x} = \frac{T}{n}$$

$$= \frac{1}{k} \sum_{i=1}^{k} \bar{x}_i$$

$$= \frac{1}{sk} \sum_{i=1}^{k} \sum_{j=1}^{s} x_{ij} \qquad (11.12)$$

Table 11.4 Arrangement of the data for a randomized block design

	Treatment 1	...	Treatment k	Row totals
Block 1	x_{11}		x_{k1}	$B_1 = \sum_{i=1}^{k} x_{i1}$:
:	:		:	
Block s	x_{1s}		x_{ks}	$B_s = \sum_{i=1}^{k} x_{is}$
Column totals	$T_1 = \sum_{j=1}^{n_1} x_{1j}$		$T_k = \sum_{j=1}^{n_k} x_{kj}$	$T = \sum_{i=1}^{k} \sum_{j=1}^{s} x_{ij}$
Sample means	$\bar{x}_1 = \frac{T_1}{n_1}$		$\bar{x}_k = \frac{T_k}{n_k}$	

and the sum of squares of all the samples, denoted by SS_x, is given by

$$SS_x = \sum_{i=1}^{k} \sum_{j=1}^{s} x_{ij}^2 \qquad (11.13)$$

The total sum of squares (TSS) can be partitioned into a sum of squares due to treatments (SS_T), a sum of squares due to blocks (SS_B) and a sum of squares due to error (SS_E) as follows:

$$TSS = SS_x - \frac{T^2}{n} \qquad (11.14)$$

$$SS_T = \frac{1}{s} \sum_{i=1}^{k} T_i^2 - \frac{T^2}{n} \qquad (11.15)$$

$$SS_B = \frac{1}{k} \sum_{j=1}^{s} B_j^2 - \frac{T^2}{n} \qquad (11.16)$$

$$SS_E = TSS - SS_T - SS_B \qquad (11.17)$$

The mean sum of squares can now be calculated. There are three mean squares of interest, the mean square due to treatments, the mean square due to blocks and the mean square due to error.

$$MS_T = \frac{SS_T}{k-1} \qquad (11.18)$$

$$MS_B = \frac{SS_B}{s-1} \qquad (11.19)$$

$$MS_E = \frac{SS_E}{(n-k-b+1)} = \frac{SS_E}{(b-1)(k-1)} \qquad (11.20)$$

Two hypothesis can be tested using this approach. The first is the hypothesis that the treatment means are equal and the second is the hypothesis that the block means are equal. (The reason for the names one-way and two-way analysis of variance should now become clear.) To test the hypothesis the applicable F ratio is calculated and compared to its value given in the table for the F distribution in Appendix C for some small, fixed, value of α. The applicable F ratios are

$$F = \frac{MS_T}{MS_E} \qquad (11.21)$$

to test the equality of the treatment means and

$$F = \frac{MS_B}{MS_E} \qquad (11.22)$$

to test the equality of the block means.

The expressions in the previous section concerning the standard deviation of the sample mean and difference between means, Eqs (11.10) and (11.11), also apply in exactly the same form here.

These ideas are now reinforced by looking at an example.

Example 11.2 Consider Example 11.1 again, but this time let us assume that we are dealing with a randomized block design in which the samples across each row are made in the same block. So Table 11.2 can be written in a slightly different form as shown in Table 11.5.

Now calculate the sum of squares:

$TSS = 7584.1$ (as before)
$SS_T = 346.9$ (as before)
$SS_B = (336.8^2 + 322.6^2 + \cdots + 243.5^2)/5 - 2611.9^2/40 = 6099.5$
$SS_E = 7584.1 - 346.9 - 6099.5 = 1137.7$

The ANOVA table can then be constructed (Table 11.6).

Table 11.5 Data for Example 11.2

	Treatment 1	Treatment 2	Treatment 3	Treatment 4	Treatment 5	Row totals
Block 1	57.0	64.8	70.7	68.3	76.0	336.8
Block 2	55.0	66.6	59.4	67.1	74.5	322.6
Block 3	62.1	69.5	64.5	69.1	76.5	341.7
Block 4	74.5	61.1	74.0	72.7	86.6	368.9
Block 5	86.7	91.8	78.5	90.6	94.7	442.3
Block 6	42.0	51.8	55.8	44.3	43.2	237.1
Block 7	71.9	69.2	63.0	53.8	61.1	319.0
Block 8	51.5	48.6	48.1	40.9	54.4	243.5
Column totals	500.7	523.4	514.0	506.8	567.0	2611.9
Sample means	62.6	65.4	64.2	63.4	70.9	65.3

Table 11.6 An analysis of variance table for Example 11.2

Source of variation	Degrees of freedom	Sum of squares	Mean square	Ratio	F test
Blocks	7	6099.5	871.4	21.4	$F_{7,28,0.05} = 2.36$
Treatments	4	346.9	86.7	2.14	$F_{4,28,0.05} = 2.71$
Error	28	1137.7	40.6		
Total	39	7584.1			

From Table 11.6 it can be concluded that there is no evidence to reject the hypothesis that there is no significant difference between the treatments at the 5 per cent level. There is, however, a significant effect between blocks, but due to the way in which we have organized the design we have not allowed this variation to mask the effect of different treatments.

Let us also look at the 95 per cent confidence interval for the treatment means as we did in the last example. The confidence interval is

$$\pm\, 2.365* \sqrt{\frac{40.6}{8}} = \pm\, 5.3$$

and the confidence interval for the difference between means is

$$\pm\, 2.365* \sqrt{40.6\left(\frac{1}{8} + \frac{1}{8}\right)} = \pm\, 7.5$$

The increased accuracy of the randomized block design over the completely randomized design is apparent in these results.

11.4.3 Factorial design

In the experimental designs considered in the last section the treatment effects are compared under a fixed set of conditions. The results of such experiments are applicable only under the conditions under which they were carried out, and if these conditions change the results may be completely altered. Only by varying the treatments can wider results be obtained. In the *factorial design* the conditions under which the treatments are investigated are varied. This is used to determine to what extent different conditions acting together and individually contribute to the results. By using this approach, the consistency of each effect may be tested and, where it is shown to be dependent on the other treatments, any interrelation can be studied. If the sets of factors do not interact, then all may be used in making treatment comparisons. If, however, some interaction is found, then attention may have to be restricted to particular combinations.

The conditions that are thought to affect the output of interest are called *factors*. The various settings of these factors are termed *levels* and the set of factor–level combinations defines a treatment. To illustrate the use of these terms consider an investigation into the effects of three different routing algorithms in a communications network at, say, low and high levels of traffic intensity. In this example two factors are being analysed: the routing algorithm and the traffic load. There are three levels for the routing algorithm and two levels for the traffic intensity, giving us a total of $3 \times 2 = 6$ treatments.

One practical problem with factorial experiments is that the number of sets of factors grows large very quickly because each possible combination of the factors is covered. For n factors each at k levels there is a total of n^k sets of factors, and so the complexity of the analysis grows exponentially. The complexity can sometimes be reduced by combining factors or by omitting those combinations that are not sensible. Even so, a factorial experiment is likely to require a lot of time.

Another problem is that the ANOVA tests assumes that either the results produced at the different factor levels are independent of each other or else they are matched on all factors apart from the ones of interest and that these vary independently of the rest. Neither assumption is completely true for simulation models and so some care has to be exercised when analysing the results. Ideally, a statistical software package should be used for analysis, but even then, the results may be inconclusive because the conditions for the statistical tests may not be completely satisfied.

Let us look in more detail at one type of factorial experiment, the 2^3 design. This design compares all combinations of three factors each at two levels. Suppose we have treatments A, B and C and that the higher level of each treatment is denoted by A, B, C and the lower level by a, b, c. Then the $2^3 = 8$ treatment combinations are $abc, Abc, aBc, abC, ABc, AbC, aBC, ABC$. Given any set of treatment combinations the effects and interactions can be explored by comparing half of the samples with the other half. Suppose we wish to examine the effect of treatment A. Then the mean of treatment combinations with a high level of treatment A are compared to those with a low level of treatment A, i.e. the mean of $Abc + ABc + AbC + ABC$ is compared to the mean of $aBC + abC + aBc + abc$. Call this effect (A); then

$$(A) = \overline{Abc + ABc + AbC + ABC} - \overline{aBC + abC + aBc + abc} \quad (11.23)$$

In a similar vein we have

$$(B) = \overline{aBc + ABc + aBC + ABC} - \overline{AbC + abC + Abc + abc} \quad (11.24)$$

and

$$(C) = \overline{abC + aBC + AbC + ABC} - \overline{ABc + Abc + aBc + abc} \quad (11.25)$$

Now consider the first-order effects in which factors act together in pairs. This consists of the interaction between A and B, A and C and B and C formed from half the change in the effect of any factor by the introduction of another, as follows:

$$(AB) = \overline{ABc + ABC + abC + abc} - \overline{Abc + aBc + AbC + aBC} \quad (11.26)$$

$$(BC) = \overline{aBC + ABC + Abc + abc} - \overline{abC + aBc + ABc + AbC} \quad (11.27)$$

$$(AC) = \overline{AbC + ABC + aBc + abc} - \overline{Abc + abC + ABc + aBC} \quad (11.28)$$

Finally, a second-order interaction is present when all three factors interact. It is given by half the difference of any first-order interaction in the presence and absence of a third factor. Using the above notation,

$$(ABC) = \overline{ABC + Abc + aBc + abC} - \overline{abc + aBC + AbC + ABc} \quad (11.29)$$

These seven relationships summarize all the possible interactions that can take place. They are each independent of one another and of equal accuracy, so can be used to determine the significant interactions in a factorial design. This will be illustrated in the following example.

Example 11.3 In this example we consider a 2^3 factorial design in five blocks of the eight treatment combinations, giving a total of $8 \times 5 = 40$ samples. The source data is given in Table 11.7. Each column in the table is headed with the treatment combination. So the first column consists of those samples made when the three factors were all at their low levels. Each row consists of those samples made in the same block using the approach of the randomized block design.

Table 11.7 Data for Example 11.3

	abc	Abc	aBc	ABc	abC	AbC	aBC	ABC	Row total
Block 1	46.8	69.2	70.7	64.8	86.6	57.0	36.8	41.2	473.1
Block 2	42.6	48.6	59.4	66.6	94.7	55.0	22.6	32.1	421.6
Block 3	41.7	44.3	64.5	69.5	43.2	12.7	34.7	34.6	345.2
Block 4	49.0	53.8	63.0	72.7	61.1	34.2	39.0	31.3	404.1
Block 5	43.5	40.9	48.1	90.6	54.4	42.0	23.5	23.2	366.2
Col total	223.6	256.8	305.7	364.2	340.0	200.9	156.6	162.4	2010.2
Means	44.72	51.36	61.14	72.84	68.0	40.18	31.32	32.48	50.26

Our initial step in the analysis is to estimate the treatment effects from the treatment totals as shown in Table 11.8. We first write down the order of the treatments in the left-hand column. Note the order used, which must be adhered to. In the next column we enter the total for each treatment. The third column contains the sums in pairs of the totals in the first four positions and the difference in the second four positions. Hence we have the total for $ABC + ABc$ in the first position, the total for $AbC + Abc$ in the second position and so on. In the fifth position we have the difference $ABC - ABc$, in the sixth position $AbC - Abc$. In this way we continue for the rest of the column.

Now the second difference column is generated in the same way, but based on the values in the first difference column, not the treatment totals. So the first position contains $(ABC + ABc) + (AbC + Abc)$, the second position $(abC + aBc) + (abc + abC)$ and so on.

The third difference column repeats this operation on the second difference column. The first position in this column contains the sum of all the terms $((ABC + ABc) + (AbC + Abc)) + ((aBC + aBc) + (abC + abc))$. The other positions give the effect of the various combinations of factors. For example, the second position contains the sum $((ABC - ABc) + (AbC - Abc)) + ((aBC - aBc) + (abC - abc))$, which gives us Eq. (11.25) for the effect of factor C by itself. If there were more than three factors then more columns would be required, but with only three the process is stopped here.

A good check on the accuracy of the calculation so far is that the first position of the third column should be the overall total. The main effects and interactions can now be calculated from the third difference column by dividing by half the number of samples, which in this example is half of 40 or 20. These values go in the final column.

We are now in a position to draw some conclusions from this data. The basic results for A, B and C are all negative, indicating that individually at least they all

Table 11.8 Calculation of the main effects for the data in Example 11.3

Label	Total	Sums and differences			Effect	Mean
ABC	162.4	526.6	984.3	2010.2	Total	
ABc	364.2	457.7	1025.9	−290.4	(C)	−14.5
AbC	200.9	462.3	−257.7	−32.4	(B)	−1.6
Abc	256.8	563.6	−32.7	−411.4	(BC)	−20.6
aBC	156.6	−201.8	68.9	−41.6	(A)	−2.1
aBc	305.7	−55.9	−101.3	−225.0	(AC)	−11.3
abC	340.0	−149.1	−145.9	170.2	(AB)	8.5
abc	223.6	116.4	−265.5	119.6	(ABC)	6.0

act to decrease the effects. Of these individual effects, the effect for C is the strongest. The individual effects of A and B cause the smallest reduction. However, when A and B are combined they show the largest increase. The effect of C is relatively weak when A and B are combined.

The overall conclusion then (assuming decreases are of interest) is that the most beneficial results are to be obtained from having factor C at a high level. The effect is reinforced if factor B is also at a high level. There is significant disadvantage in having factor A at a high level.

Although the above comments apply irrespective of the errors involved, as with all statistical data it is necessary to determine the accuracy of these results. We must determine which of the results are significantly different from zero and cannot be explained from chance variation alone. To do this we calculate the standard deviations via an ANOVA as depicted in Table 11.9. The style is the same as for the randomized block type of analysis from the previous section, so

$$T = 2010.2$$
$$TSS = (46.8^2 + 69.2^2 + \cdots + 23.2^2) - 2010.2^2/40$$
$$= 114626.36 - 101022.6 = 13603.8$$
$$SS_T = (473.1^2 + 421.6^2 + \cdots + 366.2^2)/8 - 2010.2^2/40$$
$$= 102266.6 - 101022.6 = 1244.0$$
$$SS_B = (223.6^2 + 256.8^2 + \cdots + 162.4^2)/5 - 2010.2^2/40$$
$$= 109779.1 - 101022.6 = 8756.5$$
$$SS_E = 7584.1 - 346.9 - 6099.5$$
$$= 13603 - 8756.5 - 1244.0$$
$$= 3602.5$$

We can then construct the ANOVA table (Table 11.9).

Table 11.9 An analysis of variance table for Example 11.3

Source of variation	Degrees of freedom	Sum of squares	Mean square	Ratio
Blocks	4	8756.5	2189.1	17.0
Treatments	7	1244.0	177.7	1.38
Error	28	3602.5	128.7	
Total	39	13603.0		

The standard deviations of the treatment effects may now be calculated from

$$\sqrt{4s^2/N} \tag{11.30}$$

where s is the mean square of the error term and N is the number of samples (here 40). This becomes

$$\sqrt{\left(\frac{4*128.7}{40}\right)} = \pm 3.59$$

when the values from the example are substituted. From the table of Student's t distribution given in Appendix C the 1 per cent level of significance for 28 degrees of freedom is 2.76. The result, when 2.76 is multiplied by the standard deviation, 3.59, is 9.91. Hence the effects (A), (B), (AB) and (ABC) are not significantly different from zero at the 1 per cent level, all the rest are.

Similar results are obtainable by calculating the sum of squares for each component separately. The sum of squares is obtained by squaring the values in the third difference column of Table 11.8 and dividing by the number of samples, i.e. 40. The resulting partition of the sum of squares is shown in Table 11.10. In practice we would not bother with such a partition since it tells us nothing which cannot be calculated directly.

Finally, tables of means and their standard deviations must be prepared. Often, only the significant differences are of interest, but, where the experiment is one of a series, other tables may be required. These tables of means may be constructed directly from the treatment totals or may be derived from the calculated effects. The latter approach is preferable when there are large numbers of factors.

Table 11.10 Partition of treatment sum of squares

	Degrees of freedom	Sum of squares
(B)	1	2108.3
(C)	1	26.2
(BC)	1	4231.4
(A)	1	43.3
(AC)	1	1265.6
(AB)	1	4231.2
(ABC)	1	742.2
Treatments	7	12648.2

Table 11.11 Two-way table of means for factors B and C

	Without C	With C	Mean
Without B	48.01	54.11	51.06
With B	67.01	31.91	49.46
Mean	57.51	43.01	50.26

The overall mean $\bar{x}$ in this example is 50.26. Knowing this, the effect of the different factors can be determined. Suppose we wanted to look at the mean effect with and without factor C. Then we calculate

$$\text{Mean effect with } C = \bar{x} + \tfrac{1}{2}(C) = 50.26 - 7.25 = 43.01$$
$$\text{Mean effect without } C = \bar{x} - \tfrac{1}{2}(C) = 50.26 + 7.25 = 57.51$$

In a similar fashion a table to show the interaction of, say, factors C and B could be constructed. If we do this we get

$$\text{Mean effect with B and } C = \bar{x} + \tfrac{1}{2}[(C) + (B) + (CB)] = 31.91$$
$$\text{Mean effect with C but without B} = \bar{x} + \tfrac{1}{2}[(C) - (B) - (CB)] = 54.11$$
$$\text{Mean effect without C but with B} = \bar{x} + \tfrac{1}{2}[-(C) + (B) - (CB)] = 67.01$$
$$\text{Mean effect without C or B} = \bar{x} + \tfrac{1}{2}[-(C) - (B) + (CB)] = 48.01$$

which is presented in Table 11.11.

This experiment has relatively few factors so these tables can be constructed directly from the treatment totals. In larger experiments the need to perform the above analysis is very time consuming, but the use of statistical software packages takes the drudgery out of much of this work.

11.5 REGRESSION ANALYSIS

Samples taken of an output variable of a model for some fixed values assigned to the model input variables form a probability distribution. Different values assigned to the input variables would normally culminate in a different distribution. The line which joins the mean values of these distributions is called the *regression curve*, as illustrated in Fig. 11.1.

The purpose of *regression analysis* is to obtain the best form of equation to predict the value of the dependent variable, y, as a function of a set of *predictor variables* $\{x_1, ..., x_n\}$. 'Best' in this sense means that the errors associated with the prediction must be a minimum. This task would be almost trivial if the curve

Distributions of the output variable

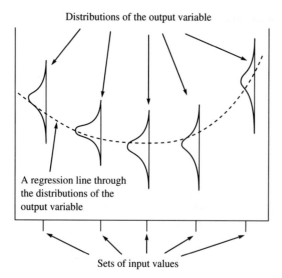

A regression line through
the distributions of the
output variable

Sets of input values

Figure 11.1 The concept of regression.

could be determined directly from the simulation outputs but, because stochastic variables all have some degree of 'noise', we are forced to use statistical techniques.

We assume that the general form of the relationship between the variables is

$$y = \text{deterministic function of } \{x_1, ..., x_n\} + \text{random error}$$

and that the mean value of the random error is zero, so that the expected value of y (the long-term average value) is equal to the deterministic component, i.e.

$$E(y) = \text{deterministic function of } \{x_1, ..., x_n\}$$

The first step in regression analysis is to hypothesize the form of $E(y)$, the deterministic function of $\{x_1, ..., x_n\}$. Only the simplest case in which $n = 1$ and the form of $E(y)$ is a linear function of x will be considered here. The approach can be generalized to *non-linear regression* by considering other than simple linear relationships. However, the basic steps are the same, irrespective of the form of the regression formula. Additional simplifications are made by considering only a single predictor variable, as opposed to the more general technique of *multiple regression*, in which several predictor variables are used. In practice this would be a severe restriction, but it enables a clearer explanation of the method. These more elaborate variants can be found in Wetherill (1986).

The decision to use a particular form of regression formula might be based on theoretical grounds, in which a known or hypothesized mathematical relationship between variables is to be verified. However, in simulation the form of the simulation model is very often unknown. It then becomes necessary to guess the functional form by inspection of the scatter diagram and then calculate the values of the parameters of the equation. An example scatter diagram is given in Fig. 11.2. This rather hit-and-miss approach may also have to be repeated several times before an adequate fit is found. This is why it is useful to have a software package that will perform the time-consuming calculations necessary.

Since we are concerned with only one predictor variable, the regression curve reduces to $f(x)$ and the relationship between y and x becomes

$$y = f(x) + \varepsilon \tag{11.31}$$

in which ε is the error term. In Eq. (11.31) $f(x)$ is deterministic, so for a fixed value of x we always obtain the same value of y. The problem is then to determine $f(x)$ in the presence of ε. When we restrict our attention to linear regression Eq. (11.31) reduces to

$$y = \beta_0 + \beta_1 x + \varepsilon \tag{11.32}$$

A plot of x against y might look something like the scatter diagram of Fig. 11.2. Here a straight line has been drawn through the set of sample points in such a way that the error is a minimum. So the line represents the *best possible* linear fit with the observed data.

Referring to Fig. 11.2 and Eq. (11.32) we find that

- y is the dependent variable
- x is the predictor variable (the independent variable)
- β_0 is the y-axis intercept of the line and
- β_1 is the slope of the line.

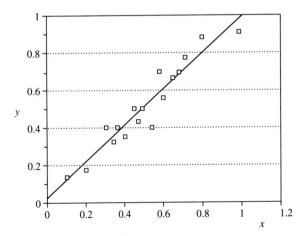

Figure 11.2 Example of linear regression.

Suppose that a set of samples $(x_1, y_1), ..., (x_n, y_n)$ are taken. By fitting a straight line to the data we can specify a corresponding set of *fitted points* $(x_1, Y_1), ..., (x_n, Y_n)$. Then the minimum error occurs when the sum of the squares of the distances

$$\frac{1}{n} \sum_1^n (y_i - Y_i)^2 = \frac{1}{n} \sum_1^n (y_i - (\beta_0 + \beta_1 x_i))^2 \tag{11.33}$$

is a minimum. Hence we have

Definition 11.1 The particular values $\hat{\beta}_0$ and $\hat{\beta}_1$ that minimize Eq. (11.33) are the *least squares values* of the parameters β_0 and β_1 and the straight line $\hat{\beta}_0 + \hat{\beta}_1 x$ is the corresponding *least squares line*.

The parameters of the least squares line can be obtained by differentiating the term for the error component $\Sigma (y_i - Y_i)^2$ and equating it to zero. We will not bother with the algebraic manipulations, but simply state the results:

$$\hat{\beta}_1 = \frac{\text{Cov}(x,y)}{\sigma_x^2}$$

$$= \frac{\displaystyle\sum_{i=1}^n (x_i - \bar{x})(y_i - \bar{y})}{\displaystyle\sum_{i=1}^n (x_i - \bar{x})^2}$$

$$= \frac{\displaystyle\sum_{i=1}^n x_i y_i - n\bar{x}\bar{y}}{\displaystyle\sum_{i-1}^n x_i^2 - n\bar{x}^2} \tag{11.34}$$

and

$$\hat{\beta}_0 = \bar{y} - \bar{x}\beta_1 \tag{11.35}$$

We must now estimate the form of the error component. It would be convenient to assume that it is normally distributed with zero mean and constant variance σ^2. This is shown in Fig. 11.3. The validity of this assumption can be tested and if it is found to be suspect the regression parameters can be recalculated using techniques other than least squares. We will not delve into these complications here though. In practice, the assumptions need not hold exactly for the least squares approach still to be useful.

To determine the probability distribution for ε assuming it is normally distributed with zero mean we must estimate the variance. The estimate s^2 of the

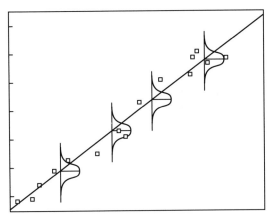

Figure 11.3 Variation of the error distribution.

true variance σ^2 can be calculated from the sum of the squared errors (SSE) between data points (x,y) and the value of the regression line at (x,Y). This is then divided by the number of degrees of freedom. This is 2 less than n, the number of samples, because the intercept and slope has been obtained with them. Hence

$$s^2 = \frac{SSE}{n-2} \qquad (11.36)$$

in which

$$SSE = \sum_{i=1}^{n} (y_i - Y_i)^2$$

$$= n\sigma_y^2 - \beta_1 n \, \text{Cov}(x,y) \qquad (11.37)$$

and

$$\sigma_y^2 = \frac{1}{n} \sum_{i=1}^{n} y_i^2 - \bar{y}^2 \qquad (11.38)$$

Having established the parameters of a regression model it becomes necessary to determine how accurately it describes the data. Since the probability distribution for the error component has been established it can be used to make statistical inferences about the regression model's adequacy in describing the mean $E(y)$ and for predicting values of y for given values of x. A test statistic can be generated for the null hypothesis that the value of x does not contribute to the value of y. We would hope to be able to reject the null hypothesis in favour of the alternative hypothesis that the value of x contributes to the value of y as approximated by the regression line. However, if we had got it completely wrong

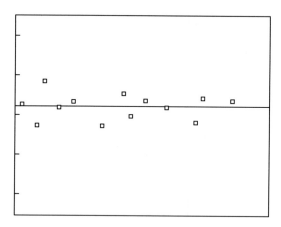

Figure 11.4 Distribution of point data for independent Tx and y.

and the variable y did not depend on x at all, then the regression line would have no x term, so that β_1 would be zero. This is equivalent to saying that the slope of the regression line is zero and that $y = \beta_0 + \varepsilon$. The distribution of the point data might then appear as shown in Fig. 11.4.

Hence, to test the hypothesis that x does not contribute to the value of y against the alternative hypothesis that x does contribute to the value of y, we test:

$$H_0 : \beta_1 = 0$$

against

$$H_1 : \beta_1 \neq 0$$

and if the data does not support the null hypothesis we can conclude that x contributes to the value of y (although of course, other forms of regression equation may give a more accurate match to the sampled data).

The test statistic is derived from the sampling distribution for the least squares estimator of β_1, $\hat{\beta}_1$. If the error terms are normally distributed with zero mean and constant variance σ^2, then the sampling distribution of $\hat{\beta}_1$ will be normally distributed, with mean β_1 and variance

$$\sigma_{\hat{\beta}_1}^2 = \frac{\sigma^2}{n\sigma_x^2} \tag{11.39}$$

which can be estimated by

$$s_{\hat{\beta}_1}^2 = \frac{s^2}{n\sigma_x^2} \tag{11.40}$$

since σ^2 is usually *unknown* a Student's t statistic can be calculated from:

$$t = \frac{\hat{\beta}_1 - \beta_1}{s_{\hat{\beta}_1}} \qquad (11.41)$$

The table of Student's t distribution in Appendix C can be used to obtain the percentage points for t.

If the test statistic causes us to reject the null hypothesis the regression model can be used to estimate the value of y for different values of x. If, on the other hand, the null hypothesis is not rejected, then we must accept the possibility that x does not contribute to the value of y. But, if such a conclusion contradicts what we already know or strongly suspect about the relationship between x and y, then it may be that a linear model is inadequate, in which case we need to consider more complex models. Alternatively, we may seek more data in order to reduce the margin for error, since a single test statistic which supports the null hypothesis does not, by itself, mean that the null hypothesis is necessarily true.

We can also establish a confidence interval for β_1. This follows from Eq. (11.41) as

$$\hat{\beta}_1 \pm t_{\alpha/2}(n-2)s_{\hat{\beta}_1} \qquad (11.42)$$

The confidence interval should confirm the alternative hypothesis, i.e. that the slope of the regression line, β_1, is not zero.

Example 11.4 Let us apply regression analysis to the set of samples in Table 11.12 overleaf. Assume that they have been obtained from a simulation model of a queuing system and relate the total system time against the service time.

The data in Table 11.12 is displayed in the scatter diagram of Fig. 11.5. It appears to be quite linear and we know from theoretical considerations that such a relationship should be linear in the steady state.

The first thing to do is calculate the means and variances of the dependent and independent variables:

$$\bar{x} = (6 + \cdots + 1)/6 = 3.5$$
$$\sigma_x^2 = (1.0^2 + \cdots + 6.0^2)/6 - 3.5^2 = 2.92$$
$$\bar{y} = (4.1 + \cdots 34.5) = 18.6$$
$$\sigma_y^2 = (4.1^2 + \cdots + 34.5^2)/6 - 18.6^2 = 92.6$$

Now the covariance is calculated which, from (10.25), is

$$\text{Cov}(x,y) = \tfrac{1}{6}(-2.5)(-14.5) + \cdots + (2.5)(15.9) = 16.1$$

Table 11.12   Data for Example 11.4

Service time	1.0	2.0	3.0	4.0	5.0	6.0
Total time	4.1	12.3	14.8	22.1	23.7	34.5

and from Eqs (11.34) and (11.35) the least squares estimates are

$$\hat{\beta}_1 = 16.1/2.92 = 5.51$$

$$\hat{\beta}_0 = \bar{y} - \hat{\beta}_1 \bar{x} = 18.6 - 5.51*3.5 = -0.69$$

We can now test the hypothesis that the value of x contributes to the value of y. From Eq. (11.42)

$$t = \frac{\hat{\beta}_1}{s_{\hat{\beta}_1}} \tag{11.43}$$

assuming the test is against an hypothesized slope (β_1) of zero. The estimated standard deviation is, from Eqs (11.36) and (11.37),

$$s^2 = (6*92.6 - 5.51*6*16.1)/4 = 5.83$$

So, from Eq. (11.40)

$$s_{\hat{\beta}_1} = \sqrt{\frac{5.83}{6*2.92}} = 0.58$$

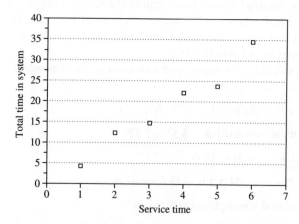

Figure 11.5 Scatter diagram for the data in Table 11.12.

then from Eq. (11.42)

$$t = 5.51/0.58 = 9.5$$

Choosing $\alpha = 0.05$, the rejection region is

$$- t_{0.025}(4) > t \qquad \text{and} \qquad t < t_{0.025}(4)$$

and $t = 9.5$ falls in the upper rejection region and so we can accept the alternative hypothesis that x contributes to the value of y. Finally, the 99 per cent confidence limits for the slope are

$$5.51 \pm 4.604*0.58 = 5.51 \pm 2.7$$

11.6 SUMMARY

In this chapter we looked at the design and analysis of experiments and regression analysis. This is particularly relevant for simulation work when we are taking measurements on a real system for the purposes of parameter estimation and model validation and for determining the experimentation to be performed with a model.

The term treatment was introduced to indicate a set of controlled variables and the value they have been assigned during a single execution of the experiment. The single execution of an experiment is termed a trial. An experimental unit can be thought of as the environment or configuration of the experiment.

An important method of analysis is ANOVA. The ANOVA procedure tests the hypothesis that a number of means are all equal against the alternative hypothesis that two or more are different. This is often used with the variance–ratio test (the F test), carried out by calculating variances and using the ratios of each mean square to the error mean square. Tables of the F distribution are used to decide when such ratios are significant.

Three types of experimental design were discussed: the completely randomized design, the randomized block design and the factorial design. The completely randomized design minimizes the sampling bias. In a randomized block design all comparisons are made within a block and not from block to block. The result is additional precision compared to the completely randomized design. Factor analysis is used to determine to what extent different factors acting together and individually contribute to the results. By using this approach, the significance of each effect may be tested and, where it is dependent on the other treatments, any interrelation can be studied.

The purpose of regression analysis is to obtain a mathematical expression of the relationship between random variables. However, this cannot be determined directly from the simulation outputs because of 'noise' which masks the nature of the dependence. Instead, regression analysis fits the best deterministic function to the sampled data. Best in this sense is defined as minimizing an error term based on the sum of the squared deviation of the data points from the deterministic function. We call the deterministic function a mathematical model of the data.

11.7 EXERCISES

11.1 Perform a one-way ANOVA for the following data. Calculate a 95 per cent confidence interval for the treatment means.

Treatment 1	Treatment 2	Treatment 3	Treatment 4	Treatment 5
125.3	135.4	78.0	67.0	56.2
56.4	176.2	87.2	56.1	67.0
162.9	203.9	67.3	67.0	34.6
123.6	167.3	56.2	51.3	38.8
210.1	173.0	91.8	63.9	43.1

11.2 Perform a two-way ANOVA for the following data. Calculate a 99 per cent confidence interval for the difference between treatment means.

Block	Treatment 1	Treatment 2	Treatment 3	Treatment 4	Treatment 5
1	23.1	23.6	27.6	41.7	52.8
2	24.1	21.1	42.3	36.2	46.3
3	31.7	23.8	36.5	37.8	51.3
4	31.1	13.6	41.8	31.9	49.1
5	32.7	27.1	33.7	41.8	59.1

11.3 Measurements were made on the yield produced by three different fertilizers. The following results were obtained:

Block	abc	Abc	aBc	ABc	abC	AbC	aBC	ABC
1	57.2	48.9	67.6	52.4	67.1	43.6	49.4	64.8
2	63.6	49.3	56.6	51.1	66.3	54.5	55.6	54.9
3	54.3	45.9	58.9	56.6	49.8	59.4	53.0	64.3

Analyse these results using the two-way ANOVA procedure and produce a table comparing the effect of fertilizer A against fertilizer B.

11.4 Determine a linear regression line for the following set of data. Calculate the 99 per cent confidence interval for the slope.

X:	1.0	2.0	4.0	6.0	8.0	10.0	12.0
Y:	2.1	6.7	12.3	14.8	22.1	26.7	34.5

11.5 Add functions to the simulation library to calculate linear regression parameters. Add a function *add_rgsn_data( )* which can be called to log each (x_i, y_i) sample pair, a function *calc_intcpt( )* to calculate the value of the intercept β_0 of the least squares line and *calc_slope( )* to calculate the value of the slope β_1 of the least squares line. A data structure should be designed to record the regression parameters and a function *make_regression( )* added which will create and return a new, initialized, regression data structure.

12

CASE STUDY

In this chapter we look at a case study which examines the performance of a common local area network protocol called Ethernet. This involves a rather complex model, the development of which is discussed in detail and the source code shown. The developed model is then used to derive performance data for the protocol in the steady state.

12.1 CSMA/CD PROTOCOLS

Some CSMA protocols have already been introduced in Exercises 10.7 and 10.8. A slightly more sophisticated variant of those protocols, called CSMA/CD, is described in this chapter. The CD postfix stands for collision detection. To recapitulate (for a complete account see Tanenbaum (1988)), when a station wants to transmit in the 1-persistent CSMA scheme it listens to the channel. If the channel is busy because some other station is transmitting, the station waits until the channel goes idle. When the channel is sensed idle the station attempts a transmission with probability 1 (i.e. always). If two or more stations happen to transmit simultaneously their transmissions will collide, resulting in unintelligible frames, and so they will have to be retransmitted. Retransmissions are scheduled to occur a random time after the collision took place. This cycle is repeated until either the station gives up because it has exceeded the maximum number of possible attempts or the transmission has been successful.

Collision detection increases the efficiency of the protocol by eliminating the amount of time wasted transmitting a garbled frame. If a collision is detected, then instead of continuing the transmission and sending out useless information the transmission is immediately curtailed. The retransmission is then made in the normal way a random time later.

An important parameter in determining performance in CSMA/CD protocols is the slot width τ. A slot width is the time it takes a signal to travel from one end of the maximum length of cable to the other. The reason why this parameter is so important is because to be certain that a frame has been correctly received by all stations on the LAN no other frames must be received by the transmitting station for two slot periods after the transmission has started. To understand why this is so, imagine there is a transmitting station, call it A, at one end of the cable and an interfering station, call it B, at the other. After A has started sending the frame it will take τ seconds to reach B. Just before it does so, assume B decides to send a frame. But as B starts to transmit, A's frame is detected and so B aborts his transmission. Now the corrupted frame from B takes another τ seconds to reach A. So, up to 2τ seconds may pass before A detects B's corrupted frame and realizes that his own transmission must have been garbled.

12.2 ETHERNET

There are several LAN specifications published by the IEEE in standard 802. One of these standards, 802.3, covers a range of 1-persistent CSMA/CD protocols from 1 to 10 Mbps. Ethernet corresponds to the 10 Mbps variety. Stations on an Ethernet LAN are connected by a cable. The Ethernet cable can consist of up to five sections, each at most 500 m long, connected by repeaters. To accommodate the worst-case propagation delay through the cables (at 0.67 times the speed of light or approximately 0.2 km/μs) and the delay through the repeaters, the slot size is set to 51.2 μs, which corresponds to 512 bit times (64 bytes) at 10 Mbps. To make sure that all stations on the cable are aware that a collision has taken place, the detecting station transmits a short noise burst. Typically this noise burst is 20 bit times long which, at 10 Mbps, equates to 2 μs.

The algorithm used for calculating the retransmission delay is termed *binary exponential backoff* and is designed to adapt to the number of users on the LAN. The backoff in terms of the number of slots is defined as a uniformly distributed number between 0 and n, where

$$
\begin{aligned}
n &= 2^i - 1 && \text{for} && 1 \leqslant i \leqslant 10 \\
&= 1023 && \text{for} && 10 < i \leqslant 16
\end{aligned}
\qquad (12.1)
$$

where i is the number of transmissions made so far. If no successful transmission is made after the sixteenth try the controller assumes that a fatal error has occurred and reports a failure. Any recovery at this stage is left up to higher-level protocols to perform.

12.3 THE SIMULATION

We will now describe the model and its development in detail, using as a framework the study tasks defined in Chapter 2.

12.3.1 Study definition

Our first task is to determine what the simulation study is to do. As mentioned in Chapter 2, this is normally based on a client's own requirements. For the purposes of this study assume that the client has agreed that the objective of the simulation is to determine the performance of the Ethernet protocol in the steady state. The output is to be a set of curves showing:

1. Average transmit delay in milliseconds against protocol efficiency in per cent for a frame size of 1024 and 256 bytes.
2. Protocol efficiency (percentage of usable capacity employed) for frame sizes of 1024 and 256 bytes against average number of users waiting to transmit in the range 0 to 8.

We will also make the following assumptions:

1. The channel is noiseless and the stations are perfectly reliable.
2. Frames travel along the cable from the transmitting station in both directions and are absorbed at the cable ends.
3. The time between the end of one transmission attempt and the beginning of the next is exponentially distributed.
4. Protocol efficiency is required with all stations working continuously, i.e. no idle periods.
5. The results are to be given with a 95 per cent confidence interval.

The initial evaluation of the required inputs to the model based on the above objectives are:

- *Frame size*. This is the size of a frame in bytes with values of 256 or 1024 bytes.
- *Number of users*. This is the number of users on the LAN.
- *Time between transmissions*. This is the mean idle time after a frame has been either transmitted or discarded (because 16 attempts have been made) until the next transmission attempt. During this time the station is dormant. Obviously, in the maximum load case this time will be zero, but for loads less than the maximum a positive, non-zero value must be assigned to this parameter.

The required outputs are:

- *Number of stations waiting to transmit*. This is the average number of stations which are waiting for a lull in the network traffic so that they can attempt a transmission. This variable will be used to characterize protocol efficiency.

- *Transmit delay*. This is the time between the initial attempt to transmit a frame and the time when a successful transmission starts; it does not include the time it takes to actually send out the frame. This will take into account the collisions and retransmissions but it will obviously apply only to successful frames. The delay for each successful frame can be measured in the model and added together to get the total delay T_D. The average time delay per frame is then T_D/N, where N is the number of successful frames.
- *Protocol efficiency*. This is the ratio of the number of successful frames to the maximum number possible when the LAN is being operated at its maximum rate, in other words when all stations are 100 per cent busy trying to send frames—there are no slack periods. If the model is run for t seconds of simulated time, then the maximum number of frames that could be successfully sent is

$$N_{max} = \frac{10^7 . t}{8B} \tag{12.2}$$

where B is the size of the frame in bytes. So the protocol efficiency is then

$$E = \frac{N}{N_{max}} = 8.B.\frac{N}{10^7 . t} \tag{12.3}$$

Another parameter that may affect performance, but one that we have not been asked to investigate at the moment, is the cable length. If delays introduced by signal propagation down the cable were to have any effect on the results it would seem logical to suppose that the worst case as far as performance is concerned is to assume maximum delay. Ethernet specifies a maximum delay of 51.2 μs but this is supposed to include the transit delay through repeaters; the actual delay through cable is limited to the delay offered by 5 × 500 m lengths. However, to simplify matters the length of cable can be assumed to have the maximum delay equally distributed throughout its entire length so that the apparent length is 51.2 μs × 200 m/μs, which is approximately 10 km.

Now let us now consider the kind of experimentation we need to perform. First of all it should be clear that this experimentation must involve repetition in order that suitable confidence intervals are obtained. Also, since we are not involved in a comparison of alternatives, we can assume that the runs can be independent. The method of block means is a convenient way to obtain independent samples of the mean from each run. It is necessary, of course, to determine the duration of a block and the duration of the initial transient phase, but it is not possible to provide an estimate of these values at this time. Instead, we must wait until we have a working model and are able to carry out some preliminary test runs. In the final model, then, the additional input variables required are:

- *Transient duration.* This is the duration of the initial transient phase which is to be ignored as far as results are concerned.
- *Simulation duration.* This is the duration of each block which is assumed to run in the steady-state phase.
- *Number of blocks.* This is the number of blocks per run.
- *Random number seed.* This is the seed for random number streams so that separate runs can be made independent.

12.3.2 System analysis

A useful starting point to comprehend a system, especially one as complicated as this, is to draw an std for the more complex object classes. This provides a useful visualization of the dynamics involved. In the Ethernet protocol there are clearly two important classes of objects to contend with—*stations* which communicate with each other on the LAN and *frames* with which they communicate.

Five states can be identified for a station based on the description above. These are:

1. *Idle.* In this state the station is doing nothing. When a frame transmission request is received the station goes to the Wait state.
2. *Wait.* In this state a frame is available to be transmitted and the station is waiting for a quiet channel to do so. When a quiet channel is detected the station can start to transmit the frame and proceed to the Listen state.
3. *Listen.* In this state the station monitors the channel to see if any other transmissions take place which corrupt the frame being transmitted. If no other frames are detected within two slot periods then the transmission will be successful and the station can adopt the Finish state. If a colliding frame is detected within this interval, the state must revert to Contention.
4. *Contention.* This state is entered if, during the initial two slot delay, a corrupting frame is detected. In this state a random delay is calculated, after which the station assumes the Wait state again in order to obtain a free channel for retransmission. However, if the maximum number of retransmissions have been attempted already, then the transmission has failed, the frame is discarded, and the station reverts to the Idle state.
5. *Finish.* This state is entered after a successful two-slot delay in which no corrupting frames were detected. For frames smaller than $51.2 \times 10^{-6} \times 10^{7}$ bits (i.e. 128 bytes) two slots are sufficient to completely transmit the frame so the station can immediately adopt the Idle state. For longer frames there is

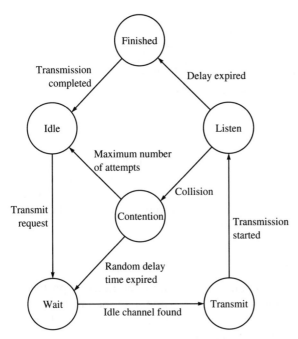

Figure 12.1 State-transition diagram for a station.

still some time left before the frame finally departs. When the frame has been transmitted the station can go to the Idle state once more.

The std for the station can be generated from the description of the states. It is shown in Fig. 12.1. The arrows indicate the possible next state, given the present state, and the inscription on the arrows gives the event which has caused the state transition.

There are three states for frames at any given station:

1. *Arrival*. In this state the start of a frame has arrived at a station. The frame will propagate to the neighbour unless it is at the end of the cable in which case there is no neighbour to go to. If the station is in the Listen state at the time a frame is received, then a collision occurs and the station moves to the Contention state.
2. *Departure*. In this state the end of a frame is leaving a station and propagating towards a neighbour.
3. *Transit*. In this state a frame is travelling past a station. Note that this state can be modelled only implicitly because it will occur when the departure of a frame entity from a station is pending (i.e. is in the calendar). As soon as the frame entity is activated (i.e. becomes the current entity) it assumes the Departure state.

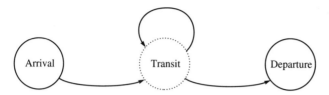

Figure 12.2 State-transition diagram for a frame.

The std for the frame is shown in Fig. 12.2. It is simpler than the std for the station but this does not necessarily mean that the realization in terms of code in the model is easier. The description of the arrival state, for example, illustrates that there are complex interactions between the received frame and the station which is bound to complicate the model logic.

12.3.3 Parameter estimation

Fortunately for the purposes of parameter estimation, the Ethernet protocol is documented in international standard IEEE 802.3 and so the parameters for our model are well defined. For instance, the standard specifies a 10 Mbps transmission rate and a slot width of 51.2 μs.

The propagation time delay between stations is an important figure which must be determined. In the model, a simplifying assumption can be made regarding the distribution of stations on the cable. It can be assumed that a cable of length l metres long has m stations uniformly distributed along its length. In this case, the distance between adjacent stations is $l/(m-1)$ metres and so the propagation time between stations in microseconds is

$$\frac{0.005*l}{(m-1)} \tag{12.4}$$

(using a propagation speed of 0.2 km/μs or 200 m/μs). The benefit of this assumption is that it gives us a constant time delay between adjacent stations and is therefore simple to model.

12.3.4 Model development

It is normally at this stage in the simulation that a firm decision is made as to the modelling approach to be adopted. Of course this decision is irrelevant if some kind of modelling package is used which does not offer any choice. However if alternatives are available, then from the analysis made of the target system it should be possible to select the most appropriate strategy. In this case study there are only two classes of active objects, so it might be useful to consider a process-oriented model. Based on the analysis of the system it is clear that this will be a fairly complex model and that flexibility and efficiency could be crucial factors. In view of this let us also agree to use explicit queuing.

The development is to start with a simplified version of the model and then to refine it in a number of steps. The first decision, then, must be to determine exactly what constitutes the initial model. It should not be trivial, but at the same time it should ignore the most complex characteristics of the system and allow a model framework to be constructed which can be built upon. However, making extensive changes to the model as the added detail is incorporated is both wasteful and error prone. Therefore each subsequent step should be essentially additive, and not significantly change what has been already been developed.

From the analysis of the system it would appear that the principal area of difficulty concerns the modelling of frame collisions and the resulting retransmission strategy since this is the source of most of the interactive effects. So in the first step this aspect of the system can be completely ignored; every transmission will be assumed to be completely successful. The initial transient phase can also be ignored. Having developed the initial model the complications of the retransmission strategy can be incorporated in a second step and the necessary data collection and analysis functionality in a third step.

Note that the decision to use three steps is dictated more by the constraint of available room in a book of this size than by consideration of an optimum development strategy. In a large modelling exercise in the real world we would probably have many more steps, and for really big models different parts of the model may even be farmed out to separate development teams.

Step 1: The initial model Rather than rush straight into coding it is normally a good idea to determine the logic of the model in fairly detailed pseudocode. The pseudocode shown here is as used in Chapter 3. It mixes C programming constructs with English functional descriptions, allowing the basic logic to be determined at a higher level of abstraction than can be done with a straight programming language. The initial model will be presented in this form, only the source code for the full model will be given. However, the accompanying disk also contains the source of the intermediate models as well.

We have already looked at the dynamics of the station and frame entities so we can sketch out a high-level design. We start off by considering the station entity. The behaviour of this entity is shown in Fig. 12.3. It consists of a continuous cycle in which the station attempts to transmit a frame which may have to be repeated several times in the case of collisions. After this it becomes dormant for a period and then the cycle is repeated.

Once a station entity record has been created it exists permanently for the life of the simulation and is involved in a succession of transmission attempts. This can be done because each transmission request is unique. In other words,

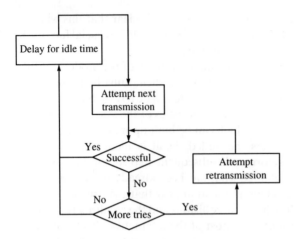

Figure 12.3 Overview of the behaviour of a station.

each station will be involved with at most one transmission request at any one time. However, for frames the situation is different since a station may potentially be responsible for several frames currently on the LAN. So frame entity records must be created for each transmission request and therefore destroyed when the frames reach the end of the cable.

The following pseudocode represents a station entity:

```
a_station()
{
    while (active)
    {
        switch (PHASE_OF(current))
        {
        case Idle:
            <<Set phase to Wait.>>
            <<Add this entity to the list of conditional entities.>>
            break;
        case Wait:
            if <<The channel is free - in this simple model we assume>>
                    <<that it always is.>> {
                <<Create and transmit two frames - one propagating to the>>
                    <<left and one to the right.>>
                <<Schedule the activation of this station in two slot>>
                    <<times in state Listen.>>
            }
            else {
                <<Continue waiting.>>
            }
            break;
```

```
        case Listen:
            ⟨⟨The frame has been (or will be) successfully⟩⟩
                ⟨⟨transmitted so add some statistics.⟩⟩
            If ⟨⟨Both frames have been transmitted⟩⟩ {
                ⟨⟨Set phase to Finish.⟩⟩
            else {
                ⟨⟨Wait until both frames have left this station.⟩⟩
            }
        case Contention:
            ⟨⟨Do nothing - this state is empty in this model⟩⟩
            break;
        case Finish:
            ⟨⟨Set state to Idle.⟩⟩
            ⟨⟨Suspend activity for an exponentially distributed amount of time⟩⟩
            break;
        }
    }
}
```

The station entity follows quite straightforwardly from the std, although it is still necessary to determine how the frame and station entities will interact. This interaction is required in the following situations:

1. When the last frame has left the station and is propagating down the cable the station must be reactivated so that the next transmission can be made, possibly after an intervening dormant period. Note that in the case of very short frames of less than 128 bytes, this would not be performed because by the time the station was activated after the initial two-slot delay both frames would already have been transmitted.
2. When a station has initiated the transmission of a frame the frame entity must be activated so that it can independently propagate to neighbours.

This suggests that there should be some static data related to each station. Since the number of stations can vary an obvious solution would be to implement this as a dynamically allocated array such as:

```
    :
station *LAN_user;
    :


    :
LAN_user = (station *)malloc(sizeof(station) * num_stations);
    :
```

Individual stations can then be identified by integer indexes into this array.

So what should this data structure contain? The first thing to add is a pointer to the entity record representing the station responsible for originating a frame. This can be accessed by a departing frame which will handle the first of the outstanding problems described above. We also postulated some statistics concerning successful transmissions. This is the obvious place to record them. With this in mind we have the following partial type definition.

```
typedef struct
{
    :
    int     state;         /* The state of a station */
    entity *ent_rec;       /* The transmitting station entity */
    int     successful;    /* The number of frames sent */
    :
} station;
```

Since the channel is duplex frames can travel independently in either direction. For convenience the directions are labelled *Left* and *Right*. In the arrival state, a frame arriving at a station from a right neighbour must be transmitted to the left neighbour and vice versa. However, if a frame arrives at the end of the cable it will not be passed along as there is no neighbour on the outgoing side.

From the above descriptions it is clear that a frame needs to know which station it is arriving at and from which station it is departing. Hence, there has to be some information associated with each instance of a frame that contains the identity of the arrival station and the departure station. Direction also has to be recorded since a frame entity should be able to determine which neighbour to propogate to. In addition, a frame entity must be able to determine the originating station and distinguish it from stations that it is just transiting. Hence, the following type declaration could form the basis of the attributes required for such a frame:

```
typedef struct
{
    :
    int     source;        /* The sender of the frame */
    int     direction;     /* The direction of propagation */
    int     arr_sta;       /* The station arriving at */
    int     dep_sta;       /* The station leaving from */
    :
} frame;
```

Now let us look at the frame entity. Based on the analysis of the system we can sketch the following outline:

```
a_frame ( )
{
    while (active)
    {
        switch (PHASE_OF(current))
        {
```

```
case Arrival:
    if (⟨⟨Frame going from right to left.⟩⟩)
    {
        if (⟨⟨Frame not at end of cable.⟩⟩) {
         ⟨⟨Schedule arrival of this frame at left neighbour.⟩⟩
        }
        else {
            ⟨⟨The start of the frame is at the leftmost station⟩⟩
            ⟨⟨so don't pass it on.⟩⟩
        }
    }
    else /* The frame is going from left to right. */
    {
        if (⟨⟨Frame not at end of cable.⟩⟩) {
            ⟨⟨Schedule arrival of this frame at right neighbour.⟩⟩
        }
        else {
            ⟨⟨The start of the frame is at the rightmost station⟩⟩
            ⟨⟨so don't pass it on.⟩⟩
        }
    }
    break;
case Departure:
    if (⟨⟨This station is transmitting this frame⟩⟩)
    {
        ⟨⟨Flag that a frame has been transmitted.⟩⟩
        if (⟨⟨This station has now finished transmitting both frames.⟩⟩)
        {
            if (⟨⟨The station is not in phase Listen⟩⟩)
                ⟨⟨Schedule activation of the station for the⟩⟩
                ⟨⟨next frame.⟩⟩
        }
    }
    if (⟨⟨The frame is going from right to left.⟩⟩)
    {
        ⟨⟨The (right to left) frame has gone now − so reset flag.⟩⟩
        if (⟨⟨The frame can be sent left.⟩⟩) {
            ⟨⟨Schedule the departure of this frame from⟩⟩
                ⟨⟨the left neighbour.⟩⟩
        }
        else {
            ⟨⟨The end of the frame is at the leftmost station⟩⟩
            ⟨⟨already so don't pass it on.⟩⟩
        }
    }
    else /* The frame is going to the right */
    {
        ⟨⟨The (left to right) frame has gone now − so reset flag.⟩⟩
        if (⟨⟨The frame can be sent right.⟩⟩)
        {
```

```
                        <<Schedule the departure of this frame from>>
                            <<the right neighbour.>>
                    }
                    else
                    {
                        <<The end of the frame is at the rightmost station>>
                            <<already so don't pass it on.>>
                    }
                }
                break;
            }
        }
    }
```

We have already seen that it is necessary to know when both frames have departed from a station so that the next transmission can be scheduled. This can be done by maintaining a flag that is set on the instigation of frame transmission and reset on frame departure from the transmitting station. Alternatively, a pointer to the frame entity scheduled for the departure event can be used. This will be set to NULL when the frame has departed. The latter approach is preferable since it may be necessary to access frame departure events in order to handle collisions. So to transmit a frame its arrival at a neighbour is scheduled when it has had time to travel the distance between the two stations, and its departure from the transmitting station is scheduled after all *frame_size*∗8 bits have been output onto the LAN at a speed of 10 Mbps. The gaps in the station data structure can now be filled in:

```
typedef struct
{
    int    state;          /* State that a station is in */
    int    successful;     /* The number of frames sent */
    int    left_to_right;  /* To indicate a frame passing to left */
    int    right_to_left;  /* To indicate a frame passing to right */
    entity *end[2];        /* Departure of frames sent from this station */
    entity *act_rec;       /* The station entity that transmitted the frame */
} station;
```

As stated in Chapter 2, one of the problems of simulation is that large and complex models such as this take a long time to run. Staring at a static screen for an hour or more is extremely tedious but, more importantly, we need to be able to distinguish between the model running normally (albeit slowly) and when it has hung (got into an infinite loop) due to the presence of a bug. Such information can be obtained by adding a special 'heart beat' event to the model which prints the current simulated time at regular intervals. This tells us two things. First of all, the duration of the run (in real time) can be estimated from a knowledge of the terminating value of simulated time. Second, we can be sure that the model has not hung because the time value will periodically update. Adding this kind of feedback is highly recommended in all simulation models. The implementation can be very simple, as demonstrated by the code in Listing 12.1 of function *print_ time( )* used in this model.

```
/* Echo current simulated time */
void print_time ()
{
    int i;
    /* Erase old time */
    for (i = 0;i < 10;i++) putchar ( 0x08 );

    /* Print new time */
    printf("%10.3f", sim_clock );
    fflush(stdout);
    wait (echo_delay);
}
```

Listing 12.1 Function to print the current simulated time.

At the opposite end of the spectrum, this animation could be made far more complex. The logical extension of the idea is to provide some form of moving graphics that depict an evolving image of the state of the model. However, this level of sophistication would reduce portability and significantly increase the running time so it will not be attempted here.

If this initial model is compiled, linked and executed the output will be as shown in Fig. 12.4. The output consists of a 'Simulation started' message from the simulation kernel followed by the incrementing value of simulated time. At some time value beyond the defined simulation duration the simulation will stop and the number of successful transmissions from each station will be printed. So now we have a basic working model that can be augmented with the remainder of the model logic and data generation.

Step 2: Modelling collisions A simulation which models the Ethernet retransmission strategy precisely is complicated by the degree of interference between the different entities in the model. These complexities must now be added. The detection of a collision in a real protocol implementation is performed by reading the frame as it is being transmitted. When the transmitted frame is different from that read the interface controller knows that a collision has occurred. However, in the model only the sequence of events that causes a collision can be detected. This sequence of events occurs when a frame is being transmitted and, at the same time, a colliding frame is being received. To model these additional complexities we must:

1. Provide a means whereby frames may be retransmitted with appropriate delays.

```
c:>ethernet 1 1000 10 10 1024 1500 343 1

Simulation started at 0.000000

Simulation stopped - end time reached at 1002.1247010
Actual time taken  - 42.000000 seconds
*** RESULTS ***
Number of stations      = 10
Frame inter tx time     = 10.000000 mS
Frame size              = 1024.000000 bytes
Time to transmit frame  = 0.819200 mS
                 Successful
Station 0 -> 90
Station 1 -> 98
Station 2 -> 104
Station 3 -> 109
Station 4 -> 93
Station 5 -> 103
Station 6 -> 103
Station 7 -> 109
Station 8 -> 108
Station 9 -> 87
TOTALS    -> 1004
```

Figure 12.4 Output from the initial Ethernet model.

2. Enable stations to detect an idle channel so that they may attempt a transmission.
3. Provide a means whereby a frame being transmitted can be truncated and flagged as invalid when there has been a collision.
4. Provide a means whereby a station can tell the difference between a transmission attempt that was successful and one that has been abandoned because all 16 attempts have failed.
5. Incorporate the effect of the noise burst following invalid frames.

We will now consider these points in a little more detail.

Once a collision has occurred a time delay must be calculated after which a retransmission can be attempted. However, if the maximum number of attempts have already been made, the transmission request must be rejected. Thus, each station must know how many attempts it has made so far. This value should be incremented for each additional attempt and then reset to zero when a frame has either been successfully transmitted or is rejected. The function *retrans_time( )* in Listing 12.2 calculates the retransmission time. A random number between 0 and 2^{num} is generated, where *num* depends on the number of retransmission attempts made by the station so far. Up to 16 retransmission attempts can be made and for each the value of *num* is increased by 1 but, for the last six attempts, the value of *num* is limited to 10.

```
/* Calculate the time to backoff - binary exponential */
float retrans_time ( int this_station )
{
      long    t;
      int     num;
      float   maximum;

      num   = ++LAN_user[this_station].number_retrans;
      if (LAN_user[this_station].number_retrans > Max_Value)
          num = Max_Value;
      /* 2 to the power i */
      maximum = (float)(1 << num);
      t = (long)uniform(s2, 0.0, maximum);
      return slot_size * t;
}
```

Listing 12.2 Retransmission delay.

In the real system, when a station is in the *Wait* state the channel must be monitored continuously. As soon as no traffic is detected the channel is considered idle and the transmission can take place. Therefore, in the model a station entity must be transferred to the conditional entity list when in the *Wait* state so that it can check the state of the channel after every event has occurred, since one of those events will be the departure of the frame which frees the channel. When this particular event has taken place the station can be removed from the conditional entity list and the frame transmission performed. This is illustrated in Listing 12.3, where the function *channel_clear_at( )* is used to check if the channel is idle. This function returns True if both the flags *left_to_right* and *right_to_left* are False, indicating that there is no frame transiting the station.

```
void a_station()
{
      :
int    channel_clear_at ( int this_station );
      :
      while (active)
      {
            switch (PHASE_OF(current))
            {
            case Idle:
                 /* Wait for free channel */
                 PHASE_OF(current)           = Wait;
                 LAN_user[this_station].state = Wait;
                 passivate ( current );
                 hold ( current );
                 break;
```

```
case Wait:
        /* Transmit only if channel free. */
        if (channel_clear_at(this_station))
        {
                transmit(left, this_station - 1, this_station );
                transmit(right, this_station + 1, this_station );

                LAN_user[this_station].state = Listen;
                PHASE_OF(current)            = Listen;

                /* Transmit on next slot */
                passivate(current);
                schedule(current, 2.0*slot_size);
        }
        else
                active = 0;
        break;
case Listen:
        :
        :
}

int channel_clear_at ( int this_station )
{
        return ((LAN_user[this_station].left_to_right == 0) &&
        (LAN_user[this_station].right_to_left == 0) );
}
```

Listing 12.3 Detecting the idle channel.

Now let us consider what needs to be done once a collision has been detected. The code for this is shown in Listing 12.4. The first thing to do is curtail the frame transmission and then flag the frame as corrupted. The test for a collision in the frame arrival phase is carried out by checking the state of the station. If the state is *Listen*, then we know that the two-slot period after the start of the transmission has not yet passed and so a collision has occurred. If, in addition, the flag *last_ok* is 1, then the collision has not yet been reported and it must be handled now.

To carry out the retransmission, we first of all curtail the frame with *invalidate_frame( )*. This uses the pointers to the scheduled frame departure events (the pointers *end[Left]* and *end[Right]*). With these pointers, the future frame departure events can be extracted from the calendar and rescheduled after an appropriate delay modelling the noise burst. This effectively chops the frame transmission. The frame can then be flagged as corrupt so that when it has been received by all the stations on the LAN the correct statistics can be updated.

```
void a_frame ( )
{
      :
      void   retransmit( int this_station );
      void   invalidate_frame ( int this_station );
      :
      while (active)
      {
            switch (PHASE_OF(current))
            {
            case Arrival:
                  this_station = this_frame->arr_sta;
                  /* If transmitting then we have a conflict. */
                  if ((LAN_user[this_station].state == Listen) &&
                        LAN_user[this_station].last_ok)
                  {
                        invalidate_frame( this_station );
                  }
                  :
                  :
      }
}

void invalidate_frame ( int this_station )
{
      entity *frm;
      /* This transmission failed */
      LAN_user[this_station].last_ok = 0;

      /* Flag frame as corrupted and abort transmission */
      frm = LAN_user[this_station].end[Left];
      if (frm)
      {
            ((frame *)ATTRIBUTES(frm))->corrupted = 1;
            /* Remove from calendar */
            passivate(frm);
            /* Immediate departure after noise burst - chop frame */
            schedule(frm, noise_burst);
      }
      frm = LAN_user[this_station].end[Right];
      if (frm)
      {
            ((frame *)ATTRIBUTES(frm))->corrupted = 1;
            /* Remove from calendar */
            passivate(frm);
            /* Immediate departure - chop frame */
            schedule(frm, noise_burst);
      }
}
```

Listing 12.4 Frame collision.

Note that the above code for *a_frame( )* is dealing with a frame arrival and so the identity of the station concerned with the arrival is

```
this_station = this_frame->arr_sta;
```

In contrast, for a departure event the identity of the station concerned is

```
this_station = this_frame->dep_sta;
```

The identities of the arrival and departure station are initialized when the frame is created, and updated as the frame propagates down the cable from station to station.

The actual retransmission is performed with *retransmit( )*, which is called from *a_station( )* in phase *Listen* after the two-slot delay. To communicate the fact that a frame transmission has failed the flag *last_ok* is set to 0, indicating that instead of waiting for the normal departure of frames from the station the current frame can, instead, be retransmitted. This is shown in Listing 12.5. The only decision to make in the case of a successful transmission is whether to wait for the frame to be transmitted because it is longer than 128 bytes or immediately to assume the Finish phase.

```
void a_station()
{
       :
       while (active)
       {
               switch (PHASE_OF(current))
               {
               :
               :
               case Listen:
                       if (LAN_user[this_station].last_ok) {
                               if (tx_finished(this_station)) {
                                       PHASE_OF(current) = Finish;
                               }
                               else {
                                       LAN_user[this_station].state = Finish;
                                       PHASE_OF(current) = Finish;
                                       passivate(current);
                               }
                       }
                       else
                               retransmit(this_station);
                       break;
                       :
       }

       void retransmit( int this_station )
       {
```

```
/* Have maximum number of attempts been made? */
if (LAN_user[this_station].number_retrans )= Max_Retrans)
{
        PHASE_OF(current) = Finish;
}
else /* Try again.*/
{
        /* Set up retransmission */
        PHASE_OF(current)          = Contention;
        LAN_user[this_station].state = Contention;

        wait ( retrans_time(this_station) );
}
}

int tx_finished ( int this_station )
{
        return !(LAN_user[this_station].end[Left]
          (LAN_user[this_station].end[Right]);
}
```

Listing 12.5 Frame departure from a station.

The model is now logically complete. If it is compiled linked and executed the output will be identical to the previous version of the model but it will run much slower. The reason for this of course is that the model now includes frame collisions; whereas previously there may have only been a few events involved with the transmission of a frame, there are now probably dozens.

Step 3: Adding data collection We know the sort of data we want to obtain from the simulation, so we now need to add a suitable monitoring code in order to generate that data. To satisfy the modelling objectives we should output:

1. Delay data:
   - The total transmit delay suffered by all successful frames (T_D)
   - The mean transmit delay, the total delay divided by the number successful ($\bar{T}_d = T_D/N$).
2. Efficiency data:
   - Protocol efficiency obtained from Eq. (12.3).
3. Load data:
   - The average number of stations waiting to transmit.

It is often a good idea to supplement the data generation beyond that which is required to satisfy the modelling objectives, as long as this does not extend the running time unduly. The additional data can help to convince a sceptical client of the reliability of the model and may even been found useful in its own right because it reveals unexpected behaviour. For example outputting the frame statistics on a per station basis will show how well the load is distributed between stations. If a few stations are consistently hogging the bandwidth, then it clearly demonstrates a logical error in the model.

None of the results listed above are difficult to obtain. All that must be done in most cases is that counts must be incremented in the appropriate places, such as when a frame has been discarded or successfully transmitted. In the case of frame transmit delay, a station entity can be time stamped when a transmission is first attempted. It is then only necessary to work out the time difference from then until the instant that the frame was considered as successfully received less the duration of the fixed two-slot delay. In order to calculate the mean number of stations waiting we can use a weighted histogram and log a count that gets incremented each time a station enters the wait state and decremented each time a station enters the Listen state.

The output function to display the results is shown in Listing 12.6.

```c
void print_results ()
    {
        int i;
        float num_slots;
        long total_successful, total_failed, total, total_time;

        /* Take last sample */
        add_hdata(wtt_stats, num_waiting_tx, 1.0);
        /* Get total simulated time excluding transient phase */
        total_time = sim_clock — transient;

        /* Initialize */
        num_slots       = total_time/frame_trans_time;
        total_successful = 0L;
        total           = 0L;
        total_failed    = 0L;

        printf(" \n*** PARAMETERS *** \n \n");
        printf("Number of stations      = %d \n",num_stations);
        printf("Inter transmission time = %f mS \n",idle_time);
        printf("Frame size              = %f bytes \n",frame_size);
        printf("Time to transmit frame  = %f mS \n",frame_trans_time);
        printf("Number of tx intervals  = %f \n",num_slots);
        printf("Number of backoffs      = %ld \n",num_backoffs);
        printf(" \n*** OVERALL RESULTS *** \n \n");
        printf("                 Requests Successful Failed \n");
        for (i = 0;i < num_stations;i++)
        {
            total            += (long)LAN_user[i].total;
            total_successful += (long)LAN_user[i].successful;
            total_failed     += (long)LAN_user[i].failed;
            printf("Station %d → %-11d %-11d %-11d \n",i,
```

```
                LAN_user[i].total
                ,LAN_user[i].successful
                ,LAN_user[i].failed);
    }

    printf("TOTALS-)%-111d %-111d %-111d \n\n"
            ,total
            ,total_successful
            ,total_failed);
    printf("Total delay         = %f \n", total_delay);
    printf("Mean total delay    = %f mS/frame \n",
            total_delay/((float)total_successful));
    printf("Mean normalized delay = %f \n",
            total_delay/((float)total_successful)/frame_trans_time);
    printf("Efficiency (%%)       = %f \n",
            ((float)100.0*total_successful)/num_slots);
    printf("Successful (%%)       = %f \n", 100.0*total_successful/total );
    print_histogram(stdout, wtt_stats, "Number of stations waiting to transmit");

    printf("\n*** BATCH RESULTS *** \n\n");
    print_summary ( stdout,delay_stats, "Transmit delay statistics (msec)");
    print_summary ( stdout,efficiency_stats, "Protocol efficiency statistics (%)");
    print_summary ( stdout,throughput_stats, "Throughput statistics (bps)");
}
```

Listing 12.6 Displaying output results.

Probably the simplest means of obtaining values for model input parameters is to input them on the command line. We will therefore initialize the variables *duration, frame_size, idle_time* and *num_stations* in this way. The *duration* specifies how long each block is to be. The *frame_size* gives the size of a frame in bytes. The variable *idle_time* gives the average time between transmission attempts and *num_stations* is the number of stations on the LAN.

From the values input and the fixed parameters such as bit rate the values *frame_trans_time* and *num_tx_slots* can be derived. The *frame_trans_time* is the length of time it takes to transmit a frame of size *frame_size* bytes. The variable *num_tx_slots* is the absolute maximum number of frames that can be transferred in the simulation period. This is N_{max} in Eq. (12.2).

The parameters *total_delay, num_waiting_tx*, and *num_backoffs* are measured along with individual station statistics. The value of total delay is calculated as

```
total_delay += (TIME_SPENT(current)-2.0 * slot_size);
```

in function *a_station( )* modelling a station entity. Twice *slot_size* is subtracted because the time delay is only required from the first transmission attempt until the successful frame starts to transmit.

The determination of *num_waiting_tx* giving the average number of stations waiting to transmit is performed by having a global count of waiting stations which is increased whenever a station enters the Wait phase and decremented whenever a station moves out of the Wait phase. A histogram is used to show the distribution of this variable and determine the time-weighted average.

Num_backoffs is a simple count that is increased every time a frame transmission is rescheduled due to collision. Station statistics give additional counts for successful and failed attempts. From this it is possible to determine the protocol efficiency since the sum of successful frames for all stations is the total number of successful frames. Using Eq. (12.3) the protocol efficiency can be calculated as the percentage of those successful to the absolute maximum possible.

The complete model is given in Listing 12.7 and on the disk supplied.

```
/*                            */
/*Simulation model of ethernet protocol.*/
/*                            */
#include <stdio.h>
#include <stdlib.h>
#include "sim_lib.h"
#include "random.h"
#include "results.h"


/* Values for ethernet */
float      v = 201000000.0;          /* Signal propagation speed (m/s) */
float      slot_size = 0.0512;       /* The slot size (mseconds)*/
float      frame_size;               /* The size of a frame (bytes) */
float      LAN_speed = 10000000.0;   /* LAN speed bps */
int        Max_Retrans = 16;         /* Max number of retransmissions */
int        Max_Value = 10;           /* Max retrans delay = 2^10-1 slots */
long       num_backoffs;             /* Total number of retransmissions */
int        num_blocks;               /* Number of blocks in a run */
float      noise_burst;              /* Duration of a noise burst 920 bits) */
int        buffer_size;              /* The size of the input buffers */
float      duration;                 /* The duration of steady state */
float      transient;                /* The duration of transient state */
float      scale_factor = 1000.0;    /* Assume the clock is in milliseconds */
float      total_delay = 0.0;        /* The total delay of all frames */
float      echo_delay;               /* Delay for echoing sim time to scrn */
#define    False            0
#define    True             1


/* Directions for frame propagation */
#define    Left             0
#define    Right            1

/* States of a station */
#define    Idle             0
#define    Wait             1
```

```
#define     Finish          2
#define     Listen          3
#define     Contention      4

/* States of a frame */
#define     Arrival         0
#define     Departure       1

/* Attributes of a frame */
typedef struct
{
      int       corrupted;      /* Has this frame clashed with another? */
      int       source;         /* The sender of the frame */
      int       direction;      /* The direction of propagation */
      int       arr_sta;        /* The station arriving at */
      int       dep_sta;        /* The station leaving from */
} frame;


/* Attributes of a station */
typedef struct
{
      int       number_retrans; /* Number of retransmissions so far */
      int       successful;     /* Number of OK transmissions from this station */
      int       total;          /* Total number of frames offered */
      int       failed;         /* Number failed */
      int       state;          /* State that this station is in */
      int       left_to_right;  /* A frame is passing this station */
      int       right_to_left;  /* A frame is passing this station */
      int       last_ok;        /* Whether last transmission was successful */
      entity    *act_rec;       /* The entity representing current transmission
                                   request*/
      entity    *end[2];        /* Frames propagating from this station */
} station;



extern     entity    *current;
extern     int        active;
extern     float      sim_clock;


/*                         */
/*Parameters of the model.*/
/*                  */
int        num_avg;           /* The number of moving averages */
int        num_stations;      /* Number of users on the LAN */
float      idle_time;         /* Frame inter-arrival time */
float      frame_trans_time;  /* Time to transmit frame */
float      neighbour_delay;   /* Time to travel between stations */
station    *LAN_user;         /* The set of all stations on the LAN */
int        num_waiting_tx;    /* The number of stations waiting to transmit */
histogram  *wtt_stats;
```

```
/*                      */
/* Random number streams. */
/*                      */
stream     *s1;                    /* Arrival process */
stream     *s2;                    /* For calculating backoff */

void       get_next_queued ( int this_station ); /* Get next frame to transmit*/
void       a_station ( void );              /* A station on the LAN */
void       a_frame ( void );                /* Frame in transit on LAN*/
void       init( int argc, char *argv[] );  /* Initialize simulation*/
void       print_results ( void );          /* Output results */
void       reset ( int this_station );      /* Reset station */
void       print_time ( void );             /* Echo time */
void       make_station( int this_station ); /* Make entity record for station */
float      retrans_time ( int this_station ); /* Calculate backoff */
float      idle_interval ( void );          /* Calculate idle time */

/* Sample logging routines */
void       log_samples ( void );
void       reset_batch_samples ( void );

summary    *delay_stats,
                 *efficiency_stats,
                 *throughput_stats;
long       num_success;
float      last_delay, last_sim_clock;

main ( int argc, char *argv[] )
{
     int i;
     float t;
     init( argc, argv );
     t = sim_clock+duration;
     for (i = 0;i < num_blocks;i++)
     {
          reset_batch_samples();
          printf("BATCH %d ... \n",i+1);
          run_sim(t, 0);
          log_samples();
          t = t + duration;
     }
     print_results();
     return 0;
}

void init( int argc, char *argv[] )
{
     int i, seed;
     int n;
     float cable_length;
```

```
/* Get command line parameters              */
if (argc != 9)
{
     printf("%s - ethernet simulation \n", argv[0]);
     printf("arg1: seed \n");
     printf("arg2: number of stations on LAN \n");
     printf("arg3: mean idle time (mSecs) \n");
     printf("arg4: frame size (bytes) \n");
     printf("arg5: simulation duration (mSecs) \n");
     printf("arg6: transient duration (mSecs) \n");
     printf("arg7: number of times to print sim clock per block \n");
     printf("arg8: number of blocks \n");
     exit(0);
}
else
{
     cable_length = 10000;
     seed         = atoi(argv[1]);
     num_stations = atoi(argv[2]);
     idle_time    = atof(argv[3]);
     frame_size   = atof(argv[4]);
     if (num_stations > 1)
            neighbour_delay = scale_factor*cable_length/(num_stations-1)/v;
     else {
            printf("Not enough stations \n");
            exit(0);
     }
     frame_trans_time = scale_factor*frame_size*8.0/LAN_speed;
     duration     = atof(argv[5]);
     transient    = atof(argv[6]);
     n            = atoi(argv[7]);
     num_blocks   = atoi(argv[8]);
}
init_sim();

/* Ensure scan conditional entities after each bound entity has run. */
scan_always(1);

/* Number of stations waiting to transmit statistics */
num_waiting_tx   = 0;
wtt_stats        = make_histogram (0.0, 1.0, 10, WEIGHTED );

delay_stats      = make_summary();
efficiency_stats = make_summary();
throughput_stats = make_summary();

/* Initially all is peace and quiet on the LAN */
LAN_user = (station *)malloc(sizeof(station) * num_stations);
for (i = 0;i < num_stations;i++)
{
```

```
                LAN_user[i].left_to_right = 0;
                LAN_user[i].end[Right]    = NULL;
                LAN_user[i].end[Left]     = NULL;
                LAN_user[i].right_to_left = 0;
                LAN_user[i].total         = 0;
                LAN_user[i].successful    = 0;
                LAN_user[i].failed        = 0;
                LAN_user[i].number_retrans= 0;
        }

        s1 = make_stream (seed, 0);
        s2 = make_stream (seed+1, 0);

        /* A noise burst is 20 bits long */
        noise_burst = 20.0/LAN_speed;

        /* Add preliminary events */
        for (i = 0;i < num_stations;i++)
        {
                make_station ( i );
        }
        echo_delay = (transient+duration)/n;
        make_scheduled_entity( print_time, (void *)NULL,
                               echo_delay, 0, 0, 1, NULL );
        printf("Transient phase \n");

        /* Run for transient period */
        run_sim ( transient, 0);

        /* Reset results */
        for (i = 0;i < num_stations;i++)
        {
                LAN_user[i].total      = 0;
                LAN_user[i].successful = 0;
                LAN_user[i].failed     = 0;
        }
        printf("Steady-state phase \n");
        total_delay = 0.0;
}

void log_samples ()
{
  float num_slots, batch_time, delay;
  batch_time      = sim_clock - last_sim_clock;
  num_slots       = batch_time/frame_trans_time;
  delay           = total_delay - last_delay;
  add_sdata (delay_stats, delay/(float)num_success);
  add_sdata (efficiency_stats, 100.0*num_success/num_slots);
  add_sdata (throughput_stats, num_success*8*frame_size*scale_factor/batch_time
}
```

```
void reset_batch_samples ()
{
  num_success      = 0L;
  last_sim_clock   = sim_clock;
  last_delay       = total_delay;
}

/* Calculate the idle time between transmission attempts */
float idle_interval ()
{
      if ( idle_time == 0.0 )
            return 0.0;
      return idle_time * exponential ( s1 );
}
/* Echo current simulated time */
void print_time ()
{
      int i;
      for (i = 0;i < 10;i++) putchar ( 0x08 );
      printf("%10.3f", sim_clock );
      fflush(stdout);
      wait (echo_delay);
}

/* A transmit request */
void make_station( int this_station )
{
      LAN_user[this_station].act_rec =
            make_scheduled_entity( a_station, (void *)this_station,
            idle_interval(), Idle, 0, 1, NULL );
}

/* Model a station on the LAN in state :                        */
/*   Idle - doing nothing                                       */
/*   Wait - waiting for a lull in the traffic to transmit       */
/*   Finish - finished transmitting a frame                     */
/*   Contention - has clashed with another frame               */
/*   Listen - frame transmitting, making sure received everywhere */
void a_station()
{
      int    this_station;
      void   retransmit( int this_station );
      void   transmit (int direction, int arr_station, int dep_station);
      int    channel_clear_at ( int this_station );

      this_station = (int)ATTRIBUTES(current);
      while (active)
      {
            switch (PHASE_OF(current))
            {
```

```
case Idle:
        LAN_user[this_station].total++;
        stamp_current();
        /* Add number waiting to transmit */
        add_hdata(wtt_stats, num_waiting_tx, 1.0);
        num_waiting_tx++;
        /* Wait for free channel */
        PHASE_OF(current)            = Wait;
        LAN_user[this_station].state = Wait;
        passivate ( current );
        hold ( current );
        break;
case Wait:
        /* Transmit only if channel free */
        if (channel_clear_at(this_station))
        {
                /* Add number waiting to transmit */
                add_hdata(wtt_stats, num_waiting_tx, 1.0);
                num_waiting - tx--;
                /* Two frames - one propagating to the left and one to the right.*/
                transmit(Left, this_station-1, this_station);
                transmit(Right, this_station+1, this_station);
                /* Listen for two slots */
                LAN_user[this_station].state   = Listen;
                LAN_user[this_station].last_ok = 1;
                PHASE_OF(current) = Listen;
                passivate(current);
                schedule(current, 2.0*slot_size);
        }
        else
                active = 0;
        break;
case Listen:
        if (LAN_user[this_station].last_ok)
        {
                /* Transmission successful */
                LAN_user[this_station].successful++;
                num_success++;
                /* time spent queueing */
                total_delay += (TIME_SPENT(current) - 2.0*slot_size);
                if (tx_finished(this_station)) {
                        /* Transmission finished */
                        PHASE_OF(current) = Finish;
                }
                else {
                        /* Transmission on-going: wait for finish */
                        LAN_user[this_station].state = Finish;
                        PHASE_OF(current) = Finish;
                        passivate(current);
                }
```

```
            }
            else
                retransmit(this_station);
            break;
      case Contention:
            /* Add number waiting to transmit */
            add_hdata(wtt_stats, num_waiting_transmit, 1.0);
            num_waiting_transmit++;
            LAN_user[this_station].state = Wait;
            PHASE_OF(current)           = Wait;
            passivate ( current );
            hold ( current );
            break;
      case Finish:
            reset(this_station);
            PHASE_OF(current) = Idle;
            schedule (current, idle_interval() );
            break;
        }
    }
}


/* Model a frame travelling along the cable, visiting neighbouring stations */
void a_frame ( )
{
    frame *this_frame;
    int    this_station;
    int    source;
    int    direction;
    int    transmission_finished ( int this_station );
    void   invalidate_frame ( int this_station );
    int    frame_ok ( int this_station );

    this_frame = (frame *)ATTRIBUTES(current);
    source     = this_frame->source;
    direction  = this_frame->direction;
    while (active)
    {
        switch (PHASE_OF(current))
        {
        case Arrival:
            this_station = this_frame->arr_sta;
            /* If this station is transmitting then we have a conflict. */
            if ( ( LAN_user[this_station].state == Listen ) &&
                   ( LAN_user[this_station].last_ok ) )
            {
                /* chop current frame */
                invalidate_frame( this_station );
            }
```

```
      /* Frame going from right to left */
      if (direction == Left)
      {
          /* A frame is transitting this station - set flag */
          LAN_user[this_station].right_to_left++;
          /* Send a frame left if possible */
          if (this_station > 0)
          {
              this_frame->arr_sta = this _ station-1;
              wait(neighbour_delay);
          }
          else
          /* The start of the frame has reached the first station */
          {
              /*Free frame data when last frame reaches cable end.*/
              ATTRIBUTES(current) = NULL;
              terminate(current);
          }
      }
      /* Frame going from left to right */
      else
      {
          /* A frame is transitting from left to right - set flag */
          LAN_user[this_station].left_to_right++;
          /* Send a frame right if possible */
          if (this_station < num_stations-1)
          {
              this_frame->arr_sta = this_station+1;
              wait(neighbour_delay);
          }
          else
          /* The start of the frame has reached the last station */
          {
              /*Free frame data when last frame reaches cable end.*/
              ATTRIBUTES(current) = NULL;
              terminate(current);
          }
      }
      break;
 case Departure:
      this_station = this_frame->dep_sta;
      /* Are we transmitting this frame? */
      if (source == this_station)
      {
          /* Dereference pointers */
          LAN_user[this_station].end[direction] = NULL;
          /* Has this station now just finished transmitting? */
          if (transmission_finished(this_station))
          {
              /* Was this frame ok? */
```

```
                    if (!this_frame->corrupted)
                    {
                         if (LAN_user[this_station].state == Finish)
                                activate(LAN_user[this_station].act_rec);


                         }
                      }
                   }
                   if (direction == Left)
                   {
                         /* The frame has gone now - reset flag */
                         LAN_user[this_station].right_to_left--;
                         /* Send end of frame left if possible */
                         if (this_station > 0)
                         {
                                this_frame->dep_sta = this_station-1;
                                wait(neighbour_delay);
                         }
                         else
                         {
                                /* We've reached the end of the line */
                                terminate(current);
                         }
                   }
                   else /* The frame has gone right */
                   {
                         LAN_user[this_station].left_to_right--;
                         /* Send end of frame right if possible */
                         if (this_station < num_stations-1)
                         {
                                this_frame->dep_sta = this_station+1;
                                wait(neighbour_delay);
                         }
                         else
                         {
                                /* We've reached the end of the line */
                                terminate(current);
                         }
                   }
                   break;
            }
      }
}

/* Has this_station finished transmitting a frame left and right? */
int transmission_finished ( int this_station )
{
      return !(LAN_user[this_station].end[Right]
         LAN_user[this_station].end[Left]);
}
```

```
/* Retransmit frame after collision */
void retransmit( int this_station )
{
     /* Have maximum number of attempts been made? */
     if (LAN_user[this_station].number_retrans >= Max_Retrans)
     {
          LAN_user[this_station].failed++;
          /*The transmission failed - get rid of the transmission request */
          PHASE_OF(current)            = Finish;
     }
     else /* Try again.*/
     {
          /* Count the number of backoffs */
          num_backoffs++;
          /* Set up retransmission */
          PHASE_OF(current)            = Contention;
          LAN_user[this_station].state = Contention;
          /* Schedule the next transmission attempt */
          wait(retrans_time(this_station));
     }
}


void reset ( int this_station )
{
     LAN_user[this_station].number_retrans = 0;
     LAN_user[this_station].state        = Idle;
     LAN_user[this_station].end[Left]    = NULL;
     LAN_user[this_station].end[Right]   = NULL;
}

/* Transmit a frame on the LAN */
void transmit ( int direction, int arr_station, int dep_station )
{
     frame *transmitted_frame;
     frame *make_frame ( int arr_sta, int dep_sta, int direction );

     if (direction == Left)
     {
          /* Is there any one to transmit to ? */
          if (dep_station < 1)
               return;
          else
               LAN_user[dep_station].right_to_left++;
     }
     if (direction == Right)
     {
          /* Is there anyone to transmit to ? */
          if (dep_station > num_stations-2)
               return;
          else
               LAN_user[dep_station].left_to_right++;
```

```
    }
    /* Schedule arrival at neighbour and departure from this_station */
    transmitted_frame = make_frame( arr_station, dep_station, direction );
    make_scheduled_entity ( a_frame, transmitted_frame, neighbour_delay,
        Arrival, 0, 1, free);
    /* Keep pointers in case of contention */
    LAN_user[dep_station].end[direction] =
        make_scheduled_entity ( a_frame, transmitted_frame, frame_trans_time,
        Departure, 0, 1, free);
}
  /* Build a new frame to transmit */
  frame *make_frame ( int arr_sta, int dep_sta, int direction )
  {
      frame *new_frame;

      new_frame        = (frame *)malloc(sizeof(frame));
      new_frame->arr_sta   = arr_sta;
      new_frame->dep_sta   = dep_sta;
      new_frame->direction = direction;
      new_frame->corrupted = 0;
      new_frame->source    = dep_sta;
      return (new_frame);
  }

  /* Calculate the time to backoff - binary exponential */
  float retrans_time ( int this_station )
  {
      long  t;
      int   num;
      float maximum;

      num = ++LAN_user[this_station].number_retrans;
      if (LAN_user[this_station].number_retrans > Max_Value)
          num = Max_Value;
      /* 2 to the power i */
      maximum   = (float)(1 << num);
      t         = (long)uniform(s2, 0.0, maximum);
      return slot_size * t;
  }

  /* Curtail the transmission of the current frame due to collision */
  void invalidate_frame ( int this_station )
  {
      entity *frm;

      /* This transmission has failed */
      LAN_user[this_station].last_ok = 0;
      /* Flag frame as corrupted and abort transmission */
      frm = LAN_user[this_station].end[Left];
      if (frm)
      {
```

```
                ((frame *)ATTRIBUTES(frm))->corrupted = 1;
                /* Remove from calendar */
                passivate(frm);
                /* Chop frame — add noise burst */
                schedule(frm, noise _ burst);
        }
        frm = LAN_user[this_station].end[Right];
        if (frm)
        {
                ((frame *)ATTRIBUTES(frm))→corrupted = 1;
                /* Remove from calendar */
                passivate(frm);
                /* Chop frame — add noise burst */
                schedule(frm, noise_burst);
        }
}

int channel_clear_at ( int this_station )
{
        return   ((LAN_user[this_station].left_to_right == 0) &&
                 (LAN_user[this_station].right_to_left == 0) );
}


void print_results ()
{
        int i;
        float num_slots;
        long total_successful, total_failed, total, total_time;

        /* Take last sample */
        add_hdata(wtt_stats, num_waiting_tx, 1.0);

        /* Get total simulated time excluding transient phase */
        total_time = sim_clock — transient;

        /* Initialize */
        num_slots        = total_time/frame_trans_time;
        total_successful = 0L;
        total            = 0L;
        total_failed     = 0L;
        printf(" \n*** PARAMETERS *** \n \n");
        printf("Number of stations      = %d \n",num_stations);
        printf("Inter transmission time = %f mS \n",idle_time);
        printf("Frame size              = %f bytes \n",frame_size);
        printf("Time to transmit frame  = %f mS \n",frame_trans_time);
        printf("Number of tx intervals  = %f \n",num_slots);
        printf("Number of backoffs      = %ld \n",num_backoffs);

        printf(" \n*** OVERALL RESULTS *** \n \n");
        printf("            Requests   Successful Failed      \n");
        for (i = 0;i < num_stations;i++)
```

```
{
    total            += (long)LAN_user[i].total;
    total_successful += (long)LAN_user[i].successful;
    total_failed     += (long)LAN_user[i].failed;
    printf("Station %d -> %-11d %-11d %-11d \n",i,
            LAN_user[i].total
            ,LAN_user[i].successful
            ,LAN_user[i].failed);
}
printf("TOTALS    -)%-11ld %-11ld %-11ld \n \n"
        ,total
        ,total_successful
        ,total_failed);
printf("Total delay              = %f \n", total_delay);
printf("Mean total delay         = %f mS/frame \n",
        total_delay/((float)total_successful));
printf("Mean normalised delay    = %f \n",
        total_delay/((float)total_successful)/frame_trans_time);
printf("Efficiency (%%)           = %f \n",
        ((float)100.0*total_successful)/num_slots);
printf("Successful (%%)           = %f \n", 100.0*total_successful/total );
print_histogram(stdout, wtt_stats, "Number of stations waiting to transmit");

printf(" \n*** BATCH RESULTS *** \n \n");
print_summary ( stdout,delay_stats, "Transmit delay statistics (msec)");
print_summary ( stdout,efficiency_stats, "Protocol efficiency statistics (%)");
print_summary ( stdout,throughput_stats, "Throughput statistics (bps)");
}
```

Listing 12.7 The complete Ethernet model.

12.3.5 Experimentation and results gathering

We now turn our attention to experimentation performed with the model. The first step is to determine the duration of the transient phase. Having done this we can perform a number of runs to accumulate the data needed.

Detecting the steady state The steady state can be determined using one of the methods described in Chapter 10. We will select the moving averages method and measure the average frame delay. The routine to do this is shown in Listing 12.8. The array *mov_avg[ ]* to hold the averages has been created when the model was initialized and its size is another model parameter entered on the command line. This flexibility is necessary, as in higher traffic level conditions the number of samples in the moving average can be increased in order to reduce the amount of data we have to sift through.

The moving average value is recorded in a time series histogram rather than being printed as a numeric value. In general, it is a good idea to at least display some of the system variables as a time series. This clarifies that the model is behaving like the system and makes it easier to judge when the steady state is dominant.

```
/* Add a value to the moving average and print when complete */
void add_to_avg ( float amount )
{
        static int cnt = 0;
        static int index = 0;
        static float avg = 0.0;

        /* replace old value with new value */
        avg -= mov_avg[index];
        mov_avg[index] = amount;
        avg += amount;
        index = (index + 1) % num_avg;
        cnt++;

        /* print it every index number of samples */
        if (!index)
                add_hdata(h, 1.0, avg );
}
```

Listing 12.8 A function to collect the moving average.

The elimination of the transient phase must be done for all input conditions, i.e. for all network load levels and frame sizes. However, if values can be assigned to the input parameters which maximizes the transient duration, then we can take the view that no combination of input variables can be worse than this and therefore only the transient response for the worst case needs to be identified. In this model, the transient behaviour can be determined for the maximum network load level and for the worst-case frame size. The highest level of network load clearly occurs when the time between transmission attempts is zero. The worst-case frame size can be assumed to be 1024 byte frames since they take the longest time to transmit and so must prolong the transient duration.

The time series histogram of transmit delay with the above input values for a network of 10 stations is shown in Fig. 12.5. It is difficult to say when the transient period has subsided from this graph because there is no steady state in this system! If the waiting time before a successful transmission is measured, we find low values between sudden peaks. This effect results from alternating periods of frame collisions and frame transmissions. In cases where the stations on the LAN were not continuously trying to transmit, we would also find idle periods when there was no LAN traffic. Hence, it must be accepted that a steady state on a micro scale does not exist. Instead periods of contention are interspersed with periods of relative inactivity.

```
   0.00     44.52#########################
  40.00     43.68#########################
  80.00     43.79##########################
 120.00     46.26###########################
 160.00     49.49#############################
 200.00     97.66###############################################################
 240.00     98.96#################################################################
 280.00     88.86##########################################################
 320.00     87.08########################################################
 360.00     81.59####################################################
 400.00     69.27###########################################
 440.00     63.82######################################
 480.00     61.67#####################################
 520.00     56.17#################################
 560.00     59.77####################################
 600.00     59.98####################################
 640.00     57.63##################################
 680.00     57.25##################################
 720.00     61.83#####################################
 760.00     63.85#######################################
 800.00     62.26######################################
 840.00     74.03###############################################
 880.00     82.17####################################################
 920.00     72.14############################################
 960.00     69.05##########################################
1000.00     74.01###############################################
1040.00     68.25##########################################
1080.00     70.32############################################
1120.00     67.80##########################################
1160.00     70.01###########################################
```

Figure 12.5 Time series histogram of the moving average of waiting times.

In situations like this the initial transient cannot be determined by looking for the convergence of measured values to a single mean because the probability distributions are never stationary, rather a judgement has to be made as to when the pattern of troughs and peaks in the measured values seems to start. Alternatively, we can take a time-averaged mean value in an attempt to smooth out the pattern. This could average out most of the variations we see during the steady-state phase but would tend to be more conservative.

A value for the transient duration for the Ethernet model can be estimated from the histogram of waiting times. In the model all stations start at time $t = 0$ by trying to transmit a frame. Obviously they will all collide and retransmit some time later. This is the reason for the large spike at around 240 ms. Very soon the stations become unsynchronized and start to transmit at different times. At this point the transient phase can be considered to have subsided. From inspection of the time-series histogram the transient phase seems to last for around 400 ms. This figure seems to remain fairly constant when these runs are repeated with up to 100 users.

Collecting data The performance of the protocol is to be categorized in relation to the average number of stations waiting to transmit. However, there is no way

Table 12.1 Relationship between the average number waiting and the number of stations on the LAN

Idle time = 0 (ms)	1024 byte frames	256 byte frames	1024 byte frames	256 byte frames
Num stations	200	200	20	20
Num waiting	7.5	2.4	0.7	0.2

of establishing this figure at the start of a simulation run, so it must be measured. The actual value measured depends on the values assigned to the input parameters such as the number of stations on the LAN, so to ensure that a suitable range is covered it is necessary to make some initial trial runs. This will enable the number of stations on the LAN to be related to the average number waiting. The result of such trial runs is shown in Table 12.1. Here we have tried a high and low value for the number of stations in order to get a rough idea of the variation of the average number of stations waiting to transmit. Trying additional values between these two extremes shows that the variation in delay time and efficiency is much more pronounced for low load levels, therefore LAN populations of 10, 20, 60 and 200 stations will be used.

It is also necessary to determine how many blocks to have and how long each should run. In order that the sampling distribution for the mean is reasonably accurate 30 blocks can be used. A good value for the run length of each block is to make it slightly longer than the transient duration, let us assume 500 ms of simulated time.

We have been directed to obtain results for frame sizes of 256 and 1024 bytes. For each frame size the number of stations on the LAN can be increased

Table 12.2 Assignment of input values

Run	Number stations	Number blocks	Block duration (ms)	Transient duration (ms)	Idle time (ms)	Frame size
1	200	30	500	400	0.0	1024
2	200	30	500	400	0.0	256
3	60	30	500	400	0.0	1024
4	60	30	500	400	0.0	256
5	20	30	500	400	0.0	1024
6	20	30	500	400	0.0	256
7	10	30	500	400	0.0	1024
8	10	30	500	400	0.0	256

Table 12.3 Results

Run	Efficiency			Delay (ms)			Number waiting		
	Mean (%)	Std dev	95% Conf	Mean	Std dev	95% Conf	Mean	Std dev	95% Conf
1	83.06	0.85	0.31	36.0	3.83	1.38	7.22	5.13	2.40
2	60.01	0.94	0.34	29.5	1.23	0.22	2.25	3.01	1.15
3	84.35	0.73	0.26	16.4	2.06	0.74	2.26	2.00	0.81
4	61.82	0.90	0.32	12.2	0.80	0.29	0.80	1.1	0.29
5	88.23	0.51	0.18	5.13	1.01	0.36	0.75	0.96	0.27
6	78.90	1.26	0.45	2.41	0.39	0.14	0.23	0.53	0.08
7	92.80	0.32	0.12	1.44	0.64	0.23	0.33	0.60	0.12
8	90.55	0.79	0.28	0.47	0.18	0.06	0.08	0.30	0.03

from 10 to 200 and the mean time between frame transmission attempts kept at zero for the maximum load scenario. Thus the values to be assigned to input variables for the initial set of runs is as shown in Table 12.2.

The results from these runs are shown in Table 12.3. Each output value has an associated mean and standard deviation calculated from the sampling distribution, from which the given 95 per cent confidence intervals are derived.

These results are displayed in Figs 12.6 and 12.7 and are given with the 95 per cent confidence interval shown as an 'I'. It is clear from these results that Ethernet works well for large frame sizes but as the frame size decreases the performance of the protocol degrades.

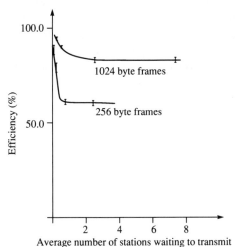

Figure 12.6 Protocol efficiency.

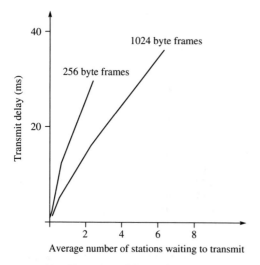

Figure 12.7 Throughput delay performance.

The above results also show that the delay increases with the traffic load as one might expect. However, the delay, even in the worst case, is not excessive. This is due to the fact that we are measuring the time to acquire the channel by a successful frame. In a real system access to the protocol itself would be controlled by a queuing mechanism that holds outstanding transmission requests. The delay experienced by a member of this queue would be much higher. In fact, if the traffic demand was greater than that which could be supported by the network (greater than about 9 Mbps) then queues would grow without bound. Clearly a real system would only have finite resources for a queue and therefore transmission requests would be dropped when the queue was full, but these effects cannot be measured in the current model because we have ignored the explicit queuing of transmission requests. However, it requires only minor changes in the model to add a queuing mechanism and to queue external transmission requests in order to explore these other dimensions. Thus, the results might lead us to ask other questions about the performance of this system such as the following:

- What happens to the average number of stations waiting to transmit as the average time between transmission attempts increases above zero?
- How does the protocol work for very small frames, say 64 bytes long?
- What is the effect as experienced by an external user who has to join a queue to gain access to the protocol?

This may require another iteration of the development loop.

12.4 SUMMARY

A case study involving the simulation of the Ethernet protocol was described. The study consisted of the following:

- A study definition where the aims of the study were determined.
- Systems analysis which examined the structure and dynamics of the subject system (the Ethernet protocol) with the help of state-transition diagrams.
- Parameter estimation, which assigned values to parameters required in the model.
- Model development, in which the model was designed in a series of steps. The initial model, lacking any representation of frame collisions, was simple and easily verifiable. Subsequent extensions to the base model allowed it to handle frame collisions and retransmissions and added data collection functions.
- Experimentation and results gathering in which the model was exercised and the outputs recorded.

The result of the simulation showed that performance of the protocol was good for large frame sizes (1024 bytes) but deteriorated for smaller frame sizes (256 bytes).

12.5 EXERCISES

12.1 Redo the model of the Ethernet protocol described in this chapter, but this time use the method of antithetic variates to try and obtain similar results more efficiently. How effective is the method in this case?

12.2 Despite the fact that Ethernet is the most widespread of LAN protocols, it has a number of significant disadvantages, such as the lack of guaranteed private communication and excessive delays as traffic intensity increases. For this reason, effort has been applied in recent years to finding ways in

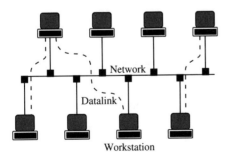

Figure 12.8 Connected data links on a LAN.

which the basic Ethernet protocol can be improved. One proposition is the use of *connected data links*, which are illustrated in Fig. 12.8.

In this proposal, data links are inserted between pairs of stations on the LAN. Typically, station pairs with high bandwidth communications requirements between them are selected. When a station wants to transmit a frame to a particular destination it first checks the list of stations that it knows it is directly connected to. If the intended destination is present in this list then a transmission across the data link is made. If no such link is available, then a broadcast transmission is made in the normal way.

Modify the Ethernet model to incorporate connected data links and compare the performance with and without them. The modified model should allow an analyst to specify the number of users on the LAN and the connectivity of the connected data links (in terms of the stations on each end of the link) in a configuration file. For the purposes of this model, assume that there are four data links and 40 stations and compare the performance when the traffic carried by the data links is 1 per cent, 5 per cent and 25 per cent respectively of the total system traffic. Assume that the data link transmission rate is 10 Mbps as for standard Ethernet.

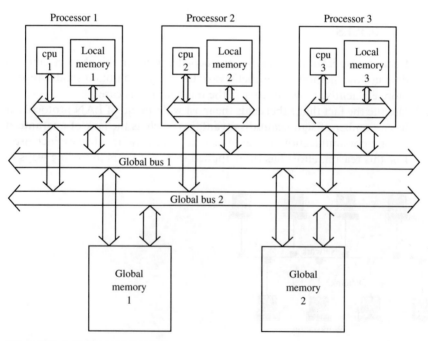

Figure 12.9 A multiprocessor system.

12.3 Figure 12.9 illustrates a multiprocessor system consisting of three processors, two global memories and two global buses. Each processor has a local environment consisting of memory and IO ports and can access a global memory via one of the buses. The workload for each processor consists of a period of activity in its local environment described by an exponential distribution with mean L time units, and then access to a global memory unit for a period of one time unit. Access to global memory requires that the processor first of all acquires a bus, queuing up for the first one free if they are all in use, and then accesses the selected memory unit if it is free. If the selected memory unit is busy, the processor joins a FIFO queue until it can be given access. Memory units are selected with equal probability so, for example, if there are four memory units then a processor will select memory unit i, $1 \leqslant i \leqslant 4$, with probability 0.25.

Develop a model of this system that takes as inputs the number of processors p, the number of buses b, the number of global memory units m and the load factor ratio w which is given by $1/L$. The output of the model is to be processing power, that is the average number of processors active either in local or global environments which, if T is the total time that *all* processors are active, is given by $P = T/D$, where D is the duration of the simulation.

Use the model to determine the following relationships between the input and output variables:

- Processing power P as a function of number of processors when $b = m = 2$ and $w = 0.1$, 0.2 and 0.4 for p in the range $2 \leqslant p \leqslant 20$.
- Processing power P as a function of number of buses when $p = 50$, $b = m$, $w = 0.1$, 0.3 and 0.5 for b in the range $2 \leqslant b \leqslant 20$.
- Processing power P as a function of load factor ratio w in the range $0 \leqslant w \leqslant 0.8$ when $p = 12$, $b = 2$ and $m = 2$.

Design suitable experimentation, either using the method of antithetic variates or control variates (with the load factor w acting as control variate) and obtain all results with a 95 per cent confidence interval.

APPENDIX A:
SIMULATION LIBRARY

This appendix comprises a user guide for the simulation library. Installation guidelines are given for a variety of development systems along with a cross-reference summary grouped by file.

A.1 INSTALLATION

The disk distributed with this book is organized as follows:

READ.ME	(Read me file with last minute changes and updates to the source code)
\CSIM	(Source for simulation library)
ABP	(Models of the alternating bit protocol)
AUTO	(Calculation of auto-covariance)
BATCH	(Model of a batch computer system)
CSMA–CD	(Ethernet model)
VER0	(The simple Ethernet model)
TRANS	(Model to discover transient phase)
ETHERNET	(The full Ethernet model)
PHILOS	(Model of the dining philosophers problem)
PROT–4	(Model of a sliding window protocol)
PR_Q	(Model of a priority queue)
SIMPLEQ	(Model of a simple M/M/1 queue)
STEADY	(Detecting steady state)
MOV_AVG	(Detecting steady state using moving average)
STD_DEV	(Detecting steady state using std deviation)

EXERCISE	(Exercises from the text)
EX5–2	
EX6–1	
EX6–2	
EX6–4	
EX7–4	
EX7–5	
EX8–4	
EX8–5	
EX8–7	
EX9–2	
EX9–3	
EX9–5	
EX10–5	
EX12–3	

The top-level directory \CSIM contains the library source code, which is split into a number of files as follows:

- *SIM_LIB.H*. Provides declarations for the simulation library as a whole and for handling entities and queues.
- *SIM_LIB.C*. Provides the executive, entity manipulation and queue handling.
- *RANDOM.H*. Provides declarations for random number streams.
- *RANDOM.C*. Provides functions for handling random numbers and generating random numbers from various statistical distributions.
- *RESULTS.H*. Provides declarations for handling results.
- *RESULTS.C*. Provides functions to record and display results in the form of histograms.
- *RESOURCE.H*. Provides declarations for resource handling.
- *RESOURCE.C*. Provides functions for resource handling.
- *STATS.H*. Provides declarations for statistics functions (confidence intervals).
- *STATS.C*. Provides functions to calculate confidence intervals.
- *ERROR.H*. Provides definitions of error codes used by other components of the simulation library for reporting error and warning conditions.
- *ERROR.C*. Contains a function to handle errors and a function to handle warnings.

There are a number of subdirectories off the main \CSIM directory. Each child subdirectory contains a related set of source code files. These may comprise an example model or code to perform analysis described in the text such as the determination of the onset of steady state.

The following are basic installation guidelines designed to aid the relative novice C programmer. If you are an experienced C user you will no doubt have set up and be familiar with your own C development environment and should find building the simulation library and the various example executables quite easy.

DOS

On a DOS-based system you can run the supplied *INSTALL.BAT* batch file from the parent directory that is to receive the source code files. To do this type the following command lines at the DOS prompt (example assumes the source is to be located in *C: \C \SOURCE \CSIM*):

```
C:)CD C: \C\SOURCE\CSIM
C:)COPY A:\CSIM\INSTALL.BAT .
C:)INSTALL
```

This will copy the files to the \C \SOURCE \CSIM subdirectory, creating additional directories as appropriate. The install batch file assumes that the source disk is in drive A:.

To create the library and executables proceed as follows:

1. Compile the **.c* files in the *CSIM* directory (sim_lib.c, etc.) with the /c (i.e. compile only) switch. Note that the macro _MSDOS_ is assumed to be defined for DOS environments. If your system does not use this particular macro name then add it as an argument to the compiler. For example, with the MIX Power C compiler add the argument

   ... /d_MSDOS_ ...

2. Combine the object **.o* files produced into a library file with the *librarian* (if there is one) supplied with the development system. Call it *sim.X*, where the *X* depends on the particular C compiler used. For example, Microsoft C users will probably use the extension *.lib* giving *sim.lib*. If no librarian is supplied with your development system then you must give the name of each object file to the linker in order to create an executable. Consult your compiler documentation to see how to do this.

   You have several options in dealing with include files. You can copy the header files from the *CSIM* directory to the directory used to keep the system header files like *stdio.h*. This is normally given by an environment variable with a name like *INCLUDE* and should be described in your compiler documentation. To incorporate a header file such as *sim_lib.h* in a model in this case add the line

```
#include <sim_lib.h>
```

to the source code.

Alternatively, you can add the full path name to the *CSIM* directory in a compile option to tell the compiler in which directories to look for header files. This would require something like

```
.... /ic:\c\source\csim ....
```

on the compile command line to which you must sometimes also add the directory holding the standard headers such as *stdio.h*.

Another option is to hard code the path name to the directory that the header files are in directly in the source. So, you could use the absolute path name:

```
#include "c:\c\source\sim\sim_lib.h"
```

or the relative path name:

```
#include "..\sim_lib.h"
```

this latter approach is how the models on the distribution disk reference header files.

3. For each of the subdirectories, compile the *.c files and link them with the library file *SIM.LIB* or with the *.o files produced in Step 1 if your system does not have a librarian.

UNIX

On a UNIX system you must use whatever facility is provided by the system to copy DOS formatted $3\frac{1}{2}$ inch data disks. Do not forget to strip carriage return/line feed sequences into the single line feed character required by UNIX. There is normally a system utility provided for this purpose. For example, on HP-UX, commands such as

```
$ doscp /dev/floppy:/csim/sim_lib.c x
$ dos2ux x > sim_lib.c
```

can be used. If you do not use the same directory structure as the distribution disk, then the model source files must be edited so that header files can be located.

To create the library and executables proceed as follows:

1. Compile the *.c files in the *CSIM* directory (sim_lib.c, etc.) with the -c (i.e. compile only) switch using the command

```
cc -c *.c.
```

2. Run the archiver to generate an archive file using the command

```
ar -r *.o sim.a
```

3. For each of the model subdirectories compile and link the source using

```
cc -o 'model' *.c 'pathname'/sim.a
```

Where '*model*' must be replaced by the name of the executable to be produced and '*pathname*' must be replaced by the pathname to the archive file *sim.a* produced in Step 2.

A.2 CROSS-REFERENCE SUMMARY

This section provides a cross-reference to the functions, macros, data types and public variables, listed by file.

Functions

sim_lib.h: activate
add_event
append
clear_queue
clear_sim
delete_event
dump_conditional
dump_pending
dump_queue
extract
hold
init_sim
make_conditional_entity
make_entity
make_queue
make_scheduled_entity
passivate
prepend
queue_back
queue_front
quit
quit_terminate
reactivate
reinstate

	remove_back
	remove_front
	reset
	run_sim
	scan_always
	schedule
	stamp
	stamp_current
	terminate
	wait
	withdraw
random.h:	binomial
	chi_square
	draw_continuous
	draw_discrete
	erlang
	exponential
	f_distr
	gamma
	geometric
	laplace
	log_normal
	make_stream
	make_table
	neg_binomial
	normal
	poisson
	reset_stream
	student_t
	triang
	uniform
	uniform01
	weibull
resource.h:	acquire
	make_resource
	release
	reset_resource
results.h:	add_hdata
	add_sdata
	clear_histogram

	clear_summary
	make_histogram
	make_summary
	print_cumulative
	print_histogram
	print_summary
	print_table
	set_fill_char
stats.h:	large_sample_conf_int
	small_sample_conf_int

Macros

sim_lib.h:	ATTRIBUTES
	BRANCH
	IS_ACTIVE
	IS_CLOSED
	IS_CONDITIONAL
	IS_EMPTY
	IS_PASSIVE
	IS_PENDING
	IS_QUEUED
	QEMPTY
	QSIZE
	PHASE_OF
	PRIORITY_OF
	TIME_OF
	TIME_SPENT
resource.h:	AMOUNT_LEFT
	AMOUNT_USED
	IS_AVAILABLE
	IS_EMPTY
	IS_FULL

Type declarations

random.h:	stream
resource.h:	resource
results.h:	table
	histogram
	summary

sim_lib.h: entity
               queue

Variables

sim_lib.h: active
               current
               sim_clock

APPENDIX B:
SIMULATION LIBRARY REFERENCE

This appendix contains an alphabetic reference to all the functions provided in the library.

B.1 FUNCTION REFERENCE

The function descriptions contain the following information:

- *Function name.* The function summary begins with the function name. This is the name that must be used to call the function.
- *Include file.* After the function name is an #*include* directive. This is the header file that is included at the top of any source file that uses the function. The header file gives the function prototype (i.e. function declaration) and associated type declarations.
- *Function prototype.* The function prototype is given as it appears in the header file. The function tells the compiler what arguments are expected and what the return value is so that automatic type checks can be performed.

    A function can be declared either by including the header file or by typing the function declaration as shown. However, the function very often needs to access data types or variables declared in the header file, so it is generally easier just to include the header file.

    The ANSI standard for function prototypes is used:

    `type_name func_name '(' ((type_name arg {',' type_name arg}) 'void')')' ';'`

    The type of the return value *type_name* may be any defined data type. *Func_name* is the name of the function. The sequence of *type_name arg* pairs are the data types and names of the arguments that you must supply in order to call the function. In the absence of any such parameters, the keyword *void* must be used.

- *Function description.* Following the function prototype comes the function description. The description will make reference to the arguments declared in the function prototype to explain the purpose and behaviour of the function.
- *Function return value.* The section following the function description gives the return value and how the output value, if there is one, depends on the input values. If the function does not return a value it is declared as returning *void*.
- *See also.* The last section lists some associated functions that might be of interest.

acquire()

```
#include <resource.h>
int acquire ( resource *r, float a );
```

Description: This function decrements the amount of resource *r* available by an amount *a*.

If the amount left is negative the warning message

```
**** warning : negative resource remaining ****
```

is printed but the simulation allowed to continue. If the resource *r* is NULL the error message

```
**** run-time error : NULL resource pointer ****
```

is printed and the simulation terminated.
Returns: TRUE if the resource *r* is non-NULL, FALSE otherwise.
See also: release().

activate()

```
#include <sim_lib.h>
int activate ( entity *e );
```

Description: If the entity record pointer *e* is non-NULL this function schedules *e* for activation as soon as the currently active entity is no longer running. It does this by putting *e* at the front of the calendar to be activated at the current value of simulated time. The current state of *e* must be *PASSIVE* for the operation to succeed.

If *e* is NULL the message

```
**** run-time error : NULL entity ****
```

is printed and the simulation stopped.
Returns: TRUE if *e* was found to be in one of the required states, FALSE otherwise.
See also: add_event(), delete_event(), extract(), hold(), passivate(), reactivate(), reinstate(), schedule(), withdraw().

add_event()

```
#include <sim_lib.h>
entity *add_event ( void (*event)(), float t );
```

Description: This function creates a new entity record and adds it to the calendar to become active a time *t* later than current simulated time. No attribute data is required, since only the function pointed to by *event* defining the code to be executed when the event occurs is added to the entity record created. The entity record is initialized to the *PENDING* state.

If memory for the entity record cannot be obtained then the error message

```
**** run-time error : cannot allocate memory for new entity ****
```

is printed and the simulation is stopped.

Returns: A pointer to the entity record created.

See also: activate(), delete_event(), extract(), hold(), passivate(), reactivate(), reinstate(), schedule(), withdraw().

add_hdata()

```
#include <results.h>
void add_hdata ( histogram *h, float x, float y );
```

Description: If the histogram *h* is non-NULL, this function adds a sample to the histogram *h*. If the histogram is an *UNWEIGHTED* histogram, the particular column is determined from the *x* coordinate value and the value of *y* is added to the running total for the column.

If the histogram is *WEIGHTED* the column is selected in the same way but the value added is the *y*-value times the length of time the value has persisted, which is taken to be the time between the last sample and current simulated time.

If the histogram type is *TIME_SERIES*, the column is selected based on the current time, and the value of *y* is added to this column.

If the value of *h* is NULL the error message

```
**** run-time error : NULL histogram ***
```

is printed and the simulation is stopped.

Returns: Nothing.

See also: clear_histogram(), make_histogram(), print_cumulative(), print_histogram(), print_table().

add_sdata()

```
#include <results.h>
void add_sdata ( summary *s, float v );
```

Description: If the summary statistics *s* is non-NULL this function adds a sample

v to the summary data structure pointed to by s. If the value of v is 0.0 then the count of zero entries is incremented. In all other cases, the value is added to *sum_ xf* and the value squared added to *sum_xxf*. The count of samples recorded is incremented by 1.

If s is NULL the error message

```
**** run-time error : NULL summary ****
```

is printed and the simulation stopped.
Returns: Nothing.
See also: clear_summary(), make_summary(), print_summary().

append()

```
#include <sim_lib.h>
int append ( queue *q, entity *e );
```

Description: If both the queue pointer q and the entity record pointer e are non-NULL this function adds the entity to the end of the queue, in a position based on the entity priority. The current state of e must be either *ACTIVE* or *PASSIVE*, in which case e will be added after all entities currently in the queue with a higher or equal priority. All existing queued entities of a lower priority will be positioned behind e. The state of e will be changed to *QUEUED*.

If q is NULL the simulation is stopped and the error message

```
***** run-time error : NULL queue ****
```

is printed. If e is NULL the simulation is stopped and the error message

```
**** run-time error : NULL entity ****
```

is printed.
Returns: TRUE if the entity was found to be in one of the required states, FALSE otherwise.
See also: clear_queue(), dump_queue(), extract(), make_queue(), prepend(), queue_back(), queue_front(), remove_back(), remove_front().

beta()

```
#include <random.h>
float beta (stream *rs, float a, float b);
```

Description: This function returns a random floating point number drawn from the beta distribution with parameters a and b. The value returned will be in the range $(0, 1)$.

If the random number stream is NULL the message

```
**** run-time error : NULL random number stream ****
```

is printed and the simulation stopped.

Returns: A floating point number from the beta distribution.
See also: binomial(), chi-square(), erlang(), exponential(), f_distr(), gamma(), geometric(), laplace(), log_normal(), neg_binomial(), normal(), poisson(), student_t(), triang(), uniform(), uniform01(), weibull().

binomial()

```
#include <random.h>
float binomial ( stream *rs, float q, unsigned int n );
```

Description: This function returns a random integer-valued floating point number from a binomial distribution of n trials each having probability q of success. The argument rs is a random number stream used as a source of random fractions from which the desired variate is obtained.

If the pointer to the random number stream rs is NULL the error message

```
**** run-time error : NULL random number stream ****
```

is printed and the simulation stopped.
Returns: An integer-valued sample as a *float* drawn from a binomial probability distribution.
See also: beta(), chi_square(), erlang(), exponential(), f_distr(), gamma(), geometric(), laplace(), log_normal(), neg_binomial(), normal(), poisson(), student_t(), triang(), uniform(), uniform01(), weibull().

chi_square()

```
#include <random.h>
float chi_square ( stream *rs, unsigned int n );
```

Description: This function returns a random floating point number drawn from a χ^2 distribution with n degrees of freedom. The stream rs is used as the source of random fractions to generate the required number.

If the pointer to the random number stream rs is NULL the error message

```
**** run-time error : NULL random number stream ****
```

is printed and the simulation stopped.
Returns: A random floating point number drawn from a χ^2 distribution.
See also: beta(), binomial(), erlang(), exponential(), f_distr(), gamma(), geometric(), laplace(), log_normal(), neg_binomial(), normal(), poisson(), student_t(), triang(), uniform(), uniform01(), weibull().

clear_histogram()

```
#include <results.h>
void clear_histogram ( histogram *h );
```

Description: If the histogram pointer *h* is non-NULL this function resets all the statistics data so far gathered to zero.

If *h* is NULL then the error message

```
**** run-time error : NULL histogram ****
```

is printed and the simulation aborted.

Returns: Nothing.

See also: add_hdata(), make_histogram(), print_cumulative(), print_histogram(), print_table().

clear_queue()

```
#include <sim_lib.h>
void clear_queue ( queue *q );
```

Description: This function clears the queue pointed to by *q* by removing and terminating all the entities that are currently enqueued.

If the queue pointer *q* is NULL the message

```
**** run-time error : NULL queue ****
```

is printed and the simulation stopped.

Returns: Nothing.

See also: append(), dump_queue(), extract(), make_queue(), prepend(), queue_back(), queue_front(), remove_back(), remove_front().

clear_sim()

```
#include <sim_lib.h>
void clear_sim ( void );
```

Description: This function clears the current simulation environment. All pending entities in the calendar and all conditional entities are terminated.

Returns: Nothing.

See also: run_sim().

clear_summary()

```
#include <results.h>
void clear_summary ( summary *s );
```

Description: If the statistics summary *s* is non-NULL this function resets all the statistics data so far gathered in *s* to zero.

If *s* is NULL the error message

```
**** run-time error : NULL summary ****
```

is printed and the simulation stopped.

Returns: Nothing.
See also: add_sdata(), make_summary(), print_summary().

delete_event()

```
#include ⟨sim_lib.h⟩
int delete_event ( entity *event );
```

Description: If the entity record pointer *event* is non-NULL and in the state *PASSIVE* this function terminates it and frees the memory occupied. No attempt is made to free memory associated with attributes.

If *event* is NULL then the message

```
**** run-time error : NULL entity ****
```

is printed and the simulation stopped.
Returns: TRUE if *event* was in the *PASSIVE* state and was deleted, FALSE otherwise.
See also: activate(), add_event(), extract(), hold(), passivate(), reactivate(), reinstate(), schedule(), withdraw().

draw_continuous()

```
#include ⟨random.h⟩
float draw_continuous ( stream *rs, table *ts );
```

Description: If stream pointer *rs* and table pointer *ts* are both non-NULL this function determines a random floating point number based on the table of values *ts*. The argument *rs* is used to perform interpolation between sample points.

If the stream pointer *rs* is NULL then the message

```
**** run-time error : NULL random number stream ****
```

is printed. If the pointer to the table of sample values *ts* is NULL then the message

```
**** run-time error : NULL table ****
```

is printed. In both cases the simulation will be stopped.
Returns: A random floating point random number from a table of samples.
See also: draw_discrete(), make_table().

draw_discrete()

```
#include ⟨random.h⟩
float draw_discrete ( stream *rs, table *ts );
```

Description: If stream pointer *rs* and table pointer *ts* are both non-NULL this function determines a random number from table *ts*. The argument *rs* is used to select one of the sample points in the table to return.

If the stream pointer *rs* is NULL then the message

```
**** run-time error : NULL random number stream ****
```

is printed. If the pointer to the table of sample values *ts* is NULL then the message

```
**** run-time error : NULL table ****
```

is printed. In both cases the simulation will be stopped.
Returns: A random floating point number from a table of samples.
See also: draw_continuous(), make_table().

dump_conditional()

```
#include <sim_lib.h>
void dump_conditional ( void );
```

Description: This function is a diagnostic routine that prints the contents of the conditional entity list. Each entity is printed in the format

[POSN] ENTITY ATTRIBUTES EVENT

where:

- *POSN* is the position in the list,
- *ENTITY* is the address of the entity record,
- *ATTRIBUTES* is the value of the *attr* components (which is normally a pointer),
- *EVENT* is the pointer to the function to be executed when the entity is active.
Returns: Nothing.
See also: dump_pending(), dump_queue().

dump_pending()

```
#include <sim_lib.h>
void dump_pending ( void );
```

Description: This function is a diagnostic routine that prints the contents of the calendar. Each entity in the calendar is printed in the format

[DEPTH] ENTITY PRIORITY TIME ATTRIBUTES EVENT

where:

- *[DEPTH]* is the depth in the tree implementing the calendar that the entity is located,
- *ENTITY* is the address of the entity,
- *PRIORITY* is the priority of the entity,

- *TIME* is the activation time for the entity,
- *ATTRIBUTES* is the *attr* component of the entity,
- *EVENT* is the function that is to be executed when the entity is activated.

Returns: Nothing.

See also: dump_conditional(), dump_queue().

dump_queue()

```
#include ⟨sim_lib.h⟩
void dump_queue ( *q );
```

Description: This function is a diagnostic routine that prints the contents of the queue pointed to by *q*. Each member of the queue is printed in the format

[DEPTH] ENTITY PRIORITY ATTRIBUTES EVENT

- *[DEPTH]* is the depth in the tree implementing the queue that the entity is located,
- *ENTITY* is the address of the entity,
- *PRIORITY* is the priority of the entity,
- *ATTRIBUTES* is the *attr* component of the entity,
- *EVENT* is the current pointer to the event or entity routine.

Returns: Nothing.

See also: dump_conditional(), dump_queue().

erlang()

```
#include ⟨random.h⟩
float erlang ( stream *rs, unsigned int k );
```

Description: This function returns a random floating point number drawn from a *k*-stage Erlang distribution with a mean of 1.0. If a distribution with a mean other than 1.0 is required, then the value returned must be multiplied by the required mean. The stream *rs* is used as the source of random fractions to generate the required number.

If the pointer to the random number stream *rs* is NULL the error message

```
**** run-time error : NULL random number stream ****
```

is printed and the simulation stopped.

Returns: A non-negative floating point random number from an Erlang-*k* distribution.

See also: beta(), binomial(), chi_square(), exponential(), f_distr(), gamma(), geometric(), laplace(), log_normal(), neg_binomial(), normal(), poisson(), student_t(), triang(), uniform(), uniform01(), weibull().

exponential()

```
#include <random.h>
float exponential ( stream *rs );
```

Description: This function returns a random floating point number from an exponential distribution with a mean of 1.0. If a distribution with a different mean is required, then the value returned must be multiplied by the required mean. The stream *rs* is used as the source of random fractions to generate the required number.

If the pointer to the random number stream *rs* is NULL the error message

```
**** run-time error : NULL random number stream ****
```

is printed and the simulation stopped.

Returns: A random floating point number from an exponential distribution.

See also: beta(), binomial(), chi_square(), erlang(), f_distr(), gamma(), geometric(), laplace(), log_normal(), neg_binomial(), normal(), poisson(), student_t(), triang(), uniform(), uniform01(), weibull().

extract()

```
#include <sim_lib.h>
int extract ( queue *q, entity *mbr );
```

Description: If the entity record pointer *e* and the queue pointer *q* are both non-NULL and the state of the entity is *QUEUED*, this function removes *e* from the queue and changes the state to *PASSIVE*.

If either the queue or the entity is NULL the simulation is stopped and the error message

```
**** run-time error : cannot add or remove with NULL queue or entity ****
```

is printed.

Returns: TRUE if the entity was queued, FALSE otherwise.

See also: activate(), add_event(), delete_event(), hold(), passivate(), reactivate(), reinstate(), schedule(), withdraw().

f_distr()

```
#include <random.h>
float f_distr ( stream *rs, unsigned int n1, unsigned int n2 );
```

Description: This function returns a random floating point number drawn from an *F* distribution with *n1* and *n2* degrees of freedom. The stream *rs* is used as the source of random fractions to generate the required number.

If the random number stream *rs* is NULL the error message

```
**** run-time error : NULL random number stream ****
```

is printed and the simulation stopped.

Returns: A random floating point number drawn from an *F* distribution.

See also: beta(), binomial(), chi_square(), erlang(), exponential(), gamma(), geometric(), laplace(), log_normal(), neg_binomial(), normal(), poisson(), student_t(), triang(), uniform(), uniform01(), weibull().

gamma()

```
#include ⟨random.h⟩
float gamma ( stream *rs, float alpha, float beta );
```

Description: This function returns a random floating point number from a gamma distribution with parameters alpha and beta. The stream *rs* is used as the source of random fractions to generate the required number.

If the random number stream *rs* is NULL the error message

```
**** run-time error : NULL random number stream ****
```

is printed and the simulation stopped.

Returns: A floating point random number from a gamma distribution.

See also: beta(), binomial(), chi_square(), erlang(), exponential(), f_distr(), geometric(), laplace(), log_normal(), neg_binomial(), normal(), poisson(), student_t(), triang(), uniform(), uniform01(), weibull().

geometric()

```
#include ⟨random.h⟩
float geometric ( stream *rs, float p );
```

Description: This function returns a random integer-valued floating point number drawn from a geometric distribution with probability of success *p*. The stream *rs* is used as the source of random fractions to generate the required number.

If the random number stream *rs* is NULL the error message

```
**** run-time error : NULL random number stream ****
```

is printed and the simulation stopped.

Returns: An integer-valued floating point random number from a geometric distribution.

See also: beta(), binomial(), chi_square(), erlang(), exponential(), f_distr(), gamma(), laplace(), log_normal(), neg_binomial(), normal(), poisson(), student_t(), triang(), uniform(), uniform01(), weibull().

hold()

```
#include ⟨sim_lib.h⟩
int hold ( entity *e );
```

Description: If the entity record pointer *e* is non-NULL this function adds it to the list of conditional entities. The entity must be in the state *PASSIVE* for the operation to be successful.

If the entity is NULL the message

```
**** run-time error : NULL entity ****
```

is printed and the simulation stopped.

Returns: TRUE if the entity record pointer *e* was *PASSIVE*, FALSE otherwise.

See also: activate(), add_event(), delete_event(), extract(), passivate(), reactivate(), reinstate(), schedule(), withdraw().

init_sim()

```
include ⟨sim_lib.h⟩
void init_sim ( void );
```

Description: This function prepares the simulation library and must be called before the simulation starts. It initializes all pointers required and sets up global variables private to the simulation environment.

Returns: Nothing.

See also: run_sim(), clear_sim().

laplace()

```
#include ⟨random.h⟩
float laplace ( stream *rs );
```

Description: This function returns a floating point random number from a Laplace distribution with a mean of 0.0 using stream *rs*.

If the random number stream *rs* is NULL the error message

```
**** run-time error : NULL random number stream ****
```

is printed and the simulation stopped.

Returns: A floating point number from a Laplace distribution.

See also: binomial(), chi_square(), erlang(), exponential(), f_distr(), gamma(), geometric(), log_normal(), neg_binomial(), normal(), poisson(), student_t(), triang(), uniform(), uniform01(), weibull().

large_sample_conf_int()

```
#include ⟨stats.h⟩
float large_sample_conf_int ( confidence_level cl, float std_dev, int n );
```

Description: This function returns the large sample confidence interval for a given standard deviation *std_dev* and number of samples *n*. The confidence level required is given by the argument *cl*. Two values of confidence level are defined, *PERCENT_99* and *PERCENT_95*, which are declared in *stats.h*. The actual confidence interval spans *mean − large_sample_conf_int( )* to *mean + large_sample_conf_int( )*.

If the standard deviation *std_dev* is negative the warning message

```
**** warning : negative standard deviation ****
```

is printed and the value 0.0 returned.

If the number of samples *n* is less than two then the warning message

```
**** warning : insufficient samples ****
```

is printed and the value 0.0 returned.

Returns: A floating point number representing half the width of the confidence interval.

See also: small_sample_conf_int().

log_normal()

```
#include <random.h>
float log_normal ( stream *rs, float mean, float std_dev );
```

Description: This function generates a random floating point number from a log-normal distribution with mean *mean* and standard deviation *std_dev* from the stream *rs*.

If the random number stream *rs* is NULL the error message

```
**** run-time error : NULL random number stream ****
```

is printed and the simulation stopped.

Returns: A floating point number from a log-normal distribution.

See also: beta(), binomial(), chi_square(), erlang(), exponential(), f_distr(), gamma(), geometric(), laplace(), neg_binomial(), normal(), poisson(), student_t(), triang(), uniform(), uniform01(), weibull().

make_conditional_entity()

```
#include <sim_lib.h>
entity *make_conditional_entity ( void (*event)(), void *at, int phase,
          int priority, void (*destroy)(void *attr) )
```

Description: This function creates a new entity dynamically using *malloc( )* and adds it to the conditional list. The entity when created will be initialized to the *CONDITIONAL* state. Argument *event* is a function declared as returning void and is the function to be executed when the entity is running. *At* is a pointer to some arbitrary data structure declared and used in the model to represent the attributes of the entity. *Phase* is the phase that will be assigned to the entity when activated. *Priority* is the assigned priority of the entity. *Destroy* is a pointer to a function that can be called to deallocate the memory assigned for attributes. In many cases, this last function will in fact be the standard *C* function *free( )* which releases memory allocated by *malloc( )*.

If memory could not be obtained the message

```
**** run-time error : cannot allocate memory for new entity ****
```

is printed and the simulation is stopped.

Returns: A pointer to the entity created.

See also: make_entity(), make_scheduled_entity().

make_entity()

```
#include <sim_lib.h>
entity *make_entity ( void (*event)( ), void *at, int phase, int priority,
          void (*destroy)(void *attr) );
```

Description: This function creates a new entity record dynamically using *malloc( )*. The entity when created will be initialized to the *PASSIVE* state. Argument *event* is a function declared as returning void and is the function to be executed when the entity is running. *At* is a pointer to some arbitrary data structure declared and used in the model to represent the attributes of the entity. *Phase* is the phase that will be assigned to the entity when activated. *Priority* is the assigned priority of the entity. *Destroy* is a pointer to a function that can be called to deallocate the memory assigned for attributes. In many cases, this last function will in fact be the standard *C* function *free( )* which releases memory allocated by *malloc( )*.

If memory cannot be allocated to create the entity record the error message

```
**** run-time error : cannot allocate memory for new entity ****
```

is printed and the simulation is stopped.

Returns: A pointer to the entity created.

See also: make_conditional_entity(), make_scheduled_entity().

make_histogram()

```
#include <results.h>
histogram *make_histogram ( float start, float width,
          int num_columns, int mode );
```

Description: This function creates a histogram data structure dynamically using *malloc( )* and returns a pointer to it. The histogram created has *num_columns* columns, each of width *width*, and they range from *start* to *start + width*num_* *columns.* The *mode* argument defines either a *WEIGHTED, UNWEIGHTED* or *TIME_SERIES* histogram. Memory is allocated for the histogram structure and to record the values for each of the columns.

If the memory cannot be obtained the error message

```
**** run-time error : cannot allocate memory for new histogram ****
```

is printed and the simulation is stopped.

Returns: A pointer to the histogram created.

See also: add_hdata(), clear_histogram(), print_cumulative(), print_histogram(), print_table().

make_queue()

```
#include <sim_lib.h>
queue *make_queue ( void );
```

Description: This function creates and initializes a new queue data structure dynamically using *malloc( )* and returns a pointer to it.

If memory cannot be allocated the error message

```
**** run-time error : cannot allocate memory for new queue ****
```

is printed and the simulation is stopped.

Returns: A pointer to the queue created.

See also: append(), clear_queue(), dump_queue(), extract(), prepend(), queue_back(), queue_front(), remove_back(), remove_front().

make_resource

```
#include <resource.h>
resource *make_resource ( float a );
```

Description: This function creates a resource dynamically using *malloc( )* with an initial amount *a* and returns a pointer to it.

If memory cannot be obtained the error message

```
**** run-time error : cannot allocate memory for new resource ****
```

is printed and the simulation is stopped.

Returns: A pointer to the resource created.

See also: acquire(), release(), reset_resource().

make_scheduled_entity()

```
#include <sim_lib.h>
entity *make_scheduled_entity ( void *proc, void *at, float t, int phase,
          int priority, int number );
```

Description: This function creates *number* new entities dynamically using *malloc( )* and adds them to the calendar to become active a time *t* later than the current clock time. The entities are initialized to state *PENDING*. Argument *event* is a function declared as returning void and is the function to be executed when the entity is active. *At* is a pointer to some arbitrary data structure declared and used in the model to represent the attributes of the entity. *Phase* is the phase that will be assigned to the entity when activated. *Priority* is the assigned priority of the entity. *Destroy* is a pointer to a function that can be called to deallocate the memory assigned for the attributes. In many cases, this last function will in fact be the standard *C* function *free( )* which releases memory allocated by *malloc( )*.

   If memory cannot be allocated to create the entity record the error message

```
**** run-time error : cannot allocate memory for new scheduled entity ****
```

is printed and the simulation is stopped.

Returns: A pointer to the entity created.

See also: make_conditional_entity(), make_entity().

make_stream()

```
#include <random.h>
stream *make_stream ( unsigned int seed, int antithetic );
```

Description: This function creates a stream data structure, used for generating random numbers, dynamically using *malloc( )* and returns a pointer to it. The argument *seed* is used to initialize the stream. Argument *antithetic* is used to control the generation of antithetic random variables. If *antithetic* has a value of zero, then a stream of random numbers $x_1, x_2, x_3, \ldots$ is produced. If *antithetic* has a non zero value, then a stream $1 - x_1, 1 - x_2, 1 - x_3, \ldots$ is produced.

   If memory for the stream cannot be allocated the error message

```
**** run-time error : cannot allocate memory for new stream ****
```

is printed and the simulation stopped.

Returns: A pointer to the stream created.

See also: reset_stream().

make_summary()

```
#include <results.h>
stats *make_summary ( void );
```

Description: This function creates a summary statistics data structure dynamically using *malloc( )* and returns a pointer to it.

   If memory cannot be allocated the error message

```
**** run-time error : cannot allocate memory for new statistics summary ****
```

is printed and the simulation is stopped.

Returns: A pointer to the *stats* data structure created.
See also: add_sdata(), clear_summary(), print_summary().

make_table()

```
#include ⟨random.h⟩
table *make_table ( int number, float *x_axis, float *y_axis );
```

Description: This function creates a table data structure which is used to generate arbitrarily distributed random numbers. Argument *number* specifies the number of point pairs used to define the empiric distribution function. The *x* and *y* values for each point are in the arrays *x_axis* and *y_axis* respectively. The function defined by the point pairs must be monotonically non-decreasing, there must be more than 1 point pair and the last *y* value must be 1.0. The arrays *x_axis* and *y_axis* must be declared static because only the pointers are stored in the table data structure.

If the conditions for the data are not met then one of error messages

```
**** run-time error : y values must be increasing in tabulated function ****
**** run-time error : x values must be increasing in tabulated function ****
**** run-time error : y values must be in range 0 to 1.0 in tabulated function ***
```

is printed and the simulation stopped.

The table data structure is created dynamically using *malloc( )*. If memory cannot be allocated the error message

```
**** run-time error : cannot allocate memory for new table ****
```

is printed and the simulation is stopped.
Returns: A pointer to the table structure created.
See also: draw_continuous(), draw_discrete().

neg_binomial()

```
#include ⟨random.h⟩
float neg_binomial ( stream *rs, float p, unsigned int r);
```

Description: This function returns a integer-valued random floating point number drawn from a negative binomial distribution with parameters *p* and *r*. The stream *rs* is used as the source of random fractions to generate the required number.

If the random number stream *rs* is NULL the error message

```
**** run-time error : NULL random number stream ****
```

is printed and the simulation stopped.
Returns: An integer-valued floating point number from a negative binomial distribution.

See also: binomial(), chi_square(), erlang(), exponential(), f_distr(), gamma(), geometric(), laplace(), log_normal(), normal(), poisson(), student_t(), triang(), uniform(), uniform01(), weibull().

normal()

```
#include 〈random.h〉
float normal ( stream *rs, float mean, float std_dev );
```

Description: This function returns random floating point numbers from a normal distribution with mean *mean* and standard deviation *std_dev* from the stream *rs*. If the random number stream *rs* is NULL the error message

```
**** run-time error : NULL random number stream ****
```

is printed and the simulation stopped. In addition, there are checks on the values of the mean and standard deviation. If these are out of the defined range the messages

```
**** run-time error : negative mean in normal distribution ****
```

or

```
**** run-time error : negative standard deviation in normal distribution ****
```

is printed.
Returns: A floating point number drawn from a normal distribution.
See also: binomial(), chi_square(), erlang(), exponential(), f_distr(), gamma(), geometric(), laplace(), log_normal(), neg_binomial(), poisson(), student_t(), triang(), uniform(), uniform01(), weibull().

passivate()

```
include 〈sim_lib.h〉
int passivate ( entity *e );
```

Description: If the entity record pointer *e* is non-NULL this function changes its state from *CONDITIONAL, PENDING* or *ACTIVE* to *PASSIVE*. If the state is initially *CONDITIONAL* then *e* is removed from the conditional entity list, if it is *PENDING* then it is removed from the calendar and if it is *ACTIVE* the state is changed directly.

If the entity *e* is NULL then the error message

```
**** run-time error : NULL entity ****
```

is printed and the simulation stopped.
Returns: TRUE if the entity was found to be in one of the required states, FALSE otherwise.

See also: activate(), add_event(), delete_event(), extract(), hold(), reactivate(), reinstate(), schedule(), withdraw().

poisson()

```
#include <random.h>
float poisson ( stream *rs, float mean );
```

Description: This function returns integer-valued random floating point numbers from a Poisson distribution having mean *mean*. The stream *rs* passed as an argument is used as the source of the random variate.

If the random number stream *rs* is NULL the error message

```
**** run-time error : NULL random number stream ****
```

is printed and the simulation stopped.

Returns: Integer-valued floating point numbers from a Poisson distribution.

See also: beta(), binomial(), chi_square(), erlang(), exponential(), f_distr(), gamma(), geometric(), laplace(), log_normal(), neg_binomial(), normal(), student_t(), triang(), uniform(), uniform01(), weibull().

prepend()

```
#include <sim_lib.h>
int prepend ( queue *q, entity *e );
```

Description: If both the entity *e* and the queue *q* are non-NULL this function adds entity *e* to queue *q*, at a position based on the priority of the entity. The current state of *entity* must be either *ACTIVE* or *PASSIVE* in which case it will be added in front of all entities currently in the queue with a lower or equal priority. All existing queued entities of a higher priority will remain in front of the entity *e*. The state of *entity* will be changed to *QUEUED*.

If either *e* or *q* is NULL the error message

```
**** run-time error : cannot add or remove with NULL queue or entity ****
```

is printed and the simulation stopped.

Returns: TRUE if the entity was found to be in one of the required states, FALSE otherwise.

See also: append(), clear_queue(), dump_queue(), extract(), make_queue(), queue_back(), queue_front(), remove_back(), remove_front().

print_cumulative()

```
#include <results.h>
void print_cumulative ( FILE *fp, histogram *h, char *title );
```

Description: If the histogram *h* is non-NULL this function prints the histogram data accumulated in *h* to the file that has file pointer *fp*, as a cumulative frequency histogram. The file pointer *stdout* can be specified to send output to the console. Argument *title* is a string used as a title banner. The statistical information printed comprises mean, variance, standard deviation, the sum of the observed frequencies, the minimum value and the maximum value, as well as the histogram itself in the following format:

```
TITLE STRING
  mean   =   xx.xxx, variance =    xx.xxx, std_dev =   xx.xxx
  sum of frequencies            = xxxx
  min val =   xx.xxx    max val =    xx.xxx
  x-val    y-val#######################################################
     :
```

The character used to fill the columns has the default value '#'. This can be changed by calling the function *set_fill_char( )* with the required character as a parameter such as

```
set_fill_char ( "=" );
```

If the histogram is NULL the error message

```
**** run-time error : NULL histogram ****
```

is printed and the simulation stopped.
Returns: Nothing.
See also: add_hdata(), clear_histogram(), make_histogram(), print_histogram(), print_table(), set_fill_char().

print_histogram()

```
#include <results.h>
void print_histogram ( FILE *fp, histogram *h, char *title );
```

Description: If the histogram *h* is non-NULL the function prints the histogram data accumulated in *h* to the file with file pointer *fp*, as a frequency histogram. The file pointer *stdout* can be used to send output to the console. Argument *title* is a string used as a title banner. The statistical information printed comprises mean, variance, standard deviation, the sum of the observed frequencies, the minimum value and the maximum value, as well as the histogram itself in the following format:

```
TITLE STRING
  mean   =   xx.xxx, variance =    xx.xxx, std_dev =   xx.xxx
  sum of frequencies            = xxxx
  min val =   xx.xxx    max val =    xx.xxx
  x-val    y-val#######################################################
     :
```

The character used to fill the columns has the default value '#'. This can be changed by calling the library routine *set_fill_char( )* with the required character as a parameter such as

```
set_fill_char ( "*" );
```

If the histogram is NULL the error message

```
**** run-time error : NULL histogram ****
```

is printed and the simulation stopped.
Returns: Nothing.
See also: add_hdata(), clear_histogram(), make_histogram(), print_cumulative(), print_table(), set_fill_char().

print_summary()

```
#include <results.h>
void print_summary ( FILE *fp, stats *s, char *title );
```

Description: If the summary statistics data structure *s* is non-NULL this function prints the data accumulated in *s* to the file with *file* pointer *fp*. The file pointer *stdout* can be used when output is required to the console. Argument *title* is a string used as a title banner. The data comprises the mean, standard deviation, variance, the number of samples that had a value of zero and the total number of samples in the following format:

```
TITLE STRING
mean =  xx.xxx, variance =   xx.xxx, std_dev =  xx.xxx
number of zero entries   = xxx
total number of entries  = xxx
```

If the statistics summary pointer *s* is NULL the error message

```
**** run-time error : NULL statistics ****
```

is printed and the simulation stopped.
Returns: Nothing.
See also: add_sdata(), clear_summary(), make_summary().

print_table()

```
#include <results.h>
void print_table ( FILE *fp, histogram *h, char *title );
```

Description: If the histogram pointer *h* is non-NULL this function prints the histogram data accumulated to the file with *file* pointer *fp* in a tabular format. The file pointer *stdout* can be used when output is required to the console. Argument *title* is a string used as a title banner. The statistical information printed comprises mean, variance, standard deviation, the sum of the observed frequencies, the minimum value and the maximum value and the histogram data in the following format:

```
TITLE STRING
  mean  =  xx.xxx, variance =   xx.xxx, std_dev =  xx.xxx
  sum of frequencies          = xxxx
  min val = xx.xxx   max val =   xx.xxx

     Range              Observed     Per cent    Cumulative    Cumulative
                         value       of total    percentage    remainder
 xx.xx  →     xx.xx     xxx.xx        xxx.xx       xxx.xx        xxx.xx
     :
```

If the histogram pointer *h* is NULL the error message

```
**** run-time error : NULL histogram ****
```

is printed and the simulation stopped.
Returns: Nothing.
See also: add_hdata(), clear_histogram(), make_histogram(), print_cumulative(), print_histogram().

probability()

```
#include <random.h>
int probability ( stream *rs, float p );
```

Description: This function returns a 1 with probability *p* and 0 with probability $1 - p$ using random fractions sampled from the stream *rs*.
If the random number stream *rs* is NULL the error message

```
**** run-time error : NULL random number stream ****
```

is printed and the simulation stopped. If the probability is not in the range 0 to 1.0 the error message

```
**** run-time error : probability values must be in range 0 to 1.0 ****
```

is printed and the simulation stopped.
Returns: 1 with probability *p*, 0 with probability $1 - p$.
See also: uniform(), uniform01().

queue_back()

```
#include <sim_lib.h>
entity *queue_back ( queue *q );
```

Description: This function returns a pointer to the last entity in the queue pointed to by *q*. The queue and the entity returned are not modified. If the queue is NULL or empty then the return value is also NULL.

Returns: A pointer to the first entity or NULL if the queue is empty or NULL.

See also: append(), clear_queue(), dump_queue(), extract(), make_queue(), prepend(), queue_front(), remove_back(), remove_front().

queue_front()

```
#include <sim_lib.h>
entity *queue_front ( queue *q );
```

Description: This function returns a pointer to the first entity in the queue pointed to by *q*. The queue and the entity returned are not modified. If the queue is NULL or empty then the return value is also NULL.

Returns: A pointer to the first entity or NULL if the queue is empty or NULL.

See also: append(), clear_queue(), dump_queue(), extract(), make_queue(), prepend(), queue_back(), remove_back(), remove_front().

quit()

```
#include <sim_lib.h>
void quit ( void );
```

Description: This function immediately terminates the current simulation run. The calendar and conditional entity list are not modified.

Returns: Nothing.

See also: run_sim(), quit_terminate().

quit_terminate()

```
#include <sim_lib.h>
int quit_terminate ( entity *e );
```

Description: If the entity record pointed to by *e* is non_NULL, this function removes it from the simulation if it is in state *PASSIVE* or *ACTIVE*, in the same way as the *terminate()* function. The termination count is then decremented and if the count is 0 or less then the simulation is stopped.

If the entity is NULL then the message

```
**** run-time error : NULL entity ****
```

is printed and the termination stopped.

Returns: TRUE if the entity is in the require state, FALSE otherwise.

See also: run_sim(), quit(), terminate().

reactivate()

```
#include <sim_lib.h>
int reactivate ( void );
```

Description: If the current entity is *ACTIVE* then it is scheduled for activation again at the current simulated time. If the current entity is in any other state this function has no effect.

Returns: TRUE if the current entity is in the correct state and FALSE otherwise.

See also: activate(), add_event(), delete_event(), extract(), hold(), passivate(), reinstate(), schedule(), withdraw().

reinstate()

```
#include ⟨sim_lib.h⟩
int reinstate ( entity *e );
```

Description: This function is used in collaboration with the *withdraw( )* function to control whether a conditional entity record pointed to by e is executable. If the entity e is non-NULL and it is in the state *CLOSED*, then e is made accessible and its state changed to *CONDITIONAL*. In any other state the function has no effect.

If the entity is NULL the message

```
**** run-time error : NULL entity ****
```

is printed and the simulation stopped.

Returns: TRUE if the current entity is in the correct state and FALSE otherwise.

See also: activate(), add_event(), delete_event(), extract(), hold(), passivate(), reactivate(), schedule(), withdraw().

release()

```
#include ⟨resource.h⟩
void release ( resource *r, float a );
```

Description: This function increases the amount of the resource pointed to by r by an amount a.

If the resource r is NULL the message

```
**** run-time error : NULL resource ****
```

is printed and the simulation stopped.

Returns: Nothing.

See also: acquire().

remove_back()

```
#include ⟨sim_lib.h⟩
entity *remove_back ( queue *q );
```

Description: If the queue pointer q is non-NULL this function extracts the last entity from the queue pointed to by *q* and returns a pointer to it. The state of the returned entity is changed to *PASSIVE*.

If the queue is NULL the error message

```
**** run-time error : cannot add or remove with NULL queue and/or entity ****
```

is printed and the simulation stopped.

Returns: A pointer to the entity removed or NULL if the queue is empty.

See also: append(), clear_queue(), dump_queue(), extract(), make_queue(), prepend(), queue_back(), queue_front(), remove_front().

remove_front()

```
#include <sim_lib.h>
entity *remove_front ( queue *q );
```

Description: If the queue is non-NULL this function extracts the first entity from the queue and returns a pointer to it. The state of the returned entity is changed to *PASSIVE*.

If the queue is NULL the error message

```
**** run-time error : cannot add or remove with NULL queue and/or entity ****
```

is printed and the simulation stopped.

Returns: A pointer to the entity removed or NULL if the queue is empty.

See also: append(), clear_queue(), dump_queue(), extract(), make_queue(), prepend(), queue_back(), queue_front(), remove_back().

reset_resource()

```
#include <resource.h>
void reset_resource ( resource *r );
```

Description: This function resets the amount of resource *r* available to its initial value.

If the resource is NULL the error message

```
**** run-time error : NULL resource ****
```

is printed and the simulation terminated.

Returns: Nothing

See also: make_resource().

reset_stream()

```
#include <random.h>
void reset_stream ( stream *rs, unsigned int seed );
```

Description: This function initializes the stream *rs* by reseeding it with *seed*. If the random number stream *rs* is NULL the error message

```
**** run-time error : NULL random number stream ****
```

is printed and the simulation stopped.
Returns: Nothing.
See also: make_stream().

run_sim()

```
#include <sim_lib.h>
void run_sim ( float t, int count );
```

Description: This function starts the simulation. The simulation only stops when either:

1. the simulated time becomes equal to or greater than *t* or
2. the termination count becomes equal to or less than zero when function *quit_terminate( )* is called or
3. function *quit( )* is called or
4. a run-time error occurs.

If the time *t* is less than zero then the message

```
**** run-time error : negative simulation duration ****
```

is printed and the simulation stopped.
Returns: Nothing
See also: clear_sim(), init_sim(), quit(), quit_terminate().

scan_always()

```
#include <sim_lib.h>
void scan_always ( int yes )
```

Description: This function controls how the scheduler selects the entity records from the calendar. If *yes* is greater than zero, the scheduler reports entity records one at a time even if there are several that have the same activation time. The result is that the conditional entity list is scanned after every event.

If *yes* is less than or equal to zero, the scheduler will report all entity records that occur concurrently (i.e. have the same activation time) together. The conditional entity list in this case will only be scanned once after the last event has completed.

The default mode after *init_sim( )* has been called is to identify all concurrent entity records together.
Returns: Nothing.
See also: make_conditional_entity().

schedule()

```
#include ⟨sim_lib.h⟩
int schedule ( entity *e, float t )
```

Description: If the entity record pointer *e* is non-NULL and in the state *PASSIVE* this function places it in the calendar to become active a time *t* later than the current clock time. In any other state the function has no effect.

If *e* is NULL the error message

```
**** run-time error : NULL entity ****
```

is printed and the simulation stopped. Also, if the value of the delay *t* is less than zero, the message

```
**** run-time error : negative rescheduling delay ****
```

is printed and the simulation stopped.

Returns: TRUE if *e* was *PASSIVE* and FALSE in all other cases.

See also: activate(), add_event(), delete_event(), extract(), hold(), passivate(), reactivate(), reinstate(), withdraw().

set_fill_char()

```
#include ⟨results.h⟩
void set_fill_char ( char fc );
```

Description: This function sets the character used to print histogram bars to the character passed as an argument. The default value is the hash symbol '#'.

Returns: Nothing.

See also: print_cumulative(), print_histogram().

small_sample_conf_int()

```
#include ⟨stats.h⟩
float small_sample_conf_int ( confidence_level cl, float std_dev, int n );
```

Description: This function returns the small sample confidence interval for a given standard deviation *std_dev* and number of samples *n*. The confidence level required is given by the argument *cl*. Two values of confidence interval are defined, *PERCENT_99* and *PERCENT_95*, which are declared in *stats.h*. The actual confidence interval spans *mean − small_sample_conf_int( )* to *mean + small_sample_conf_int( )*.

If the standard deviation *std_dev* is negative the warning message

```
**** warning : negative standard deviation ****
```

is printed and the value 0.0 returned.

If the number of samples *n* is less than 2 then the warning message

```
**** warning : insufficient samples ****
```

is printed and the value 0.0 returned.

Returns: A floating point number representing half the width of the confidence interval.

See also: large_sample_conf_int().

stamp()

```
#include ⟨sim_lib.h⟩
void stamp ( entity *e );
```

Description: If the entity *e* is non-NULL this function adds a time stamp to it. A time stamp is the current value of simulated time. This value may then be accessed in the model with the macro *TIME_OF(e)* or the difference between the time stamp and the current time may be accessed with the macro *TIME_SPENT(e)*, both of which are declared in *sim_lib.h*.

If the entity *e* is null then the message

```
**** run-time error : NULL entity ****
```

is printed and the simulation stopped.

Returns: Nothing.

See also: stamp_current().

stamp_currrent()

```
#include ⟨sim_lib.h⟩
void stamp_current ( void );
```

Description: This function stamps the current entity. It is functionally equivalent to *stamp(current)*.

If the entity *e* is NULL the message

```
**** run-time error : NULL entity ****
```

is printed and the simulation stopped.

Returns: Nothing.

See also: stamp().

student_t()

```
#include ⟨sim_lib.h⟩
float student_t ( stream *rs, unsigned int n );
```

Description: This function returns a floating point number drawn from a Student-*t* distribution with *n* degrees of freedom. The stream *rs* is used as the source of random fractions to generate the required number.

If the pointer to the random number stream *rs* is NULL the error message

```
**** run-time error : NULL random number stream ****
```

is printed and the simulation stopped.

Returns: A random floating point number drawn from Student's *t* distribution.

See also: beta(), binomial(), chi_square(), erlang(), exponential(), f_distr(), gamma(), geometric(), laplace(), log_normal(), neg_binomial(), normal(), poisson(), triang(), uniform(), uniform01(), weibull().

terminate()

```
#include <sim_lib.h>
int terminate ( entity *e );
```

Description: If the entity *e* is non-NULL and in the state *PASSIVE* or *ACTIVE*, this function removes it from the simulation. Memory allocated for *e* is released by calling *free()*. If the attribute data associated with *e* is non-NULL the memory occupied by it is released by calling the *destroy()* function that was passed as an argument to the function creating *e*.

If *e* is NULL, the error message

```
**** run-time error : NULL entity ****
```

is printed and the simulation stopped.

Returns: TRUE if *e* is in the correct state, FALSE otherwise.

See also: quit_terminate().

triang()

```
#include <random.h>
float triang ( stream *rs, float mode );
```

Description: This function returns a floating point number from a triangular distribution having mode *mode*. The argument *rs* is used as the source of random fractions from which the desired random number is drawn.

If the value of *mode* is out of range the error message

```
**** run-time error : mode out of range in triangular distribution ****
```

is printed and the simulation terminated. If the random number stream *rs* is NULL the error message

```
**** run-time error : NULL random number stream ****
```

is printed and the simulation stopped.

Returns: A random floating point number in the range 0 to 1 drawn from a triangular distribution.

See also: beta(), binomial(), chi_square(), erlang(), exponential(), f_distr(), gamma(), geometric(), laplace(), log_normal(), neg_binomial(), normal(), poisson(), student_t(), uniform(), uniform01(), weibull().

uniform()

```
#include <random.h>
float uniform ( stream *rs, float lower, float upper );
```

Description: This function returns a random floating point number from the uniform distribution in the range *lower* to *upper* from the stream *rs* passed as an argument.

If the random number stream *rs* is NULL the error message

```
**** run-time error : NULL random number stream ****
```

is printed and the simulation stopped. The limits of the distribution must be such that lower < upper. If this is not the case the error message

```
**** run-time error : must have upper limit > lower limit in uniform distribution ****
```

is printed and the simulation terminated.
Returns: A floating point number from a uniform distribution.
See also: beta(), binomial(), chi_square(), erlang(), exponential(), f_distr(), gamma(), geometric(), laplace(), log_normal(), neg_binomial(), normal(), poisson(), student_t(), triang(), uniform01(), weibull().

uniform01()

```
#include <random.h>
float uniform01 ( stream *rs );
```

Description: This function returns a floating point number from a uniform distribution defined over the range 0 to 1 using the stream *rs* passed as an argument.

If the random number stream *rs* is NULL the error message

```
**** run-time error : NULL random number stream ****
```

is printed and the simulation stopped.
Returns: A random floating point number from a uniform distribution in the range 0 to 1.
See also: beta(), binomial(), chi_square(), erlang(), exponential(), f_distr(), gamma(), geometric(), laplace(), log_normal(), neg_binomial(), normal(), poisson(), student_t(), triang(), uniform(), weibull().

wait()

```
#include <sim_lib.h>
int wait ( float t );
```

Description: If the current entity is in the *ACTIVE* state this function causes it to be scheduled a period *t* later than the current simulated time.

If the time delay *t* is less than 0.0 then the error message

```
**** run-time error : negative rescheduling delay ****
```

is printed and the simulation stopped.

Returns: TRUE if the current entity is in the ACTIVE state, FALSE otherwise.
See also: schedule().

weibull()

```
#include <random.h>
float weibull ( stream *rs, float a, float b );
```

Description: This function returns a random floating point number from a Weibull distribution with parameters *a* and *b*. The stream *rs* passed as an argument is used as the source of the random variate.

If the random number stream *rs* is NULL the error message

```
**** run-time error : NULL random number stream ****
```

is printed and the simulation stopped.

Returns: A floating point number from a Weibull distribution.
See also: beta(), binomial(), chi_square(), erlang(), exponential(), f_distr(), gamma(), geometric(), laplace(), log_normal(), neg_binomial(), normal(), poisson(), student_t(), triang(), uniform(), uniform01().

withdraw()

```
#include <sim_lib.h>
int withdraw ( entity *e );
```

Description: If the entity record pointer *e* is non-NULL and in the state *CONDITIONAL* this function changes its state to *CLOSED*, which prevents it from being called during a scan of the conditional entity list. In any other state it has no effect.

If *e* is NULL then the error message

```
**** run-time error : NULL entity ****
```

is printed and the simulation stopped.

Returns: TRUE if the entity is in the required state, FALSE otherwise.
See also: activate(), add_event(), delete_event(), extract(), hold(), passivate(), reactivate(), reinstate(), schedule().

APPENDIX C: STATISTICAL TABLES

C.1 THE AREA OF THE STANDARD NORMAL DISTRIBUTION

Values in Table C.1 give the shaded area under the curve representing the probability $P[0 \leqslant z \leqslant b]$ that z is between 0 and b.

Table C.1 Area of the standard normal distribution

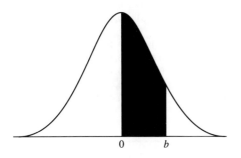

x	0.00	0.01	0.02	0.03	0.04	0.05	0.06	0.07	0.08	0.09
0.0	0.0000	0.0040	0.0080	0.0120	0.0160	0.0199	0.0239	0.0279	0.0319	0.0359
0.1	0.0398	0.0438	0.0478	0.0517	0.0557	0.0596	0.0636	0.0675	0.0714	0.0753
0.2	0.0793	0.0832	0.0871	0.0910	0.0948	0.0987	0.1026	0.1064	0.1103	0.1141
0.3	0.1179	0.1217	0.1255	0.1293	0.1331	0.1368	0.1406	0.1443	0.1480	0.1517
0.4	0.1554	0.1591	0.1628	0.1664	0.1700	0.1736	0.1772	0.1808	0.1844	0.1879
0.5	0.1915	0.1950	0.1985	0.2019	0.2054	0.2088	0.2123	0.2157	0.2190	0.2224
0.6	0.2257	0.2291	0.2324	0.2357	0.2389	0.2422	0.2454	0.2486	0.2517	0.2549
0.7	0.2580	0.2611	0.2642	0.2673	0.2703	0.2734	0.2764	0.2794	0.2923	0.2852
0.8	0.2881	0.2910	0.2939	0.2967	0.2995	0.3023	0.3051	0.3078	0.3106	0.3133
0.9	0.3159	0.3186	0.3213	0.3238	0.3264	0.3289	0.3315	0.3340	0.3365	0.3389
1.0	0.3413	0.3438	0.3461	0.3485	0.3508	0.3531	0.3554	0.3577	0.3599	0.3621
1.1	0.3643	0.3665	0.3686	0.3708	0.3729	0.3749	0.3770	0.3790	0.3810	0.3830
1.2	0.3849	0.3869	0.3888	0.3907	0.3925	0.3944	0.3962	0.3980	0.3997	0.4015
1.3	0.4032	0.4049	0.4066	0.4082	0.4099	0.4115	0.4131	0.4147	0.4162	0.4177
1.4	0.4192	0.4207	0.4222	0.4236	0.4251	0.4265	0.4279	0.4292	0.4306	0.4319
1.5	0.4332	0.4345	0.4357	0.4370	0.4382	0.4394	0.4406	0.4418	0.4429	0.4441
1.6	0.4453	0.4463	0.4474	0.4484	0.4495	0.4505	0.4515	0.4525	0.4535	0.4545

Table C.1 *Cont.*

x	0.00	0.01	0.02	0.03	0.04	0.05	0.06	0.07	0.08	0.09
1.7	0.4554	0.4564	0.4573	0.4582	0.4591	0.4599	0.4608	0.4616	0.4625	0.4633
1.8	0.4641	0.4649	0.4656	0.4664	0.4671	0.4678	0.4686	0.4693	0.4699	0.4706
1.9	0.4713	0.4719	0.4726	0.4732	0.4738	0.4744	0.4750	0.4756	0.4761	0.4767
2.0	0.4772	0.4778	0.4783	0.4788	0.4793	0.4798	0.4803	0.4808	0.4812	0.4817
2.1	0.4821	0.4826	0.4830	0.4834	0.4838	0.4842	0.4846	0.4850	0.4854	0.4857
2.2	0.4861	0.4864	0.4868	0.4871	0.4875	0.4878	0.4881	0.4884	0.4887	0.4890
2.3	0.4893	0.4896	0.4898	0.4901	0.4904	0.4906	0.4909	0.4911	0.4913	0.4916
2.4	0.4918	0.4920	0.4922	0.4925	0.4927	0.4929	0.4931	0.4932	0.4934	0.4936
2.5	0.4938	0.4940	0.4941	0.4943	0.4945	0.4946	0.4948	0.4949	0.4951	0.4952
2.6	0.4953	0.4955	0.4956	0.4957	0.4959	0.4960	0.4961	0.4962	0.4963	0.4964
2.7	0.4965	0.4966	0.4967	0.4968	0.4969	0.4970	0.4971	0.4972	0.4973	0.4974
2.8	0.4974	0.4975	0.4976	0.4977	0.4977	0.4978	0.4979	0.4979	0.4980	0.4981
2.9	0.4981	0.4982	0.4982	0.4983	0.4984	0.4984	0.4985	0.4985	0.4986	0.4986
3.0	0.4987	0.4987	0.4987	0.4988	0.4988	0.4989	0.4989	0.4989	0.4990	0.4990

C.2 THE AREA OF THE STUDENT'S t DISTRIBUTION

Values in Table C.2 give the shaded area under the curve for the t distribution with v degrees of freedom.

Table C.2 Area of the Student's t distribution

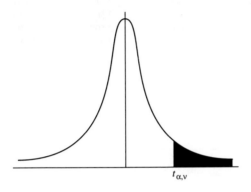

$t_{\alpha,v}$

Degrees of freedom	$t_{0.100}$	$t_{0.050}$	$t_{0.025}$	$t_{0.010}$	$t_{0.005}$
1	3.078	6.314	12.706	31.821	63.657
2	1.886	2.920	4.303	6.965	9.925
3	1.638	2.353	3.182	4.541	5.841
4	1.533	2.132	2.776	3.747	4.604
5	1.476	2.015	2.571	3.365	4.032
6	1.440	1.943	2.447	3.143	3.707
7	1.415	1.895	2.365	2.998	3.499
8	1.397	1.860	2.306	2.896	3.355
9	1.383	1.833	2.262	2.821	3.250
10	1.372	1.812	2.228	2.764	3.169
11	1.363	1.796	2.201	2.718	3.106
12	1.356	1.782	2.179	2.681	3.055
13	1.350	1.771	2.160	2.650	3.012
14	1.345	1.761	2.145	2.624	2.977
15	1.341	1.753	2.131	2.602	2.947
16	1.337	1.746	2.120	2.583	2.921
17	1.333	1.740	2.110	2.567	2.898
18	1.330	1.734	2.101	2.552	2.878
19	1.328	1.729	2.093	2.539	2.861
20	1.325	1.725	2.086	2.528	2.845

Table C.2 *Cont.*

Degrees of freedom	$t_{0.100}$	$t_{0.050}$	$t_{0.025}$	$t_{0.010}$	$t_{0.005}$
21	1.323	1.721	2.080	2.518	2.831
22	1.321	1.717	2.074	2.508	2.819
23	1.319	1.714	2.069	2.500	2.807
24	1.318	1.711	2.064	2.492	2.797
25	1.316	1.708	2.060	2.485	2.787
26	1.315	1.706	2.056	2.479	2.779
27	1.314	1.703	2.052	2.473	2.771
28	1.313	1.701	2.048	2.467	2.763
29	1.311	1.699	2.045	2.462	2.756
∞	1.282	1.645	1.960	2.326	2.567

C.3 THE AREA OF THE χ^2 DISTRIBUTION

Values in Tables C.3.1 and C.3.2 give the shaded area under the curve for the χ^2 distribution with v degrees of freedom.

Table C.3.1 Area of the χ^2 distribution

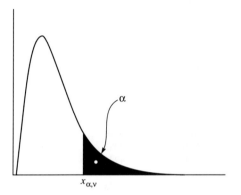

α

$x_{\alpha,v}$

Degrees of freedom	$\chi^2_{0.995}$	$\chi^2_{0.990}$	$\chi^2_{0.975}$	$\chi^2_{0.950}$	$\chi^2_{0.900}$
1	0.0000393	0.0001571	0.0009821	0.0039321	0.0157908
2	0.0100251	0.0201007	0.0506356	0.102587	0.210720
3	0.0717212	0.114832	0.215795	0.351846	0.584375
4	0.206990	0.297110	0.484419	0.710721	1.063623
5	0.411740	0.554300	0.831211	1.145476	1.61031
6	0.675727	0.872085	1.237347	1.63539	2.20413
7	0.989265	1.239043	1.68987	2.16735	2.83311
8	1.344419	1.646482	2.17973	2.73264	3.48954
9	1.734926	2.087912	2.70039	3.32511	4.16816
10	2.15585	2.55821	3.24697	3.94030	4.86518
11	2.60321	3.05347	3.81575	4.57481	5.57779
12	3.07382	3.57056	4.40379	5.22603	6.30380
13	3.56503	4.10691	5.00874	5.89186	7.04150
14	4.07468	4.66043	5.62872	6.57063	7.78953
15	4.60094	5.22935	6.26214	7.26094	8.54675
16	5.14224	5.81221	6.90766	7.96164	9.31223
17	5.69724	6.40776	7.56418	8.67176	10.0852
18	6.26481	7.01491	8.23075	9.39046	10.8649

Table C.3.1 *Cont.*

Degrees of freedom	$\chi^2_{0.995}$	$\chi^2_{0.990}$	$\chi^2_{0.975}$	$\chi^2_{0.950}$	$\chi^2_{0.900}$
19	6.84398	7.63273	8.90655	10.1170	11.6509
20	7.43386	8.26040	9.59083	10.8508	12.4426
21	8.03366	8.89720	10.28293	11.5913	13.2396
22	8.64272	9.54249	10.9823	12.3380	14.0415
23	9.26042	10.19567	11.6885	13.0905	14.8479
24	9.88623	10.8564	12.4011	13.8484	15.6587
25	10.5197	11.5240	13.1197	14.6114	16.4734
26	11.1603	12.1981	13.8439	15.3791	17.2919
27	11.8076	12.8786	14.5733	16.1513	18.1138
28	12.4613	13.5648	15.3079	16.9279	18.9392
29	13.1211	14.2565	16.4071	17.7083	19.7677
30	13.7867	14.9535	16.7908	18.4926	20.5992
40	20.7065	22.1643	24.4331	26.5093	29.0505
50	27.9907	29.7067	32.3574	34.7642	37.6886
60	35.5346	37.4848	40.4817	43.1879	46.4589
70	43.2752	45.4418	48.7576	51.7393	55.3290
80	51.1720	53.5400	57.1532	60.3915	64.2778
90	59.1963	61.7541	65.6466	69.1260	73.2912
100	67.3276	70.0648	74.2219	77.9295	82.3581

Table C.3.2 Area of the χ^2 distribution

Degrees of freedom	$\chi^2_{0.100}$	$\chi^2_{0.050}$	$\chi^2_{0.025}$	$\chi^2_{0.010}$	$\chi^2_{0.005}$
1	2.70554	3.84146	5.02389	6.63490	7.87944
2	4.60517	5.99147	7.37776	9.21034	10.5966
3	6.25139	7.81473	9.34840	11.3449	12.8381
4	7.77944	9.48773	11.1433	13.2767	14.8602
5	9.23635	11.0705	12.8325	15.0863	16.7496
6	10.6446	12.6916	14.4494	16.8119	18.5476
7	12.0170	14.0671	16.0128	18.4753	20.2777
8	13.3616	15.5073	17.5346	20.0902	21.9550
9	14.6837	16.9190	19.0228	21.6660	23.5893
10	15.9871	18.3070	20.4831	23.2093	25.1882
11	17.2750	19.6751	21.9200	24.7250	26.7569
12	18.5494	21.0261	23.3367	26.2170	28.2995
13	19.8119	22.3621	24.7356	27.6883	29.8194
14	21.0642	23.6848	26.1190	29.1413	31.3193
15	22.3072	24.9958	27.4884	30.5779	32.8013
16	23.5418	26.2962	28.8454	31.9999	34.2672
17	24.7690	27.5871	30.1910	33.4087	35.7185
18	25.9894	28.8693	31.5264	34.8053	37.1564
19	27.2036	30.1435	32.8523	36.1908	38.5822
20	28.4120	31.4104	34.1696	37.5662	39.9968
21	29.6151	32.6705	35.4789	38.9321	41.4010
22	30.8133	33.9244	36.7807	40.2894	42.7956
23	32.0069	35.1725	38.0757	41.6384	44.1813
24	33.1963	36.4151	39.3641	42.9798	45.5585
25	34.3816	37.6525	40.6465	44.3141	46.9278
26	35.5631	38.8852	41.9232	45.4617	48.2899
27	36.7412	40.1133	43.1944	46.9630	49.6449
28	37.9159	41.3372	44.4607	48.2782	50.9933
29	39.0875	42.5569	45.7222	49.5879	52.3356
30	40.2560	43.7729	46.9792	50.8922	53.6720
40	51.8050	55.7585	59.3417	63.6907	66.7659
50	63.1671	67.5048	71.4202	76.1539	79.4900
60	74.3970	79.0819	83.2976	88.3794	91.9517
70	85.5271	90.5312	95.0231	100.425	104.215
80	96.5782	101.879	106.629	112.329	116.321
90	107.565	113.145	118.136	124.116	128.299
100	118.498	124.342	129.561	135.807	140.169

C.4 THE AREA OF THE *F* DISTRIBUTION

Values in Tables C.4.1 and C.4.2 give the shaded area under the curve for the *F* distribution with v_1 degrees of freedom of the numerator and v_2 degrees of freedom of the denominator.

Table C.4.1a Area of the *F* distribution ($\alpha = 0.01$) for v_1 in the range 1 to 9

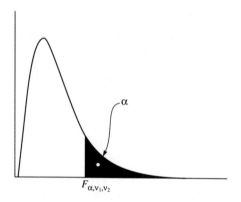

v_2	v_1 1	2	3	4	5	6	7	8	9
1	4052.2	4999.5	5403.4	5624.6	5763.6	5859.0	5928.4	5981.1	6022.5
2	98.50	99.00	99.17	99.25	99.30	99.33	99.36	99.37	99.39
3	34.12	30.92	29.46	28.71	28.24	27.91	27.67	27.49	27.35
4	21.20	18.00	16.69	15.98	15.52	15.21	14.98	14.80	14.66
5	16.26	13.27	12.06	11.39	10.97	10.67	10.46	10.29	10.16
6	13.75	10.92	9.78	9.15	8.75	8.47	8.26	8.10	7.98
7	12.25	9.55	8.45	7.85	7.46	7.19	6.99	6.84	6.72
8	11.26	8.65	7.59	7.01	6.63	6.37	6.18	6.03	5.92
9	10.56	8.02	6.99	6.42	6.06	5.80	5.61	5.47	5.35
10	10.04	7.56	6.55	5.99	5.64	5.39	5.20	5.06	4.94
11	9.65	7.21	6.22	5.67	5.32	5.07	4.89	4.74	4.63
12	9.33	6.93	5.95	5.41	5.06	4.82	4.64	4.50	4.39
13	9.07	6.70	5.74	5.21	4.86	4.62	4.44	4.30	4.19
14	8.86	6.51	5.56	5.04	4.69	4.46	4.28	4.14	4.03
15	8.68	6.36	5.42	4.89	4.56	4.32	4.14	4.00	3.89
16	8.53	6.23	5.29	4.77	4.44	4.20	4.03	3.89	3.78
17	8.40	6.11	5.18	4.67	4.34	4.01	3.93	3.79	3.68
18	8.29	6.01	5.09	4.58	4.25	4.01	3.84	3.71	3.60

Table C.4.1a *Cont.*

v_2	v_1 1	2	3	4	5	6	7	8	9
19	8.18	5.93	5.01	4.50	4.17	3.94	3.77	3.63	3.52
20	8.10	5.85	4.94	4.43	4.10	3.87	3.70	3.56	3.46
21	8.02	5.78	4.87	4.37	4.04	3.81	3.64	3.51	3.40
22	7.95	5.72	4.82	4.31	3.99	3.76	3.59	3.45	3.35
23	7.88	5.66	4.76	4.26	3.94	3.71	3.54	3.41	3.30
24	7.82	5.61	4.72	4.22	3.90	3.67	3.50	3.36	3.26
25	7.77	5.57	4.68	4.18	3.85	3.63	3.46	3.32	3.22
26	7.72	5.53	4.64	4.14	3.82	3.59	3.42	3.29	3.18
27	7.68	5.49	4.60	4.11	3.78	3.56	3.39	3.26	3.15
28	7.64	5.45	4.57	4.07	3.75	3.53	3.36	3.23	3.12
29	7.60	5.42	4.54	4.04	3.73	3.50	3.33	3.20	3.09
30	7.56	5.39	4.51	4.02	3.70	3.47	3.30	3.17	3.07
40	7.31	5.18	4.31	3.83	3.51	3.29	3.12	2.99	2.89
60	7.08	4.98	4.13	3.65	3.34	3.12	2.95	2.82	2.72
120	6.85	4.79	3.95	3.48	3.17	2.96	2.79	2.66	2.56
∞	6.63	4.61	3.78	3.32	3.02	2.80	2.64	2.51	2.41

Table C.4.1b Area of the F distribution ($\alpha = 0.01$) for v_1 in the range 10 to ∞

v_2 \ v_1	10	12	15	20	24	30	40	60	120	∞
1	6055.8	6106.3	6157.3	6208.7	6234.6	6260.6	6287.0	6313.0	6339.0	6366.0
2	90.40	99.42	99.43	99.45	99.46	99.47	99.47	99.48	99.49	99.50
3	27.23	27.23	26.87	26.69	26.60	26.50	26.41	26.32	26.22	26.13
4	14.55	14.55	14.20	14.02	13.93	13.84	13.75	13.65	13.56	13.46
5	10.05	10.05	9.72	9.55	9.47	9.38	9.29	9.20	9.11	9.02
6	7.87	7.87	7.56	7.40	7.31	7.23	7.14	7.06	6.97	6.88
7	6.62	6.62	6.31	6.16	6.07	5.99	5.91	5.82	5.74	5.65
8	5.81	5.81	5.52	5.36	5.28	5.20	5.12	5.03	4.95	4.86
9	5.26	5.26	4.96	4.81	4.73	4.65	4.57	4.48	4.40	4.31
10	4.85	4.85	4.56	4.41	4.33	4.25	4.17	4.08	4.00	3.91
11	4.54	4.54	4.25	4.10	4.02	3.94	3.86	3.78	3.69	3.60
12	4.30	4.30	4.01	3.86	3.78	3.70	3.62	3.54	3.45	3.36
13	4.10	4.10	3.82	3.66	3.59	3.51	3.43	3.34	3.25	3.17
14	3.94	3.94	3.66	3.51	3.43	3.35	3.27	3.18	3.09	3.00
15	3.80	3.80	3.52	3.37	3.29	3.21	3.13	3.05	2.96	2.87
16	3.69	3.69	3.41	3.26	3.18	3.10	3.02	2.93	2.84	2.75
17	3.59	3.59	3.31	3.16	3.08	3.00	2.92	2.83	2.75	2.65
18	3.51	3.51	3.23	3.08	3.00	2.92	2.84	2.75	2.66	2.57
19	3.43	3.43	3.15	3.00	2.92	2.84	2.76	2.67	2.58	2.49
20	3.37	3.37	3.09	2.94	2.86	2.78	2.69	2.61	2.52	2.42
21	3.31	3.31	3.03	2.88	2.80	2.72	2.64	2.55	2.46	2.36
22	3.26	3.26	2.98	2.83	2.75	2.67	2.58	2.50	2.40	2.31
23	3.21	3.21	2.93	2.78	2.70	2.62	2.54	2.45	2.35	2.26
24	3.17	3.09	2.89	2.74	2.66	2.58	2.49	2.40	2.31	2.21
25	3.13	3.06	2.85	2.70	2.62	2.54	2.45	2.36	2.27	2.17
26	3.09	2.96	2.81	2.66	2.58	2.50	2.42	2.33	2.23	2.13
27	3.06	2.93	2.78	2.63	2.55	2.47	2.38	2.29	2.20	2.10
28	3.03	2.90	2.75	2.60	2.52	2.44	2.35	2.26	2.17	2.06
29	3.00	2.87	2.73	2.57	2.49	2.41	2.33	2.23	2.14	2.03
30	2.98	2.84	2.70	2.55	2.47	2.39	2.30	2.21	2.11	2.01
40	2.80	2.66	2.52	2.37	2.29	2.20	2.11	2.02	1.92	1.80
60	2.63	2.50	2.35	2.20	2.12	2.03	1.94	1.84	1.73	1.60
120	2.47	2.34	2.19	2.03	1.95	1.86	1.76	1.66	1.53	1.38
∞	2.32	2.18	2.04	1.88	1.79	1.70	1.59	1.47	1.32	1.00

Table C.4.2a Area of the *F* distribution ($\alpha = 0.05$) for v_1 in the range 1 to 9

v_2 \ v_1	1	2	3	4	5	6	7	8	9
1	161.45	199.50	215.71	224.58	230.16	233.99	236.77	238.88	240.54
2	18.51	19.00	19.16	19.25	19.30	19.33	19.35	19.37	19.38
3	10.13	9.55	9.28	9.12	9.01	8.94	8.89	8.85	8.81
4	7.71	6.94	6.59	6.39	6.26	6.16	6.09	6.04	6.00
5	6.61	5.79	5.41	5.19	5.05	4.95	4.88	4.82	4.77
6	5.99	5.14	4.76	4.53	4.39	4.28	2.21	4.15	4.10
7	5.59	4.74	4.35	4.12	3.97	3.87	3.79	3.73	3.68
8	5.32	4.46	4.07	3.84	3.69	3.58	3.50	3.44	3.39
9	5.12	4.26	3.86	3.63	3.48	3.37	3.29	3.23	3.18
10	4.96	4.10	3.71	3.48	3.33	3.22	3.14	3.07	3.02
11	4.84	3.98	3.59	3.36	3.20	3.09	3.01	2.95	2.90
12	4.75	3.89	3.49	3.26	3.11	3.00	2.91	2.85	2.80
13	4.67	3.81	3.41	3.18	3.03	2.92	2.83	2.77	2.71
14	4.60	3.74	3.34	3.11	2.96	2.85	2.76	2.70	2.65
15	4.54	3.68	3.29	3.06	2.90	2.79	2.71	2.64	2.59
16	4.49	3.63	3.24	3.01	2.85	2.79	2.66	2.59	2.54
17	4.45	3.59	3.20	2.96	2.81	2.70	2.61	2.55	2.49
18	4.41	3.55	3.16	2.93	2.77	2.66	2.58	2.51	2.46
19	4.38	3.52	3.13	2.90	2.74	2.63	2.54	2.48	2.42
20	4.35	3.49	3.10	2.87	2.71	2.60	2.51	2.45	2.39
21	4.32	3.47	3.07	2.84	2.68	2.57	2.49	2.42	2.37
22	4.30	3.44	3.05	2.82	2.66	2.55	2.46	2.40	2.34
23	4.28	3.42	3.03	2.80	2.64	2.53	2.44	2.37	2.32
24	4.26	3.40	3.01	2.78	2.62	2.51	2.42	2.36	2.30
25	4.24	3.39	2.99	2.76	2.60	2.49	2.40	2.34	2.28
26	4.23	3.37	2.98	2.74	2.59	2.47	2.39	2.32	2.27
27	4.21	3.35	2.96	2.73	2.57	2.46	2.37	2.31	2.25
28	4.20	3.34	2.95	2.71	2.56	2.45	2.36	2.29	2.24
29	4.18	3.33	2.93	2.70	2.55	2.43	2.35	2.28	2.22
30	4.17	3.32	2.92	2.69	2.53	2.42	2.33	2.27	2.21
40	4.08	3.23	2.84	2.61	2.45	2.34	2.25	2.18	2.12
60	4.00	3.15	2.76	2.53	2.37	2.25	2.17	2.10	2.04
120	3.92	3.07	2.68	2.45	2.29	2.18	2.09	2.02	1.96
∞	3.84	3.00	2.60	2.37	2.21	2.10	2.01	1.94	1.88

Table C.4.2b Area of the F distribution ($\alpha = 0.05$) for v_1 in the range 10 to ∞

v_2	v_1 10	12	15	20	24	30	40	60	120	∞
1	241.88	243.91	245.95	248.01	249.05	250.10	251.10	252.20	253.30	254.30
2	19.40	19.41	19.43	19.45	19.45	19.46	19.47	19.48	19.49	19.50
3	8.79	8.74	8.70	8.66	8.64	8.62	8.59	8.57	8.55	8.53
4	5.96	5.91	5.86	5.80	5.77	5.75	5.72	5.69	5.66	5.63
5	4.74	4.68	4.62	4.56	4.53	4.50	4.46	4.43	4.40	4.36
6	4.06	4.00	3.94	3.87	3.84	3.81	3.77	3.74	3.70	3.67
7	3.64	3.57	3.51	3.44	3.41	3.38	3.34	3.30	3.27	3.23
8	3.35	3.28	3.22	3.15	3.12	3.08	3.04	3.01	2.97	2.93
9	3.14	3.07	3.01	2.94	2.90	2.86	2.83	2.79	2.75	2.71
10	2.98	2.91	2.84	2.77	2.74	2.70	2.66	2.62	2.58	2.54
11	2.85	2.79	2.72	2.65	2.61	2.57	2.53	2.49	2.45	2.40
12	2.75	2.69	2.62	2.54	2.51	2.47	2.43	2.38	2.34	2.30
13	2.67	2.60	2.53	2.46	2.42	2.38	2.34	2.30	2.25	2.21
14	2.60	2.53	2.46	2.39	2.35	2.31	2.27	2.22	2.18	2.13
15	2.54	2.48	2.40	2.33	2.29	2.25	2.20	2.16	2.11	2.07
16	2.49	2.42	2.35	2.28	2.24	2.19	2.15	2.11	2.06	2.01
17	2.45	2.38	2.31	2.23	2.19	2.15	2.10	2.06	2.01	1.96
18	2.41	2.34	2.27	2.19	2.15	2.11	2.06	2.02	1.97	1.92
19	2.38	2.31	2.23	2.16	2.11	2.07	2.03	1.98	1.93	1.88
20	2.35	2.28	2.20	2.12	2.08	2.04	1.99	1.95	1.90	1.84
21	2.32	2.25	2.18	2.10	2.05	2.01	1.96	1.92	1.87	1.81
22	2.30	2.23	2.15	2.07	2.03	1.98	1.94	1.89	1.84	1.78
23	2.27	2.20	2.13	2.05	2.01	1.96	1.91	1.86	1.81	1.76
24	2.25	2.18	2.11	2.03	1.98	1.94	1.89	1.84	1.79	1.73
25	2.24	2.16	2.09	2.01	1.96	1.92	1.87	1.82	1.77	1.71
26	2.22	2.15	2.07	1.99	1.95	1.90	1.85	1.80	1.75	1.69
27	2.20	2.13	2.06	1.97	1.93	1.88	1.84	1.79	1.73	1.67
28	2.19	2.12	2.04	1.96	1.91	1.87	1.82	1.77	1.71	1.65
29	2.18	2.10	2.03	1.94	1.90	1.85	1.81	1.75	1.70	1.64
30	2.16	2.09	2.01	1.93	1.89	1.84	1.79	1.74	1.68	1.62
40	2.08	2.00	1.92	1.84	1.79	1.74	1.69	1.64	1.58	1.51
60	1.99	1.92	1.84	1.75	1.70	1.65	1.59	1.53	1.47	1.39
120	1.91	1.83	1.75	1.66	1.61	1.55	1.50	1.43	1.35	1.25
∞	1.83	1.75	1.67	1.57	1.52	1.46	1.39	1.32	1.22	1.00

C.5 THE K_n^+ AND K_n^- DISTRIBUTIONS

Table C.5 shows the probability of obtaining a value for K_n^+ or K_n^- which is less than or equal to the value indicated in n samples.

Table C.5 Percentage points for the K_n^+ and K_n^- distributions

n	$p=0.01$	$p=0.05$	$p=0.25$	$p=0.50$	$p=0.75$	$p=0.95$	$p=0.99$
1	0.01000	0.05000	0.2500	0.5000	0.7500	0.9500	0.9900
2	0.01400	0.06749	0.2929	0.5176	0.7071	1.0980	1.2728
3	0.01699	0.07919	0.3112	0.5147	0.7539	1.1017	1.3589
4	0.01943	0.08789	0.3202	0.5110	0.7642	1.1304	1.3777
5	0.02152	0.09471	0.3249	0.5245	0.7674	1.1392	1.4024
6	0.02336	0.1002	0.3272	0.5319	0.7703	1.1463	1.4144
7	0.02501	0.1048	0.3280	0.5364	0.7755	1.1537	1.4246
8	0.02650	0.1086	0.3280	0.5392	0.7797	1.1586	1.4327
9	0.02786	0.1119	0.3274	0.5411	0.7825	1.1624	1.4388
10	0.02912	0.1147	0.3297	0.5426	0.7845	1.1658	1.4440
11	0.03028	0.1172	0.3330	0.5439	0.7863	1.1688	1.4484
12	0.03137	0.1193	0.3357	0.5433	0.7880	1.1714	1.4521
15	0.03424	0.1244	0.3412	0.5500	0.7926	1.1773	1.4606
20	0.03807	0.1298	0.3461	0.5547	0.7975	1.1839	1.4698
30	0.04354	0.1351	0.3509	0.5605	0.8036	1.1916	1.4801
> 30			$y_p - 1/(6\sqrt{n}) + 0(1/n)$, where $y_p^2 = \frac{1}{2}\ln(1/(1-p))$				
y_p	0.07089	0.1601	0.3793	0.5887	0.8326	1.2239	1.5174

ANSWERS TO SELECTED EXERCISES

CHAPTER 3

3.1 Event | Description

Receive start	The start of a packet is received on one of the incoming communications links.
Receive end	A complete packet has been received on one of the incoming communications links.
Transmit start	A packet has started transmission from one of the outgoing communications links.
Transmit end	A complete packet has been transmitted from one of the outgoing communications links.

CHAPTER 4

4.2 See Listing 10.1.

CHAPTER 5

5.2 Refer to distribution disk.

5.5 From the table the value of V is

$$V = 1010844/1000 - 1000$$
$$= 10$$

This value of V would occur between 90 per cent and 10 per cent of the time assuming randomness and so is not significant at the 5 per cent level. There is no reason to reject the hypothesis that the numbers are random.

5.6. The empirical cdf is shown in Table 1.

Table 1

x	$F_n(x)$	x	$F_n(x)$
−2.81927	0.04	0.01993	0.56
−2.40518	0.08	0.25350	0.60
−2.03294	0.12	0.94021	0.64
−1.35628	0.16	1.20343	0.68
−1.31765	0.20	1.37423	0.72
−1.22142	0.24	1.54942	0.76
−1.15846	0.28	1.69495	0.80
−1.10567	0.32	1.98628	0.84
−1.10007	0.36	2.29519	0.88
−0.98310	0.40	2.44434	0.92
−0.94245	0.44	2.62720	0.96
−0.25637	0.48	2.72929	1.00
−0.02860	0.52		

Abscissae of a normal distribution with mean 0 and variance 2.5 can be translated to the standard normal distribution using

$$x' = \frac{x - 0}{\sqrt{2.5}}$$

The values of the cdf of the standard normal distribution at the points of interest are shown in Table 2.

Table 2

x	x'	$F(x)$	x	x'	$F(x)$
−2.81927	−1.783	0.038	0.01993	0.013	0.504
−2.40518	−1.522	0.064	0.25350	0.160	0.564
−2.03294	−1.287	0.100	0.94021	0.595	0.722
−1.35628	−0.858	0.195	1.20343	0.761	0.776
−1.31765	−0.834	0.203	1.37423	0.870	0.808
−1.22142	−0.773	0.221	1.54942	0.980	0.837
−1.15846	−0.732	0.233	1.69495	1.072	0.858
−1.10567	−0.700	0.242	1.98628	1.257	0.896
−1.10007	−0.696	0.243	2.29519	1.453	0.927
−0.98310	−0.622	0.268	2.44434	1.546	0.938
−0.94245	−0.596	0.278	2.62720	1.663	0.952
−0.25637	−0.162	0.436	2.72929	1.727	0.958
−0.02860	−0.018	0.492			

By comparing $F(x)$ and $F_n(x)$ the K–S test statistics are:

$$K_n^+ = 5*0.162 = 0.81 \text{ (occurs at } x = -0.94245)$$
$$K_n^- = 5*0.096 = 0.48 \text{ (occurs at } x = 1.20343)$$

The table in Appendix C gives the chance of getting 0.81 about 75 per cent. Therefore the result is not significant at the 1 per cent level and there is no basis to reject the hypothesis that the data is normally distributed with 0 mean and variance 2.5.

CHAPTER 6

6.1 Refer to distribution disk.
6.2 Refer to distribution disk.
6.4 Refer to distribution disk.

CHAPTER 7

7.4 Refer to distribution disk.
7.5 Refer to distribution disk.

CHAPTER 8

8.2 Utilization $= 4.22/5.4 = 0.78$
Mean number in system $= 0.78/(1-0.78) = 3.54$
Mean time in system $= 3.54*5.4 = 19.12$
Mean time queuing $= 19.12 - 4.22 = 14.90$
8.4 Refer to distribution disk.
8.5 Refer to distribution disk.
8.7 Refer to distribution disk.

CHAPTER 9

9.2 Refer to distribution disk.
9.3 Refer to distribution disk.
9.5 Refer to distribution disk.

CHAPTER 10

10.1 Confidence interval $= \pm 1.96*\sqrt{1339.8/42}$
Lower limit $= 2.941 - 1.7 = 1.241$
Upper limit $= 2.941 + 1.7 = 4.641$
10.2 Data A:
Number of samples $= 30$
Mean $= 4.737$

s^2 $= 4.254$

Data B:

Number of samples	$= 12$
Mean	$= 7.691$
s^2	$= 43.78$
Combined estimate of variation	$= 15.123$
$t_{0.025}(40)$	$= 1.96$
Confidence interval	$= \pm 1.96 * \sqrt{15.12(\frac{1}{30} + \frac{1}{12})}$
Lower limit	$= 2.95 - 2.603 = 1.241$
Upper limit	$= 2.95 + 2.603 = 4.641$

10.5   Refer to distribution disk.

CHAPTER 11

11.1   The totals and means are:

	Treatment 1	Treatment 2	Treatment 3	Treatment 4	Treatment 5
Total	678.30	855.8	380.50	305.30	239.50
Mean	135.66	171.16	76.10	61.06	47.90

Overall mean $= 98.3$
Overall total $= 2459.60$

$$TSS = (125.3^2 + \cdots + 43.1^2) - 2459.6^2/25 = 72574.8$$
$$SS_T = (678.3^2 + \cdots + 239.7^2)/5 - 2459.6^2/25 = 55600.5$$
$$SS_E = 72574.8 - 55600.5 = 16974.4$$

ANOVA table:

	Degrees of freedom	Sum of squares	Mean sum of squares	Ratio
Treatments	4	55600.5	13900.1	13.1
Error	15	16974.3	1060.9	

From tables of the F distribution $F_{4,16,0.05} = 3.01$. Thus 13.1 is significant at the 5 per cent level and therefore the treatments are different. A 5 per cent confidence interval for treatment means is

$$\pm 3.01*\sqrt{1060.8/5} = \pm 43.8$$

and for the difference between two treatment means is:

$$\pm 3.01*\sqrt{1060.8(\tfrac{1}{5} + \tfrac{1}{5})} = \pm 62$$

11.4 The means are:

$$\bar{x} = 6.0$$
$$\bar{y} = 17.0$$

The slope and intercept are:

$$\beta_1 \text{ (slope)} = 297.3/113 = 2.63$$
$$\beta_0 \text{ (intercept)} = 17.0 - 6.0*2.63 = 1.22$$

The covariance is:

$$\text{Cov}(x,y) = 279.1/7 = 39.9$$
$$\sigma_y^2 = 2811.48/7 - 289 = 112.64$$
$$\sigma_x^2 = 365/7 - 36 = 16.14$$

Therefore:

$$\text{SSE} = 7*112.64 - 2.63*7*39.9 = 53.92$$
$$s^2 = 53.92/5 = 10.78$$
$$s_{\beta_1}^2 = 10.78/(7*16.14) = 0.095$$

Confidence interval of slope =

$$2.63 \pm t_{0.005}(5)*0.31 = 2.63 \pm 4.032*0.31 = 2.63 \pm 1.25$$

CHAPTER 12

12.3 Refer to distribution disk.

REFERENCES

Aho, A.V., J.E. Hopcraft and J.D. Ullman (1974) *Data Structures and Algorithms*, Addison-Wesley.

Alford, M.W. (1977) A Requirements Engineering Methodology in Real-Time Processing Requirements, *IEEE Trans.*, January.

Anderson, G.E. (1984) The Coordinated Use of Five Performance Evaluation Methodologies, *Comm. ACM*, Vol. 27(2), 119–125.

Andrews, D. and D. Ince (1991) *Practical Formal Methods with VDM*, McGraw-Hill, London.

Banks, J., J.S. Carson II and J.N. Sy (1989) *Getting Started with GPSS/H*, Wolverine Software Corp., Annandate, VA.

Bell, D., I. Morrey and J. Pugh (1987) *Software Engineering. A Programming Approach*, Prentice-Hall, Englewood Cliffs, NJ.

Bell, P.C. (1987) Visual Interactive Modelling in Operational Research: Successes and Opportunities, *J. Ops. Res. Soc.*, Vol. 36, 975.

Birtwistle, G. and J. Kendall (1986) *AI Graphics and Simulation*, Society for Computer Simulation, San Diego, CA.

Birtwistle, G.M., O.J. Dahl, B. Myhrhaug and K. Nygaard (1973) *SIMULA BEGIN*, Auerbach, Philadelphia, PA.

Box, G.E.P. and M.E. Muller (1958) A Note on the Generation of Normal Deviates, *Ann. Math. Statist.*, No. 28, 610–614.

Bruno, G. (1984) Using Ada for Discrete Event Simulation, Software—Practice and Experience, Vol. 14(7), 685–695.

Buxton, J. and J.G. Laski (1962) Control and Simulation Language, *The Computer J.*, Vol. 5, 194–199.

CACI (1991) *A Quick Look at COMNET II.5*, CACI Products Division, Watchmoor Park, Riverside Way, Camberley, Surrey, UK.

Carrie, A. (1988) *Simulation of Manufacturing Systems*, Wiley, New York.

Chan, A.W. (1982) Interactive Computer Modelling for Conveyor Systems, *CIM Bulletin*, November, 81–83.

Clementson, A.T. (1966) Extended Control and Simulation Language, *The Computer J.*, Vol. 9, 215–220.

Cochran, W.G. and G.M. Cox (1957) *Experimental Design* (2nd edn), Wiley, New York.

Conway, A.E. and N.D. Geoganas (1989) *Queueing Networks—Exact Computational Algorithms: A Unified Theory Based on Decomposition and Aggregation,* MIT Press, Cambridge, MA.

Conway R., W. Maxwell and S. Warona (1986) *XCELL: Factory Modelling System,* Scientific Press, USA.

Cootner, P.H. (ed.) (1964) *The Random Characterization of Stock Market Processes,* MIT Press, Cambridge, MA.

Cormen, T.H., C.E. Leiserson and R.L. Rivest (1989) *Introduction to Algorithms,* MIT Press, Cambridge, MA.

Cox, D.R. and H.D. Miller (1965) *The Theory of Stochastic Processes,* Wiley, New York.

Dagpunar, J. (1988) *Principles of Random Variate Generation,* Oxford University Press, Oxford, UK.

Dahl, O.J. and K. Nygaard (1966) SIMULA—An ALGOL Based Simulation Language, *Comm. ACM,* Vol. IX(9).

Davies, H. and R.M. Davies (1987) A Simulation for Planning Renal Services in Europe, *Ops. Res. Soc.,* Vol. 38, p. 693.

Devroye, L. (1986) *Non Uniform Random Variate Generation,* Springer-Verlag, Berlin.

Dill, W.R., D.P. Gaver and W.L. Webster (1965) Models and Modelling for Manpower Planning, *Man. Sci.* Vol. 13, p. B-142.

Donovan, J.J., M.M. Jones and J.W. Alsop (1969) A Graphical Facility for an Interactive Simulation System, *Proc IFIP Congress,* North Holland.

Dudewicz, E.J. and S.N. Mishra (1988) *Modern Mathematical Statistics,* Wiley, New York.

Easteal, C. (1989) *Software Engineering: Analysis and Design,* McGraw-Hill, London.

Emshoff, J.R. (1971) *Design and Use of Computer Simulation Models,* Macmillan, London.

Fishman, G.S. (1978) *Concepts and Methods in Discrete Event Digital Simulation,* Wiley, New York.

Fishman, G.S. and P.J. Kiviat (1967) The Analysis of Simulation Generated Time Series, *Man. Sci.,* Vol. XIII(7), 525–557.

Fox, M. (1965) A Simplified Model for the Formation, Movement and Dissipation of Fair Weather Cumulus Clouds, *J. App. Prob.,* Vol. 2, p. 178.

Frost, R.A. and M.M. Peterson (1982) A Short Note on Binary Search Trees, *Computer J.,* Vol. 25(1), p. 158.

Gelenbe, E. and G. Pujolle (1987) *Introduction to Queueing Networks,* Wiley, New York.

Gordon, G. (1969) *System Simulation,* Prentice-Hall, Englewood Cliffs, NJ.

Gordon, G. (1975) *The Application of GPSS V to Discrete System Simulation*, Prentice-Hall, Englewood Cliffs, NJ.

Hac, A. (1984) PL/1 as a Discrete Event Simulation Tool, *Software—Practice and Experience*, Vol. 14(7), pp. 697–702.

Halsall, F. (1988) *Data Communications Computer Networks and OSI*, Addison-Wesley, Reading, MA.

Hewlett-Packard (1985) *X.25: The PSN Connection An Explanation of Recommendation X.25*, Hewlett-Packard France, 5, Avenue Raymond Chanas, 38320 Eybens, France.

Hills, P.R. (1966) Simon—A Computer Simulation Language in Algol, Digital Simulation in Operational Research, R. Hollingdale (ed.), English Universities Press, London.

Holmes, W.M. (ed.) (1985) *Artificial Intelligence and Simulation*, Society for Computer Simulation, San Diego, CA.

Horvath, W.J. (1966) Stochastic Models of Behaviour, *Man. Sci.*, Vol. 12, p. 513.

Huff, D. (1960) *How to Take a Chance*, Gollancz, London.

Hurrion, R.D. (1980) An Interactive Visual Simulation System for Industrial Management, *Eur. J. Ops. Res.*, Vol. 5, p. 86.

Jackson, M.A. (1983) *System Development*, Prentice-Hall, Englewood Cliffs, NJ.

Jackson, M. (1988) *Advanced Spreadsheet Modelling with Lotus 123*, Wiley, New York.

James, A. (ed.) (1978) *Mathematical Models in Water Pollution Control*, Wiley, New York.

Jennergen, P. (1984) *Discrete Event Simulation in Pascal MT+ on a Microcomputer*, Student-Litteratur, Chartwell-Bratt, Lund, Sweden.

Jones, C.B. (1980) *Software Development: A Rigorous Approach*, Prentice-Hall, Englewood Cliffs, NJ.

Karian, Z.A. and E.J. Dudewicz (1991) *Modern Statistical, Systems and GPSS Simulation, The First Course*, Freeman, New York.

Kernigan B. and D. Richie (1988) *The C Programming Language* (2nd edn), Prentice-Hall, Englewood Cliffs, NJ.

Killbridge, M. and L. Webster (1966) An Economic Model for the Division of Labour, *Man. Sci.*, Vol. 12, p. B-255.

Klein, L.R., R.J. Ball, A. Hazlewood and P. Vandome (1961) *An Econometric Model of the UK economy*, Blackwell, Oxford.

Kleinrock, L. (1975) *Queueing Systems Volume 1: Theory*, Wiley-Interscience, New York.

Kleinrock, L. (1976) *Queueing Systems Volume 2: Computer Applications*, Wiley-Interscience, New York.

Knuth, D.E. (1973a) *The Art of Computer Programming: Volume 1, Fundamental Algorithms*, Addison-Wesley, Reading, MA.

Knuth, D.E. (1973b) *The Art of Computer Programming: Volume 3, Sorting and Searching*, Addison-Wesley, Reading, MA.

Knuth, D.E. (1981) *The Art of Computer Programming: Volume 2, Seminumerical Algorithms*, Addison-Wesley, Reading, MA.

Kwatney, H.G. and W.A. Konopacki (1977) The Modelling of Once-Through Steam Generator for System Dynamics and Control Studies, *1977 Joint Automation and Control Conference*, Part I, IEEE, pp. 323–331.

Lapin, J.E. (1987) *Portable C and Unix System Programming*, Prentice-Hall, Englewood Cliffs, NJ.

Law, A.M. and D. Kelton (1982) *Simulation Modelling and Analysis*, McGraw-Hill, London.

Lehmer, D. (1951) Mathematical Methods in Large Scale Computing Units, *Harvard University Computation Laboratory Annals*, Vol. 26, pp. 141–146.

Linington, P.F. (1983) Fundamentals of Layer Service Definitions and Protocol Specifications, *Proc. IEEE*, Vol. 71, pp. 1341–1345.

Little, J.D. (1961) A Proof of the Queueing Formula $L = \lambda W$, *Operations Research*, Vol. 9, pp. 383–387.

Markowitz, H., B. Hausner and H. Karr (1963) *SIMSCRIPT: A Simulation Programming Language*, Prentice-Hall, Englewood Cliffs, NJ.

Marsden, B.W. (1984) A Standard Pascal Event Simulation Package, *Software—Practice and Experience*, Vol. 14(7), pp. 659–684.

Mihram, G.A. (1972) *Simulation: Statistical Foundations and Methodology*, Academic Press, London.

Newby, W.J. (1964) Planning Refinery Production, *Conference on Computable Models*, British Computer Society, London, UK.

Ogilvie, J.W.L. (1990) *Advanced C Struct Programming*, Wiley, NewYork.

O'Keefe R.M. and J.W. Roach (1987) Artificial Intelligence Approaches to Simulation, *J. Ops. Res. Soc.*, Vol. 38, pp. 713–722.

Oren, I.I. (1977) Software for Simulation of Combined Continuous and Discrete Systems: A State of the Art Review, *Simulation*, Vol. 28, No. 2.

Page-Jones, M. (1988) *Practical Guide to Structured Systems Design*, Prentice-Hall, Englewood Cliffs, NJ.

Parks, G.M. (1964) Development and Application of a Model for the Suppression of Forest Fires, *Man. Sci.*, Vol. 10, pp. 760–764.

Pidd, M. (1988) *Computer Simulation in Management Science* (2nd edn), Wiley, Chichester, UK.

Pidd, M. (ed.) (1989) *Computer Modelling for Discrete Simulation*, Wiley, Chichester, UK.

Press, W.H., B.P. Flannery, S.A. Teukolsky and W.T. Vetterling (1988) *Numerical Recipes in C*, Cambridge University Press, Cambridge, UK.

Pressman, R.S. (1987) *Software Engineering: A Practitioner's Approach* (2nd edn), McGraw-Hill, London.

Pritsker, A.A.B. (1975) *The GASP IV Simulation Language*, Wiley-Interscience, New York.

Pritsker, A.A.B. and G. Hurst (1973) GASP IV: A Combined Continuous—Discrete FORTRAN based Simulation Language, *Simulation*, Vol. 21, No. 3.

Reitman, J. (1971) *Computer Simulation Applications; Discrete Event Simulation for Synthesis and Analysis of Complex Systems*, Wiley, New York.

Reynolds, J. (1981) *The Craft of Programming*, Prentice-Hall, London.

Roberts, N., D. Anderson, R. Deal, M. Garret and W. Shaffer (1983) *Introduction to Computer Simulation: A Systems Dynamics Modelling Approach*, Addison-Wesley, Reading, MA.

Robins, H. and J. Van Ryzin (1975) *Introduction to Statistics*, Science Research Associates, London, UK.

Rozanov, Y.A. (1969) *Probability Theory: A Concise Course*, Dover, New York.

Salsburg, M.A. (1988) The Performance Evaluation of a Transaction Processing Application, *Proc. CMG 88*, Dallas, Texas, December, pp. 444–449.

Sauer, C.H. and L. Woo (1977) *Hybrid Simulation of a Distributed Network*, IBM Research Report RC 6341, IBM T. J. Watson Research Center, Yorktown Heights, New York.

Schriber, T.J. (1990) *An Introduction to Simulation Using GPSS/H*, Wiley, New York.

Sedgewick, R. (1988) *Algorithms*, Addison-Wesley, Reading, MA.

Shannon, R.E., R. Mayer and H.H. Adelsberger (1985) Expert Systems and Simulation, *Simulation*, Vol. 44(6), pp. 275–284.

Sherman, S.W. (1976) Trace Driven Modelling: An Update, *Proc. Symp. Simulation of Computer Systems*, pp. 87–91, National Bureau of Standards, Boulder, CO.

Smith, C.U. (1990) *Performance Engineering of Software Systems*, Addison-Wesley, Reading, MA.

Spinelli de Carvalho, R. (1976) *Cellular Simulation*, PhD Thesis, University of Lancaster, UK.

Stahl, I. (1990) *Introduction to Simulation with GPSS*, Prentice-Hall, Englewood Cliffs, NJ.

Tanenbaum, A.S. (1988) *Computer Networks*, Prentice-Hall, Englewood Cliffs, NJ.

Teheri, H.R. and B.J. Askins (1991) Simulating the Performance of a Multiprocessor Operating System, *IEEE Winter Sim. Conf.*, pp. 81–90.

Tysso, A. (1979) Modelling and Parameter Estimation of Ship Boilers, *5th IFAC Symposium on Identification and System Parameter Estimation*, Darmsadt, pp. 949–960.

Wall, F.T., L.A. Hiller, D.J. Wheeler and W.F. Atchinson (1954) Statistical Computation of Mean Dimensions of Macro Molecules, I–III, *J. Chem. Phys.*, Vol. 22, pp. 1036–1041.

Watson, H.J. and J.H. Blackstone (1989) *Computer Simulation* (2nd edn), Wiley, New York.

Wetherill, G.B. (1986) *Regression Analysis with Applications*, Chapman and Hall, London, UK.

Wilf, H.S. (1986) *Algorithms and Complexity*, Prentice-Hall, Englewood Cliffs, NJ.

Williams, J.W.J. (1964) The Elliot Simulation Package, *The Computer J.*, Vol. 6(4).

Wirth, N. (1986) *Algorithms and Data Structures*, Prentice-Hall, London, UK.

Yazdani, M. (ed.) (1986) *Artificial Intelligence: Principles and Applications*, Chapman and Hall, London, UK.

INDEX

1-persistant CSMA protocol, 275, 309

A phase, 27, 35, 145
accessibility, 7
accuracy, 214
acknowledgement, 47
acquire(), 128, 325
activate(), 120, 325
ACTIVE, 120
Ada, 25
add_event(), 49, 161, 326
add_hdata(), 183, 326
add_sdata(), 184, 326
ALGOL, 25
Aloha protocol, 193
alternating bit protocol, 47
alternative hypothesis, 215
analysis of variance:
   (ANOVA), 246
   one-way, 248
   table, 250, 254, 259
   two-way, 252
antithetic variates, 231, 237
append(), 121, 158, 327
applications, 1
arrival pattern, 148
   process, 149
   rate, 153
   time dependent, 166
assumptions, 12
autocorrelation, 67, 228
average (*see* mean)

average interarrival time, 149
average service interval, 149

B phase, 29, 32
balking, 160
batch computer system, 169
batch means, 232
   advantages, 234
   batch size, 233
   disadvantages, 234
Bayesian inference, 63
benchmark, 15, 169
benefits of simulation, 7
Bernoulli trial, 90, 91, 93
beta(), 93, 327
bias, 247
binary exponential backoff, 273
binary tree, 138, 140
   complexity, 140
binomial(), 96, 328
binomial coefficient, 93
birth-death process, 150
birth-death system, 151
bit error rate (ber), 50

C, 7, 25, 28, 39
   ANSI, 43
C phase, 32, 35, 122
calendar, 29, 137
cdf (*see* cumulative distribution function)
cellular simulation, 121
Central Limit Theorem, 198

chi-squared test, 71
chi_square(), 101, 328
class intervals, 177
clear_histogram(), 184, 328
clear_queue(), 159, 329
clear_sim(), 329
clear_summary(), 184, 329
client information, 14
CLOSED, 120
collisions, 272, 285
COMNET, 25
CONDITIONAL, 120
conditional event routines, 32
confidence interval, 217
  for difference of means, 223
  with known variance, 217, 223
  large sample, 219, 224
  for slope of regression line, 267
  small sample, 220
  treatment mean, 249, 251
  with unknown variance, 221, 225
  of variance, 222
confidence level, 215
controlled variables, 12
control variates, 234
correlation, 14, 228
correlation coefficient, 228
cost effectiveness, 7
covariance, 228
CSMA protocols, 242
CSMA/CD protocol, 272
cumulative distribution function, 63
cumulatuve frequency histogram, 180
current entity, 120
customer, 148

data communications, 47
decision variables, 12
dedicated simulation packages, 24
degrees of freedom, 71, 102, 221
delete_event(), 49, 330
difference equations, 151
dining philosophers problem, 128–134
discrete event simulation, 5
  advantages of, 7
distribution disk, 316
distribution function (*see* cumulative
  distribution function)
distributions,
  beta, 87

binomial, 90
chi-squared, 70, 100, 359
empirical, 103
Erlang, 88
exponential, 84
F, 102
gamma, 85
generalised lambda, 112
geometric, 91
Laplace, 99
lognormal, 96
negative binomial, 92
normal, 96
Poisson, 93
selection of, 115
standard normal, 96
standard uniform, 80
Student's t, 101, 357
triangular, 83
uniform, 82
variance ratio (*see* distributions, F)
Weibull, 98
documentation, 20
domain specific tools (*see* dedicated simulation
  packages)
DOS, 318
draw_continuous(), 107, 330
draw_discrete(), 107, 330
dump_conditional(), 331
dump_pending(), 331
dump_queue(), 332

efficiency metric, 185
entity, 13, 27, 35, 117
  attributes, 118
  blocked, 39
  bound, 37
  conditional, 35
  creation of, 122
  record, 118
  routine, 35, 118
  state, 119
erlang(), 88, 332
Ethernet cable, 310
Ethernet protocol, 272
event routine, 32, 118
event scheduling, 29
events, 14, 15, 134
  bound, 29, 32
  conditional, 32, 118

customer arrival, 31
customer departure, 31
simultaneous, 144
executive (*see* scheduler)
expected value, 223
experimental designs
  completely randomized, 247
  factorial, 246, 255
  randomized block, 251
  unifactor, 246
experimental unit, 245
experimentation, 11, 307
explicit queueing, 38, 40
exponential(), 84, 333
extract(), 120, 158, 333

f_distr(), 103, 333
F ratio, 249
factors, 256
first come first served (FCFS), 149
first in first out (FIFO), 149
fitted points, 264
floor function, 95, 181
FORTRAN, 25
fourth moment, 192

gamma(), 85, 237, 334
GASP, 25
general purpose language (GPL), 24, 26
geometric(), 91, 334
goodness of fit, 123, 128
  chi-squared, 108
  Kolmogorov-Smirnov, 109
GPSS, 25
granularity, 3

histogram, 103–107, 177–181
  classes, 177
  cumulative frequency, 189
  cumulative relative frequency, 104
  frequency, 103, 178
  printing of, 186–192
  tables, 189
  time series, 177, 187
  unweighted, 178
  weighted, 178
historic data, 17, 113
hold(), 120, 335

IEEE standard 802, 278
implicit queuing, 38

independence, 14, 232
independent random variables, 223
inductive probabilty, 61
inheritance, 35
init_sim(), 49, 335
initial transient, 200
  duration, 202
input variables, 12
inter-process communication, 35
interrupt queue, 165
idle time, 184

Kolmogorov-Smirnov test, 109–111
Kolmogorov-Smirnov distribution, 367

laplace(), 99, 335
large_sample_conf_int(), 219, 336
latency, 15
least squares, 264
  estimates, 268
  line, 264
level of significance, 215
levels, 255
librarian, 318
library routines, 325–354
linear congruential generator, 68
linked list, 138
  complexity, 139
Little's result, 153
log_normal(), 96, 336

M/M/1 queue, 155
  size, 156
  throughput delay, 156
  time in system, 157
main(), 43
make_conditional_entity(), 123, 336
make_entity(), 123, 337
make_histogram(), 183, 337
make_queue(), 338
make_resource(), 127, 338
make_scheduled_entity(), 123, 338
make_stream(), 237, 339
make_summary(), 184, 339
make_table(), 107, 340
manufacturers specifications, 15
Markov chain, 150
  stationary, 150
Markov process, 150
maximal period, 69
mean, 64

continuous, 65
discrete, 65
mean square, 249
    due to blocks, 253
    due to error, 253
    due to treatments, 249, 253
memoryless, 150
model development, 16, 278–307
model structure
    logical, 4
    mathematical, 4
model template, 44
modelling approach, 28
modelling strategy (*see* modelling approach)
modelling units, 19
models, 1–3
modulus, 68, 77
moving averages, 210
multiplier, 68

naive experimentation, 245
nameing convention for queues, 152
neg_binomial(), 92, 340
negative correlation, 228, 231
noise burst, 273
non-terminating simulation, 201
normal(), 96, 237, 341
null hypothesis, 215

object oriented techniques, 35
objectives, 10
observation (*see* sample)
one-tailed test, 216
output variables, 12

p-persistant CSMA protocol, 242
parameter estimation, 11, 14
    for Ethernet model, 278
passivate(), 49, 120, 341
PASCAL, 25
PASSIVE, 120
path length estimations, 15
peformance metrics
    idle time, 208
PENDING, 136
performance metrics, 19, 154, 185
phases of simulation study, 11
PL/1, 25
poisson(), 93, 342
Poisson process, 93, 149

population mean, 65
population size, 148
positive correlation, 228, 238
power (of simulation), 7
pre-emptable server, 165
predictability, 2
predictor variables, 261
prepend(), 158, 342
prime, 69
prime factorization, 69
print_cumulative(), 189, 342
print_histogram(), 186, 343
print_summary(), 192, 344
print_table(), 189, 344
priority queue, 149
priority scheduling, 144
probability, 61
probability(), 50, 345
probability density function (pdf), 62
probability distribution function (*see*
    cumulative distribution function)
process interaction, 35
process oriented, 35
program structure, 43
pseudo-random, 61
pure birth system, 151
pure death system, 151

queue_back(), 121, 158, 345
queue_front(), 121, 158, 346
queue behaviour, 159
queue swapping, 159
QUEUED, 120
queueing discipline (*see* service policy)
queuing systems, 148
queuing theory, 149
queues, 14, 27, 143
queue implementation, 157
quit(), 346
quit_terminate(), 121, 124, 346

race condition, 144
random number generator, 27, 68–69
    desirable qualities, 67
    URN13, 76
random number stream, 60
random numbers, 51, 54, 60
random variables, 60
    antithetic, 76
    continuous, 60, 107
    discrete, 60, 106

randomization, 247
randomized block design, 247, 251
randomness, 59
reactivate(), 120, 346
reactivation pointer, 35, 118
regenerative behaviour, 200
regenerative point (*see* renewal point)
regenerative state, 200
regression analysis, 261
  multiple, 262
  non-linear, 262
regression curve, 261
regression model, 265
reinstate(), 121, 347
rejection region, 215
relative cumulative frequency histogram, 180
relative frequency, 178
release(), 128, 347
remove_back(), 120, 158, 347
remove_front(), 120, 158, 348
reneging, 161
renewal point, 200
repetition, 230
  no autocorrelation, 261
  with autocorrelation, 262
report, 21
reset_resource(), 348
reset_stream(), 348
residency time, 153
residual, 259
resource.h, 145
resource record, 127
resources, 27, 127, 148
response time, 184
response variables, 12
results, 27
retransmissions, 286
run, 17
run_sim(), 49, 124, 349

sample, 17
sample mean, 65
  variance, 66
sampling, 111, 198
sampling distribution for the mean, 198
sampling distribution for the variance, 199
scan_always(), 145, 349
schedule(), 120, 161, 350
scheduler, 27, 137
  dynamic algorithms, 138
  static algorithms, 138

scope (of simulation), 7
seed, 68, 77
semi-Markov process, 150
sensitivity analysis, 17
sequence number, 47
  demand, 149
  distribution, 149
  facility, 148
  policy, 149
  pre-emption, 162
  times, 15
set_fill_char(), 187, 350
significance testing, 215
SIMON, 25
simple queue, 31
SIMULA, 25
simulation clock, 29
  library, 26
    cross reference, 320–323
    strategy (*see* modelling approach)
small_sample_conf_int(), 231, 350
solvability, 3
special purpose language (SPL), 25
spectral analysis, 240
spreadsheet, 3
stack, 152
stamp(), 125, 351
stamp_current(), 125, 351
standard deviation, 66
  error, 217
  normal, 218, 235
state transition diagram (std), 119
  for frames in Ethernet model, 278
  for stations in Ethernet model, 277
stationary Markov chain, 150
  probability distributions, 197
statistical probability, 61
steady state, 17, 46, 197
  detection using moving averages, 204
  detection using standard deviation, 210
steady state behaviour, 197
stochastic process, 150
stratified sampling, 251
student_t(), 101, 351
study definition, 11
sum of squares, 248
  due to blocks, 253
  due to error, 249, 253
  due to treatments, 249, 253
  total, 248, 253
summary record, 183

system throughput, 185
systematic errors (*see* bias)
systems analysis, 11, 13, 276

terminate(), 49, 121, 352
TERMINATED, 120
terminating simulation, 201
tertiary tree, 143
testing, 16
tests of randomness
    coupon collectors test (a), 74
    coupon collectors test (b), 74
    empirical, 72
    gap test, 72
    poker test, 73
    run test, 75
    serial correlation test, 76
    spectral test, 76
    theoretical, 75
    uniformity test, 72
thinning, 168
third moment, 195
three phase, 32
throughput:
    of alternating bit protocol, 49
time dependent rates, 165
time scales (*see* modelling units)
time stamps, 125
timeout, 47
trace driven simulation, 5

tracing program, 5
transient behaviour, 199, 239
transient state, 46
treatment, 245
trial, 245
triang(), 84, 352
two phase (*see* event scheduling)
two-tailed test, 216, 224

unbiased estimate, 199
uniform(), 78, 353
uniform01(), 84, 269, 353
UNIX, 43, 319

validation, 16
variability, 3
variance, 64
variance-ratio test (*see* F-test)
variance reduction, 234
verification, 16

wait(), 120, 353
weibull(), 98, 354
withdraw(), 121, 354
workload, 18
world view (*see* modelling approach)

X.25, 117
XCELL, 25